THE
NEIGHBORHOOD
OF GODS

SOUTH ASIA ACROSS THE DISCIPLINES

A series edited by Muzaffar Alam, Robert Goldman, and Gauri Viswanathan
Dipesh Chakrabarty, Sheldon Pollock, and Sanjay Subrahmanyam, founding editors

Funded by a grant from the Andrew W. Mellon Foundation and jointly published by the University of California Press, the University of Chicago Press, and Columbia University Press.

South Asia across the Disciplines is a series devoted to publishing first books across a wide range of South Asian studies, including art, history, philology or textual studies, philosophy, religion, and the interpretive social sciences. Series authors all share the goal of opening up new archives and suggesting new methods and approaches, while demonstrating that South Asian scholarship can be at once deep in expertise and broad in appeal.

Recent South Asia across the Disciplines titles:

The Hegemony of Heritage: Ritual and the Record in Stone
by Deborah L. Stein (California)

Language of the Snakes: Prakrit, Sanskrit, and the Language Order of Premodern India
by Andrew Ollett (California)

Modernizing Composition: Sinhala Song, Poetry, and Politics in Twentieth-Century Sri Lanka
by Garrett Field (California)

Hindu Pluralism: Religion and the Public Sphere in Early Modern South India
by Elaine M. Fisher (California)

Reading the Mahāvaṃsa: The Literary Aims of a Theravada Buddhist History
by Kristin Scheible (Columbia)

Building Histories: The Archival and Affective Lives of Five Monuments in Modern Delhi
by Mrinalini Rajagopalan (Chicago)

Negotiating Languages: Urdu, Hindi, and the Definition of Modern South Asia
by Walter N. Hakala (Columbia)

THE NEIGHBORHOOD OF GODS

*The Sacred and the Visible at
the Margins of Mumbai*

WILLIAM ELISON

THE UNIVERSITY OF CHICAGO PRESS • CHICAGO AND LONDON

The University of Chicago Press, Chicago 60637

The University of Chicago Press, Ltd., London

© 2018 by The University of Chicago

Published 2018

Printed in the United States of America

27 26 25 24 23 22 21 20 19 18   1 2 3 4 5

ISBN-13: 978-0-226-49487-6 (cloth)

ISBN-13: 978-0-226-49490-6 (paper)

ISBN-13: 978-0-226-49506-4 (e-book)

DOI: https://doi.org/10.7208/chicago/9780226495064.001.0001

Library of Congress Cataloging-in-Publication Data

Names: Elison, William, author.

Title: The neighborhood of gods : the sacred and the visible at the margins of Mumbai / William Elison.

Other titles: South Asia across the disciplines.

Description: Chicago ; London : The University of Chicago Press, 2018. | Series: South Asia across the disciplines

Identifiers: LCCN 2018006744 | ISBN 9780226494876 (cloth : alk. paper) | ISBN 9780226494906 (pbk. : alk. paper) | ISBN 9780226495064 (e-book)

Subjects: LCSH: Mumbai (India)—Religion. | Motion pictures—India—Mumbai.

Classification: LCC BL1153.7.M83 E45 2018 | DDC 294.5/350954792—dc23

LC record available at https://lccn.loc.gov/2018006744

♾ This paper meets the requirements of ANSI/NISO Z39.48–1992 (Permanence of Paper).

For

Gayatri Chatterjee

Mary Ann Newman

Ramu Pandit

Andy Rotman

Friends and teachers

CONTENTS

PREFACE

This book is about a holy city. There are many in India. Mumbai is not usually considered one of them.

The very image may seem incongruous. To say that Mumbai does not look like a holy city is to evoke what it does tend to look like, in images that circulate across India and abroad: it's a commercial metropolis, a glittering Bollywood backdrop; conversely, it's a slumland dystopia. But for many if not most of the people who live in the city (of whom there are over twelve million and counting),[1] the neighborhood streets, lanes, and yards are shared with local gods and other agents of divine power.

As practiced by its less well-off residents, in the main, the work of consecrating the city is in large part a visual project. A site is marked apart with religious symbols and objects. As it flourishes, the site grows in visibility and definition, from a display to a shrine to a full-blown temple. To be sure, such efforts transgress boundaries that are salient for more prosperous residents—the boundaries middle-class citizens rely on to maintain their own vision of the city—lines dividing interior from exterior, private from public. And this transgressive tendency indicates some of what is at stake in imagining Mumbai as a sacred geography, as opposed to simply a town that contains a lot of temples.

When labor migrants settle in shantytowns, or when local villages are swallowed up in sprawl, it is the community's guardian deities that stake out the fault lines of urban development. Highlights of the tour offered in these pages include the dense downtown wards where even divine beings squat in slum housing; the cult of Sai Baba of Shirdi, whose saintly embrace reaches throughout the city and across sectarian divisions; Filmistan Studios in the suburbs, where an image factory has been built over a village; and the forest reserve that borders another studio, Film City, where tribal residents are being expelled on the grounds that they cannot be told apart from urban squatters.

Contestation among urban groups over which spaces look sacred—or which spaces are recognized as sacred even if they don't look like it—is often discussed by local observers in terms of what is real and what fake. What is that booth-like structure in the middle of the sidewalk? About the size of a cash machine, it has a store-bought icon of Sai Baba installed more or less where the touchscreen would go. Evidently, it's a Sai Baba temple. But is it a *real* Sai Baba temple? And this play of real and fake informs some curious juxtapositions. I have just alluded to a film studio complex, a facility incorporating a camera-ready temple that has been built on top of a village with a temple of its own. Another site to be discussed is that of an elaborate Hindu structure, an exact replica of a distant pilgrimage center, whose officiating priests are dressed as Brahmins but actually hail from lower-caste Muslim and Buddhist families.

As my own thinking about spaces like these progressed, however, *real* and *fake* receded as analytic categories. What took their place was a pair of terms learned from colloquial Hindi. *Pakka* is an adjective meaning cooked, proper, or clearly defined. *Kaccha* is its opposite: raw, ad hoc, blurry. In this book I view people's struggles to make and keep homes for themselves in India's exemplary city as a bid for recognition in the eyes of the powerful. (What may look like an optical metaphor here is not a metaphor.) I am interested in the cultural work that Mumbai's marginalized communities put into making their *kaccha* persons, spaces, and deities *pakka*, or visible.

To give an illustration that has little, on the surface, to do with religion: viewed in this way, a squatter colony is a *kaccha* settlement that may ascend, by degrees, to the status of a *pakka* neighborhood. Such a process involves the securing of official recognition through certification on paper, and this paper trail advances alongside a sort of material solidification: as plastic sheeting and scrap lumber get replaced with brick and concrete, the outlines of houses grow straighter and clearer, and the claim to the land becomes permanent. What this process has to do with temples (and with Muslim and Christian sites too) is the central question of *The Neighborhood of Gods*. The clue to foreground here is that the human agents of the state are not the only viewing subjects that have the power to bestow recognition.

The exposition is organized around two sets of field sites where subaltern communities (some Hindu, some non-Hindu, and some whose identity is under negotiation) use religious images and symbols to mark urban space. One effect of this activity is to claim scarce turf in this famously congested city—to signal "this space is taken" to other urban constituencies in terms that are legible to them. Another is to tame it—to make a territory viable for settlement by creating a base for a community's gods alongside its human members.

To say that "folk" or "village" religion is centered on the cults of locally based gods is not exactly news to scholars of religion in India. But what becomes of these territorial deities once they migrate, along with their human subjects, to the metropolis? And what becomes of visual worship, known in Hinduism as *darshan*, once transplanted from its locus classicus—a Brahmin-run temple in a village or pilgrimage town—into urban public space? Theorizing sacred space is a well-established project within the field of religious studies, but my own emphasis in this study has not been on space as such. Rather, what I have done here, drawing on insights from anthropology and semiotics, is to focus on the power of the images that demarcate discrete sites as sacred. And I should make it clear that reading such signs for their meaning is not my primary concern; my interest in images is not iconographic. I focus on visual operations in two directions: on the sacred image's relation to the space that surrounds it and on its relation to its spectator, or addressee.

This train of thought leads to another question. Should *darshan* be understood as a strictly Hindu practice? I believe it is better to think in terms of norms of relating to certain kinds of spaces and images, norms that have more to do with subject positions within Indian society than with confessional distinctions. Note that this question of classification is of importance not only to the academic study of religion. In the present day, the tone and terms of official and public discourses in India are increasingly dominated by Hindu nationalist ideology, which centers on a program of sorting out who is and who is not authentically Indian on the basis of Hindu identity. In taking seriously the reality of gods and other superhuman agencies in the experiences of ordinary people in an Indian city, my study pursues a sort of posttheological ethnography. Given the political climate, a project like this one risks being misread by the exponents of Hindutva—or its critics—as religious apologia.

It is imperative to clarify what kind of intervention I am proposing in this book. The place to start is with the category of *religion* and its applications in modern South Asian contexts: analytic, political, and legal. In both the academic discipline of religious studies and in official India in its capacity as heir to the British colonial archive, there has been a pervasive and longstanding emphasis on a scripturalist model of religion. Religious communities on this model are defined as bounded collectivities composed of individual subjects, each beholden to the collectivity by virtue of his or her belief in a discourse that is codified, paradigmatically, in the form of scripture. These internal loyalties are expressed socially through participation in ritual and the veneration of sacred symbols—visual artifacts and other sorts of signs that are understood to refer back to the foundational dogma or theology exclusive to, and definitive of, a discrete tradition.

Let's not mince words. This is a model that has privileged belief over practice, text over performance, discourse over embodiment, meaning over affect, and—to telegraph some points of special importance to the argument that awaits—abstract conceptualization over concrete particularity and descriptive iconography over the visual projection of effects. This book is committed to the delineation of an alternative system of norms. A perspectival shift to the secondary terms in these pairings can draw out commonalities in the everyday practices of members of Hindu, Muslim, Christian, Buddhist, and other religious communities, practices normally elided by the scripturalist model. With sacred space as its canvas, the system reveals itself in a complex palette of visual media.

My study follows two parallel investigations. One concerns the Warli community, a so-called tribal group whose modest settlements on the fringes of Mumbai occupy land claimed by other interests, including two film studios. According to the Warlis the land is their ancestral territory, and they mark it as such with the dwelling places of tribal gods. Initially drawn to the landscape by Bollywood's uncanny re-marking of it with the icons of national spaces—empty temples, Potemkin villages—I moved on in my fieldwork to problematize the effects of spectacles like these in erasing the local sacred geography.

The other inquiry takes up the unauthorized construction by city residents of shrines on the public streets. In the fall of 2003, acting in enforcement of a Bombay High Court ruling, municipal authorities set about knocking them down in the name of secularism and public order. As the demolitions met with citywide resistance, it became clear that, just as with the gods of the tribals, the "illegal religious structures" marked contested ground. From a subaltern perspective, I argue, the spiritual presences stationed at these outposts operate as local agents of surveillance, preserving their turf against the outsiders—rival communities, urban planners, citizen busybodies—who would trespass against them.

This book itself straddles boundaries, of a disciplinary sort. And after the manner of a Mumbai streetscape, it engages diverse publics. *The Neighborhood of Gods* has plenty to say about India but offers much that applies across the postcolonial world. The research presented here is based on fieldwork but the project is not conventionally anthropological. The book is a study in visual culture that emphasizes the social visibility and invisibility of human subjects. It celebrates the city but critiques liberal notions of cosmopolitanism and civil society.

Finally, it analyzes practices that are generally considered "religious" and "Hindu" but in so doing destabilizes the two categories. The argument pivots, nevertheless, on one of the classic concerns of the academic study of Hinduism: namely, the complex relation between local, non-elite symbols and cults and the translocal "great tradition" that has historically been defined by elites (mostly Brahmins, mostly in Sanskrit). And the book recasts, in a modern context, a question central to the history of Hindu thought: if the divine is manifest in the phenomenal world, then where and in what form do we recognize God— and with what sort of insight or authority?

Transliteration and Other Conventions

In transliterating words from Hindi and other South Asian languages I have chosen to dispense with diacritics, relying instead on the semistandard style of romanization associated with India's English-language press. My view is that this set of popular conventions is not only less abstruse than the system favored by philologists but also truer to the ad hoc, hybrid character of Mumbai speech. Where I have excerpted material from sources in which diacritics are used, I have preserved the original style.

In naming the city in present-day—that is to say, post-1995—contexts I have opted to go with the official default setting, *Mumbai*. I use *Bombay* when citing historical conjunctures and when reproducing the voices of others who, for various reasons, might favor the no-longer-official version of the name. References to *Thane* and *Thana* follow the same rule.

In 2003 the exchange rate shuttled between forty-seven and forty-eight Indian rupees to the US dollar. A rough-and-ready conversion for US readers encountering the rupee amounts in these pages, therefore, is Rs 50 = (just over) $1.00.

INTRODUCTION

That nick in the rock
is really a kick in the side of the hill.
It's where a hoof
struck

like thunderbolt
when Khandoba
with the bride sidesaddle behind him on the blue
horse

jumped across the valley
and the three
went on from there like one
spark

fleeing from flint.
To a home that waited
on the other side of the hill like a hay
stack.

ARUN KOLATKAR, "The Horseshoe Shrine"

Arun Kolatkar belonged to a celebrated group of Bombay-based modernist poets. He wrote in English, like his colleagues Nissim Ezekiel and Dom Moraes. But Kolatkar also wrote in Marathi, which is to say that he also knew his city as *Mumbai*. Unlike the Jewish Ezekiel or the Catholic Moraes—exemplary voices of the metropolis—he came from a Hindu family with Maharashtrian roots, from the southern city of Kolhapur. His best-known poems are double-sided ones, in which the English-educated urbanite confronts the vernacular dimensions of his environment and self.[1]

Jejuri, which supplies the epigraph here, is emblematic of this reflexivity. First published in 1976, this is his most celebrated work, an English-language poem cycle named after a backcountry Maharashtrian pilgrimage center. The modernist makes for an ambivalent pilgrim. Recounting his progress, bored and baffled by turns, he sifts through the dust and the rural pieties and is surprised by fleeting revelations—glimpses of the divine force on the landscape the locals seem to take as a given. At a time when Western hippies were flocking to India in search of the transcendent, Kolatkar takes his own strange trip to Bombay's backyard and discovers something immanent. The quest feels quintessentially Hindu.

With a keen observational eye and a no-less-acute self-awareness, Kolatkar was a flaneur at large in a messier town than Paris, and there's much in his work to commend it to ethnographers of India. In fact, the poet could himself be described as an armchair ethnographer—with the semantic compass of *armchair* defined by the small set of chairs in which he might actually have sat, as was his habit every Thursday, taking in the scene from the Wayside Inn, which used to stand at the main crossroads of the downtown area called Kala Ghoda.

In 2004, two years after the Wayside Inn closed (it gave way to an Asian fusion place), Kolatkar published *Kala Ghoda Poems*. The collection brings his hunt for the sublime home to the urban landscape—to the café's doorstep, in fact. Its centerpiece is a long poem called "Breakfast Time at Kala Ghoda." Annapoorna, the subaltern heroine of this mock epic, is an itinerant vendor of *idli*s, South Indian–style rice cakes. On a concrete parking barrier she sets an "aluminium box full of idlis / —lying / like an infant Krishna," and the poet looks on from his window as the neighborhood comes to life. For an enchanted moment, the crossroads plays host to a communion of diverse characters, sharing in the bounty of "Our Lady of Idlis" (Kolatkar 2010, 130). And in due course the spell is broken: "The pop-up cafeteria / disappears / like a castle in a children's book . . . as soon as the witch / shuts the book on herself" (144).

Most of Kala Ghoda's buildings date back to the late colonial period. Architecturally speaking, the neighborhood is dominated by the downtown art museum, an example of the trademark "Indo-Saracenic" style of the British Raj. As with many other Mumbai landmarks, this institution has officially been renamed after Chhatrapati Shivaji, the seventeenth-century king who is the great Maharashtrian culture hero, but local people generally know it as the Prince of Wales Museum, for its construction and dedication had commemorated the visit in 1905 of the future George V. And yet oddly enough it is a different monarch—his father—whose legacy defines the neighborhood as a whole. The best-known equestrian statue in the city is the triumphal image of Edward VII that stood before the museum for decades after the Raj's departure. In 1965 the authorities relocated horse and rider to the municipal zoo. Kolatkar gives an account of the displacement in his poem "David Sassoon," but the really notable thing about the statue is not its physical removal from the spot but its symbolic adherence to it. For if the king has been deposed in the city's memory, his mount has not: *kala ghoda* means "black horse."

What sort of associations does this ghost horse carry? The symbolism of horsemen as figures of heroism and mastery resonates deeply across South Asia.[2] My fieldwork was in its beginning stage when the Kala Ghoda came up in a conversation I was having with a leftist intellectual, a longtime resident of Mumbai. She told me that a similar monument stood some blocks to the north, in the garden at the center of another outpost of the old imperial city, Horniman Circle. But if anyone paid attention to the statue in Horniman Circle anymore, it was the day laborers and other lumpen types drawn to the neighborhood by the promise of menial work. They looked at Lord Cornwallis and saw, not the eighteenth-century governor-general, but Khandoba—the master of Jejuri, the Maharashtrian guardian god who patrols the frontiers of rural settlements on horseback. They prayed before it and left offerings at its base, she said. The site was thought to be efficacious as a dispenser of luck to gamblers.

The tone in which my friend gave these details was sardonic. She offered them in illustration of the false consciousness of the masses. It was well known that if you set a stone down on the street in Mumbai—or in any Indian city—you had no more than to wait overnight to find some simple fellow worshiping it as a god the next morning. But I thought I saw something else in the story and the stereotype behind it. Wasn't this an indication of subaltern agency?[3] If not precisely an act of resistance, surely it was a reclamation of urban space? Let's revisit Kolatkar's project in *Jejuri* for a moment. The wit of his observations builds on the premise that it makes sense for an inhabitant of the big, modern city to travel to the country, to the *desh*, to seek God. But as I was coming to understand, some of those *deshi* gods had come home to roost in the city.

To start thinking about what a public statue does as an idol of Khandoba it is helpful to consider what it was supposed to be doing as an effigy of Marquess Cornwallis. This is an exercise made simpler by historical and ideological distance from the British regime. There must be hardly anybody in Mumbai anymore who would claim membership in the sort of public envisioned by the monument's designers: imperial subjects who would recall Cornwallis's career as a soldier and administrator, celebrate his work and vision, and feel cued to experience a sense of shared purpose in an enterprise spanning the globe. Yet one thing the comparison makes clear is that at stake here is a claim to spatial order. The flip side of the global vista of empire is the local claim to territorial sovereignty: joining with people in Canada and Africa admiring the same sort of statue begins with admiring "our" own statue, *here*. And at one level, worshiping the statue as Khandoba accomplishes a similar recognition of territorial sovereignty, at once translocal and local. The lord of Jejuri is also lord here. Thus invoked at the same site is a different geography of the imagination—not that of Great Britain's imperial dominion but that of a Hindu Maharashtra.

But the comparison is only just getting started, because as it stands this is a false equivalence. For one thing, the sort of quasi-nationalist vision advanced by the Maratha-chauvinist Shiv Sena Party—the enforcers of the city's official renaming as Mumbai and many of its attractions after Shivaji—is certainly a force to be reckoned with in these pages. But Shivaji was a king (indeed, he has his own equestrian statue down by the Gateway of India), and Khandoba is a god. There is more to the idea of Maharashtra than an ideology of territorial sovereignty, and more to qualifying it as Hindu than the practice of identity politics along religious lines, or what in India is known as "communalism."

For another thing, the British Empire is defunct as a political project, but that is not to say the Horniman statue is empty of meaning or power for anyone in the present day who understands it to correspond to a historical personage named Cornwallis. It could well embody a certain nostalgia for the past, nostalgia not exactly for the colonial system or for the authority of white gentlemen in formal costume but for an idealized era when the construction of such spaces as Horniman Circle showed confidence in a narrative of progress. As such, this nostalgia also projects a desire for the future. According to some, once upon a time Mumbai, or rather Bombay, seems to have been a more modern place. Well before Independence, the city cultivated an image as India's premier city, its window to the West—"Urbs Prima in Indis," as the motto goes—and a certain picture of a well-designed, well-run metropolis continues to be cherished among the postcolonial elite. It is a place inhabited by disciplined, civil citizens and is organized according to rational principles, such as the distinction between public spaces (for example, a garden in a municipal park) and private ones (for example, a house of worship).[4] And it is a place as legible as it is sensible, defined with conceptual clarity, such that it looks on the ground the way it does on the map, and its constituent features correspond to their labels. Buses run on schedule, for example. The numbers on your electricity bill reflect the amount that you've used, people do not loiter or pee where the sign tells them not to, and statues are who it says they are on the plaque. Most of these notices are in English.

By contrast with this semiotic relation between viewer-as-reader and statue-as-text, what happens when a person identifies the statue as Khandoba involves a more intimate, visceral bond.[5] Describing the bond concisely for the purposes of this introduction is difficult, since theorizing it is one of the principal tasks of this book. But the readiest way to gloss the interaction that takes place at sites like these between a human subject and a materially emplaced deity is to use the Hindu term *darshan*, which designates the ritual of visual worship. An aspect of *darshan* with important implications for my work is that in granting the connection to the worshiper, the deity is perceived to gaze back. This is a visual exchange, then, between subject and master, and as such it invites analysis as a gesture of mutual recognition. In pursuing this argument in this study I will be looking to a body of work on the gaze and its operations whose inspiration goes back to Jacques Lacan.[6]

Two more factors may be mentioned that complicate the autonomy of the viewing subject. The first is that, according to the logic of *darshan* which obtains among many Hindus (and also others, perhaps, who do not self-identify as such), the exchange of glances is accomplished as an exchange of personal substance. As in other rituals, participation in *darshan* renders the organism porous. The second is implied when gamblers attribute control over their fortunes to Khandoba and consequently attempt to win his favor through ritual transactions. To interact in this way with powerful nonhuman persons is to participate in a system of negotiating and redistributing agency. It follows that to localize the presence of these divine agents alongside oneself and one's fellow human dependents is to inhabit a landscape contoured by flows of decentered and distributed agency.[7]

It seems that the earlier proposition about what is at stake in the identity of the lord of Horniman Circle—what I had termed spatial orders, or geographies of the imagination—is in need of some reformulation. Clearly, the question is not merely one of rival maps, differences of interpretation at the conceptual level. What is called for is the elaboration of models of space that are interdependent with models of the self. To ask, "What kind of space is this?" would then be to ask, "What kind of bodies inhabit it—and to what kind of regime are they subject?" Again, I propose that the recognition the statue compels in the viewing subject (is it Lord Cornwallis or Lord Khandoba?) is not a simple matter of reading the image's iconography. As Louis Althusser (1971) and others following his lead have shown, ideology makes its appeal at a deeper level—affective, embodied, and performative. Local sovereignty is indeed in contention, but this is sovereignty in the sense of a structural dispensation that has the power to organize normative personhood. It configures the subject in relation to the experience of space. And this relation is mediated at discrete and concrete sites within the city, through an ideological appeal that is delivered visually.

Such, in broad outline, are the analytic contours of the study that will take up the chapters to follow. My project is not the same as Kolatkar's; I am not looking for gods in the streets. But it is an empirical fact that many people in Mumbai do see gods in the streets. As my ethnographic research advanced, it was around these people's practices that my inquiry took shape—around their participation in the city's selective enchantment and around the effects of those practices across the urban canvas and beyond, into the broader domain of Indian public culture.

Rather than following through at Horniman Circle, however, I turned my attention to some of the many shrines to be found elsewhere in public space. I focused on what, in reflection of the clash of geographies noted above, the municipal authorities and the English-language press generally describe as "illegal religious structures": displays put up on the street with the apparent purpose of attracting attention from foot traffic. I came to think that what brought the shrines' clients together as a collectivity was neither a set of beliefs that could be classified under the rubric of Hinduism nor a common attachment to the *desh* of Maharashtra. Their diversity overspilled the bounds of religious or regional affiliation. But the very precarity of the illegal shrines seemed to mirror the precarity of the only housing available to half of Mumbai's population— namely, the slums. I took up research on the figure whose face invites *darshan* from most of these local stations, Sai Baba of Shirdi, revered by Hindus and Muslims alike. And I sought critical purchase on a different dimension of the city's enchantment: the nationwide projection of Mumbai as the showcase of Indian modernity.

This is a phenomenon that is related to but distinct from the postcolonial nostalgia I remarked above. It is an effect of the pervasive reach of commercial mass media—above all, of one of the city's flagship industries, the Hindi popular cinema. "Mumbai" or "Bombay" in this sense, as William Mazzarella (2003, 179) states, "hypostasizes in one signifier the transformative allure of the modern, both material (a new life in the city, the possibility of making a life—however precarious—on one's own terms) and phantasmic (the spectacular imaginaries of Bollywood, which increasingly play with the place of Indianness within a globalizing world)." He breaks the image down further: "Bombay is a dazzling microcosm of the diversity of the nation. But Bombay is also nothing like 'the real India,' the India of half a million villages. In India, Bombay is everywhere and nowhere. Writes Amrit Gangar: 'Bombay is often called Mayapuri, the city of *maya*—of illusion. . . . It is a generic city that exists everywhere in India in various forms.'"[8]

The Sanskritic name Mayapuri, with its derivation from classical philosophy, is indeed a potent figuration, inasmuch as the concept of *maya* packs in both illusion's attractiveness—the glamour of a certain lifestyle, the glitter of wealth—and its essential emptiness.[9] And like its American corollary Tinseltown, it enfolds an internal critique—and targets show business as the engine of illusion.

The *B* in Bollywood stands for Bombay, of course. And yet, as it turned out, where my fieldwork was concerned the "wood" part proved to be no less telling, because the film studios are located in suburban tracts cleared from land that was forest just decades ago. Of the two studios where I worked, one was set in the middle of a neighborhood, and the other, much larger, sprawled into a wooded area bordering a forest reserve. At both sites I learned that the facilities had been built over villages, over the settlements of a community indigenous to the forest, the Warlis. Indeed, in the very spaces where the film producers staged their glossy fantasies, the Warlis were trying to maintain their own geography as best they could by attending to their tribal gods.

In the conflict I followed downtown, the rival camps could be identified as middle-class advocates for the "public interest," on the one hand, and the client communities of the shrines, people largely based in slums, on the other. In the parallel conflict that had developed in the suburbs, another public-interest group had pressed, as part of an environmentalist agenda, to free the forest from human habitation. (Warli settlement patterns had historically not taken into account legal boundaries of the sort that separate neighborhoods, film studios, and nature preserves.) Both of these conflicts were made official in courts of law. The urban petitioners (plaintiffs) filed to have the city government remove the shrines from the street, and the suburban petitioners filed to have the state forestry department remove the tribals from the forest.

Organizing my exposition around these two lawsuits has resulted in a book that falls into complementary halves. And when I took on the task of sorting through the legal files, the tedium of my research was relieved by an insight that has provided one of the key elements of my analytic scheme. If the visual interface of Mumbai's sacred geography was the shrines and other public religious displays, and that of Mumbai as spectacular fantasy was commercial and entertainment media, then what sort of imagery, I needed to ask, mediated the city's rationalized, postcolonial geography? The answer was official paperwork—legal documents, government forms and licenses, maps and planning diagrams—or, more precisely, the visual idiom of paperwork. To return to an earlier point in this discussion, the focus of attention at this level was not on the statue of Lord Cornwallis so much as on the label on the statue. English text in black type on white paper was how the viewing subject encountered the city's "techno-juridical grid" (Pinney 1997b, 855);[10] as my fieldwork would demonstrate, the perception of its authority was just as great, if not greater, among residents who did not read English.

The idea that Mumbai is made up of layers of space is refracted in an image the novelist Michael Chabon once proposed for a different citadel of the British Empire. In a 2005 essay about Sherlock Holmes, he investigates the detective's phantasmic milieu, where respectable housefronts shield parlors and cellars with secrets, tracing its origins beyond Victorian London back to Conan Doyle's childhood home. For Chabon, it is Edinburgh that truly embodies the split: a city whose elegant eighteenth-century grid was constructed over an auld Scots ancestor realm, a medieval warren notorious for its squalor.

The tale of three cities I tell here will offer a contrast. Mumbai's own warren will be depicted as neither anarchic nor archaic but organized according to principles of its own. The rational grid strains to contain this alternative landscape. And in the city's "modern" façades, as smoothed out and flattened through spectacularized representations in the cinema and other organs of mass media, I will locate a third stratum with phantasmic characteristics of its own.

Critical Terms and Debates

If you ride taxis in Mumbai, you learn that the landmarks the cabbies steer by tend to fall into three categories: big government buildings, houses of worship, and cinema halls.[11] Thus far in this introduction, I have proposed a model of official space, the rationally conceived, rationally operating city of planners and administrators. I have distinguished that realm from a second domain that I call sacred space. This is conceived as a network of sites that are endowed with a special sort of value, one distinct from the calculus of the real estate market. In this case, the agents of appreciation are invisible persons—the divine affiliates of human communities—who have been settled at these spots (and thus brought into visibility) by the human beings who live alongside them.[12] And I have identified a third realm: the gleaming metropolis of aspirational modernity, which I call spectacularized space.

At this point it is important, however, to make it clear that this threefold scheme is not a critical element of my argument. I will be making much use of this official-sacred-spectacular triad in the chapters to follow. But it is a heuristic, not an analytic. What I have laid out in the preceding pages is an expository device, a conceptual map of sorts.

I have been led to look at the city in this multilayered way by Arjun Appadurai, whose theorizing of space marks a pivotal moment in the anthropology of modern societies, and nowhere more so than in the study of Mumbai, his native city. Appadurai's (1995) concept of the "production of locality" directs attention at the cultural work involved in "transforming spaces into places" and at the interdependency between the agents of this work and the places they construct; put simply, in producing locality, people define themselves as local subjects.[13] Expanding out from the neighborhood level, Appadurai recasts this dynamic at two translocal removes: at the level of the nation-state and at the potentially globalized level of the "virtual neighborhood." These three levels, which are interactive, will be seen to line up with my own categories: the sacred, the rationalized, and the spectacular, respectively.[14]

Through the course of my fieldwork, Appadurai's production of locality served as a guiding rubric. Again, however, the points I will argue in this book are not primarily directed as interventions in scholarly debates about space. This cautionary note needs to be sounded especially clearly with regard to sacred space. In the broadest terms, to be sure, I have found inspiration in two approaches to the problem that are well recognized in religious studies. The project of making sense of the cosmos by inscribing it with binaries through religious discourse and ritual activity—the operative categories being sacred and profane, or pure and impure—applies to the organization of physical space in the religious systems theorized by Émile Durkheim (1995) and Mary Douglas ([1966] 2002). And in foregrounding perception, the phenomenologically inflected ideas of Mircea Eliade ([1954] 2005) and Gaston Bachelard ([1964] 1994) open the way to thinking about the effects of sacred space on the human subjects who experience it as such—individually and collectively. Yet given the sort of complex ethnographic milieu I am navigating, these models of space afford an analytic project like mine no more than the bluntest of instruments.

There are many reasons for this. In this study, sacred spaces tend to appear more as bones of contention than as sites of cohesion. Questions of power and agency go unaddressed in the traditional models, as does another central concern of my research: failure. What if you build a shrine—and nobody comes? Is that space somehow not authentically sacred? (Conversely, what if you build it for wholly mercenary purposes—say, to shield an illegal connection to a municipal water main—and this "fake" shrine attracts cultic attention?) Again, the sites of my interest are located in a contemporary urban context that is complex and dynamic. Multiple constituencies may be involved in contesting and negotiating a claim to sacrality. And yet more problematically, some of these groups may fail altogether to recognize the terms of the claim—the logic behind it or the symbols that mark it. A recent argument that advances very much in line with my sympathies here is that of Jacob N. Kinnard (2014) in his *Places in Motion*, an ethnography of pilgrimage places that explores New York's Ground Zero alongside several Indian sites. The emphasis in Kinnard's book is on the processual, socially negotiated dimension of what he calls the religious "charging" of sites; he eschews the language of the sacred altogether.

Kinnard goes so far as to cite a pronouncement handed down by Claude Lévi-Strauss: the sacred is "a value of indeterminate signification, in itself empty of meaning and therefore susceptible to the reception of any meaning whatsoever."[15] Now, this may well be so of the term when proposed as a universal category. But I do not retain *sacred*—and incorporate it in this book's title—solely for its rhetorical utility. It is my position that within the cultural context of my ethnography—Mumbai and, more broadly, South Asia—there is in fact a common understanding of sacred space that obtains across boundaries of class, caste, regional origin, or religion. The question "What makes a space sacred?" has a pretty concrete answer: it is the locally established presence of a superhuman personality. Some essence, emanation, or fragment of a deity, saint, or spirit has become emplaced in material space and is there made perceptible and accessible to human subjects.[16] (Readers familiar with the Sanskrit terminology will recognize here *pitha*, sacred space in the sense of the "seat" of a deity, as opposed to *tirtha*, a "ford" or crossing place, but the logic of the *pitha* is not to be confined to classical Hindu teachings, or even primarily attributed to them; again, the gods and saints of a diversity of traditions have been seated across the city, and I never heard the term *pitha* used in a fieldwork context.)[17] To be sure, in lived practice, the number of humans who recognize the presence specific to a given spot will be circumscribed in various ways, and the number of those wishing to participate in relationships with it at that spot will of course be defined yet more tightly. But in Mumbai, recognizing the principle of the spirit-presence is a simple matter of cultural literacy.

Rounding out the discussion of my spatial heuristic, I should identify some of the sources that support the other two legs of the triad. Both rationalized space and spectacular space owe their initial formulation to well-known works of Marxist theory. What eventually took shape as rationalized space originated in Henri Lefebvre's (1991) concept of "abstract space" in *The Produc-*

tion of Space. My way of thinking about spectacular space was inspired by Guy Debord's (1994) *The Society of the Spectacle* (see also Baudrillard 1993; Eco 1986; Kracauer 1995). But as this study advanced, the question of what capitalism does to the city came to seem less germane than the question of what post-colonial administration does to it (see Ong 2011, 2–3). In the end, the insights that have come to define rationalized space can be traced primarily to Michel Foucault's (1991, 1995, 2010) work on surveillance, governmentality, and the archive (see also J. C. Scott 1998). Two other sources that must also be named as part of this conversation are theoretically oriented essays about Mumbai itself. Jim Masselos's (1991) "Appropriating Urban Space" offers insights about the experience of space in colonial Bombay that prove eminently applicable to the postcolonial city of the present. Appadurai's (2002) "Deep Democracy" upends the Foucauldian model of governmentality to analyze slum-based methodologies of local administration "from below."

It will be noted that with the ideas of many of the theorists named above— Foucault, Scott, and Appadurai, and also Debord and his associates—a concern with visuality comes to the fore. Visual forms represent, mark, and cite different kinds of space, defining and configuring them not only in representational archives but "on the ground," and serving to reproduce them. Here at last is the analytic turf, as it were, on which I stake out my own intervention.[18] If my inquiry into how diverse Mumbai residents convert urban space into discrete places is aimed at making a contribution to social theory, it is in problematizing the visual mediation of the experience of space. The picture comes into relief wherever people make the same space into different places. (The reader will encounter many such scenarios in this book.) As my analysis will demonstrate, the question of which place that might be for what kind of people becomes a question of showing and seeing, of what the space looks like to whom. A central proposition of my argument will be that distinct constituencies within the city's population inhabit distinct urban geographies—that the recognition by the viewer of a certain kind of place is to be related to that viewer's conditioning as a member of a social group.

But the problem is less straightforward than lining up models of space with discrete social constituencies bounded by lines of class or caste (to specify two important ways of grouping people in the Mumbai context). In other words, I am not simply proposing that poor people see sacred space where middle-class people see rationalized space, although I am satisfied to put that notion forward as a provocative starting point. As the discussion of *darshan* in the first part of this introduction has suggested, neither term in the relation of recognition is stable. I understand recognition as a moment of subjectification, in which an authoritative sight, once construed as such, helps configure the subject position of the beholder.

Organizing the analysis in this way around visual relations makes engagement possible with four important factors. Two of these have already been touched on in the discussion of *darshan*. The first is the role of distinct visual idioms in mediating the relation between the manifold urban geography and the human subjects who navigate it. The second is the potential for failure—that is, failure in the process of subjectification, failure in the ideological appeal of the visual signal to the viewer. Examples are the advertisement that persuades no one to buy anything, the public No Spitting sign stained red with betel juice, the *murti*, or god image, that sits unadorned and unadored. And related to this problem is a third factor, one that received some attention in this book's preface: the relative legibility or illegibility of the visual medium. No less important than the question of the viewing subject's receptivity to the ideological appeal is the formal capacity of the viewed image to project it. It has been in developing this aspect of my analysis that I have pressed into service two terms from everyday Hindi: *kaccha* (raw, blurry, sketchy, among other things) and *pakka* (finished, proper, concrete).

Finally, there is the question of the public. This word will be encountered frequently as my argument unfolds. In this book's first chapters, especially, *public* will appear in the exposition as an adjective. Thus, I will use *public space*, in the sense of material spaces that fall legally under the purview of the state, as, for example, with city streets, and also in the sense of spaces that may be privately owned but are traversed by people from all walks of life.[19] Thus also, I will employ *the public interest*, a high-minded figuration salient in the language of the lawsuits I have followed. At the theoretical level I will work with the abstractions of the *public sphere*, as propounded by Jürgen Habermas ([1962] 1989), and of *public culture*, as formulated by Arjun Appadurai and Carol Breckenridge (1988) in response to Habermas, with postcolonial conditions exemplified by the Indian case very much on their minds.[20]

But when deployed analytically in its noun form—as the fourth factor brought into play by the argument's emphasis on visual relations—*public* is a unit of social categorization. Used in this sense, the word flags a way of examining how groups of people are brought together that emphasizes the socially constructive force of cultural forms in mass circulation. And in investigating how these forms perform their work of mediating an individual's relation to a collectivity, it is also crucial to note *where* they do so—for mass circulation is by definition not limited to spaces configured or regulated by any particular collectivity.[21] Exemplary, then, are public spaces such as streets and cinema screens, as opposed to circuits of transmission confined to kinship or caste networks or pedagogical or other institutional contexts. As for exemplary forms, for the purposes of this study they include movies, newspapers, and popular religious art; within the scholarly conversation my work follows, salient arguments have centered on novels, satirical newsletters, and even devotional song.[22] Guided by Michael Warner's (2002) seminal "Publics and Counterpublics," I understand discrete and diverse publics to be unevenly integrated within the discordant concert of modern public culture.

In principle a dynamically bounded collective, a *public* in this sense can be defined as a social constituency whose members respond in like fashion to the way a given set of cultural forms "hails" or addresses them. In my framework, the stress will be placed on recognition—as opposed to rational discourse à la Habermas or to consumption practices per the public-culture model. Here, as a step toward enacting this realignment, let's double the terms on each side of the recognition relation. Expanding from two to four makes clearer the complementarity of the relation's visual and social dimensions. The viewing subject (1) may thus be seen as an individual representative of a broader social constituency (2); and the viewed image (3) emerges as a cultural artifact that mediates the call of a deity or other ideological master figure (4). Unpacking the connection in this manner between the mediating image and its target audience can open the way to more general propositions about social constituencies, on the one hand—which may well correlate with received categories of group identity such as caste and class—and about ideologized subject positions, on the other.

More needs to be said about the last point. I do not rule out ideological positions conventionally identified as such within contemporary Indian political discourse—for example, "secularist" or "Hindu nationalist." The model of ideology I favor, however, is one that goes both broader and deeper, and in this regard I situate my project within a tradition of scholarship on subjectification that builds on the insights of theorists already named in this discussion: Althusser, Lacan, and Foucault. I brought in the concept of the ideological dispensation earlier, in connection with the question of sovereignty; here, let me break down what is at stake in an individual's subjection to a given dispensation with some questions formulated from the position of the subject—that is, of the interpellated public.

One list of questions pertinent to this study might look like this: What are the rules that govern the environments I inhabit—the city of Mumbai, Indian society as a whole, the cosmos? What sort of agency do I have as an individual to engage those rules? Who is empowered to enforce them? (And how and where are those persons emplaced within the city, society, the cosmos?) What, then, is the relation of my community—of kindred subjects—to the state? Questions of this kind revolve around a concern that I will gloss as *sovereignty*.[23]

Another pair of questions might look like this: How does what I see relate to realities beyond the limited compass of my vision? How do signs signify things; how does signification relate to reality? These concerns will be addressed under the rubric of *signification*.

Here is how my framework accommodates the problem of sovereignty, or polity. I have found that the ideologically laden images of my research tend to engage this concern in either of two ways. Correspondingly, where my argument enters a sustained discussion of the public—in chapter 1—it develops a comparison between two distinct subject positions. The point of this divergence is the state; these collectivities are defined against each other in the contrasting modes of their membership within the urban (and, at one remove, national) sociopolitical order that, in combination, they compose. And this is not to say that their divergence in the matter of temporal authority does not have implications for subjects' relations to divine authority—it most emphatically does. But, in a word, what divides the two camps is the question of citizenship. I examine one of them, accordingly, under the label of *citizens*, and the other under that of *subalterns*.

In retaining this sort of binary at the basis of an analysis of postcolonial society, I find support in the thinking of three members of the Subaltern Studies collective, all of whom have moved on to complicate the Marxian preconceptions that characterized the collective in its heyday in the 1980s and 1990s.[24] As chapters 1 and 2 will make clear, I have been inspired by some of Sudipta Kaviraj's insights pertaining to the organization of public spaces in Kolkata. Of primary importance to the way I conceptualize publics in chapter 1, however, is the theory of Indian political life formulated by Partha Chatterjee (2004b) in *The Politics of the Governed*. Chatterjee's distinction between civil society and political society marks the decisive shift from a structural bifurcation to a model based on ideological orientations. It must be said that my own pool of subalterns—as I use the term to designate a subject position—fits imperfectly within Chatterjee's scheme, inasmuch as it will be seen to encompass populations too marginal to aspire to the sort of instrumentalist activity that characterizes participation in political society. And in this connection, I share the concern enunciated by Dipesh Chakrabarty (2000) with the subaltern tendency to attribute political agency to divine powers, an apparent outsourcing of personhood that has long vexed scholars pursuing a traditionally leftist historiography.

One more name, and this overview of my book's analytic apparatus can be considered complete. Alongside the problem of sovereignty, I have indicated a second aspect of the recognition relation where attention to visual-cultural artifacts unlocks implications for the construction of social subjects. This is the problem of signification. How does the image that marks a given site represent or educe a greater reality? What is the logic behind the spectacle's generation of an effect on the viewer? In construing the visual interfaces of my interest—cinema, paperwork, cultic displays—I have turned to the semiotics of Charles S. Peirce for terms that can categorize how such forms mediate the relation between ideological dispensations and their subjects. Peirce's well-known triad of *icon*, *index*, and *symbol* will come into play as the argument takes shape from chapter 2 onward.

"One very important triad is this," explains Peirce ([1885] 1993, 243), "it has been found that there are three kinds of signs which are all indispensable in all reasoning; the first is the diagrammatic sign or *icon*, which exhibits a similarity or analogy to the object of discourse; the second is the *index*, which like a pronoun demonstrative or relative, forces the attention to the particular object intended without describing it; the third is the general name or description [*symbol*] which signifies its object by means of an association of ideas or habitual connection between the name and the character signified." This is an early formulation that sorts out "signs" (what I have called images or forms) on the basis of distinct logics connecting them to their objects. Peirce refined and elaborated this elementary scheme in the years that followed. What I do in this book is very far from a systematic or rigorous Peircean analysis, but— after the manner of other scholars in anthropology and film studies who have sought inspiration in Peirce—I have borrowed his triad as a tool for the analysis of visual culture.[25] My particular interest here is in visual artifacts that have been imbued (or "charged," as Kinnard would have it) with the power of the sacred. For the purposes of this introduction, the way I apply Peirce's categories to the variety of ways such an image projects an address can be illustrated with a familiar example.

Who is the master of Horniman Circle? Let me invite the reader to step into the shoes of a hypothetical observer. (And as you work through the illustration, bear in mind that for Peirce all three modes are technically present in any instance of a sign-object relation, although one of the three will tend to dominate.) You enter the park and encounter an impressive personage in stone. As established at the start of this introduction, whether you see in the image a British sahib or a *deshi* deity depends on your frame of reference. But complicating things for the sake of argument, let's say your background is something like Arun Kolatkar's; you are a person capable of recognizing both Marquess Cornwallis and Khandoba. The leverage Peirce's categories bring to a problem like this is in excavating the logic behind the image's triggering of a given association. Here it's a question of crossed wires, which can be traced back to the sign's iconic function. The shape of the marble presents a formal resemblance, on the one hand, to an East India Company official and, on the other, to the horseman god of Maharashtrian Hinduism[26] (in his earlier writings, Peirce refers to icons as *appearances*). To the degree that this spectacle is encountered as an icon, then, it has failed to make an authoritative address.

What of the indexical level, where signification is enacted on the basis of a causal relation or of a "spatiotemporal contiguity" (Parmentier 1994, 6)? Let's say there are offerings, perhaps fruit or flowers, laid at the statue's base. These are indexical traces of the devotion of others; someone else has recognized a deity at the site. How does this reframing affect your perception? A more direct identification could be made if among the offerings was turmeric powder, because turmeric and its golden color are trademark features of the cult of Khandoba. Now, to be sure, simply registering that someone else has seen Khandoba will not necessarily cue you to recognize him there yourself. But perhaps you are familiar with the teaching that the god makes his presence manifest in turmeric (the origin stories of some Khandoba temples state that he chose the site by causing spice to flow from the ground), and as you stand there, taking in the whole picture, the wind picks up the powder and brushes you with it. Or it may be that a shaft of sunlight strikes the statue just then, backlighting it in a telltale gold-yellow tone. Indices of this sort would have put Kolatkar on notice, summoning an affective response if not a full-blown *darshan* experience. (In the poem "The Butterfly" from *Jejuri*, Khandoba's gesture to Kolatkar is a wink-like "pinch of yellow," delivered as the insect flits by.)

Finally, there is the symbolic relation, where the sign indicates its object on the basis of a strictly conventional association, as, for example, written letters stand in for sounds, or names for persons. This would be the case with a plaque labeling the statue in roman letters: *Cornwallis*. It may be superfluous to add here that not everybody in Mumbai can read, and of course not everybody who reads does so in English. In this connection, however, let me suggest that regard for the truth claim of this inscription is not necessarily predicated on the ability to read it.

Let's switch back from the relation between the sign and its object to reexamine the way the sign engages the viewing subject, and conclude the exercise by inviting two reflections from you, the observer. The first has to do with authority. The symbolic identification the label performs is not free of ideology. If your impulse on reading the answer spelled out in the word *Cornwallis* is to deem it satisfactory, or "correct"—resolving the dilemma the statue poses at the iconic level, in supersession of signals received at the indexical level—then let's ask what that says about your standard of evidence. And to take it one step further: what are the implications of mediation-by-symbol for the way you make sense of the city you inhabit?[27] These questions should recall to mind the line of inquiry introduced just before this discussion moved on to Peirce: the project proposed in this book of analyzing subject positions in terms of sovereignty.

The second reflection has to do with affect. The statue's illustration of different modes of signification should also suggest different reactions at the level of subjective experience. Peirce's system does in fact offer phenomenological categories (Firstness, Secondness, and Thirdness) to be matched up with the semiotic triad, although to impose this taxonomy on my research would be taking things a step too far in a programmatic direction.[28] Nevertheless, the key point, to state the obvious, is that visual stimuli engage rational, affective, and embodied kinds of attention in varying proportions. To interpret a monument's meaning by reading the label feels very different from participation in the exchange of *darshan*. Of particular interest for this study are those moments when a privileged (or otherwise anomalous) spectacle stands out in relief, as it were, from the quotidian landscape and commands your gaze such that you are reaffirmed in your subject position. Or—yet more interesting—you are shifted into an alternative state in which your sense of self and your surroundings are transformed. What set of variables would need to converge for you to perceive Khandoba there, looking back at you?

This concludes the semiotic exercise. But there are two details left to add about the statue's history that will further complicate what, and how, it signifies.

The first is that the chain of associations that led my friend from Kala Ghoda to the story about Horniman Circle was, I have learned, more subtle than I thought, for the statue's form is not actually equestrian. Cornwallis is depicted on foot, like other largely forgotten colonial figures. It is a literally pedestrian image that has become imbued with the cavalier's qualities of vigilance and martial prowess. At Horniman Circle it used to occupy a colonnaded structure topped by a canopy, and it seems this framing device helped to set it apart. The parasol-like canopy cited the classical *chhatri*, the iconographic accoutrement of a deity or king, and the overall arrangement would have resembled those of the sacred idols housed in shrines, large and small, at public sites throughout the city. It thus turns out that the display corresponded, at the iconic level, more straightforwardly with a generic category of god images than with any particular god.

The second point is that it has not actually stood in the garden since the 1960s. Cornwallis was swept up in the same purge of antinational statuary that claimed Edward VII. What remains today is an unlabeled patch of flagstones. And nevertheless, according to my friend and many others in Mumbai, the spot continues to command ritual attention.[29] As at Kala Ghoda, it seems a ghost rider patrols here too; for a certain subset of the local population, at least, the sacred geography is still evident. In this, the present-day scenario at Horniman Circle gives a preview of many examples I will present from my fieldwork, where divine presence is indexed to specific plots of ground. Swollen forms on the landscape like anthills show Hindu goddesses in the process of "self-manifesting"; other spots hint that they contain the as-yet-unmemorialized remains of Muslim saints. The problem at sites like these, however, where the iconic and symbolic dimensions have remained undefined or become erased, is that it can be hard for people outside the local cult community to see anything special about them. And when it comes to sites demarcated as public, as my research will demonstrate, this can be quite a big problem.

Plan of the Book

The analytic program outlined above unfolds throughout the book's exposition. But the basic framework has been set in place by the end of chapter 3. The first three chapters establish the main components of the framework: the discussion of multiple spatial orders; the retirement of the spatial model as an analytic in favor of relating the experience of space to multiple subject positions; the stress on the visual mediation thereof; the definition of the problem of formal visibility or legibility; the discussion of the public and the recasting of the subaltern; the theorization of *darshan* in terms of reciprocal recognition; and the turn to Peircean semiotics in the analysis of "sacred spaces" and other ideological spectacles.

Chapter 1 introduces a multilayered and quintessentially Mumbai sort of space, a Bollywood studio. Filmistan Studios occupies a five-acre compound in Goregaon, one of the city's outer suburbs. One of the leading production houses of the Hindi cinema's so-called Golden Age in the 1950s and 1960s, Filmistan in the present day is a facility consisting of sound stages and outdoor lots that are rented out to producers for their shoots. The chapter begins by tracking my own encounter with this space through successive layers. The first layer is an official, rationalized space of work—one that in some regards instantiates a liberal model of public space better than other sites juridically defined as public, such as the city streets. At the same time, Filmistan is also a community, or "urban village," whose human members organize themselves in relation to the exercise of power on the grounds by parahuman agents such as gods and ghosts. And there is, of course, a third layer at work here as well: the dimension of cinematic spectacle, wherein component elements of the studio space—or the façades thereof—represent coordinates within the formulaic Bollywood landscape of the Indian nation and its exemplary city, Mumbai.

The studio is traversed by a diversity of constituencies that I cast as a microcosm of the city that surrounds it. These include the studio management and their clients, the film producers, and the workers employed by both. In addition to these groups, there are also two others that present an arresting contrast: hypervisible Bollywood talent and a community of all-but-invisible people who actually live on the grounds. This contrast sets up a theme that will become increasingly apparent in the chapters to follow: namely, that of the attainment, precisely, of visibility. But the group with which this chapter is mainly concerned is the production crew workers, known as "light boys." Building on some observations about the light boys, their own negotiation of distinct spatial layers, and the visual interfaces that mediate those relations, I put forward some theoretical propositions about publics, political society, and subalterns.

The next two chapters cohere around a conflict defined (and materially exacerbated) by a lawsuit adjudicated in the Bombay High Court. Demonstrating a cleavage between the city's citizens and subalterns, the conflict was precipitated by a citizen's rights group asserting a grievance in the name of the public. In the ruling handed down in Writ Petition 2063 of 2002, *Janhit Manch v. State of Maharashtra*, Mumbai's municipal administration was ordered to act on its mandate to keep the urban grid clear of material and symbolic clutter by demolishing what the court and the press both referred to as "illegal religious structures." I devote chapters 2 and 3 to a consideration of these wayside shrines, which neighborhood residents had been accustomed to erect in public space to house the various deities and protective spirits—Hindu and otherwise—who watch over their streets.

Chapter 2 relies on an ethnographic walking tour of South Mumbai to provide narrative movement. The specific sites I describe represent a typology of the so-called "illegal religious structures" consigned to demolition by the High Court ruling, and among my featured attractions are some that did indeed end up in the fall of 2003 at the business end of a backhoe. At the analytic level this chapter fills in much of the groundwork for the book's argument by laying out two sets of categories. The first, which anchors each end of an axis on which to plot a given site's visibility—or semiotic legibility—is the versatile pair of Hindi words mentioned earlier: the oppositional terms *kaccha* and *pakka*. More technical is the second set of categories, Peirce's taxonomy of sign-object relations: the triad of icon, index, and symbol.

In chapter 3 I build on this typology of street shrines to examine the predominance of a single figure as their divine occupant: Sai Baba of Shirdi. This historical holy man's appeal has come to transcend his affiliations with Hindu and Islamic traditions to endow the spaces he marks with a sort of generically sacred quality. An investigation of the Baba icon's history in Mumbai, which originates with a photograph—a *pakka* visual form—introduces several points for complicating the study of *darshan*, or visual worship. Drawing on some insights from Lacan and his interlocutors, I move on to theorize the *darshan* encounter in terms of reciprocal recognition. I examine the sacred image's legibility, or *pakka* quality, as one important factor in the recognition relation. And the saint's early twentieth-century teachings enjoining iconic representation as an efficacious conduit of *darshan* are related to the contemporary context, in which urban public space has become saturated with copies of his portrait.

In chapter 4 I return to Filmistan. Conversations with a person I call Vikas, who lives in a corner of the studio grounds that is familiarly designated "the Village" (and sometimes filmed as such), reveal that the whole operation was built on top of a hamlet, or *pada*, settled by members of the Warli community, one of Maharashtra's so-called Scheduled Tribes. In excavating Filmistan's tribal history I pay particular attention to the studio's temples, of which one, through a process of "*pakka*-fication," has in effect undergone a conversion from a site dedicated to a tribal goddess to an outpost of modern Brahminical Hinduism.

Vikas's living situation presents a predicament that involves a lawsuit of his own. He believes the ruling in a case dating back several decades vindicates his ancestral claim to the Filmistan grounds. In arguing this, he cites not only matters of property and title—evidence given form through paperwork—but also his standing as a son of the soil, as the scion of the village headman's lineage, and as the local medium who communes with territorial deities. In making my own argument, I theorize my interlocutor's emergence from the social margins into civil society as a problem of visual definition akin to the tribal goddess's transformation into a Hindu icon.

What, indeed, would it take for the powerful interests that contend over the space to recognize Vikas in his patrimony? The question frames my interlocutor's reflections on a number of related themes: on the Indian legal system as a colonial inheritance; on the anarchic state of "terror" that would prevail in the absence of law; on contact with locally emplaced deities as a source of power and affective transport in his life; and on cinema as a modern, "scientific" innovation with the capacity to produce similar effects.

Chapter 5 takes up the history of the Warlis, a tribal (*adivasi*) community that stakes a claim of autochthony to coastal stretches of western India extending from southern Gujarat to Thane District in Maharashtra and—a problem whose ramifications are explored in some detail—parts of the Mumbai (Suburban) District. Central to the exposition here is a mythohistorical narrative I call the "Oxhide Tale." The tale explains the Warlis' lot as inhabitants of the wilderness as the result of a crooked legal contract that has banished them beyond the realm of polity and thus beyond that of the public. The distinction between spaces of culture and spaces of nature is a trope with a long history in Indian intellectual and literary discourses. I take it up as an organizing principle by which the state and affiliated elites have constructed the tribals as people defined (against the thrust of the "Oxhide Tale") by a naturalized bond with the raw, *kaccha* space of the forest. The visualization of this bond in terms of religious beliefs and practices that differ from the norms professed by caste Hindus is a corollary that has important implications for the course I chose to take in my work among Mumbai Warlis.

In 1995 an environmentalist group, acting in the name of the public interest, initiated an effort to have all residents evicted from the Sanjay Gandhi National Park (SGNP), a national forest that abuts the suburb of Goregaon. Chapter 6 is about the inhabitants of the *pada*s in the wooded areas to the west of Filmistan: the SGNP, the Aarey Milk Colony, and the Film City production facility. The key points of the crisis were laid bare in a series of legal arguments presented before the Bombay High Court over an eight-year period. Writ Petition 925 of 2000, *Manik Rama Sapte v. State of Maharashtra*, filed by members of a tribal-rights organization on behalf of the Warlis and other indigenes of the SGNP, is the narrative pivot of this last part of my study. In the ruling handed down in this case in 2003, the right to remain in the forest was reserved to residents who could demonstrate before the authorities that they were "bona fide tribals." In other words, what was at issue was not the principle of tribal people's privileged access to natural space but the recognition of the case's petitioners as persons who could claim that right in the first place. And recognition in this sense, in practice, turned out to be a visual problem.

Working with Warli interlocutors, and guided by Peirce's semiotic triad, I develop some propositions about the visual mediation of space. Within this forest area, as at Filmistan, what instantiates a *pada* as a claim to space is not only the presence of human residents but the recognition alongside them of kindred spirit-beings—gods, ancestors, ghosts—that dwell within discrete landmarks. Some of these sites, such as the Film City–based temple of the local goddess (*gaondevi*) that provides a cultic hub for the area's *pada*s, incorporate material markings and embellishments. Others are natural features that have been framed as sites of power without the intervention of human hands—rocks, hills, trees.

To be sure, such methods of sacralizing space have historically been prevalent among non-Brahminized village communities across western India and beyond. What is coming to identify them as distinctively "tribal," as opposed to part of what might be called "folk Hinduism," is a set of political and economic imperatives. At the same time, casting tribal religion as the site of a distinct identity is a project that must be contextualized against a powerful countervailing trend. Typical of *adivasi* communities across India is the way that Mumbai's Warlis, in the past generation, have become increasingly integrated within metropolitan Hinduism. Even when tribals are not made the target of strategically directed proselytization campaigns—the Hindi term is *ghar wapsi*, literally "return home"—hegemonic Hinduism extends its reach through the penetration of images and symbols from calendar art, cinema, and other popular media. It is thus the case, once again, that establishing the cultural alterity of the tribal community is a matter of visual culture.

If one index of bona fide tribal status is a spiritual connection to natural space, that standard has been proving hard to imagine in a *pakka* form that others can recognize. As an alternative, some activists have begun looking to symbols of tribal culture already in public circulation as potential vehicles of empowerment. One site of intervention I consider in the final chapter is the graphic form commonly known as "Warli art," a visual idiom that has moved from *pada*-based ritual contexts into metropolitan and even transnational art markets. Another source of current visual and narrative tropes defining the "tribal," to uncanny effect, is the very film industry whose facilities have overrun Warli villages. All but displaced from their ancestral hunting grounds, could

Mumbai's tribals find room for tactical "poaching" within these modern media environments?

The major events described in this ethnography happened over a decade ago. Since then, one trend that has only become exacerbated is the spectacularization of the city: its iconic reproduction in its more camera-ready angles, to the further marginalization of the ragged edges. Several factors have contributed to the ascendancy of this meta-Mumbai. Notable among them are selective flows of capital, the pervasive spread of digital technologies, and a governing ideology that has two evident priorities: sponsorship of hegemonic Hinduism in the public sphere and a national development policy premised on massive corporate investment.

In a brief conclusion, I make use of several vignettes from the present day to reflect on the conditions presented in my study. The occultation of the slum communities and other "encroachments" from this market-friendly vision of progress in no wise reflects the actual distribution of the city's population. Yet to assume that participation in the fantasy is confined to a middle-class public would be to miss something vital about the way ideological spectacles work. This book begins with a discussion of sacred space in Mumbai. It revisits the concept at the end, concluding with some thoughts about this contemporary apparition of Mayapuri—the dazzling, elusive City of Illusion—and about the predicament of those on the spectacle's margins who want to recognize themselves in it.

I

—

POTEMKIN VILLAGE

SPACES AND SURFACES AT A FILM STUDIO

There's lots of fun to be had at the playhouse!

So stay near the playhouse
 Take in the world's pageant
  While you try and fill your empty stomachs—

I've got your Mumbai here for sale!

PATTHE BAPURAO KULKARNI, "Mumbaichi lavani" (The ballad of Bombay), translated by Christian Lee Novetzke and Shobha Kale

Patthe Bapurao's "The Ballad of Bombay," dated to around 1910, is a pioneering work. The poet and artist Dilip Chitre ([1995] 2000, 25), who made a partial English translation, calls it "the first Marathi poem on industrial civilization." Over a hundred years on, what is striking about the way it reads today is not, strictly speaking, its modernity. Modernity is the theme of the poem, the object of its critique; but it's the way Bapurao makes the critique that resonates in the present because of the topicality of his choices.

Many of the images and tropes introduced in his stanzas circulate in popular discourses about contemporary Mumbai. The city is glamorous, for example, but it's also a place of raw hustle. It's full of cops and robbers alike, as well as prostitutes of all nationalities. Its lifeblood is money—an element that has the power to distort human relations such that everything and everyone is up for sale—and the poet extolls the city's charms in the voice of a street vendor hawking wares, or perhaps a pimp talking up his ladies. The buildings dazzle with their glassed fronts and colorful lights. The streets and port throb with the speed and power of technological marvels.[1] Most of all—then and now—Mumbai is a show, a play of appearances that are seductive but not backed by anything substantial or genuine.

Generically speaking, Patthe Bapurao's "ballad" is a *lavani*, a performance form that typically catalogs the eroticized charms of a beautiful woman. The locus classicus of the *lavani* is, or was, the Maharashtrian *tamasha* theater, whose talent and audience alike came largely from lower-caste backgrounds (Bhagwat 1995, 116–17; Chitre [1995] 2000, 26–27). As cultural expression it is not only vernacular but demotic. The playhouse mentioned in the epigraph, then, is a reflexive image: it's at once the space in which the *lavani*'s plebeian public would hear it—a discrete site within the city—and a synecdoche for the city itself. In other words, the great, modern city is a theatrical fabrication, and to understand this truth you go to the theater.

Substitute cinema for playhouse, and the insight is as penetrating as ever—more so, in fact, for over the course of the twentieth century the film industry became identified with Mumbai to a far greater extent than the theater ever was. (If Bapurao had been born a few decades later, it's a safe bet he would have wound up in the movie business, and his lyrics would have become disseminated through *filmi* music.) To be sure, this is not the only town in India where movies are made; these days, the Mumbai-based industry is not even the most prolific. But it is certainly the richest. Its flagship product, the Hindi-language popular feature film, can claim hegemonic status across South Asia and beyond. And within India, Hindi popular cinema is recognized simultaneously as representative of Mumbai and as the chief interpreter of the city's look and sensibility. Thus, the nickname "Bollywood" brands this global rival to Hollywood with an initial *B* taken from the name of its host city.

Bombay ceased to be an official geographical designation in 1995, of course, but Bollywood is a historical phenomenon. If the name originated in the early 1970s, the ascendancy of the Bombay style of filmmaking can be traced back to the time of Independence, perhaps earlier.[2] The 1950s and 1960s are known as the Golden Age of Hindi cinema, but the story actually gets going in the decade before, when several of the best-known studios were built in what is now the Mumbai outer suburbs. Each had its sound stages and back lots and stable of talent, and each was run by a different production house. In Indian English the companies were called "banners," and of the banners that used to unfurl on the cinema screen to inaugurate the opening credits, none had more cachet in its day than Filmistan Studios.

The banners broke up in the 1960s. But Filmistan Studios remains open to this day as a production facility. Its stages and lots are booked by producers shooting scenes for features, commercials, and television shows. On any given day, multiple shoots may be in session. It was a few years before I began work on my main fieldwork project that a film producer contact introduced me to this storied space. And I discovered for myself that the stories generated at and by the studio had the effect of making it into different kinds of spaces.

My task in this chapter will be to peel back the multiple layers of this site, which is at once extraordinary and—I will argue—exemplary. There are three overlapping geographies to be charted here. I will discuss a cinematic register, in which the studio's features are mediated through the camera to emerge as elements in a spectacularized fantasy of the city and the nation. I will also theorize an official regime of abstraction and surveillance associated with the state and related agencies and interests. This is a regime of governmentality whose antecedents are colonial, whose primary medium is paper, and whose visual interface is English text—paradigmatically, the "black-letter law"—although the key example to be cited in this chapter will be an identity card. The final emphasis will be on a realm of sacred space. At the studio, this stratum is marked and inhabited primarily by the grips, service workers, and other poor people who traverse the site. Situating this group within the city's class- and community-riven sociology as representative subalterns, I will move on to discuss the studio's sacred geography as a domain claimed and made visible through religious practices, most notably through shrine-building activity.

First Exposure

If you have ever seen a movie made about moviemaking—*Singin' in the Rain, Day for Night, The Stunt Man*—you've been cued to a certain two-step movement. The camera draws your eye to the mise-en-scène: something attractive, fantastic, horrific. Then it pulls back to show what's behind the illusion: the lights, the reflectors, the extras on their cigarette break. And if you have ever been on a movie set, maybe you've carried this conditioning with you and experienced double takes as you discover, time and again, that the shiny object in front of the camera is so much plywood and duct tape from the back.

India's film industry has long been among the world's largest, and Indian filmmakers have put the technique to good use over the years, from the 1930s classic *Manoos* to the Bollywood blockbuster *Om Shanti Om*. But if the standard movement is two-step—"real" exposed as "fake"—my first visit to Filmistan involved something more complex. There were points where I felt I had completed a three-step, from real to fake and back to real again. And I found myself asking, time and again: as the spectator, just where was I standing?

At the outset, to be sure, the thing I find most disorienting about Filmistan is its apparent ordinariness. The studio occupies a compound, some five acres in area, that is surrounded on all sides by the bustling neighborhood of Goregaon. And at first glance, there seems to be nothing about the other side of the gate to mark it apart from its environs. The general disrepair is typical of Indian institutional spaces at their most drearily real: sleeping dogs, cracked windowpanes, damp-stained concrete, crooked trees that probably need more water.

Standing by the gate in a casual clump are three or four men in khaki uniforms. Idling policemen, too, are a ubiquitous feature of Indian public landscapes.[3] Do you notice them or not notice them? Walking tall with the producer's entourage, I stride through the gate and on past them. Of course, it says a great deal about your own mode of inhabiting the landscape if you can choose to make a cop invisible. In the absence of an officious word or gesture to signal that the officer is indeed on duty, the effect of their presence on a passerby like me—a foreign researcher, a sahib-class person—is generally negligible.

But there's more to be said about the police. In my anticipation of dream-factory illusion, for the first time I find myself questioning the familiar uniform. Are those real Mumbai cops? Or are they private-security men? And a short while later, when I see more uniformed men by a gateway labeled "Central Jail," a third option presents itself: could they all simply be extras costumed as cops? (One indication that the experience of a certain discombobulating feeling in the presence of the Mumbai police is not unique to me—nor to the film studio scenario—is provided by a sign that can be seen at a police outpost at the Bandra train station: "Beware of Bogus Police," it says in English, Marathi, and Hindi.)[4]

Next, to go from state to church: I see what appear to be two temples in the compound, although I can't identify the god enshrined in either one. The temples prompt the same question I had for the cops—are they real or are they fake?—but a little self-reflection shows that what's at stake in the two cases is different. When it comes to the police, I enjoy a degree of privilege on account of my own appearance, one that's even more pronounced in India than the States. And yet it feels natural to heed the authority of the uniform—when I can tell its wearer is in earnest, at any rate. Resisting the impulse takes a real effort. By contrast, I haven't internalized a reaction to images of Hindu gods, at least not those whose iconography I don't consciously read. Whether manifested in the form of a painted statuette, as in the more finished temple, or as a rock marked with red lead, as in the little shrine tucked just beyond the Central Jail, the presence of divinity on the grounds evokes equally blank reactions (fig. 1). But as an ethnographer of religion, a prospective participant observer, I want to carry myself with due respect. If, that is, the sacred sites are actually sacred.

I ask Ram Prasad, my guide from the production crew: "Those temples—

are they real or only for show?" He answers: "They're real temples. The nicer-looking one out front was built by the studio. People use it for worship, but when the script calls for a scene with a temple, and there's been no time to arrange a location shot, sometimes it's convenient to shoot there. They have a really good temple at Film City."

Film City is a much larger and more modern studio complex located about a half hour's walk away on the other, less densely built-up side of the suburb of Goregaon. Ram Prasad's matter-of-fact answer presented me with a counterpoint to my reflection about the studio cops: given the centrality of visual address to Hindu devotional practice, does asking whether a temple is "only for show" not somehow miss the point? Certainly, on one level, the question of whether a policeman or a shrine is real or fake could be resolved by an appraisal of its situation in the material economy. Who pays the men in uniform? Who takes care of the shrine and the image within it? But in terms of their ability to project visual effects, it would seem that the *fake* policeman is the figure—regardless of his employer—whose dormant presence blends into the background, the *real* policeman being the one who, through a performative display that mobilizes the authority inscribed in his uniform, successfully invokes deference in the civilian observer. In this sense, the measure of the reality of such ideological spectacles as policemen and temples is precisely the degree to which their effects are inscribed on viewing subjects (fig. 2).

One way to get started theorizing this observation is suggested by the figure of the policeman. In Louis Althusser's (1971) concept of interpellation, a person's configuration as a *subject*—a term in which Althusser collapses the basic psychoanalytic unit of identity with the basic political condition of subjection to the state—is summoned by the ideological structure within which it operates. In the case of men in khaki uniform, my modern subjectivity betrays me: the cop hails me—"Hey, you there!"—and I respond, in the paradigmatic Althusserian scenario. (I will have more to say on hailing different kinds of Mumbai subjects further on.) Why, by contrast, does the colored statuette fail to interpellate me? The obvious answer, alluded to above, is that there's nothing in my subjective makeup to be interpellated here. To put it in less highbrow terms, I don't recognize the image's address as directed toward any part of me. And I might explain this by stating that for me as an unbeliever, the ensconced figure means nothing more than whatever set of interpretations might be derived from reading an icon of a youthful-looking cowherd who happens to have three faces.

But to fixate on the question of belief—and follow through with a hermeneutical approach—would be to read right past how this sort of visual encounter actually produces its effects. After all, I no more decode the policeman's uniform than I cherish a conviction in the legitimate authority of the Government of Maharashtra. At the same time, as an ethnographer, in preparing to undertake a project conceived around popular religious practice I did not limit myself to textual study. Well before I established myself in Mumbai, I had been introduced to the somatic dimension of Hindu practice as a student in Banaras—a cityscape saturated with icons—by Brahmin friends and host family members who conscientiously observed the ritual calendar. In the temple space, when I performed *pradakshina*, or clockwise circumambulation, in anticipation of the revelatory moment of *darshan*, the visual encounter with the enshrined image, a conscious understanding of the meaning of such observances was at best secondary to the inscription of norms of conduct on my body and eyes. In short, in terms of the performance the valorized image elicits, I could claim to have been put through my paces. What proved destabilizing about the shrines at Filmistan was my inability to recognize whether the images, as framed in their respective spaces, were valorized or not.

What is then at stake, I propose, is not my belief or the lack thereof but rather the degree of my integration as a subject within what Althusser would describe as the pervasive structure of ideology. Now, Althusser conceives of ideology as a monolithic system (his is something of a unified field theory), and the complexity of the lifeworlds I encountered in my fieldwork has compelled a rethinking of interpellation in terms of multiple fields of effects. The ideological systems or dispensations in force in contemporary Mumbai are themselves multiple. And as I will argue, each becomes manifest at my field sites in a distinct visual register—a distinct set of particular kinds of images that occupy a particular kind of space and, in addressing viewing subjects, initiate a particular range of affective relations.

But if the belief paradigm is to be set aside, how do ideological subjects themselves understand their participation in these fields of effects? This chapter has already introduced one conceptual device to which Mumbai residents (and not only I) have had recourse: the categories *real* and *fake*. This is a straightforward-looking opposition that my inquiries will move on to complicate. Some other ideas presented by my fieldwork interlocutors will be addressed in chapters to come; their insights are especially illuminating when it comes to thinking about visual operations in sacred space. At this early point in the argument, however, the most direct way to address the point is with an illustration from *Camera Indica*, Christopher Pinney's landmark study of photography in India.

Taking up the question of photography's projection of divine power, Pinney (1997a, 166–67) comments on an eloquent moment of testimony. His interlocutor Tiwari is the devotee of a holy man whose photograph he petitions for blessings. Tiwari denies any connection between his personal faith and the guru's ability to transmit these effects:

> faith or belief is not necessary; desires will be fulfilled without belief (*bina vishvas*). The analogies that tumble forth from Tiwari's lips are all grounded in a technological world in which all that matters is effect: "Suppose you want to use some electric power—you make a connection, fit your tube light, lay the wiring, provide a switch, connect this to the overhead wires. If the power is available, the tube is fine, the wiring is fine, the switch is fine, the tube light will come on— (*chalega!*)—with belief and without belief"—he flicked his thumb to and fro as though switching the current on and off.

The specific technique being advocated here involves the utterance of a verbal formula before the guru's portrait. But there is no difficulty in extrapolating from Tiwari's personal cultic practice to norms of visual worship that prevail among Hindus and others in present-day Mumbai. The principle applies to the activation of a visual circuit by the supplicant's gaze whether it is augmented by words or not. The electricity metaphor is one frequently encountered in explanations of the metaphysics of popular Hinduism. It dismisses the internal condition of either term—on the one hand, the purity of faith that resides in the devotee; on the other, the meaning that resides in the sacred image—and shifts attention to the "live" quality of the connection between the two.

Now, having opened this theoretical discussion by following one subject's position—my own—as it traverses multiple fields of effects, I will draw to a close this preliminary tour of the strange space that provoked my reflections. The final stop awaits on the other side of the archway of the Central Jail. Ram Prasad leads me into a space like a courtyard, where one side is lined by rough shelters of sheet metal and canvas. Unlike the jail—which looks like a fortress from the front but turns out, from the back, to be painted boards—these structures show their seams on the surface. They could be storage units, but then again they could be rooms for people; they have a definite behind-the-scenes look. Yet the plot they occupy is right in the middle of the route to our set.

At first I don't pay much attention. In Indian cities there's nothing unusual about people living cheek by jowl with the nominally public thoroughfare. Amid the lines of drying laundry and chickens scratching the dirt, there's an old lady who wears her sari hitched up high, in a rustic style. Over the course of the day, I cross the space several times, and I see other women busy at their chores. I sense that respecting privacy has little to do with the way the production crew ignores them. Rather, it seems to me that they and their dwellings have become invisible, after the conventional manner of menial workers in Indian public establishments. They're supposed to be a part of the backdrop, like the sleeping dogs and water stains, and it's not the done thing for a guest or customer to notice them.

Norms of middle-class conduct notwithstanding, though, the time comes to find Ram Prasad. "Is that a real village, or is it only for show?" "That is a real village. It was here from before. But when the script calls for a scene with a village, and there's been no time to arrange a location shot, it's often convenient to shoot there." "And those 'villagers' up there—do they really live there, or are they just acting like they lived there?" "Of course they live there. They do odd jobs around the studio, building sets, cleaning up. But when we're shooting the village scenes, we get them to act as the villagers."

When I ask the studio managers in the office by the gate, they're not only dismissive but seem surprised I've noticed the settlers at all. "They are nothing," one of them tells me impatiently, as though trying with his words to return them to invisibility. "They are little people. Why don't you talk to the producers, the director—the people who are making the films?"

Friends, Citizens, Countrymen

In an ethnographic irony, the celebrities, seasoned self-promoters, proved easy to approach; the "little people," more elusive. I returned to the United States full of speculations about the studio's secret sharer. In 2002 my proposal to pursue field research at Filmistan was awarded funding, and I set up shop in Mumbai late in the year.[5] My return to the studio was made possible, much in the same way as before, by a director who invited me to attend a shoot booked for one of the stages. As a guest of this production I became friendly with one of the workers on the set, a man who called himself Chandra Shekhar Azad.

An energetic, powerful-looking man, Azad moved with a swagger that belied his years; he had been working in the film industry for forty years, he told me, and underneath the garish red dye he applied, his hair had apparently turned quite white.[6] His job on the set combined running errands with security work—a portfolio, one got the sense, largely of his own devising. Having equipped himself with a bamboo staff in the style of a Mumbai street cop, he patrolled the set projecting a familiar combination of affability toward ranking members of the hierarchy and officiousness toward everybody else.

Self-assured and humorous, he was an original character. But if I cite his opinions and attitudes in the pages to come, it is not only for the sake of his voice as an individual. I came to see him as representative of a whole group of people with whom I was getting acquainted at the studio. These were the workers who provide the muscle on the production crews: industry journeymen who serve as grips, carpenters, and generic heavy lifters and who might even on occasion be called on to cross over to the other side of the camera as bit players, or "junior artistes" as they are known in the simultaneously English and Hindi lexicon of Bollywood. The industry term for such jacks-of-all-trades is another distinctive coinage, "light boy." The designation applies regardless of the age of the person in question. The juvenilizing implications of both tags underscore the central distinction on which the workplace hierarchy is structured. It is a distinction that cuts along lines of linguistic and to some extent regional and caste affiliation, invokes the affect-laden rhetoric of familial seniority, but maps most meaningfully onto categories of class and culture.

This split between an English-speaking professional, managerial class and a Hindi-speaking class that serves it forms a boundary in the film industry. To cross that boundary is difficult, if possible at all. The subordinate side addresses the dominant side as "sahib" or "sir," appellations handed straight down from the colonial order. But if there is a standard mode of address to be directed at or among the blue-collar contingent, it may, oddly enough, be yet another Hindi-ized English term, "boss." It would be fair to say that *boss* means, in Mumbai, just about the opposite of what it means in American English, and this distinctive local usage is worth unpacking, inasmuch as its ramifications have much to say about social relations in the city.

The corresponding term in standard Hindi is *bhai*, or "brother." *Bhai* is indeed ubiquitous in textbook, North Indian–style Hindi as a term of familiar address. In fact, the habitual recourse to *bhai* taken by British-accented patrons summoning menials is one origin story for the colonial practice of hailing male natives as "boys." The explanation usually given for the word's unpopularity in Mumbai, however, is that it is resented as a marker of North Indian identity and what that might connote—rusticity, "backwardness," Johnny-come-lately migrant status. Moreover, the appeal to a fictive affinal bond seems also to be resisted; there is a popular sense, supported by the story lines of Bollywood films, that whatever the case may be back in the village, on the mean streets of the city all men are not brothers.[7] (It should be mentioned that along with North Indian rubes there is a second group that *bhai* connotes in Mumbai: *bhai log*, the gangster underworld, or perhaps "the Brotherhood.")

To return to the workplace milieu: the rift between *sahib* and *boss* obtaining among members of the production crew is paralleled in the cast by that segregating the credited actors from the junior artistes.[8] And here is an important point. It is also replicated, to a large extent, in offices in the corporate and NGO sectors, and it is actually formalized in government hiring policies that set a ceiling on the promotion of public employees who lack educational qualifications at Class IV; the official designation for the Class IV position is "peon." Nevertheless, the dichotomy is especially stark in the film industry, where on a shoot the workplace dynamic really does seem a matter of masters and servants. And if I dwell on this point, it is because Bollywood instantiates, in concrete, lived practice, a distinction that can be drawn through Mumbai's population as a whole—one with theoretical ramifications that will inform my argument throughout this book. This is the divide between bourgeois subject-citizens and subalterns.

Famously, the city's very name is contested: among the urban bourgeoisie, whose classrooms, offices, and (to a lesser extent) domestic parlors are English-medium environments, the no-longer-official *Bombay* is still standard usage; *Mumbai*, with its Maharashtrian and thus rustic provenance, decidedly less so. The two versions even claim rival etymologies, each rich with its own set of associations. *Bombay* is attributed to the Portuguese *boa baía*,[9] or "good bay," of the port's original colonial masters. *Mumbai* is said to be derived from Mumbadevi, the name of a local goddess (*gaondevi*), whose cult, as with other goddesses of this type in western and southern India, centers on veneration of her persona within a particular settlement as its emanation or embodiment. A pithy take on what was at stake in the 1995 name change—and the many smaller-scale renamings that led up to it—is given in *Maximum City: Bombay Lost and Found*, Suketu Mehta's literary portrait of the city. For Mehta (2004, 130), the renaming campaign, proceeding landmark by colonial-era landmark, heralded the emergence of the so-called *ghatis*—poor migrants from the Maharashtrian hill country—out of an undifferentiated, collective mass of "servants": "This is how the ghatis took revenge on us. They renamed everything after their politicians, and finally they renamed even the city. If they couldn't afford to live on our roads, they could at least occupy the road signs."

The symbolism of the name change goes deep, and to assign *Bombay* to English and *Mumbai* to Marathi is just to get started. (Hindi is the city's true lingua franca—the medium of communication between sahib and boss—and the Hindi pronunciation appropriately falls right in the middle: *Bambai*.) *Bombay* is not only colonial but imperial, even dynastic, enfolding as it does the legacies of two European masters. By the same token, *Mumbai* is not just nationalist but nativist; Marathi can be said to be the language of people indigenous to the hinterlands to the east and south, but to call it the mother tongue of the city (as many people do) is to make a tendentious claim.[10] Again, *Bombay* looks to the sea, the historical conduit of the city's wealth as well as of communities represented among its mercantile and cultural (if no longer political) elites. "Good Bay": it's a sailor's name. By contrast, *Mumbai* is a peasant's name; it looks to the earth, and not only because the specific Marathi-speaking community it metonymizes for Mehta, the "*ghatis*," are a farming caste, properly known as Maratha-Kunbis or Kunbis.[11] Recall that the word is derived from the name of a local goddess, and goddesses of this sort, as subsequent chapters will investigate in some detail, are local precisely because they are rooted in the soil. *Bombay* indexes a historical lineage; *Mumbai* indexes popular religion.

To be sure, there are plenty of elite, English-medium people who habitually say *Mumbai* and are indeed committed to its use as a political statement. And there are many among the less privileged classes who would never name their city that way—just as there are many who speak no other Marathi words either. It must be said that any blanket distinction between Bombay's haves and Mumbai's have-nots elides multiple fissures. And it is within the vast collectivity of have-nots that the rifts run deepest. Linguistic identity, as indicated above, implies a claim to a place of ancestral origin, and the populist champions of Marathi claim the whole urban area for the Marathas as the sons of the soil. Theirs is a political program that marginalizes—when not actively targeting—diverse populations that have been coming to seek work in India's economic capital for generations (and among these, native speakers of Hindi and Urdu are prominent). Another rift that is impossible to ignore is that of religion. After all, if invoking a Maharashtrian goddess in the official name is not a gesture best calculated to win over non-Maharashtrian residents, it would seem to have even less to offer the city's Muslims and other religious minorities.

A substantial mass constituency can nevertheless be seen to take shape, one bounded by shared commitments to the Marathi language, Maharashtrian regional and cultural origins, and the Hindu religion. And yet, even this picture is complicated by an internal rift: that of caste. For one thing, the goddess Mumbadevi has historically commanded a following not among the Kunbis but among the Kolis, a fishing caste that actually has a stronger claim of indigeneity to the area. (The Kolis' chief contenders in this matter are a so-called tribal community, the Warlis, who will emerge as the protagonists of the second half of this book.) A prominent subset of the Kolis are not even Hindus but Catholics. For another, a large proportion of the non-elite Maharashtrians of the city are Mahar by caste—that is, Dalits—members of a community once stigmatized as untouchable. And while a characterization of this constituency as solidly Maharashtrian and "essentially" Hindu may compel the attention of political leaders of different stripes, the repudiation of Brahminical Hinduism is a point of principle among urban Mahars, most of whom have turned to a rationalized form of Buddhism formulated in the mid-twentieth century as a vehicle of social and spiritual empowerment.

What, then, is left of Mehta's aperçu about names, masters, and servants? These observations about language, region, religion, and caste have not exhausted his comment about social categorization. Mehta's dichotomy should not be laid to rest without some discussion of the city's class structure, and that is a task I will undertake in the next section. And there is also another way to put his statement to work as a heuristic for theorizing urban citizenship, one that relies on two moves. The first move is to take seriously the image of a population made up of masters and servants (perhaps more seriously than Mehta intended) and to conceptualize these two camps as ideological subject positions. The second is to read more deeply into the rival models of urban community encapsulated in the two names for the city, the one defined in terms of a legacy of colonial rule, the other by subjection to a territorial deity. Here is the proposition. The members of one camp inhabit the city as participants in a rationally organized social compact, the heirs of a tradition of governance that is at once liberal in philosophy and colonialist in execution. This is postcolonial civil society. The members of the other camp experience urban space as the domain of sovereign powers, which may deign to recognize certain parties—individual or collective—amid the mass of their subjects and bestow material fortune or instrumental agency. This is something else.

In short, what I propose is that the master and servant classes are constructed not solely in relation to each other but also in relation to the space they inhabit—a space that they may physically share but that they perceive to be governed by distinct dispensations. Here I follow the lead of Sudipta Kaviraj (1997, 84n3), who builds an argument about contested spaces in postcolonial Kolkata on a similarly "simple and possibly misleading distinction between the elite and the others."[12] With the understanding that this kind of heuristic can distort or occlude many details of a complex urban sociology, let me cast a stark light on the site of my own study. The Mumbai of this book is a class-riven city in which an Anglophone bourgeoisie dominates a population that functions in vernacular languages—foremost among them Marathi and Hindi—and maintains ties with villages of origin in the hinterland.[13] This subordinate group settles, or-

ganizes, and makes sense of space in different ways from the liberal bourgeoisie. One point of conflict of central importance for this study involves the two
groups' rival constructions of the public and the sacred. The exemplary zone
of contestation here is the street. For a member of the elite group—whether
Hindu, Muslim, Christian, Jain, or Zoroastrian—the street beyond the front
door is a public thoroughfare, a zone to be traversed by autonomous citizens
under the neutral jurisdiction of a secular republic. But for a subaltern urbanite
of whatever religious affiliation, that street may well be the legitimate abode of
bodies both human and divine—and the divine presence would be recognized
as a presence whether honored by the subject's personal devotions or not.[14]

This dichotomy I draw, defining citizens against subalterns, maps imperfectly
onto an identification of middle and working classes grounded in an analysis
of economic relations. Many industries and government bodies employ white-
collar workers who occupy an interstitial category as members of what might
be called the vernacular middle class. This is the class whose increasing visibility
and clout have been located at the root of many aspects of Indian society's transformation over the past generation, most notably the rise of the Hindu Right,
whose principal institutional standard-bearer in Mumbai, the Maharashtrian-
chauvinist Shiv Sena Party, not coincidentally gained traction in the 1960s and
1970s by pressuring employers to admit its supporters to the ranks of their clerical workforces. To the Shiv Sena can be assigned the bulk of the responsibility
both for the event that shattered the city's long-cherished image as a place of
cosmopolitan tolerance—the traumatic Hindu-Muslim "riots" of 1992–93—and
for the official name change in 1995. With an eye to defending my heuristic,
however, I think it could be argued that the volatility and insecurity characteristic of the vernacular middle class are symptomatic, precisely, of its interstitial position, wedged as it is between the starkly alternative modes of modern
Indian identity bequeathed it by a colonial heritage. At this troubled historical
conjuncture, the cultural project of devising a self-image that negotiates both
established examples, of striking a happy medium between upper-class "deca-
dence" and lower-class "backwardness," has perhaps been marked as much by
the tension and conflict-ridden effects of Othering as by attempts at accommodation or synthesis.[15]

In fact, the Shiv Sena's modus operandi is a textbook example of "political
society" in action—political society being a concept devised by Kaviraj's fellow
Subaltern Studies alumnus, Partha Chatterjee (2004b), in explicit counterpoint
to bourgeois civil society. In Chatterjee's scheme (and the theoretical terminology that goes with it) political society is to subaltern populations what civil so-

ciety is to elite citizens. Political society parallels civil society in that it is a mode of participating in polity, and much of its engagement with the various organs of the state is mediated by representations that circulate in public. (Note that mass demonstrations like *morchas*, boiling down as they do to the mobilization of bodies in public spaces, fall under this description, inasmuch as the demonstrators' bodies are themselves representing other things—whole communities, for example.) But the two models part company on a pair of fundamentals.

First, if civil society is in principle a concert of autonomous citizens, the unit of agency in political society is not the individual but the community or, per Chatterjee, the "population." This is a group whose identity may be delineated in terms of categories already mentioned—language, caste, religion—but is given cohesion as a social formation by leadership that articulates collective aspirations and grievances. To bring in some more of Chatterjee's language, bourgeois citizens argue for the recognition of rights—rights that are everyone's due, in principle, since all citizens are equal before the law. Subaltern populations, on the other hand, agitate for their own recognition as particular groups due entitlements. Let me reiterate that religious identity is part of the mix here, and thus religious imagery is too, inasmuch as visual culture is a field on which collective identities take shape in public.

Second, civil society's relation to the state is defined, in principle, by rational discourse between interlocutors bound within a common matrix—that of the law. But this ideal is not shared by the exponents of political society, for whom the state is set above and apart as an aloof bureaucracy. "Citizens inhabit the domain of theory, populations that of policy." Thus, Chatterjee's (2004b, 34) argument recasts the state from a participatory democracy to a complex of technologies of governmentality: "This regime secures legitimacy not by the participation of citizens in matters of state but by claiming to provide for the well-being of the population. . . . Its apparatus is not the republican assembly but an elaborate network of surveillance through which information is collected on every aspect of the life of the population that is to be looked after." The scenario is not only Foucauldian but postcolonial. The predicament of political society can be put concretely like this: where gaining access to government services and resources is concerned, the capture of electoral offices by members of subaltern groups—and the political parties formed to advance their interests—is secondary to the continued dominance of the elite class over the state's technocratic and administrative agencies. And the alterity of state bureaucracy is not simply a matter of what sort of people are in charge of it; the conceptual taxonomies, the methodological protocols, and the very language of administration have been handed down from the British Raj. Here too there is a religious dimension to be highlighted, inasmuch as norms of subaltern religious practice (not at all confined to Hindu subalterns), centering as they do on a relation of recognition between sovereign and subject, offer a paradigm of submission to the state as well.[16]

In saying this, I don't wish to exoticize or mystify the encounter. On the contrary, the chapters to follow will supply ethnographic descriptions that should elucidate the attitudes and tactics of subaltern petitioners before state authority. And it also seems useful to affirm here that the sense of alienation experienced at the threshold of government offices is not exclusive to non-elite Indians—or Indians in general or even subjects of postcolonial polities in general. As a research scholar from the United States I embodied sahib privilege in many social contexts, and yet on my repeated visits to the Foreigners Registration Office in quest of a visa extension, filing multiple forms in an English jargon even I found arcane, soliciting permission to remain at my own place of residence for just a little bit longer, the question I took with me when I approached the clerk at his window was precisely one of recognition. What would it take for him or, rather, for the opaque edifice he fronted to recognize in me a person with a legitimate claim to attention?

Let's return to the question of who a subaltern is. For Chatterjee, political society is made up of subalterns. But not all subalterns participate in political society. In the descriptions that await in these pages of the trials (some of them literal) that tribal people and others meet with at the hands of the state, a major theme is the risk of failure petitioners contend with when bidding for recognition as members of a given population. I theorize this in terms of the attainment of visibility. For if there are subalterns whom the state recognizes as "players" in the game of political society, there are also myriad others who have not even entered the realm of the public. They are bereft of representation in two senses: they lack organization under leadership that can embody the community and its interests, and they lack agency in the production and circulation of cultural artifacts that signify the community in the public sphere. Notwithstanding the state's aspiration to a panoptical compass, then, it could be said that unmobilized populations are invisible populations. Exemplary are the kind of groups discussed in Sandeep Pendse's (1995) overview of Mumbai's "toilers"—the menial workers who are spread across the urban economy's informal sectors (see also Chatterjee 2004b, 62–64). In fact, in Pendse's analysis, the rubric that brings together this highly diverse congeries of urban have-nots is precisely the condition of invisibility shared by its members.

I have followed these cues in my own fieldwork inquiries. But I am mindful that, as cultural agents, my subaltern interlocutors participate in a process of consuming, reframing, and to some extent re-producing signification and spectacle in public space. And while on one level the condition of subalternity is definable as a negative quantity, in terms of degrees of exclusion from the productive end of this process of exchange—in other words, nobody more powerful than you pays attention to you; your voice is unheard, your presence on the landscape invisible—artifacts of subaltern cultural expression do have a way of leaking into circuits and spaces imagined by dominant groups as their own preserve. The neighborhood and streetside shrines that I will introduce in this chapter and describe in some detail in the next are, I will argue, examples of such artifacts.

A few more words on this model are in order before I return to the light boys and their representative, Azad. I should state that I do not assume that either subject positions or the symbolic orders that support them are stably bounded entities. Indeed, through some of the description that follows I hope to demonstrate, for example, that street temples that court patrons from elite strata constitute one kind of disruptive node at which boundaries that are normally in force may be crossed. Nevertheless, a pervasive desire for the illusion of wholeness—of the integrity of human subjects, the systematicity of discourses—is well seated in modern Indian society, although perhaps less so than in the United States (and least so among subaltern communities; to be colonized, after all, is to be subjected to the claims of different authoritative discourses). Notwithstanding a certain instability or room for play at the margins, then, the two domains I have delimited—the bourgeois and the subaltern—should be considered to function as both separate and unequal and to be defined against each other as such. *Everyone in Mumbai has a servant*: how a resident makes sense of this assertion will signal at once the width of the gap and on which side of it he or she falls.[17]

Spotlight: Light Boys

Let's sum up the theoretical framework laid out above, along with its terminology. I propose to relate the sort of social divisions I have observed in my ethnographic work to a division that obtains across the city as a whole. Building on the later work of some Subaltern Studies theorists, I repurpose *subaltern* as a designation for one of two subject positions, structurally placed in subordination to the other position, *citizen*. Visual artifacts and other cultural forms that circulate in public mediate the relations of these subject positions to the distinct ideological dispensations that configure them. Subjects collectively interpellated in this way can be viewed in the aggregate as social formations to be known as *publics*. And let it be noted that, inasmuch as publics provide a frame for conceptualizing groups around the public images and discourses that bring their members together, they present a kind of mirror image to Partha Chatterjee's "populations," which can be thought of conversely as subaltern groups made recognizable to others by public media.

Next, to move from the mediating term to the process of subjectification: if an ideological dispensation is theorized as a system that configures personhood in subjection to social and cosmic orders, enfolded within that system are norms which position that subject in relation to his or her fellow subjects, to the subjects of other dispensations, to the space they all share, and to the regime that governs it. This is the domain of *sovereignty*. The Indian state is one entity whose sovereignty over the territory occupied by Mumbai subalterns thus needs to be studied as determinative of their subjective makeup. And yet—as this chapter will move on to demonstrate—for my fieldwork interlocutors the state is not the sole sovereign agent.

The purpose of this section is to put this analytic apparatus through an ethnographic dress rehearsal. To stick with the metaphor, the scene is Filmistan, and the spotlight will be on the light boys. Filmistan will stand in for public space. The designation is technically applied, of course, to government-administered areas like streets and parks, but the casting against type in this case should yield productive insights. The light boys will feature here both as a representative subaltern population and as the "public" constituency for certain kinds of visual-cultural artifacts that circulate within the studio and beyond it. Attention to selected elements of the visual environment, and the effects they exert on the light boys, will set up the question of how the studio grounds function as the site of three distinct modalities of the production of space: spectacularized space, rationalized space, and sacred space.

Let's start by revisiting the sheer diversity of Mumbai subalterns. Within the urban citizen class, an authoritative English-language mass media and an educational system dominated by English-language instruction demarcate a shared realm of cultural flows and habitual practices. Given that there is no comparable set of institutions at work among the constituencies convened under the rubric of subalterns, it could be objected that the subaltern category is simply too broad to describe any meaningful sort of solidarity. Bourgeois residents of the city, in other words, have been disciplined, conditioned, informed, entertained, and seduced into considering themselves modern Indians. By contrast, the people who build or clean their houses, for example, remain variously Maharashtrian Kunbis, North Indian Ansaris, Buddhist ex-untouchables, or Warli tribals.

The Marxist tendency would be to look to the workplace as furnishing a common experience of labor. But as Pendse (1995) has pointed out with his alternative formulation of *toil*, the variety of tasks performed by the less prosperous members of Mumbai's workforce is as diverse as the range of their linguistic, regional, and caste affiliations. Mending sandals, hauling handcarts, cleaning other people's ears; hawking, hustling, cadging petty "commissions" for errands: much of this employment is impermanent, little of it is on the books, and a good deal of it resists description as wage labor under conditions of industrial capitalism. As Pendse (1995, 6) notes: "flux, contradictions and ambiguities in the lives and realities of members of this stratum make delimitation of precise boundaries difficult. The flux, contradictions and ambiguities are crucial in shaping the cultural identities of the toilers; they need to be recognized and understood, not dismissed as impurities or obstacles in analysis. Further, the flux is not the product of an innate characteristic of the toilers but rather a function of the changing situation—economic, political and social—of the city." Under these circumstances of fragmentation, it is not surprising that the primary frame of solidarity should be caste, village, or religious provenance or, in Pendse's (1995, 7) words, that the "numerous fractions among the toilers . . . often coincide with socio-cultural strata and thereby tend to become rigid."[18]

Given the lack of conceptual cohesion among observers (never mind collective solidarity among the observed), the Marxist-leaning old guard of Mumbai's urban studies establishment has cause to feel stymied by the events of the last thirty-odd years. Into the 1980s a prevailing image of Mumbai or, rather, of Bombay as the showcase of Indian modernity was held not just by leftist intellectuals but by politicians and technocrats, filmmakers and media types, and toiling strivers alike. The intriguing aspect for the Left was that as the locus of India's most sophisticated capitalist activity, the city was also host to a burgeoning industrial proletariat whose "feudalistic" ties to sectarian loyalties were understood to be in the process of becoming transcended by class consciousness. The laboratory of this promising development was the great mills operated by the textile industry, and when the back of the labor movement was broken in the epic textile workers' strike of 1982, Bombay's economy took a postindustrial turn that confounded the development narratives of both Marxism and modernization theory. Leftist disillusionment was cemented with the widespread co-optation of working-class Maharashtrians by the Shiv Sena, which mobilized its cadres by solidifying precisely those premodern sectarian distinctions fondly thought to have melted into air.[19]

But there is at least one prominent sector of Mumbai's economy known for sustaining a workforce whose subaltern members hail from diverse castes and creeds—from all across India, in fact. I return to the film industry and its labor pool of light boys. Against the colonial ambience suggested by the terminology of *sahibs* and *boys*, the Bollywood workplace is actually in sync, in this regard, with the projections of the prophets of Indian modernity. Indeed, alongside academics and activists, among those prophets should be numbered many of the foremost writers and directors of the post-Independence Hindi cinema, purveyors into the 1980s of a socialist-inflected populism.[20]

In film, Bombay has been depicted as a town of hard knocks and opportunity, where country boys leave the caste restrictions of the village behind to make something of themselves, in lawful society or on the streets; both are cosmopolitan realms open to young men of promise, such that the generic Hindu hero's loyal buddy may well be a Muslim and any discord between the communities is exposed, by the end of the movie, as having behind it the long arm of some mastermind (who is often marked out with Anglophile tastes and mannerisms). I was aware that when advancing the image for public consumption of a modern industry free of prejudice, Bollywood's stars and spokespeople often seem to be retailing tropes and ideals of modernity disseminated through the movies.[21] But in spite of (or because of) my awareness of the official line in these matters, it came as some surprise to hear similar attitudes voiced among the light boys. The laboring rank and file of the film industry were said to have no time for identity politics and collectively to pride themselves on their rejection of it.

What I could learn of the antecedents of the light boys I met seemed to bear out the picture of a remarkably diverse group. Thinking about the Foreign Legion–like composition of Azad's crew has led me to some theoretical propositions about what brought them together and what they find in common. With brio, Azad recounted to me how he had set out, back in 1962, penniless, illiterate, and alone, from his village near Allahabad in Uttar Pradesh to follow his dream of a glamorous future in the film industry.[22] His is the story of a young man for whom the vision of modernity disseminated across India by the cinema seems to have overwhelmed the strictly local horizon of a place in society defined by commitments to caste, clan, and community. And to the extent that this narrative resonates with his fellow light boys I suggest it does so beyond personal experience. They had indeed also traveled from across India—and in one case from Nepal—to seek their fortunes, but what rings loud and clear here is the clarion call of Bollywood romance.

Importantly, to identify cinema as the medium that delivers this "call"—or interpellation—is not to limit things to narrative. Azad's personal story may indeed owe much to stories from and about the movies, but it also bespeaks an attraction to the vision of a certain kind of place. This is the shiny modern India generated by cinematic constructions of space, where room for autonomy and libidinal license can be found within the structure of a recognizably Indian morality.[23] And in the typical Bollywood mise-en-scène, modernity is imagined in an urban idiom—and contrasted with the village, the site of tradition. Among the chief outputs of Mumbai's illusion factory, in other words, is Mumbai itself, the City of Illusion. My own take on Azad's story gives it a circular spin: drawn to Mumbai by the picture of it given in the cinema, the light boys have found their living in the city in erecting and demolishing studio sets—the very fabric of the illusion.

Now, to the degree that what is presented here is an ideologized model of space whose appeal to a group is mediated through visual forms, this is an example of what I call spectacularized space in action. But taken by itself, the spectacular doesn't have much to say about the collectivity of light boys as subalterns. On the contrary, one of the compelling aspects of Bollywood's montage of Mumbai is that the fantasy of modernity it generates tends to elide the social dichotomy. (At the same time, this tendency can generate imaginary vistas from which all traces of recognizably subaltern habitus have been erased; indeed, in this book's conclusion, I will develop the idea that the historical trend has been toward erasure.) It is a different mode of perceiving and organizing space—what I term rationalized space—that really throws into relief the distinction between the citizens who run the studio grounds and the subalterns who work for them.

This stage of the exposition will center on a modest visual artifact. However otherwise disparate, Bollywood's light boys and associated industry workers, from skilled technicians to generic toilers, do have one thing in common. This is a material thing, a token of collective identity: a Ciné Workers Union identity card. We are far from the hopeful scenario of the seeds of class consciousness germinating on the factory floor, however. Union membership in this case is more like a license to compete as a free agent in a labor market than a guarantee of job security or collective-bargaining rights.[24]

Among film industry subalterns, a minority has stable employment with a regular employer. Filmistan, where I gathered most of my information about the studio work dynamic, retains only a skeleton staff on its payroll to maintain the facilities and grounds.[25] A second group is made up of staff who are permanent members of production houses or assistants attached to professional subcontractors like the cameraman or makeup artist. In both such cases, bonds of dependency obtain between the worker and his patron that are conventionally glossed in terms of family (in like vein, domestic servants are also often understood to be part of the family, at the bottom of an expanded household hierarchy). The standard method of getting by as a light boy, however, is to go freelance. A brief description of what is involved in finding work in this way should clarify the issue of the relative unimportance of caste or religion as a determining factor of sociality among the light boys.

On the big steel gate that faces the street, underneath the letters that spell "Filmistan Studio," there is painted a warning: "No entry without cine unions identity card. Trespasser will be procecuted [sic]."[26] In the style of most such injunctions marking public space in Mumbai, the notice is written in English, the better to project the effect of official sanction that marks a boundary. In pursuit of the day's work, unsigned light boys (most of whom cannot read English and some can't read at all, notwithstanding which everyone knows well enough what the sign is there to do) arrive at the gate in the morning and present their sole credential to the security guard. They are then free to wander the enclosed grounds, all day if need be, offering themselves for hire at any of the stages or outdoor sets at which filming may be planned or already in progress. Agreements are concluded verbally and compensation is determined at a negotiable daily rate, paid in cash. The hunt is facilitated by an informal network of contacts and patrons who relay useful information and perhaps put in a helpful word with the sahib. But notwithstanding all this scope for elaboration—and room for variously interested parties to take their cut—in principle the system seems simple enough. Once through the gate, a job seeker enters a space with bounds that enclose a marketplace of labor. It is a system whose operation is predicated on a glut of unskilled labor, but that is a condition that Indian businessmen across most economic sectors have long been able to take for granted.

The union ID functions as the admission ticket to this cattle call. Having scraped together the sum of seven thousand rupees that obtains this all-important bit of paper, an individual is free to measure himself on equal terms against his peers, whose official qualifications are coterminous with his own. It is tempting to see the paper as the passport to a miniature republic, a liberal—one might say utilitarian—commons, spatially demarcated by the studio compound, within which sectarian identities are checked at the door to be superseded by a neutral certificate of citizenship. But I think an emphasis on the agency of these ostensibly free agents would be misleading, and the attribution of citizenship misplaced. Rather, I propose that the studio grounds be viewed on the lines of a postcolonial model of public space, and the light boys as a subaltern population.

To clarify: Filmistan is not an actual public space, in that entry to it is restricted and activities within its bounds are dedicated to private enterprise. Precisely because of these anomalous features, however, it functions in a way that public space is supposed to in the rationalized vision of the modern city that inspires Mumbai's chattering classes and its planners in the Municipal Corporation. The colonial heritage of this vision is traceable not only to technologies of mapping and governmentality but also to the English liberal tradition in political philosophy (see U. Mehta 1999; Parekh 1995; Stokes 1959). The mechanism of the ID cards registers the entry of subjects, at once incorporating each individual into an archive and rendering him interchangeable with his fellows. (It would be interesting to learn about how union cards are borrowed, traded, or rented; I was never told of such practices, but given the plethora of ways Mumbai residents "game" the identity-granting paperwork at the nexus of official and subaltern spheres, I have no doubt that they are prevalent.) To enter the space to join the light-boy population, in other words, you have to pass through the sahibs' radar. And thus made visible, the light boys proceed about their business as self-policing subjects of Filmistan, a realm in which—to revisit the brief discussion of their terms of address—no boy is a *bhai*, a kinsman within a discrete brotherhood, but rather all are equally *boss*.[27]

The sets and props of the studio complex, in their varied stages of completion or disrepair, present a visual environment as complex as that of any Mumbai street. The spectacle of human activity is likewise a rich one, with not everyone hard at work, but scattered groups idling here and there over tea or cigarettes or actually napping. That, too, is like the street. But the light boys are temporary occupants, circulating in the space to pass through. They will return to their homes at the end of the day to be replaced by different individuals the next morning. And *that* is a scenario the elite guardians of public order only wish they could bring to the streets, beset as the city's officially public spaces are by beggars, cowherds, pavement dwellers, and unlicensed hawkers, not to mention the incorrigible builders of unauthorized structures—the shrines and temples on the public thoroughfare, the slum dwellings or "encroachments" that range from tarps stretched over the sidewalk to whole residential blocks with concrete housefronts.[28] (A final point of contrast: the grounds of Filmistan are well served by public toilets, which are kept tolerably clean.)

From a citizen's-eye view, then, Filmistan can look like a rationally organized place. It is a landscape assimilable within the "techno-juridical grid," in Christopher Pinney's (1997b, 855) and Ronald Inden's Foucauldian term—an ordering mechanism of the modern regime of power and knowledge bequeathed by the colonial Raj. Again, the grounds are occupied by ramshackle structures whose ad hoc appearance reflects the clutter on the streets outside. But in contrast with the street, the presence of such structures on the studio landscape is planned and directed—and as temporary as that of the light boys who erect them only to tear them down once their utility expires at the end of the shoot. The point here is not to use the illusory character of the filmmaking business to make a statement about the transience of all worldly things. Rather, what the comparison highlights is the subjection at Filmistan of these visual and material artifacts, alongside their fabricators, to a scheme of rationalized calculations by the managerial class. If the street is the site of resistance, or at least of a certain defiance, to the blueprints of administrators, urban planners, and real estate developers, the studio landscape conforms to the spreadsheets imposed by the management and its film producer clients.

One reason why Filmistan demonstrates a particularly arresting perspective on the rationalization of space is that, as remarked before, the very sets that are erected and dismantled so calculatingly contribute to a topography of fantasy outside the studio gates. It should further be noted that the valorization of such sites is reinscribed on the street and elsewhere, in significant measure, by its public dissemination as a result of the shooting undertaken within the studio. Put another way, the more a kind of place is celebrated on film, through its integration in narrative or its extradiegetic presentation as an *icon* (see Kapur 1987), the more jarring the effect of seeing it get torn down. The best example I can give from Filmistan is that of a two-story building that anchors that part of the permanent studio complex known to the light boys as the Village. This building serves as the armature for a variety of façades to be donned or discarded like costumes on a mannequin: police station, rural homestead, Hindu temple. Somewhat paradoxically, it is the façades—precisely the visually marked layer that makes the building meaningful—that the sahibs' logic has rendered expendable. Further on in this book I will be able to introduce sites where, conversely, the façade has taken over the host structure.

Now, I have suggested that a movement parallel to that operating among the light boys, transforming them from members of disparate Indian communities into equivalent units of labor power, converts Filmistan's edifices from meaningful images into fungible components to be reassembled or discarded. In conceptualizing this dynamic I draw on the insights of a broadly Marxian conversation that begins with the discussion of use value and exchange value in *Capital* and has been extended to an analysis of the social construction of space, magisterially by Henri Lefebvre (1991) and more idiosyncratically by Walter Benjamin (1968) and Michel de Certeau (1984). As I have stated in the introduction and earlier in this chapter, however, I am passing over a class-based analysis in favor of an approach that foregrounds the visual mediation of the experience of space. My argument will proceed in alignment with scholarship that examines the dynamic of abstraction from a postcolonial perspective, problematizing the rationalizing "grid" and its visual prostheses by situating them in modern technologies of surveillance, classification, and dissemination instituted by the colonial regime.

The genealogy of much postcolonial critique along these lines originates in Michel Foucault's concept of governmentality. In studying the role of the Indian state I have been inspired by the work of Nicholas Dirks (2001) and Bernard Cohn (1987); and in foregrounding the visual, by that of Christopher Pinney.[29] It will be noted that in both examples I have given from the studio, the trajectory from concrete particularity to abstraction is accomplished through mediation by an artifact of visual culture. In the case of the light boys, particular identities are displaced onto bits of paper, extensions of an archival apparatus. The challenge for the workers, in a sense, is not so much how closely the pictures on their ID cards look like them as how closely they look like the pictures on their cards. In the case of the sets, generic types of places are represented by material installations that are consigned to scrap once their surfaces have been captured for reproduction on film.

This discussion of the spectacularized and rationalized dimensions of the studio space, and the place the light boys find in them, has one more turn to take through the analytic playhouse. The bourgeois regime at the studio manages the workforce by ensuring that each body entering the space is tagged to a card in a file. Similarly, the fate of constituent parts of the built environment is mediated by contractual paperwork: each lot on the grounds is let to such-and-such a production for x amount of money for y amount of time, and whatever is erected on that spot stands for only as long as the record permits it to stand. In the studio as an instantiation of rationalized space, then, the abstraction is dispositive. On the other hand, in the city outside the gates, where the corollary to the studio's sets is the slums, the violation such subaltern "encroachments" pose to civic order is precisely their lack of documentation. These scratch-built structures transgress the law on two counts: their material fabrication has not been authorized, and their occupancy of specific plots has not been registered in anyone's name. And inasmuch as their construction and upkeep involve economic transactions, that business is conducted largely off the books.

Yet in practice the mandate to remove the settlements is a ticklish one for the authorities, especially in cases where the residents who are put under threat of displacement are capable agents of political society (see Weinstein 2014). The characteristic tactic of such a population will be to file paperwork of their own—less, perhaps, to contest the official record through argument than to muddy its reflection of the facts on the ground. Of course, what is business as usual for the municipality looks, from the perspective of a public-spirited citizen, like a crisis of governmentality. But it takes a pretty diehard commitment to a law-and-order position to deny that Mumbai's prosperity, such as it is, is dependent on the presence of an enormous and cheap labor pool. There must be days when it seems that the best way to exercise bourgeois citizenship is simply to lower the shades on the windows and summon—via TV, cinema, or glossy print media—the reassuring spectacle of a modern city from which subaltern housing has been abjected.

But now let's shift perspectives. What remains to be said is that when the day's shooting wraps, and yet another shiny picture of Mumbai life has been put in the can, the light boys themselves head home to the slums. This is a blanket statement, to be sure (and the snapshot of a light boy's living situation I offer at this chapter's end will complicate the picture), but it is hardly a stretch. With one-and-a-half times New York's population shoehorned into three-fifths its area, Mumbai is an exceptionally crowded city. Not less than 60 percent of this population lives in slums, if by *slums* are meant those sprawling neighborhoods, showing up as blank blocks of gray on the map, that lack legible trace in the archive. In the end, occupancy of unauthorized housing—and the project intrinsic to it of making inhospitable terrain habitable—is perhaps the main point of common experience to be found among Mumbai's toiling populations. When the old Marxist narrative comes home to roost, it turns out, it does so precisely at home—subaltern subjectivity coalesces, not in the workplace, but rather in domestic space. Or to rephrase things with reference to Chatterjee: political society, in the urban context, is overwhelmingly a product of the slums.

If these structures make members of the citizen class psychologically uncomfortable, they of course keep the people who actually live in them physically uncomfortable. But it should be stressed that much of the ramshackle character of slum dwellings is attributable to the contingency of their continued existence. Labor, money, and durable materials will be invested in a given settlement only to the degree that the location seems likely to withstand the threat of demolition. At the same time, certain kinds of symbolic or cultural work pursued by slum residents can help to configure their space as a permanent home. One such project is the after-the-fact acquisition of a paper trail for their settlement, exemplary of the sort of tactical engagement analyzed in Chatterjee's model of political society. The gloss I propose here brings this activity in line with a visual studies approach: in assembling artifacts of textual representation, residents acquire legibility for their neighborhood within the scheme of rationalized space. The project, in other words, is a play for recognition in the eyes of others—of the state bureaucracy, of the bourgeois class that staffs its upper ranks.

But this is not the only visual practice oriented around the community's desire for recognition; nor is it the most meaningful to the community's members. It's time to move on from the concept of rationalized space to a different register: that of sacred space.

Sacred Space

Mumbai is a city that is capitalist to the core. Moreover, the experience of colonialism is central to its character as a lived community and a viewed landscape. These aspects of the metropolis will be apparent to any bourgeois visitor (and perhaps even more apparent to newcomers from subaltern backgrounds). Yet capitalist and colonial are not all Mumbai is. If abstract space, or its visual instantiations, predominate at certain locations, there are other visual registers that make urban spaces habitable in different ways. And if the logic of abstract space be summed up, after the manner of George Orwell's pigs, as "All space is homogenous, but some parcels of space are quantifiably more valuable than others," the alternative logic of sacred space proposes, "No two places are the same, but some places are more particular than others."

In the visually rich environment of Filmistan, one site had a particularity that was defined, to my eye, by a semiotic excess. This was the aforementioned Village, which occupies the southwest corner of the grounds. Its built elements consist of a few rude, shedlike structures flanked by a more *pakka*, or finished-looking, building, the one on which the light boys rig the façades for shooting. I have already remarked how my curiosity about the area was intensified by the ease with which the producers and managers ignored it. To put things in analytic terms, I came to see that what they had done was to assimilate it within the scheme of rationalized space, as one generic lot among others. With its physical components understood as bare infrastructure, they had equated the space to a blank slate that would acquire legible features only once it had been set up for shooting. As my first guide, Ram Prasad, explained, the area is used by producers chiefly for staging scenes depicting rural or small-town settings. At this level, the Village has meaning and particularity only insofar as it is a fake village.

But in this connection, consider that a Bollywood village is not just any old backdrop. Hindi cinema has a long tradition of casting the village as the foil to the dazzling city (generally named in diegesis as Mumbai), for the spectacle of city life—all its attraction and promise notwithstanding—does not always win in the movies. The village is the locus of authenticity, as opposed to urban pretentiousness and pretense; of the simple home virtues, as opposed to decadent big-city ways; of stability, as opposed to dynamism, to be sure, but also to inconstancy. Which is all to say that if the city is the site and defining image of illusion, then the village is encoded with an association with the truth. Is Filmistan's little enclave, then, all the more dishonest as a "fake village" (*nakli gaon*)—a mask disguised as an open face?

In fact, where the Filmistan light boys and other subalterns are concerned, I believe the reverse is the case. Integral to the site are certain features that— while obscure to an uninitiated eye—converge in a sort of matrix that anticipates its projection as the spectacularized all-Indian village. In other words, to see or sense these features at the Village is to recognize it as a "real village" (*asli gaon*). There is more than one well, and while these no longer function, they remain substantial features nonetheless. There are peripheral areas properly occupied by special trees, like tamarinds; such trees had indeed marked the village's contours until a generation ago. There is a "real temple" (*asli mandir*) on the premises, as opposed to the "fake temples" (*nakli mandir*) sometimes assembled for shooting. And as I have had cause to describe already, there is a community of human villagers comprising several dozen members of an extended family.

How these unofficial yet well-established residents understand and inhabit this space is a question I have, since first meeting them, pursued through ethnographic research. An account of the geography they occupy and the abjected condition to which they submit under the regime of rationalized space is reserved for chapter 4. This subsequent tour of the studio will thus explore the Village as a real village in the sense of a social unit (although, to be sure, "real village" in that sense is itself a modern construction laden with implications for ideology and governmentality). But I have not hinted at the mapping onto

Filmistan of a third mode of inhabiting space only to defer engaging with it here altogether.

Ethnographic work on popular religious practice in India, especially insofar as it bears on questions of space, has long been concentrated on village communities. One reason for this is the conceptual opposition between the village as traditional and the city as modern, a dichotomy that academics seem to have found almost as hard as filmmakers to move beyond.[30] But the emphasis on the village context should not be dismissed altogether (even if the best way to begin thinking critically about "traditional" villages may be to take a hard look at the tradition of ethnography). This is a book about the sacred dimension of a vast metropolis, India's "world-class city." I begin it with this peculiar example of a village enclave because, for my Filmistan interlocutors, what makes the Village real is not a connection with agriculture (which is nonexistent) or even, strictly speaking, with human social organization. Rather, the "realness" of the Village inheres in its capacity to provide a stable home to a community composed of human and nonhuman persons, and this is what its essential features have in common. There are human residents, who sleep in the shedlike structures. And then there are spiritual presences, which are made visible on the landscape by the material elements that emplace them: sacred trees, wells, and, of course, temples.

This is the insight that launches one of the most conceptually sophisticated village ethnographies, *Fluid Signs* by Valentine Daniel (1984): Daniel's Tamil informants and, indeed, the anthropologist himself are simultaneously inhabiting two villages at the same spot. Striving to clarify the distinction between the two spatial orders—between the village as *kiramam*, which I would call an example of official, abstract space, and the alternative category of the *ur*—he devises a map-drawing exercise:

> When asked to draw a kirāmam map, informants frequently responded with hesitation and would tell me, "Why, you can get that . . . from the village accountant or the munsif [village policeman]." Those who did agree to draw one invariably began by drawing a linear boundary in the shape of a square, rectangle, circle, or other less regularly shaped enclosing form. . . .
>
> When villagers were asked to draw ūr maps, they were considerably less hesitant to do so, already hinting at a conceptual distinction between the terms ūr and kirāmam, which are prima facie equivalents. . . . The drawing began not with the periphery of the village but at its center, with the noting of the important places, such as the temple, the priest's house, the crossroads, and so on.

Only then did attention shift to the periphery. All the respondents took great care to mark the shrines of the sentinel deities, the points at which roads or the village stream enters the village, and the haunted tamarind trees that dot the edge of the village. (74)

My own realization that Filmistan's sadly attenuated-looking village contained within it what Daniel's Tamil neighbors would recognize as an *ur* can be traced, in retrospect, to two exchanges with light boys.

The first encounter was a friendly conversation with a man I will call Nilesh. It was a slow day at Filmistan—the Shiv Sena–mandated state holiday of Maharashtra Day, in fact—and Nilesh was helping, at a leisurely pace, to strike a set at Stage Number Three. (Typically, he did not refer to the production in question by title, identifying it only as "Jackie's," after the name of the star.) With the lack of supervision, he found plenty of time to chat. I had arrived with a friend, and we had been visiting the temple installed in the outer yard of the studio. When I referred to it, he responded warmly. It was a comforting thing to have a temple on the premises, he told me; he performed his devotions (*puja*) at that temple every morning upon entering the grounds, right before reporting to work. It was when he suggested that I should take my companion to look at the other temple too that I took notice: "Over that way," he gestured.

"You mean in the Village?" I asked. "Yes, in the Village. The people who live there are *adivasi*s [tribals]," he volunteered, "you know, people from the jungle." This raised an intriguing question. "Do you observe *darshan* [visual worship] at that temple as well?" I asked. Sure, he told me. "But don't they have a different type of god?" Nilesh's response was a nonchalant assertion that the gods were "equal," or one, to him: *barabar*.

I had actually known for some months about the Warli tribal identity of the denizens of the Filmistan Village. In fact, what had tipped me off was a colleague's identification of the deity seated in the little shrine inside the Central Jail. The red rock embodied Wagh, or Waghoba, the tiger god, who guards the outskirts of villages in tribal areas of western India. Once we had recognized their god, some of the Village residents opened up to discussion of their tribal status and its implications for their claim to the space they occupied. But I was surprised to learn that the light boys knew of it too. That the tiger god, a rustic figure metonymic of the presence of Warli and other *adivasi* communities on the land, a symbol at once regionally specific and "backward," should have been recognized as the object of devotion by the likes of Nilesh, a metropolitan Hindu with a Gujarati name, offered food for thought.

I took home with me a more fundamental question, which, with reflection, I can articulate like this. Why did Nilesh find it necessary, every morning after entering the studio and before joining his crew, to check in at either temple on the grounds? Were private devotions at home, performed before his commute, somehow not adequate? Just what did he get out of observing *darshan* in that particular space?

In the second conversation my interlocutor was Azad. When I asked him about the evil-eye charm someone had fastened on the stage door he was guarding, he had a voluble response. The longer he worked at Filmistan, he told me, the more conscious he had become of the presence of spirits populating the studio grounds. Indicating the charm at the threshold—the usual bundle of chilies attached to a lemon—he explained that it was a means of providing protection for the space within from this infestation of mischievous local spir-its. And he launched into an enthusiastic telling of the tragedy that had sup-plied that building with a ghost of particular note. I will summarize the story elsewhere. The point to mark here is that between Nilesh's talk of gods and Azad's of ghosts, the two had turned me on to the view of the studio grounds as the turf of invisible residents whose presence was recognized by many of the workers.

The next time I ran into Azad he took me out of the gate and next door to a middle-class apartment building. What he wanted to show me was just inside the entryway. Right before the turn to take the stairs to the apartments, at the threshold spot generally occupied by the *chowkidar*—a building's watchman or caretaker—Azad had fitted together a shedlike structure of sheets of aluminum plate. Inside was a bright blue bas-relief of Shiva. The transparent stream of the Ganges pouring from the god's head was complemented by a three-dimensional figure of Ganga Maa, the holy river personified as Shiva's consort, seated on her crocodile mount on a shelf above the main image. At the right hand of Shiva stood a vermilion Hanuman. The whole exhibit was notable for its high-gloss finish, but as far as the iconography went, Azad had clearly taken his cues from the visual style of a North Indian temple. With aplomb, my host explained that the *linga*s, ithyphallic cult objects, installed in front of Lord Shiva were stones he had brought all the way from his home village near Allahabad.

When it came to the question of why he had chosen that particular spot, Azad attributed agency in the matter to the deity. This is a characteristic move. The origin stories of many Hindu temples identify the cult object located in the sanctum as *svayambhu*, or "self-manifested": emitted naturally at the space it occupies as a material index of that space's particularity. The explanation Azad offered was different, but it was one I was to hear reproduced in the testimony of many other freelance builders and operators of religious structures I would meet in the course of research. He had built the temple, he told me, because he had been told to do so in a dream. Mahadev ("Great God," an epithet of Shiva) had appeared to him and revealed that a *mandir* had formerly stood on the consecrated spot but had been destroyed years before. In erecting a new temple, his servant was simply restoring visible form to a presence that remained immanent.

It might also be said, by an outside observer like me, that in making over part of an apartment building in the idiom of North Indian popular Hinduism, Azad was a homesteader staking out a claim. He was planting the flag, as it were, of his natal village, marking a corner of a Mumbai plot that would remain forever the banks of the Ganges. But my friend had also added some cosmopolitan elements to the mix. The back of the shelf was faced with tiles printed with Hindu gods. These mass-produced tiles are a characteristic visual element in Mumbai's temples and are also frequently installed on walls by urban landlords for a reason I will take up in the next chapter. What was interesting was that neither of us could identify many of the icons; he shrugged and said, "They're gods from Gujarat." The impressive plaster bas-relief of Lord Shiva had been commissioned from a props department man at the studio. Indicating the conventional Himalayan horizon in the back of the scene, Azad invoked, not the context of Puranic myth, but the alternative imaginary of Bollywood: "That's Kashmir," he offered.[31] A virtuosic touch with the electric lighting and the arrangement of mirrors completed the effect of a professional Filmistan production.

Azad's zest in playing host was palpable, and it felt impolitic to press him on the details of his residence in the building. I suspect that rather than inhabiting an apartment of his own, he was retained by the management in a service capacity—perhaps he himself had a position as *chowkidar*—and may have been given no more than some small utility space to use as his private quarters.[32] But regardless of his status in the building, the point is that he had managed to impose his personal vision on a passage traversed by multiple others. Technically speaking, most of those people enjoyed at least as much right to dispose of the space as he did, if not (as seems likely) considerably more.

Tenant, staff, or squatter? If there was no straight answer where Azad himself was concerned, as applied to his god the question does shed light—from different angles—on the relation of a local deity to its space. Thanks to Azad's sponsorship, Lord Shiva had indeed become a squatter, an illegal occupant of someone else's property. And then again, inasmuch as he had been stationed in the entryway, perhaps Shiva should be seen as the building's actual *chowkidar*, the guardian of the threshold. All who would gain entry to the realm—native inhabitants as well as outsiders—had to pass under the divine gaze, and perhaps Azad was not the only one who looked into the painted eyes for a daily affirmation that he did indeed belong there.

What would not be right to say is that Shiva had moved into the building as a tenant, on an equal footing with others. Mahadev was not beholden to the rule of private property—and he was certainly no renter. Rather, the god had been set up in implicit challenge to the landlord, indeed to the whole system of rationalized space; he was the original sovereign, the master (to cite some theoretical language that will shape the analysis in the following chapters) of the dispensation that truly governed the space.

And here at the end of the chapter, let's note the most important thing about Azad's creation. For all its veneer of Bollywood glitz, it is in fact typical in its spatial arrangement as well as its visual features. My purpose in describing it is to introduce a whole class of religious displays that local entrepreneurs erect in urban spaces across India and, indeed, across South Asia. Whether dedicated to Mahadev in Banaras, Sufi saints in Lahore or Dhaka, Buddhist relics in Colombo, or Sai Baba in Mumbai (and in Mumbai, and probably only in Mumbai, the majority of shrines are indeed dedicated to the saint Sai Baba of Shirdi, for reasons I will explain in chapter 3), such spectacles perforate the official spatial order, opening windows on an alternative geography.[33]

Farther on in this study, I will connect this work of sacralizing space with norms of religious practice observed among the Warli residents of Filmistan itself, as well as in tribal enclaves elsewhere in the Mumbai suburbs. Before the argument is brought home, however, it will be useful to make a move downtown to study shrine construction on the streets of the historic part of the postcolonial city—the "Raj town" and its environs. This phenomenon requires examination in multiple contexts, including aspects of Mumbai's history, its religious diversity, the technologies and ideologies of Indian visual culture, and—not least of all—the anxiety held by citizens and subalterns alike concerning the city's perennial housing crisis. My exposition will pivot on a clash of rival geographies: the campaign of demolition the Municipal Corporation waged in the fall of 2003, not against slum housing, but against "illegal religious structures."

2

CONCRETE SPIRITS

RELIGIOUS STRUCTURES ON THE PUBLIC STREETS

The arc terminated abruptly. The man's hand shook twice and performed a deft movement in his trousers before he slipped away.

"You saw?" said Gustad. "Shameless. That's the reason for the stink. But once you draw your holy pictures, no one will dare." He glimpsed hesitation on the other's face and hastened to add, "First we will have the whole wall washed and cleaned."

The pavement artist thought for a bit, then agreed. "I can start tomorrow morning."

"Good, good. But one question. Will you be able to draw enough to cover three hundred feet? I mean, do you know enough different gods to fill the whole wall?"

The artist smiled. "There is no difficulty. I can cover three hundred miles if necessary. Using assorted religions and their gods, saints and prophets: Hindu, Sikh, Judaic, Christian, Muslim, Zoroastrian, Buddhist, Jainist."

ROHINTON MISTRY, *Such a Long Journey*

The wall that concerns Gustad forms the boundary between the urban plot on which he lives—a residential colony reserved for Parsis, a space demarcated as private in terms of both property and community exclusivity—and the street. In Rohinton Mistry's novel the wall functions as the motif of a complex accommodation between the Parsis in their bourgeois enclave and the potential danger and defilement represented by what lies beyond their front gate: Bombay at the time of the 1971 Bangladesh War, synecdoche of a vast and turbulent nation. Looking to the painter's talents, Gustad devises an entente with the city on the other side. By opening his wall to the diverse symbols under which its constituent groups find protection and recognition, he erects a shield against the public and at the same time extends a greeting, a gesture of address. And at a concrete level, of course, he prevents incontinent pedestrians of all creeds from relieving themselves on his slice of urban space.

Mistry did not invent the device of the sacred display–as–wall-mounted splashguard. His is a literary representation of a well-established Mumbai phenomenon, to be observed throughout the city at certain spots where private walls face public streets. One Juhu-based example notable only for its forthrightness bears the caption "For God's sake, don't piss here." Most of the ethnographic information on which this chapter's discussion builds will be presented in a set of descriptions of public religious displays, and I will introduce the list with an examination of a similar wall-mounted site, one located near the Dadar train station.

By way of framing that discussion, however, let me first note a counterexample. In an essay titled "Filth and the Public Sphere," Sudipta Kaviraj (1997, 84) considers a photograph printed in an English-language newspaper of "a common street scene in Calcutta":

> It showed a municipal sign proscribing urination with the order "Commit no nuisance," and a row of unconcerned citizens right underneath engaged in this odious form of civil disobedience. Even in such unreflecting moments, I shall argue, people are taking a philosophical stance, or at least a position with conceptual implications. . . . The photograph . . . shows a dissonance at many levels between two ways of dealing with and acting upon the world—of the poor and the rich, of the powerful and dominated, of those who own property and those who can only defile it. . . . It shows in an everyday form the contest between a bourgeois order of the middle class and those who flout its rules.

So coy at first blush, the locution "Commit No Nuisance" is in fact quite explicit in its citation of the Public Nuisance Act of 1860, an ordinance drawn up by Calcutta's colonial masters in part to address the problem of natives urinating in the streets (and apostrophized satirically by the Bengali essayist Ishwarchandra Gupta in his *Mutrasutra*, or "Piss Sutra").[1]

Let me begin recruiting Kaviraj's ideas to my own argument by glossing some terms he has introduced. His "row of unconcerned citizens," of course, belongs to just that group whose position within the postcolonial polity I am defining in opposition to a liberal model of citizenship: subalterns. And a formulation of their stance as a "philosophical" project is not a proposition I want to follow up on; rather, my take on what is at stake in the subaltern reformulation of officially public space stresses effects that are felt at the affective or somatic levels.[2]

In the last chapter I sketched the outlines of this problematic, identifying citizens and subalterns with distinct modes of experiencing space, and nominating Bollywood's light boys as exemplary urban subalterns. As a practice of the subaltern production of locality I highlighted the demarcation or installation of sacred spaces that establish, visually and physically, certain otherwise invisible fellow residents on the landscape. Among these parahuman neighbors, Hindu deities are but one subset to be recognized. Nevertheless, personalities identified with modern metropolitan Hinduism are prominent; indeed, they are made especially so by virtue of the aesthetic codes that have come to dominate sacred imagery as a popular genre within Indian visual culture. This is a point to which I will return. But as my epigraph from the Mistry novel indicates, one implication of my research is that sectarian distinctions among the divine figures enshrined in this sort of local context function chiefly to differentiate the social constituencies alongside whom they lay claim to space. It could be said that the diverse religions and sects are separate camps within the same subaltern public. For I hypothesize little conceptual disagreement among local subalterns professing Hindu, Muslim, or other loyalties concerning the coexistent presence of their spirit-sponsors. That is to say that however doctrinally incompatible those sponsors may seem (not to mention invisible, until materially seated), their ontological status as actual or real (*asli*) persons or powers is not in question.

One thing that the comparison between the hapless Kolkata bureaucrats and the savvier private citizens of Mumbai throws into relief is that, despite both groups falling on the same side of the citizen-subaltern divide, Mistry's Parsis and their painted wall represent a case of bourgeois citizens participating— however instrumentalist their motives—in a subaltern construction of space. There are several points to be made about this apparent irony. The first is that the Kolkata municipal signage bespeaks an official concern with policing public space. Indeed, it might even be considered to succeed in its purpose, to the extent that the notice has been posted in a place where it can attract the gaze of the kind of people who can (1) actually read it and (2) feel interpellated by it. (Interpellated, that is, if not at the level of a prohibition, then as a sort of ritual affirmation: "The street is public space; therefore, respectable citizens like us do not / must not urinate here.") These two groups will be largely the same: the resident Anglophone elite. By contrast, the interventions of Gustad and his real-life counterparts are aimed at sequestering private space, cordoning it off from the public. Far from civic-mindedness, the attitude that motivates the installation of such displays is Not In My Back Yard; a corollary to "For God's sake, don't piss here" that could run alongside it would be "Try the other side of the street."

Questions of intent or instrumentality nothwithstanding, however, such exhibits do project their effects within public space and thus function to reconfigure it. Religious imagery as a formal category of visual culture—those images, at all events, that follow the typological codes of sacrality established as standard through mass reproduction—does not imply patronage by subalterns exclusively. But of course the logic of placing such images on the street is founded on engaging a response among the subaltern publics that traverse it. And in that sense the displays can be framed as subaltern phenomena, regardless of their authorship.

This is a point that will be complicated considerably in the ethnographic descriptions to follow. It will emerge that there is actually a great deal of social diversity to be observed among both the sponsors and the patrons of religious installations that open on public space. Indeed, one might take the proposition a step beyond the multiple social contexts of individual subjects to destabilize identity at the level of subjectivity as such. That is, to the extent that this sort of religious "guerrilla marketing" can evoke attitudes of piety—however fleeting and conflicted—among transient publics with middle-class educations or bank balances, it could be said that they have the power to interpellate alternative subject positions otherwise latent within them. Nor should the question of instrumentality be allowed to divert the analytic focus from the display's effects. The motives of the actors behind the production of my diverse examples will frequently be shown to be anything but pious, but that does not necessarily detract from their effect—on at least some passersby—of incorporating the street within a circuit of divine presence and power or, at least, of citing the trace of such a system in place.

My argument in this chapter is organized along three axes that might be summed up as Site/Sight/Cite.[3] First, I present a set of ethnographic descriptions of sites in Mumbai where rival constructions of space as public and sacred collide. Second, I open an inquiry into the range of effects that such sights provoke in their viewers. Third, I set up a semiotically informed analysis of the visual and discursive fields that they cite. There is a defining event that provides the chapter with narrative cohesion: the demolition drive targeting "illegal religious structures" mounted by city authorities in the late fall of 2003.

Walking Tour, Part 1

For many months, I had a commute that was the reverse of the route taken by most of the city's white-collar workforce. I would take the Western Railway from South Mumbai, where I lived in a downtown neighborhood abutting a business district, to the outer suburbs, where my fieldwork contacts in their tribal enclaves lived alongside burgeoning housing developments and slums. It was toward the end of my time in the city that I realized that a complementary

site of inquiry stood almost literally at my doorstep. The shrines and other religious displays that offered oases of contemplation (or otherwise heightened
affect) on the downtown streets were actually mirroring the very phenomenon
I was riding the trains north to study—the beleaguered landmarks of a tribal
geography, the abodes of local sovereigns all but banished by the transformation of their territory into real estate.

This section consists of a set of descriptions of shrines and other religious
sites that occupy public space. Having introduced the examples, I will move
on to unpack what that attribution of sacrality means and does in the contexts
and fields I find most germane. If plotted on a map, most of my walking tour's
highlights will be seen to be clustered in prosperous commercial and residential
areas of South Mumbai. The transgression of bourgeois norms of public and
private is especially evident in neighborhoods that have a history as parts of the
old "Raj town" and its neighboring areas. But there is nothing exceptional about
these particular sites. They are representative of entirely commonplace features
of urban landscapes in South Asia (and possibly even farther afield).[4] The order
in which they are presented will illustrate not geographical contiguity but a typology of progressively more finished and elaborate forms.

As *Stop 1*, then, consider a large private house located a few blocks from the
Dadar train station. A low wall surrounds the property, and mounted on it, facing the street at varying heights from just above the pavement to approximately
eye level, is a series of tiles printed with religious imagery. Every tile retailer
I visited in the city could offer a wide range of designs like these, colorfully
printed to represent all the major religious communities residing in Mumbai
and, in the case of Hindu gods, local or regional deities metonymic of specific
places in India. This wall is typical in the eclecticism of its cast of characters.
Ganesh, Hanuman, the child Krishna, Durga as slayer of the Buffalo Demon, a
mosque, Jesus, the Last Supper, the Virgin Mary, the Zoroastrian sacred flame,
and Sai Baba of Shirdi are all depicted. Alongside the neighborhood's gods is
also rendered its Caesar: the seventeenth-century king Chhatrapati Shivaji,
whose icon is more potent as a metonym of modern, translocal Maharashtrian
identity than the divine or saintly alternatives; compare Khandoba (too pa-
rochial), Ganesh (too generically Hindu), Dattatreya (too Brahmin), or Tu-
karam (too humble)—or, indeed, the nearly ubiquitous modern saint Sai Baba
of Shirdi, in connection with whom a number of objections can be raised here
but will be unpacked in the next chapter. (To anticipate my argument, I submit
that the Baba functions more as an emblem of Mumbai than of Maharashtra;
that he casts his vote for the Congress over the Shiv Sena; and that while in

practice he generally "reads" as Hindu he is certainly, in this context, not nearly Hindu enough.)[5]

No true Maharashtrian or respecter of Maharashtra would relieve himself on Shivaji; conversely, if you do soil the tile, you have disrespected Maharashtra (which can be a dangerous statement to make in Dadar). The broadly eclectic reach, the strategic placement, and the rudimentary production values of the display are all features that indicate that it has been installed to mask off a private wall against public urination (and again, to have acknowledged urination as simply one of those things that can be expected to happen in public space is already to have written off a certain ideal of public space). Not only in their purpose but also in their provenance the site's sponsors reflect Mistry's story: the house belongs to a Parsi family. And it can be added that as a prominent yet numerically minuscule community, Mumbai's Parsis have historically been among the most vocal champions of what in the Indian context is called *secularism*—that is to say, an evenhanded acknowledgment in public discourse of diverse religions as authentically Indian. The eclecticism shown by public displays like this one can thus be read simultaneously as a statement of "secularism" in this sense and as a characteristically Parsi gesture.

The assertion of private property rights and the public affirmation of local or national religious pluralism may be the display's primary and secondary purposes as far as its owners are concerned. Yet there are still telltale signs that mark particular spots on the wall as sites of devotion—spots at which at least someone traversing the street has trained a gaze and sensed a force looking back. The tiles representing Ganesh and the Zoroastrian flame have been set near the top of the wall by the gate, and a shelf has been installed just beneath them to accommodate offerings. Next to them is the site's most elaborate exhibit: Sai Baba, who—in contrast with the others—has been given a three-dimensional effigy. This has been enshrined on the wall within a small booth-like structure roughly the size and shape of a cuckoo clock. The miniature *murti* has been decked with ocher-colored cloth and garlands and placed atop a metal cashbox complete with coin slot; these are typical elements I will have more to say about further on. What interests me here is the question of just whose attentions it is these accessories facilitate. Judging by the prominent position and finished, or *pakka*, quality of the additions, I would expect to find the worshipers among the household's Hindu servants, who have reserved a spot on the shelf for the fiery object of their Parsi employers' devotions. A garland of marigolds draped around the tile of Christ, which has been mounted one step from the ground (down by the gutter, if the street had a gutter), presents a more enigmatic clue.

Is the adornment the gesture of a pious passerby? Or perhaps (and this is sheer speculation) of a Christian sweeper attached to the household, made sensitive by his or her walk of life to the presence of traces of the sublime where others would avert their eyes from pollution?

With a view to framing this site as an illustration of typical forms, I offer two closing observations about Stop 1. The first is that sacred images—representations of personalities (gods, saints, and culture heroes), places (the mosque), and objects (the flame)—are not the only sights on the wall that bid for the attention of viewing publics. One side of the wall has been sold as advertising space to a courier service, whose slogans, painted in colorful English letters, surround and dwarf the tiles that share the surface. The juxtaposition can draw chuckles from passersby of diverse persuasions: the phrase "Courier booking at" is punctuated by an icon of the Virgin Mary, while "Painless Delivery" runs next to an image of Hanuman transporting the herb-bearing Medicine Mountain, a celebrated episode in the *Ramayana*.

Are these two modes of visual address complementary? Do their publics overlap? In general it could be said that as part of the official economy, to the extent that they are funded by on-the-book business transactions (or at any rate are *pakka*-looking enough to give that impression), environmental advertising and shopwindow displays are an approved part of the bourgeois model of public space. English-language advertising, in particular, can cite the visual idiom of the notices of proscription and direction exemplified by the "Commit No Nuisance" sign located by Kaviraj as an outpost (however ineffectual) of bourgeois ideology in the postcolonial city. Indeed, in Mumbai the language used on any given block will have something to say about the community identity and class aspirations of the people who traverse it—or whose traversal is welcomed by landlords and advertisers—and at that level such signage can be read along parallel lines to religious imagery that functions, as discussed above, as socially metonymic.[6]

A more interesting project would invite a comparison of ideological effects similarly mediated through visual forms and perhaps similarly poised to mobilize desire in the construction of social identities. How, and at what sort of sites, would it work to analyze the interpellative effects produced by advertising displays on subjects as consumers—"Hey, you! Buy this!"—in relation to effects produced by religious displays on subjects as worshipers? I can only gesture here at the nexus of advertising and popular religion in India as a promising target of inquiry, one that will remain to be pursued, for the most part, outside the bounds of this book.[7] Yet it must be said that advertising imagery ranks alongside religious iconography as perfect material for analysis as ideologized visual media. And inasmuch as it follows that both classes of images generate effects that contribute to the production of space, there is nothing in the purpose or instrumentality of advertising as such that keys it to a particular spatial register. The examples of advertising graphics already discussed here can be assigned variously to official space and sacred space, while corporate advertising plays a major role in the makeover of Mumbai as spectacularized space. My remarks in the conclusion will pursue the last of these points.

My final comment about Stop 1 is aimed at locating it as an exemplary site within a broader category of religious display. The wall in Dadar is remarkable for the catholicity of its embrace and for the permanent, secure quality of its installation, but as a display of two-dimensional graphics that elides the partition between public and private space it shares formal characteristics with a host of other sites. Collectively these can be categorized as the most rudimentary, nascent, or *kaccha* form of street shrine. By way of comparison I will describe two down-market counterparts.

The first can be encountered a few stops south of Dadar on the western commuter line, off the Grant Road station to the right of the Sleater Road exit. Along the street, parallel to the tracks, there stretches a row of makeshift shelters; the occupants have not been evicted because they have chosen to pitch their tents on land administered by the railway, as opposed to the municipality. Spilling onto the railings that separate the tracks from the street are devotional prints of Hindu gods. What for an even slightly more prosperous family would be contained on a shanty's internal wall or shelf—sequestered as the low-rent version of a domestic prayer room—has thus become, as the result of practical contingencies governing the arrangement of living space, an exhibit that exerts its effects in public. A more innovative work of bricolage is a pair of figurines that squat nearby on the property of a different public utility, the power company. Manufactured as images of Jesus and Mary, they have been stood next to each other inside a pillar-mounted switch box after the conventional manner of framing Rama with Sita, or the Maharashtrian god Vitthal alongside his Rakhumai.

My second site is to be found yet further downtown in the British-planned business district of Ballard Estate. There, an entrepreneurially minded young Muslim has adorned a municipal tree with a color poster of the tomb of the Sufi saint Nizamuddin Auliya, which is located in Delhi. Having thus staked a claim to the block in the name of a distinct geographical affiliation as well as a religious one, he told me of his plans to collect funds toward the upkeep—and eventual expansion—of this budding shrine from any locals who might care to contribute. The proposition that even such a rudimentary display as this one may, given adequate patronage and investment, set down roots in the neighborhood as a *pakka* landmark should contribute a sense of dynamism to this walking tour, whose progressive steps represent typological categories that can also been seen as stages on a continuum of development.

For rhetorical convenience *Stop 2* can also be located in Ballard Estate, where in November 2003 I interviewed three siblings from Satara District in southwestern Maharashtra. The trio had traveled to the city to exhibit the effigy of their village goddess in return for alms. But the type of display they represent cannot be limited to specific sites in specific neighborhoods because, along with their idol, my young interviewees were acting as the vehicles of a mobile exhibition that customarily traces a circuit along the city streets at certain times of the year. The older of the two sisters, dressed in a rustic-looking sari, carried the draped and garlanded goddess on a tray-sized platform that fit on her head. Their brother wore a loudly colored *lungi* and a lot of red pigment on his face. As street performers and exponents of a decidedly non-elite cultic practice, people like these are known in Mumbai as *zogua*, a Marathi cognate for *yogi*.

By caste these three youngsters, like almost all the other *zogua*s with whom I spoke, identified themselves as Mahadev Kolis, members of a primarily rural community listed as a Scheduled Tribe by the state of Maharashtra. *Zogua*s serve as attendants of village goddesses, or *gaondevi*s, who circulate in a sort of reverse pilgrimage in which it is the remote, rustic deity who makes the rounds of her viewers instead of the other way around. The main element of this practice, and certainly the loudest, is the ritual—or visual citation of ritual—enacted by pairs of Mahadev Kolis in which the woman bearing the *murti* beats a drum to accompany the capers of her male partner, who whips himself with a rope in imitation of a medium in a state of possession. The performance has been glossed by scholars in terms of a dramatic reenactment of the combat between Durga and the Potraj, or Buffalo Demon.[8] But none of the *zogua*s with whom I spoke seemed anxious to have their work absorbed within a Sanskritic narrative. On the other hand, in naming their deity to me as Lakshmi, the Ballard Estate trio chose one of the standard ways of eliding the local specificity of country goddesses through identification with a metropolitan persona.

In nominating the *zogua*s as representative of a class of *kaccha* display at Stop 2, I stress as the defining characteristic not so much their mobility as their transience. Now, to be sure, there is nothing anomalous about traveling images of gods in the context of Hindu temple ceremonial. The annual excursion made by the cultic object beyond the temple gates, attended by priestly and lay devotees, is the salient event in the festival calendar of many Hindu cultic centers (see, inter alia, Gomes da Silva 2010; Parish 1996; Pechelis 2009; Tanaka 1997).[9] When it comes to big cities, the outstanding study is *Landscapes of Urban Memory*, Smriti Srinivas's (2001) ethnography of Bangalore's Karaga festival, a yearly event in which the resident goddess of a local temple makes the rounds of her urban domain.

In its outlines, the performance put on by Mumbai's *zogua* visitors would seem to have a good deal in common with these kinds of festivals. In fact, the Potraj raises his head—in a variety of guises—in goddess cults across the southern part of the country. Srinivas (2001, 176) describes him thus: "Potha Raja is a ritual figure found in some parts of south India who is usually a servant or a guardian of the local goddess." But to categorize the *zoguas'* routine as a sort of snippet or trace of an elaborate ritual production like the Karaga does not straightforwardly address what it accomplishes on the field of effects. Given the comparison, it's really the points of diversion that shed light on what the *zoguas* are doing on the Mumbai streets.

Srinivas's study devotes a chapter to the *Karaga Purana*, an oral epic declaimed in Telugu and Tamil on the climactic ninth night of the festival. The recitations of the previous days have offered a telling of parts of the *Mahabharata*, with the spotlight on the heroine Draupadi, whose essential *shakti* has been channeled into the clay pot, or *karaga*, that is the focal point of the procession. Capping off the whole narrative, the *Karaga Purana* vernacularizes and localizes the Sanskritic figure of Draupadi by telling of an alliance between the wandering heroes of the *Mahabharata* and the Potraj, who has been recast as the sovereign of the local territory. Cementing connections in this way between registers of Sanskritic and vernacular symbol and myth, this multivocal narrative is presented by the ritual's virtuosi—members of a single caste group, the Vahnikula Kshatriyas—to a diverse urban public. By integrating their local goddess cult within prestigious genres of Sanskrit sacred literature, the Vahnikulas enact an annual renewal of vows, as it were, as a synecdoche of the urban community as a whole.[10]

By contrast, recall that the *zoguas* resisted association with the Potraj, and when I pressed them to name their deity, the translocal, Sanskritic identity they opted for was not Durga or Draupadi but Lakshmi. Narrative and mythology—discourse—are of central importance for Bangalore's Vahnikulas; they seem to be of no regard for the *zoguas*. Verbal communication forms no part of the show. Recall, too, that the partner who whips himself as if possessed is not actually in the throes of a possession experience. Let me reiterate that this is a display that projects the *image* of a human subject in a condition of religious ecstasy. And to follow the logic of possession in which the human body is the material vessel occupied by a divine spirit, it might also be thought of as a method of giving the deity visible form. The performance, in other words, is an exhibition—a fleeting, cursory exhibition, a citational gesture like a wink. The *zogua*s pass along the street unnoticed until they choose to announce themselves. Then *crack!* goes the whip and the drummer builds up a drone with circular motions of her drumstick. Anyone whose attention has been caught is exposed to a sacred peepshow—a flash, just possibly, of divine power—before the duo melt back into the street.

Some other differences with the Bangalore Karaga festival should be listed, all having to do with the marginality of the Mahadev Kolis relative to the Vahnikulas—a social marginality that can be thought of, within a visual-culture framework, as invisibility. The *zogua*s, like other kinds of street people, are mendicants—not even slum dwellers. By contrast, the Vahnikulas are a prominent constituency in Bangalore, upwardly mobile and well represented in city government (Srinivas's account gives a picture of deft participation in political society). The infrastructural center of the Karaga festival is a well-established temple. And the festival is held regularly at dates set by the Hindu ritual calendar, it enjoys not only official sanction but patronage by high government officials, and it commands an audience in the hundreds of thousands.[11]

Even the Karaga is dwarfed, however, by the best-known show on the streets of Mumbai: the annual festival of Lord Ganesh, Ganapati Puja. On the tenth day, the plaster effigies of the god that have been displayed over the preceding nine in *pandal*s, temporary neighborhood booths, are paraded westward through the streets to be immersed in the Arabian Sea. With attendance counted in the millions, the scale of the event demands a massive investment by the state in crowd management, traffic management, and—the day after—trash management. In 2015 special trains were provided for out-of-town visitors, and some forty-seven thousand security personnel were deployed, along with helicopters, drones, and sniffer dogs (Press Trust of India 2015).

There is a political dimension to these great public rituals, one that comes to the fore in Srinivas's discussion of the intermythological compass of the *Karaga Purana*. It is also manifested in the geographical circuit the Karaga votaries make, which takes in a diversity of Bangalore's sacred spaces, including lately sacred sites like bodies of water (compare the wells of the Village in chapter 1) and even Islamic and Christian sites; the festival embraces a whole city as a sacred geography, with the Vahnikulas as custodians of the collective vision. And politics is indeed the organizing concern of Raminder Kaur's (2005) study of the Ganesh festival, *Performative Politics and the Cultures of Hinduism*. The crux of the comparison between the case of Bangalore and that of Mumbai—a more demographically complex and densely settled city—is the part played by the Mumbai constituency that corresponds to the Vahnikulas as the sovereign god's champions before a broader public. The term is imprecise, but this is a collectivity that may be designated as *Marathas*.

From its inception as a public spectacle, Ganapati Puja has been a show of strength: a display of mass solidarity and spirit by one of the city's major constituent populations, a porous performance that invites allied groups to join in the stream even as it signals others to seal themselves off. The standard narrative credits the nationalist leader B. G. Tilak, a Maharashtrian Brahmin, with bringing Ganapati Puja out of domestic space and into the urban street in the 1890s. Tilak's project is understood as having been instrumentalist in purpose. The festival would mobilize Brahmins and Marathas together in a display of Hindu clout; to consecrate the metropolis to Ganesh was also to throw down a challenge to the British Raj (Raminder Kaur complicates this history in her chapter 2; see also Hansen 2001, 29–31; Masselos 1991, 50–52).[12] It could be said that Lord Ganesh brought Mumbai home to the streets of Bombay; in terms of the colonial segregation of space, the "native quarter" had flowed into the Raj town.

In the present day the Brahmin alliance is no longer an imperative, but the public negotiation and affirmation of Maratha identity are if anything more central to the city's political life. Thomas Blom Hansen (2001, 31–36, 41–49) gives an account of this name's shifting contours from the nineteenth century through to the present (see also Glushkova and Vora 1999). Several points may be noted here in shorthand, as it were. The first is that as a category of collective identity, *Maratha* lands somewhere between caste group and ethnolinguistic or regional group. People from Kunbi-caste families identify themselves as Maratha, as do many Kolis, Malis, and other Marathi-speaking Hindus; Brahmins do not.[13] Another important point is a certain swagger projected by the name, which resonates with a martial history; for readers of historical texts some of the affect may be conveyed in the old-fashioned spelling "Mahratta." There is the claim of indigeneity noted in the previous chapter: the Marathas are *bhoomiputra*, the "sons of the soil." Finally, let me reiterate another claim identified in chapter 1: that of the Shiv Sena Party to speak on behalf of all true Marathas, and to adjudicate just who that may be. The claim can be contested, but it has—for the past four decades—been impossible to ignore.

As an appropriation of public space in the image of a militant Maharashtrian Hinduism, Ganapati Puja plays on memories of the bloody winter of 1992–93, when over a thousand people died in sectarian violence, the vast majority of them Muslims. This episode's signal contribution to religious practice was the *maha aarati*s, or prayer rallies, that the Shiv Sena staged on streets in mixed areas as an all-too-successful incitement to riot. And the overlap between Shiv Sena *shakha*s, or neighborhood cells, and the *mandal*s, or local committees, that sponsor the Ganesh floats is a defining feature of the festival as it is celebrated these days. One newspaper article quoted party activists claiming that "over 95 percent of the mandals in Maharashtra, particularly in Mumbai and Pune, are sponsored by them" (Deshpande 2003).[14] In 2003 there was a well-remarked tendency for Ganesh *pandal*s to exhibit nationalistic tableaux featuring adversarial figures that had been colored Islamic green and labeled "terror" or "Pakistan"; the theme has, sad to say, remained topical across the years.[15]

So Ganapati Puja is politics—and politics on no small scale. What does it have in common with the guerrilla theater of the *zogua*s? In 2003 I followed the Ganapati processions with a group of Anglophone friends from the downtown crossroads of Kemp's Corner to Chowpatty Beach. The scene was carnivalesque. The euphoria and also the tension in the air—overwhelmingly masculine and charged with aggression—brought to mind a big sports event in an American city or university campus (and, of course, the festival is a homecoming of a sort).[16] Some eight years had passed since the city's renaming, and yet in that bourgeois downtown district it was as if the floodgates of the Raj town had been breached all over again; a good number of the young men thronging the avenues must have come from *mandal*s in the slums. Promenading to music blaring from truck-mounted speakers, many were visibly intoxicated, some dancing wildly in distinct citation—or possibly invocation—of a possession experience. "The *murti*s get bigger every year," my friends commented. Overall, the impression the revelers gave was of a subaltern constituency liberated by the ritual calendar to court as much attention as they could (aurally as well as visually) from middle-class residents habituated to ignoring or dismissing them.[17]

Here is the angle I want to highlight in connection with Stop 2 of my walking tour. To the extent that the Ganesh festival enables subalterns to reconfigure urban sites through summoning visual and affective registers normally elided at those sites, it presents an affinity with the yet more transient and *kaccha* exhibitions mounted by *zogua*s and their itinerant allies, such as transvestite *hijda*s (or "eunuchs"), Muslim *fakir*s, and Hindu cow-walkers. I suggest that by inviting individuals on the street to participate in a ritually mediated exchange, such marginal performers achieve recognition as fellow subjects within a shared landscape. And in so doing, within that ritually bounded window, for themselves and for those of their audience members who have become transactors within this exchange, they transform the landscape as well.[18] Although no Shiv Sena–like agency has ever shown interest in the likes of the *zogua*s, it should not be missed that in the context of citizen-subaltern relations the activities of such subalterns as these have political implications.

What is at stake at this level is not the question of who is Maratha and who isn't, or even who is Hindu and who isn't. Rather, the question posed by the performer or celebrant to the public on the street is *Do you see what I see?* Some of the ephemeral displays assigned to Stop 2, like the Ganesh floats themselves, are visual artifacts, "idols" equipped with the open eyes that court *darshan*. In other examples, such as Ganesh's dancers, the self-flagellating male half of the *zogua* team, or the *hijda*s who accost pedestrians and shopkeepers with handclaps and banter, the presenter's body in itself constitutes both divine vessel and image. (In this light, a rebuffed *hijda*'s last recourse of lifting up her skirt and flashing the inauspicious scar where the male organ used to be represents an interesting challenge: the threatened display of a normally abjected sight as a confrontational bid for the recognition that redeems the *hijda* herself from abjection.)[19] The animate-body-as-vehicle-for-divine-transactions idea is even put into action by people who can be called, for lack of a better term, cowwalkers. These are backcountry women who escort cows on the daily rounds of downtown blocks and roads, striking chords of sympathy in Hindu and Jain passersby and moving some of them to part with a few rupees for the chance to feed the beast a handful of grass. Their target clientele includes a prosperous element, and consequently not only foot traffic but also motor traffic in some South Mumbai neighborhoods is punctuated in the morning by the halts incurred by participants in this simple exchange.[20]

Finally, by way of rounding out this discussion of Stop 2, I should establish once again that the Mumbai streets present no bar to any enterprising Muslims keen to work them—none deriving from the Islamic proscription of graven images, at any rate. The typical agents of mobile address to urban Muslims are young men who travel as representatives of local Sufi saints' *dargah*s, displaying the veils that drape the tomb enshrined at the site. What is presented for scrutiny is thus neither the vessel that contains the technical object of devotion nor even a mimetic representation of that vessel but rather the material device of its obscuration. Central to this transaction too is the exchange of some kind of spiritual charge, glossed here as *barkat*, the "power" that emanates from the still-charismatic presence in the tomb. (It thus functions as an index not only of a valorized personality but also of a particular place, a point I will develop further on in this chapter.) The saint's emissaries tote a brazier that delivers scented smoke, *lobaan*—a medium of *barkat* that can be absorbed through the pores and lungs of whoever cares to make a small monetary contribution.[21]

Walking Tour, Part 2

The massive colonial-era façades of Girgaum, a South Mumbai neighborhood full of long-established offices and shops, provide this conceptual itinerary with its *Stop 3*. Near the Opera House intersection is a big apartment building where right by the entrance a three-dimensional *murti* of the baby Krishna has been mounted on the wall inside a vitrine. The sculpture's soft pastel tones and naturalistic posing are reminiscent of a pre-Independence generation of oleograph images of Hindu deities. The old-fashioned effect is reinforced by the *murti*'s glass showcase, an authoritative style of framing typical of sites associated with the colonial heritage such as museums and archives. Also worth mentioning in this context is the big Gandhi *khadi* emporium on D. N. Road, where the homespun cloth and peasant garb have been arranged in cases left by the former occupant of the space, a tropical gentlemen's outfitters. And even the exhibits of biscuits and snacks surrounding the cashier's station at any of the Irani "Restaurant and Stores" businesses run by Zoroastrian families over many generations can be seen to retain this colonial aesthetic of rationalized compartmentalization.[22]

If the concept of God-in-a-case seems peculiar, it will seem less so after a visit to a museum, in Mumbai or elsewhere, where Hindu *murti*s and other cultic objects are shown behind glass as artworks or cultural artifacts.[23] And if one of the things such authoritative framings are doing is to assimilate sacred images into official space, the effect of the Girgaum vitrine on a pedestrian spectator is rather the reverse: it punctures the official grid of the colonial city with a window into the sacred. I did not pursue inquiries at this address and thus did not establish who exactly bore the responsibility for Krishna's installation. Was it the host building's ownership or management, past or present? Or any of its tenants, legal or illegal? Any one of these would seem a likely possibility.

Another glass-fronted display once marked Girgaum's boundary at its most heavily trafficked point of entry: the pedestrian overpass that connects the neighborhood with the Western Railway's Charni Road station. In 2003 the crowds of commuters had been greeted daily by a great, metallic *murti* of Lord Ganesh framed in the window of a building overlooking the crossing. It was an eye-catching display, with an artful bit of staging behind it. The brass-colored Ganesh was as tall as a man (and, of course, considerably broader), and when viewed through the windowpane, it had a solid, three-dimensional appearance. A visit to the building that housed the image, however, showed that it was a bas-relief, both shallow and hollow, made of vac-form plastic.

Reactions among the crowd must have been mixed. Alongside those who registered a momentary transport there would have been others who read in the rotund form a generic cipher of beneficence, and moved on. And there would have been yet others, it is safe to say, who saw in the Tilak-approved emblem of Maharashtrian Hinduism no welcome. My tour of the premises made it plain that the image was intended strictly for public consumption; any would-be worshiper who actually entered the room would have been hard put to fit between Ganesh's surface and the glass. Far from having functioned as a temple or prayer room, the unit seems to have served a less elevated purpose. The caretaker told me that the tenants who installed the god had been members of a so-called "social club." The implication was that the space had been devoted to drinking and possibly gambling, in which case the image's function as a sort of mask of public piety would have come into play.

Stop 4 presents the first sites that actually fit within the category of *religious structure*, which will turn out to be a key term further on in this chapter. In 2003, two minutes' walk from my door would have brought me to a freestanding booth whose open side greeted the street with a figurine of an old man in a cross-legged pose. Its dimensions approximated those of a pillar-style mailbox. The booth was a typical example of the small shrines dedicated to Sai Baba of Shirdi that lined Nepeansea Road and other streets in my neighborhood—a well-to-do area not to be identified with any specific regional or caste community—at a density approaching one per block. It is a god kiosk, a Prayr-o-mat as it were, complete with coin slot for cash offerings. The structure was assembled and installed by a man who lived next to it behind a small, illegally constructed shop. An exposed wire stretching from the light fixture inside the *pandal*-like canopy back to the power outlet in the shop gave one clue that the shrine's upper component had actually been designed for indoor use. The effigy displayed within, somewhat lower than an average pedestrian's eye level, had been draped with a shiny cloth.

Structures of this kind are commonly known in Hindi as *mandir*, but in this case the standard English gloss of "temple" supplies a poor match because there is no priest in attendance and the structure is coterminous with the display—its environs are not formally contained or demarcated. This modest *mandir* is not so different from the *zoguas*' traveling shrine, the glassed-in exhibits, or even perhaps the row of wall-mounted tiles at Stop 1. Nevertheless, Stop 4 marks a formal departure from the categories that have preceded it, because as a fixed, three-dimensional installation, the shrine occupies not merely the flat surface of some other edifice but a parcel, however minuscule, of land. The little outpost operates both as a house of god—that is, a fixed address for the enshrined presence—and as a public place of worship, a station at which transactions with that presence are open to whoever cares to participate. And at both levels it serves its clients in the same way that a "proper" temple would.[24]

In fact, as the progress of this tour will indicate, the distinction between a proto-*mandir* like this example and a full-blown temple with an enclosure, an inner sanctum, and a priestly staff can be thought of as a transition that a thriving site makes on its trajectory from *kaccha* to *pakka*—given the right convergence of variables. I enumerate the following: (1) popularity, (2) capital investment, (3) sufficient room to expand, and (4) a blind or indulgent eye on the part of officialdom—which very likely implies other local power brokers. And as my exposition will go on to show, the authorities' forbearance can prove crucial, for the state has its own standards for adjudicating what is and what is not a proper temple, legal standards that rest on documentation within its archive. As with the slum housing described in the previous chapter, an "illegal religious structure" like the Sai Baba kiosk is illegal twice over. As an edifice, its construction has probably not been authorized. Nor, as a social entity, is it likely to have been registered as the occupant of an address under municipal jurisdiction—whether as a charitable trust, as would be the case with a legal temple, or alternatively as a private business or domicile.[25] Once again, in this connection it is vital to recall that the businesses and homes of over half of Mumbai's human population—the city's slum dwellers—are similarly deficient in documentation.

The self-service Sai Baba station at Stop 4 is exemplary of a category that contains the majority of religious displays that occupy public space in Mumbai. These installations conform to certain structural and typological standards. First, there has to be a foundation substantial enough to stake a claim to its site with credibility or, at any rate, unbudgeability. In this case, bricks have been built up around lengths of rebar driven into the pavement. The base supports a platform on which can be mounted an image or an object to function as the material focus of cultic attention: the Hindu term is *murti*. This sight is presented at an elevation that can court the gaze of a pedestrian public. Crowning all this is a superstructure to provide shelter and also to cite visually the spires or domes of architectural idioms associated with institutionally established houses of worship. Within these constraints there is as much room left for variation as the urban bricoleur's palette of scrap materials, found artifacts, and manufactured components will allow.

By way of illustrating this point I need look no farther than the other side of Nepeansea Road, where a counterpart to the brick-and-stone booth used to stand next to my bus stop. Fronting the entrance to a middle-class residential colony, it was a columnar stack of concrete slabs of varying heights and diameters that had been topped with a *shikha*, or metal pinnacle (fig. 3). An arch-shaped backdrop of painted plywood stated the structure's function: Sai Baba Mandir. Also named was its sponsoring body: the Sai Mitra Mandal, or Sai Friendship Association, an organization whose membership consisted, oddly enough, mainly of residents of a different apartment building up the block. Among this *mandir*'s accoutrements was a bell for worshipers to strike while performing their devotions, a feature shared by many of the other shrines to be found throughout the neighborhood.

Two other typical elements should be mentioned. The first is association with trees. Where the municipality planted shade trees along the street, as on Hughes Road nearby, the neighborhood's religious entrepreneurs installed their shrines beneath them. The practice can be seen as an urban expression of the widespread Hindu veneration of trees that is manifested through more developed attentions in village or forest settings (see Haberman 2013; Kent 2013; Sen Gupta 1965). There was also a practical or tactical reason for this placement, since the cement bases that often girdle the trunks of municipal trees furnish convenient platforms on which to build.[26] In other words, not only has the Municipal Corporation itself seen fit to erect an auspicious object on the public walkway—the tree—but this ready-made spirit-vessel comes equipped with its own government-issue concrete foundation. To local shrine builders this must have seemed, if not an outright invitation, at least an indication of tacit sanction of a do-it-yourself approach to the disposal of public space.

The second point to mark in connection with Stop 4 is the ubiquity of Sai Baba of Shirdi, whose likeness so dominated the *mandir*s in my old neighborhood as to have rendered any local contenders wholly superfluous. That mass-produced Sai Baba artifacts should have saturated those blocks and demographically similar parts of the city seems particularly incongruous in light of the saint's historical association with a specific location in the hinterland of Maharashtra. This is the dusty village of Shirdi, where economic activity is virtually coterminous with the pilgrimage center administered by the Shri Saibaba Sansthan Trust. Yet despite the Baba figure's manifest popularity in the metropolis, the trust's presence in Mumbai is confined to an office building in Dadar, where an upstairs prayer room does duty as the only officially run Sai Baba *mandir* in the city. In the next chapter I will offer Sai Baba some of the attention that is his due as a powerful factor in the production of sacred space in the city; among other points, I will probe the implications of his status as the resident deity of the Nepeansea Road area for its definition as a particular kind of neighborhood.

The tour concludes at *Stop 5*, which can best be represented, for my purposes, by a site I encountered well north of the area that had served as my base of operations, beyond the shabby-genteel arcades and avenues of South Mumbai, in the suburb of Juhu. The structure in question, located just behind the Sea Princess Hotel on Juhu Beach, looked at first glance like a *kaccha* eating shop of the kind that provides cheap refreshment on the street. The layout followed a standard arrangement, with a row of partitioned stalls open for business behind a paved strip facing the zone of traffic, in this case the beachfront. An awning of blue plastic sheeting stretched over the top added to the generally makeshift look of the whole complex. A man relaxing out front who might have been a fry cook discovered between shifts turned out to be, on closer inspection, the saffron-draped *pujari* of a temple whose name ran above the stalls in big Hindi letters: Shiv Sai Seva Mandir.

Beneath the main signboard, a smaller legend in English read "Welcome." "Is this your temple?" I asked, to be met with the somewhat chary reply, "It is the Lord's." When I pressed on with, "But you must have built it?" my interlocutor, whom I will call Om Prakash, told me: "It grew here bit by bit, just like that." More elaborate than previous examples, the Shiv Sai Seva Mandir boasts not only an on-site priest but also a loudspeaker system. It aims to offer a one-stop *darshan* experience to a diverse clientele. As the name indicates, the site is dedicated both to Shiva and to Sai Baba, and effigies of the two divine personalities are displayed in separate "chapels." A glossy blue Shiva has been adorned with his Ganga in the form of a stream of water that squirts out of his coif from a connection to a tank overhead. The Baba himself dominates a stall set aside for the protean Maharashtrian god Dattatreya and his avatars. (Shirdi's saint shares this status with several other historical charismatics; I will have more to say about Datta in chapter 4.)

But the site owns to other loyalties as well, which are telling. The priest's own native place of Junagadh, in Gujarat, stands at the foot of Mount Girnar and is renowned as a pilgrimage center. A shrine assigned to the goddess identified with Girnar, Amba Mata, has been decked with images of Om Prakash's hometown guru. Goddess worship is further represented by *murti*s of Durga and Kali, and the popular and pan-Indian Ganesh and Hanuman each enjoy their own displays. Also represented is Julelal, the Sindhi god of the sea, who functions alongside the Gujarati Amba and the Maharashtrian Dattatreya as a metonym of yet another prominent constituency among the Hindus of Mumbai. Finally, a central space has been reserved for an impressive-looking Christian cross. Inscribed with INRI in metallic letters and garlanded with jasmine, it is flanked on one side by Kali and on the other by a small figure of Nanak, the first Sikh guru. It was in fact the cross, the priest related, that constituted the original seed from which an entire *mandir* just sorta growed. In a claim paralleling the origin stories of many well-established Indian cultic centers, including both the Mahalaxmi Temple and Mount Mary, the premier Hindu and Catholic places of worship in coastal Mumbai, a cruciform object that may or may not have been substantially identical with the one enshrined was said to have washed up on the beach at that very place. It was at once a gift from the sea and a sign of God's blessing.

The question of which particular god is to be recognized as the face of divine agency in this case is clearly beside the point; if the Shiv Sai Seva Mandir combined a diversity of icons signifying specific regional and sectarian affiliations, what Om Prakash stressed in our conversation was the commonality of the divine essences thus stationed. "The sea is [a] god," he told me, motioning at the surf, the Hindi language's lack of articles keeping it unclear whether he was simply adding another attraction to the featured cast or making a statement about the diffusion of a unitary spirit. He then made an equivalence that, oddly enough, can be easily expressed as a pun in English, although not in the Hindi we were using. "It sends waves up to wave at us," he said, citing as evidence of the sea's divine nature precisely the sort of gesture of recognition I want to identify as central to the operation of the sites I describe in this chapter.

Whether his point is to be interpreted as attributing an immanent spirit-presence to many, most, or all places, the temple's very purpose is of course founded on the proposition that access is more easily attained at some spots than others. And in a nationalist amplification of this logic, Om Prakash went on to explain that the land of India as a whole was blessed territory. Nevertheless, he assured me that the *mandir*'s clientele was not limited to Hindus; people of all religions came to worship there. Indeed, the site's cross-sectarian embrace—as stated in principle, at any rate—was asserted in the famous words of Sai Baba that had been posted over his shrine: "Sab ka malik ek" (the Lord of All is One).

The *pujari* offered free drinking water to everyone who stopped by—"And what's a temple if not a place to quench your thirst?" He was also hospitable with his information. It was a rich Hindu resident of the neighborhood who had established the *mandir* at the spot initially marked by the cross; Om Prakash was merely a Brahmin employee of this local person of means. But far from appearing on his private property, the site so fortuitously chosen occupied public land, and it appeared that the *mandir* had been allowed to expand to its proportions owing largely to its germination on a plot belonging to the port authority—a body whose attitude toward such growths was evidently more lenient than the municipal government's.

By way of comparison, similarly elaborate arrangements at downtown sites tend to attain their level of growth through the indulgence or passivity of private landlords. Thus, some of the best-established street-front temples in crowded South Mumbai have expanded, not forward across the pavement, but backward into a host building. Among the priestly entrepreneurs whose operations fit within this category are tenants, such as two middle-class families of Forjett Street in Tardeo who have converted their adjacent ground-floor apartments into complementary Sai Baba *mandir*s. The site, Sai Krupa, has become a local institution. On Thursday, Sai Baba's special day, when devotees spill across the building's courtyard and along the street, the traffic is dense enough to support a small army of flower vendors in business at the threshold. Although the crowd is a diverse one, the major proportion is made up of well-dressed, prosperous-looking people.

The arrangements on either side of the building's entrance are similar, with each neighbor's foyer opening on a *puja* room dominated by a life-size, naturalistic sculpture of the saint, and the congregants' observances proceed along parallel tracks. At both stations, the exchange of glances enacted through *darshan* with the Baba is typically accompanied by a moment of communion through silent prayer and a complementary, material transaction: worshipers deposit offerings of cash or flowers and realize blessings conducted through food (*prasad*) or sacred ash (*vibhuti*). It is the contrasting visual idioms that dominate the two rooms—the one baroque, decked with gilt and ornament; the other clean and spare, defined by stone surfaces and green accents—that provide the most striking indications that one shrine belongs to a Hindu household and the other to a Muslim one.

Another tendency to note among establishments that colonize residential buildings in this way is that in some cases the people who operate them are the caretakers, or "supers," of the host structure. At two sites attached to upscale addresses, the entrepreneur in question had gotten his foot in the door as a maintenance or security worker—a fellow occupant nevertheless marked apart from his neighbors as a resident subaltern. The goddess shrine that flanks a posh Malabar Hill apartment house as a sort of annex had been built up over the years and looked after by a non-Brahmin man who is the son of the building's chief caretaker. Dedicated to Santoshi Maa, the deity whose cult was propagated at an all-India level through the success of a 1975 movie,[27] the installation is distinguished by an electric-lighting scheme that runs off power bootlegged from its host. My contact among the tenants, an English-language journalist, professed no particular regard for the display but nevertheless admired how the well-tended enterprise had earned its sponsor respect from other people in the neighborhood.

By contrast, the tone in which a young lawyer described the *mandir* that had taken over the ground floor of her Gamdevi residence was contemptuous, if not downright derisive. Framed in spangles and garlands, the entrance of her building is kept open all day to the street. It is possible when passing down Gamdevi Road, on foot or even by car, to peer through and be greeted by a view of the *murti* of Amba Mata ensconced within. In its essentials, the lawyer's story of how an illicit shrine expanded, shifting its position from an exterior wall to an interior one and eventually to occupancy of most of the floor space, conforms to a familiar script: *kaccha* to *pakka*. But her account was enlivened by some sensational details. The temple's founder, known by the informal title of Kaka, or "uncle," opened for business in 1971 with a modest booth-like structure. A Gujarati from a non-Brahmin background, he chose to honor an aspect of the goddess identified with his native place of Palanpur, and the norms of worship observed in the earlier days apparently indexed a regionally specific, nonmetropolitan cult, with mediums in attendance who would educe the goddess's presence through possession behavior (by contrast, Santoshi Maa, the cinematically mediated goddess of the Malabar Hill site, is a modern and translocal deity). Aided by its strategic location on a commuter route traversed by business people in cars, the site has attracted a dedicated following whose key constituency is well-to-do Gujaratis from merchant-caste families.

Much of the site's success can be attributed to these patrons' generosity. My informant described the piles of jewelry and silk saris rich women were known for leaving as offerings, naming among the site's regulars one of the matrons of the Reliance industrial empire. But she also identified a secondary, clandestine level at which the goddess mediated the circulation of the bodies of an urban public, along with its capital. For some years, the self-styled *pujari* had been using the temple as a front for a prostitution ring. Buttressed by an exposé piece printed in the now-defunct gossip tabloid *Blitz* (*Blitz* Team of Investigators 1982), her allegations made a persuasive case for Kaka's business model. The open doors of a temple could welcome a diversity of visitors—including well-turned-out young women—around the clock and for indefinite periods of time without presenting the appearance of anything irregular. Moreover, the venue of Kaka's choice boasted a respectable address on a well-trafficked road; the procurer could command access to at least two of the building's ground-floor flats; and the façade of piety served to inhibit, if not deflect altogether, any attention from the authorities or other busybodies.[28]

With the passing of the site's management to Kaka's son, Baba, my friend charted a shift in the prevailing visual and symbolic idiom. What had begun as an outpost or satellite of Ambaji of Palanpur, defined by rustic Gujarati antecedents, had received a glitzy makeover that cited film industry–derived codes designating modernity and upward mobility. And it appeared that during Baba's tenure, hookups had ceased to number among the transactions negotiated downstairs from my informant's apartment. Overseeing Amba Mata's ritual business had perhaps turned out to be adequately remunerative in its own right. In due course, like his counterpart in Malabar Hill, the Baba of Gamdevi Road seemed to have succeeded in transcending the laws of both civic and caste authorities to settle into respectability as a neighborhood priest (although his marriage to a Christian woman supplied a further note of unconventionality). The last troubling episode I was told about in connection with this site concerned Baba's collaboration in a Shiv Sena plan to stage a *maha aarati* there in 1992; in the end the block was spared the inflammatory spectacle.

Operations in Visual Culture: Attraction and Repulsion

What do all these sites have in common? None of them has been officially sanctioned by any institutional source of authority, whether the state, the Sai Baba trust that runs the pilgrimage center at Shirdi, or any body of orthodox Brahmins. And while all but the most *kaccha* sites would colloquially be referred to as *mandir*s, taken together they do complicate on several counts the conventional understanding of what a *temple* is, at least among exponents of respectable middle-class Hinduism (and perhaps among scholars who hew closely to the scripturalist model of religion). There is the absence, at all but the last stop, of specialists, Brahmin or otherwise, to provide ritual mediation between the deity and its audience. There is the feature of eclecticism, which is a well-remarked characteristic of Hinduism, but freedom from any institutional monitor of doctrinal orthodoxy has enabled these sorts of sites to experiment with such bold combinations as the Shiv Sai Seva Mandir's local and translocal deities and saints arranged around a Christian cross. And I would argue that it is inadequate to attribute these magpie assemblages to the assimilative tendency of popular Hinduism. My brief tour has taken in only two Muslim examples, but streets in different parts of the city can offer a full range of *kaccha* and *pakka* Muslim, Christian, and Buddhist sites.

There is the question of design: my lawyer acquaintance who had to share her Gamdevi building with Amba Mata denounced Baba's establishment as "not a real temple" because it did not conform to the Brahminical dicta governing the proportions of sacred structures as laid down in the *vastu shastra*s. But it is highly doubtful whether any of the bricoleur architects whose constructions crowd the streets look to Sanskrit scriptures for their blueprints. (As I will argue in the pages to follow, a more promising source of insight into their physical arrangement can be found in norms governing the disposition of space in villages in Maharashtra and further afield.) Finally, there is the elision of one of the organizing principles of modern rationalized space: the demarcation between public and private. At what point does a domestic prayer room become a public temple?

What I do identify as the common denominator among my examples is their mobilization of religious imagery to mark urban public space. Whether housed in open-faced shelters, toted on a girl's head, showcased behind glass, or simply mounted on the wall, the sacred figures displayed at these sites take advantage of sight lines organized by the built environment to address not only the cult community associated with their construction but also a transient audience within the dense and constant foot traffic on the Mumbai streets. They appeal, in other words, to diverse publics. I have already drawn the connection with the advertising graphics that similarly saturate Mumbai, and I think there is real promise in theorizing visual representations of Hindu deities along the lines of corporate branding that at once targets and constructs diverse constituencies of consumers.[29]

But there is a bigger point here. If the walking tour has ended, this chapter's argument has just gotten under way. The analytic move I propose is to theorize these shrines and related displays as a problem of visual culture. It seems appropriate to launch this exploration of visual effects by recalling some conversations with the scholar Vidya Kamat, who is also a visual artist.

I was introduced to Vidya at an urban studies workshop in 2003, at a moment when we were both developing research interests in the city's illegal religious structures. Our discussions left me with two questions I chewed over for years as my own argument found its *pakka* form. In pursuing inquiries on Dalal Street, where Mumbai's stock exchange is located, Vidya had become intrigued by the discrepancy between attendance at one Sai Baba *mandir* that enjoyed a reputation among the brokers as a wish-granting site and its less favored neighbors on adjacent blocks. If they are all dedicated to the same divine personality, she asked, why should one particular shrine project more cultic power than its neighbors?

She also made an observation about the formal characteristics of the various displays enshrined on the streets. There seemed to be a correlation between the class status of the worshiper and the mimetic precision that defined the image worshiped, whether the style in question was a kind of anthropomorphic naturalism, as in the case of most metropolitan Hindu deities; mimetic referentiality to an original *murti* seated elsewhere, as in the case of the black Krishna metonymic of the pilgrimage center of Nathdwara; or both, as in the case of Sai Baba of Shirdi. The better off the client, the slicker the aesthetic. Why should that be so?

Reviewing these questions from the other end of my research, it now seems to me that the first question concerns a contest between two sources of power that the Dalal Street shrine cites at the same time: on the one hand, the Sai Baba personality and, on the other, the particular space the shrine occupies. In the next chapter, I will analyze this sort of contest in terms of rival modes of signification: Peirce's categories of the icon and the index. The second question proposes a relation between an image's formal attributes and the social positionality of its public. My answer here has to do with a process I have conceptualized under the Hindi-English neologism of *pakka*-fication. Building on the *kaccha-pakka* dynamic introduced in this chapter, in chapter 4 I will probe what is at stake in the cultic object's attainment of formal cohesion within a valorized visual idiom.

Now, to get my argument to the point where it can engage problems like these, let me address the premise underlying Vidya's two questions. Inasmuch as these are questions of visual culture, I locate both at the nexus of Site, Sight, and Cite. They open the sacred image's operations to inquiry along three vectors: the relation of the sight to the point it marks in space; the sitedness in society of the public to which it appeals; and the fields of discourse, affect, and bodily habitus it cites as a sign or material extension. And animating all three lines of inquiry—to return to fundamentals—is a common point of concern: efficacy. Which of these factors, in combination, will enable the *mandir* to do its work? Is an efficacious temple the same thing as a real temple? How does a sacred image—or indeed any kind of ideological spectacle—succeed in its bid for the desiring gaze? I propose that answers about the image's power of address may best be sought through a rethinking of the Hindu ritual of *darshan*.

So let's begin by asking what *darshan*, which I have glossed throughout the preceding pages as "visual worship," really is. When people speak in Hindi of "doing" or "taking" *darshan* (*darshan karna, darshan lena*), this serves as a shorthand way to denote the whole sequence of interactions prescribed for a human subject who comes before a sacred image. Note that visual recognition of the deity stands alone as a fulfilling act even if other exchanges mediated through light, music, scent, and material offerings such as food are not performed. Again, vision's primacy as a channel of contact over communication through language, whether voiced or thought, is the norm observed in contemporary practice. (And let it be added here, parenthetically, that vision is also the paradigm of perception in classical Hindu epistemology.) To have engaged in *darshan*, in short, is indeed for the encounter between human and god to have "worked."

At once synecdochic and encompassing, *darshan* emerges as definitive of the experience of divine presence in Hinduism, central to the history of Indian visual culture, and undertheorized by scholars of both. John Cort (2012) gives an overview of the scholarly conversation, noting the continued centrality of Diana Eck's (1981) short monograph *Darśan*, with its emphasis on Brahminical norms and a rather totalizing concept of a Hindu "polytheistic imagination," and following up with a call for theoretical reformulations. He notes advances made from several disciplinary perspectives—calling out, along the way, the puzzling lack of engagement by art historians. Cort's own approach has been to turn to primary texts of a didactic character, a project in which he is joined by other scholars of South Asian religions: Richard Davis (1997, 26–50), with readings of Shaivite and Vaishnavite theological works from medieval South India, and Andy Rotman (2009), with ancient Buddhist didactic texts. Cort's contribution centers on medieval and modern Jain hymns. The route I have chosen follows two other approaches: an anthropological track, running from Lawrence Babb's (1981) ideas about transactional relations and Alfred Gell's (1998) theory of distributed personhood through to the corpothetics of Christopher Pinney (2002; see also Bhatti and Pinney 2011); and a parallel track that runs through media studies, especially film studies, with key texts here being Kapur 1987 and Vasudevan 2011.

One thing is clear. The contemporary Indian scene, distinguished as it is by migration to larger, more cosmopolitan cities and by the ascendancy of mass media, demands a reappraisal of *darshan* outside the "traditional" temple environment. Exploration of the contemporary urban context—along the lines undertaken in this chapter—challenges the temple scenario on multiple fronts. Let's review three points.

First, *deterritorialization*. The conception of a local deity as a presence organically connected with a particular place over which it exerts sovereignty seems straightforward enough in the rural context. Exemplary here are cases like that of the village goddess (*gaondevi*) that personifies a tribal settlement or even that of a Sufi's tomb (*dargah*), whose claim to space is anchored in the historical narrative of the saint's life. But the movement of deities, along with their worshipers, to the city and their reemplacement alongside their constituents' new homes highlight the processual character of the connection between divine power and material space and the human agency involved in maintaining it. The deterritorialization effect is particularly acute in slum neighborhoods, where the contingent and vulnerable character of housing for humans extends to the structures housing their gods (compare Dianteill 2002; Headley 2004).

Second, *reproducibility*. Modern Hindus and other Indians whose devotional practice centers on *darshan* relations with a materially seated source of divine power have been enthusiastic about adopting technologies of mass reproduction. But the attribution of authentic power to the cultic image or object is complicated in a milieu where a multitude of copies circulate (see Cohen 2017a, 2017b; Lambek 2003; Mallapragada 2010; Port 2011). The relevance of the ritual authorization of the *murti*—paradigmatically by a Brahmin priest—that would, in textbook Hinduism, be the determining factor recedes in an urban environment characterized by a multiplicity of sacred-looking images, on the one hand, and a diverse and transient client community, on the other.

Third, this brings us to *the public*. Both the spatial and the social relations presumed in the temple-centered model of *darshan* are recast in the urban scenario of the street-facing prayer booth, at which communications and transactions with the personality enshrined within are open to whoever is moved to recognize it there. Such shrines may serve their client constituencies in much the same way as a "proper," institutional temple with a priestly staff and a threshold to set off a sacred interior from a profane exterior. But their lack of state or Brahminical authorization, combined with the diverse and transient composition of the foot traffic to which they appeal, opens the question of each site's power or efficacy to adjudication by the public eye.

In sum, I contend that *darshan* attraction does indeed exert its effects in public space. What is more, I further contend that the ease with which modern technologies inscribe, reproduce, and circulate typologically correct visual material has elevated mass-mediated *darshan* to hegemonic status as a mode of worship within metropolitan Hinduism and perhaps has even encouraged a corresponding *darshan*-ization within other Indian religious communities as well. In the next chapter I will engage more closely with some of the anthropological propositions noted above. And I will move to theorize *darshan* specifically in terms of a relation of recognition in a sustained analysis of the most popular of Mumbai's divine squatters, the already much-cited Hindu-Muslim crossover figure Sai Baba of Shirdi.

To be sure, one of the things I learned in the course of fieldwork is that focusing on what happens when a privileged connection is made by a viewing subject with a visual artifact is a limiting approach. Moreover, for all its promise of theoretical elegance, the methodological task it set for my ethnography proved confounding. More readily observed and, as I have realized, of no less importance as an aspect of their operation are the conditions under which these images fail to exert an attraction.

I suggest that such negative visual effects fall into two categories: effects of abjection and effects of repulsion, or of warding off. Abjection, the opposite of subjection, involves selective blindness on the part of bourgeois subjects of the sort that relegates poor or "backward" people such as slum dwellers to a default position of invisibility. A US–based scenario I can invoke by way of comparison is the occluded presence of immigrant busboys in restaurants; and indeed, there's a complementary observation to be developed here in connection with the undocumented status of such subalterns and their invisibility in the eyes of the American state. The degree to which many of my interlocutors from Mumbai's more privileged classes shun subaltern eyesores like Sai Baba shrines as legible features of their environment is pervasive enough to point to as symptomatic of a broader subjective disposition. Of the examples I have described, perhaps the most abjected in this sense would be the rustic performers who strive through their flamboyant appearance and insistent noise to gain the attention of people who are resolutely opposed to recognizing them.[30]

The second kind of negative effect I propose is that of warding off. What I refer to here is the property that religious images and, by extension, the structures that house them have of protecting the space they occupy against persons who might approach them with impious intent. The clearest example I can offer is the Mumbai institution of the tiled or painted wall, as introduced by this chapter's epigraph from *Such a Long Journey*. The eclectic and unequivocally instrumentalist use of divine imagery states: "Sacred Space—Do Not Disturb." But the converse of this pragmatic ecumenicalism can also be seen at work in a related but less innocuous practice. This is the installation of images metonymic of specific religious identities at the boundaries of neighborhoods to stake out turf. If, for the bourgeois citizens attuned to ignoring them, the *mandir*s threaten to rupture the cherished illusion of the city as the locus of a seamless modernity, subaltern residents may well see in the Ganesh on the overpass or the cross at the street corner a warning sign: "Sacred Space—Proceed at Own Risk." These are two sides of the rebuke posed by the *mandir*s to the professed secularism of the Indian state that provides the municipality with a casus belli against them.

This function of partitioning public space among enclaves reserved for distinct communities calls to mind three contexts. The first, which I have already raised in connection with the annual Ganesh festival, is that of the *maha aarati*s, or mass street-based prayer ceremonies, that were mobilized to such bloody effect by the Shiv Sena in the violent winter of 1992–93. Happily, no doubt, I have no original ethnographic research of my own to offer on this point, and accordingly I am relegating it to third-tier status. Readers interested in pursuing the connection are directed to the work of documentation and analysis undertaken by Thomas Blom Hansen (2001), Gérard Heuzé (1995), and Kalpana Sharma (1995), as well as to the material on the *maha aarati* tactic contained in the official government inquiry on the riots ("Damning Verdict: Report of the Srikrishna Commission," n.d.). Here I will content myself with noting that several of my Anglophone interlocutors drew a correlation between the burgeoning presence of *mandir*s on the streets in the past decades and the rise to prominence of Hindu nationalism, in its various faces (Hindutva ideology takes institutional shape as the Sangh Parivar, the "family of organizations," comprising labor, professional, and cultural associations, political parties, and religious groups, among others). In the next chapter I will turn my own analysis to two roughly contemporaneous trends that can be related to the Hindutva ascendancy: the dissemination of religious imagery through modern mass media and the explosive growth of the city's slums.[31]

The second context that requires some attention is that of the boundary gods, or "sentinel deities," in Valentine Daniel's (1984) terminology, that guard the approaches to villages in much of rural India. As I advance in this book to report some aspects of the fieldwork I conducted among the Warlis whose *pada*s, or tribal settlements, have been engulfed within urban neighborhoods, this is the inquiry that will direct the course of my argument. The third point to mark is the ubiquity of Sai Baba, who, by way of contrast, often seems to be deployed within this context of contested turf as a sort of ecumenical placeholder, a nonsectarian symbol aimed at evading these divisive effects as a marker of generically religious space. Chapter 3 will examine Sai Baba of Shirdi in some detail.

It is in their capacity as warders-off of attentions of an unwelcome sort from their vicinity that the *mandir*s also feature as outposts of a seamy subaltern underground in a whole fund of middle-class lore about Mumbai neighborhoods. What bourgeois citizens and, tellingly, the sponsors of rival temples have to say about what really transpires at that *mandir* down the street may go beyond the mere collection of funds to involve its use as a cover for gambling, as with the example of the Charni Road Ganesh, or for prostitution, as in the case of the Amba temple in Gamdevi. The idea in both cases is that streetside worship provides cover for the anonymous mingling of clients and the purveyors of illicit goods and services. Another allegation, disseminated through Bollywood films such as Ram Gopal Varma's *Company* (2002) and echoing a classic trope of India-based adventure narratives running from Hollywood through *The Moonstone* back to the exploits of Mahmud of Ghazni (see Davis 1997), is that the structures or the *murti*s themselves are repositories of gangster loot: drug drops, caches of smuggled goods, hoards of ill-gotten cash sequestered from the arm of the law.

None of this is to reduce the shrines' lack of documentation to the level of a minor infraction, a technical transgression that somehow stands in for graver but less actionable offenses. Correct and legible paperwork is the very ticket of admission, as it were, into the realm of rationalized space. And yet public prayer booths do not merely subvert the official gaze by evading it. They are conspicuous by design; they are the visual interface of an alternative ideological dispensation. In the eyes of administrators, planners, and middle-class civil society, the ideological stare-down perhaps seems most acute when it comes to the way these installations stake out turf in the name of distinct religious communities—and downright egregious when the space so contested is the public thoroughfare, understood in liberal discourse as a conduit for the free transit of all. And viewed in this light, the frequency with which the shrines are condemned for their obstruction of traffic seems revealing of a more general disquiet about the civic and national narrative of progress. To the degree that the *mandir*s are seen as obstacles to society's forward march to modernity, they are manifestations of the endemic backwardness of the city's subaltern populations.

Yet the contest does not fall straightforwardly along the lines of a dichotomy between the liberal bourgeoisie and the subaltern masses. Owing to norms of piety that tend to prevail across social strata, and to the very party-line "secularism" that stresses ecumenical respect for the diversity of religious practice in India, in practice the authorities find it difficult to act to remove the structures. This is one reason for their seeming ubiquity in slum settlements, where they tend to get built in proximity to other, less valorized kinds of makeshift structures that house families or businesses, or on top of jury-rigged connections to municipal pipes or cables. Again, the sponsorship of shrines by neighborhood power brokers—for example, Shiv Sena cell leaders—who can claim allies in high places means that patronage of specific sites may, in practice, reach to the higher tiers of officialdom. This is to say that, in effect, the guardian deities actually are extending protection over their communities in very concrete, material ways.

The Crisis: Municipal Demolitions, Fall 2003

But on occasion the authorities do knock the temples down. It was in the fall of 2003 that, bowing to the decision of the Bombay High Court in the civil suit filed on 31 July of the previous year by the public-interest NGO Janhit Manch, the Brihanmumbai Municipal Corporation initiated citywide demolitions of what were defined in the suit, and subsequently described in the press, as "illegal religious structures." The demolition campaign came to my neighborhood early on the morning of 6 November. From Nepeansea Road, where I lived, past Kemp's Corner, along Hughes Road, and up to my favorite lunch spot at Chowpatty Beach, the little booths that had lined the streets, attracting the eye with their colors and textures and stimulating a variety of responses in passersby—piety in many, curiosity in me—had been reduced to heaps of rubble.

It is only to be expected that in Mumbai, where a severely congested built environment is overlaid with an intricate set of official and unofficial rules governing the recognition of tenancy, such a conflict would betray—on both sides—deep anxieties about who belongs in the city, who doesn't, and where their proper places are. In addition to appealing to the principles of secularism and the rule of law, the president of Janhit Manch, Bhagvanji Raiani, noted in his petition: "In Mumbai lakhs of people live on the pavements with the blessings of the corporators and the municipal officers at the great hardship and risk to the pedestrians and the vehicular traffic. Hundreds of gods & goddesses have also enrolled as footpath dwellers alongwith the human Occuptans [*sic*] aggravating the chaotic traffic the Mumbaikars are facing in their daily lives."[32]

Again, the concern to reserve the streets for traffic flow is a standard trope in bourgeois discourse that safeguards the city's integrity, at an epistemic level, against the encroachments of chaotic and backward subaltern elements. Curiously, however—and his sarcasm notwithstanding—in his identification of gods and goddesses with human migrants to the city, Raiani may have inadvertently reflected the perspective of his opponents.[33]

The petition took names and counted numbers. No fewer than 758 of the illegal religious structures identified on Municipal Corporation land were listed as Hindu, with 44 Christian, 20 Muslim, and 5 Buddhist entries making up the balance. Reporting these figures, the *Times of India* observed that the actual number of unlicensed structures was bound to be far higher than the total given: "The BMC [Brihanmumbai Municipal Corporation] submitted a list of 857 illegal shrines to the high court and it was later updated to 1,430. But a deputy municipal commissioner admitted on condition of anonymity that 'there are no less than 10,000 illegal shrines in the city'" (Wallia 2003). There can be little doubt that of the structures classified as Hindu, a majority were dedicated to Sai Baba of Shirdi. The tabloid *Mid Day* presented the saint's popularity as a "conundrum" for the authorities: "Interestingly, many of the illegal structures on the corporation's list are Sai Baba shrines. While demolition of any shrine invites public opposition, a Sai Baba shrine is especially difficult to touch because people from all communities can be mobilised in its support. Shirdi's spiritual master is not identified with any particular religion" (Krishnakumar 2003). As events subsequently proved, the reporter had gotten things exactly backward: Sai Baba's generic quality had left him—unlike, say, Hanuman or Mary—without a specific constituency to organize politically against his eviction from the streets. (By contrast, the Catholic Church and Muslim groups were swift to protest, followed belatedly by the Shiv Sena, which enacted a characteristic flip-flop from an initial posture in favor of cleaning up the streets to championship of the "Hindu community.") But by the same token, it had been the Baba's neutrality as a metonym of no particular religious community that had enabled his shrines to be erected in a prosperous and diversely populated neighborhood like mine in the first place. Of the illegal religious structures along the route I frequented, every single one had been a Sai Baba shrine, and every one encountered a municipal bulldozer.

As a result of Raiani's persistence, my lunchtime pilgrimage trail had been erased from the city after the manner of a slum clearance. Another skirmish had been fought in the endless battle to make the lived streets look the way they do in development plans. By the very next morning, however—7 November—each pile of broken bricks had been rededicated. Where the smaller of the two Nepeansea Road examples described at Stop 4 was concerned, the thoroughgoing demolition had left the owner with the prospect of rebuilding virtually from the ground up, but either he or a well-wisher had already garlanded an adjacent electrical switch box as an assertion of the deity's enduring claim on the site. The process of reclamation was more advanced in the case of its neighbor across the street, the Sai Mitra Mandal's shrine, where the plywood backdrop had been salvaged and the *murti* replaced inside one of the prefabricated cases sold for domestic prayer rooms (fig. 4). I discussed the demolition and the Mitra Mandal's efforts to have the structure rebuilt with my dry cleaner. As a small businessman on the block, he had been approached for contributions. Through him I ended up donating a few hundred rupees.

I have proposed that the clash between the authorities and the sponsors of such illegal religious structures can be understood as the overlap of two geographies or spatial ideologies, with the state and its instigators in civil society cast in the role of postcolonial rationalizers of space—disenchanters, to tweak a term from Max Weber. In rounding off this chapter, the theoretical move I will introduce in advancement of this case will rest on some basic principles borrowed from the semiotics of Charles S. Peirce. At this point in the discussion, I think a distinction can be made, to productive effect, between the logics of signification favored by the elite and subaltern classes in their use of visual media to mark and organize space.

As I have noted above, shrines, like the dwellings of human persons, fall into legal jeopardy when they lack either of two forms of registration: certification of the structure itself as a material object; and a record of its claim to the space it occupies in the name of a social entity—a family, a company, or (typically in the case of a temple) a charitable trust. In other words, to be accorded its place in the official spatial order, a recognizable component of the urban landscape must be tagged with at least two pieces of paper. The ascendancy this official archive achieves in terms of power effects over the material object or person it represents has become a favorite theme of postcolonial theory following Michel Foucault's (1991) critique of governmentality. A Peircean spin on the problem identifies the relation of signification thus privileged as functioning in the *symbolic* mode: that is to say, the relation between the sign and its object is strictly conventional. And while for Peirce all words are related to the things they signify on a symbolic basis, when viewed in its social context the dynamic of abstraction at work in this example appears particularly acute.

In the gaze of the bureaucrats charged with the production and maintenance of rationalized urban space, a site attains recognition as a place of residence, business, or worship not through its concrete manifestation in material space but rather in the form of writing on paper—especially English text in Roman letters. What is more, the flip side of the attention such text commands among the citizen class (recall "Commit No Nuisance") is the illegibility with which it confronts many subalterns, among whom literacy is typically confined to vernacular languages. I will have more to say about the enunciative effects of government paperwork in chapter 6, when I turn to a consideration of the efforts of tribal activists to gain legal recognition for their constituents as the indigenous inhabitants of parts of Mumbai. For the present purpose, it should suffice to invoke comparison with more classically colonial scenarios in which the authorities' heed of paper-borne graphics cues a reciprocal gesture. A celebrated example involving *adivasi*s from the eastern part of India comes from the Santal Rebellion of 1855. Its leaders Sido and Kanhu Subah stated to their British captors that they had been called to arms by written despatches of divine origin, an episode analyzed by Ranajit Guha (1983, 54–55, 248–49) and Dipesh Chakrabarty (2000, 102–6).

By contrast with the symbolic, Peirce's idea of *indexical* signification establishes meaning on the basis of a causal relation between a sign and its object.[34] I posit the indexical mode as integral to a subaltern spatial praxis that maps urban neighborhoods on the plan of a village. For while officialdom's attitude to urban space can be theorized as colonial, in the sense that the Mumbai style of governmentality is largely a British inheritance, many of the city's subalterns are actual colonists. They or their parents have arrived in Mumbai from villages elsewhere and erected their "slum colonies" (this is mainstream Indian parlance) on territory that has to be made habitable. And as with agricultural land actually cleared from the forest, ground has to be broken, boundaries have to be drawn, and claims have to be patrolled and maintained. I base my case here largely on the fieldwork I have conducted among the Warlis of the outer suburbs. These are members of an *adivasi* community that has historically practiced shifting agriculture in the wilderness, only to find, with the advance of urban sprawl, that what they inhabit is more and more a concrete jungle.[35]

Within this praxis of settlement, city blocks are established and made recognizable as habitable, not through certification by the paperwork of the state, but by a higher if unofficial imprimatur, the concretized presence of protective spirits. And here is the relevant point for this discussion of visible indices: the gods need homes too. Subtly constituted settlers no less than fleshly ones require housing, and shelters are built where such squatter gods have asserted their presence; I suspect that local country deities in particular are judged not only unfortunate if left homeless on the streets but also dangerous.[36]

The place-holding markers of the morning of 7 November gave the impression of having sprouted from the ruins spontaneously, as though the immanent divinity residing at each site could not be suppressed. To regard such a mark as an indexical trace in this way is to participate in the logic of the shrine builders, who erect their structures around material features identified as *svayambhu*, "self-manifested." The phallic projection, elephant's trunk–like protuberance, or termite mound enshrined at a particular place is there because it had appeared there by itself—or rather because a god (in the examples given, Shiva, Ganesh, and a goddess, respectively) had caused it to appear there. One example that can serve for many is the Shiv Sai Seva Mandir, whose supermarket-style eclecticism in its display of *murti*s singled it out for the particular derision of Bhagvanji Raiani of Janhit Manch (the sardonic description of it Raiani gave when I interviewed him was actually how I learned about the site's existence). It will be recalled that Om Prakash, the temple's *pujari*, had informed me that the whole panoply had grown up at his prime beachfront location around the self-manifested cross.[37]

And in fact something of the naturalizing logic of self-manifestation is actually replicated among the shrines' opponents in official quarters. One interviewee, an administrator at the Maharashtra Housing and Development Authority, cast the structures as natural growths like weeds or toadstools, subject to the laws of an organic ecology in defiance of rational principles. First, you might see a stand offering free drinking water, he related. Next, a canopy would swell over the table. It was once the growth reached the stage where it sprouted a flag over the canopy that you would be able to tell from the color—saffron or green—whether what you had on your doorstep was an embryonic Hindu temple or mosque. . . .

One thing I found telling about the way he presented the scenario was the absence of human agency. "What can we do?" his attitude conveyed. "We're just civil servants with limited resources." But agency was likewise hard to assign where the adversary was concerned. If for their own publics these structures were indices of divine power and presence, to what did the Maharashtra Housing and Development Authority trace their causality? To subaltern populations not yet recognized as players in political society, channeling their collective desire for visibility into an alternative, "backward" idiom? To the chaotic vitality of the slums, themselves invasive growths? To the structural inequity of postcolonial urban society?

It will be noted that in this chapter I have deployed only two of the three distinct categories Peirce has formulated for the analysis of sign-object relations: the indexical and the symbolic. Absent so far has been the iconic mode, in which signification is effected on the basis of a formal resemblance. This omission will be rectified in the next chapter, which builds on the points made in this one to present an argument about the city's most tenacious occupant of illegal religious structures, Sai Baba of Shirdi. It will develop that central to the history of the Sai Baba cult is the question of how his divine presence is manifested visually—a tension between two signifying logics, the indexical and the iconic.

3

SECULAR SAINT

SAI BABA OF SHIRDI AND *DARSHAN* IN THE CITY

8. If you look to me, I look to you.

SAI BABA OF SHIRDI, "Eleven Assurances"

Azad, the light boy and shrine entrepreneur, held forth to me one day on the religious diversity of his adopted city, long celebrated in Indian public culture as the national metropolis, the center of modernity and cosmopolitanism. "Koi Bhagwan ko maanta hai," he told me, "koi Allah Miyan ko maanta hai, koi God ko maanta hai, koi Sai Baba ko maanta hai."

I open this chapter about Sai Baba, the unofficial patron saint of Mumbai, with these words for several reasons. One is the bricolage of languages and affective registers typical of Mumbai street style. Going provisionally with "to believe in" as the most idiomatic way to gloss the verb *maanna*, Azad's observation can be translated thus: "Some believe in Bhagwan ["the Lord," usually denoting Vishnu or his avatars], some believe in Allah Miyan [a formulation connoting affectionate regard, something like "Mr. Allah"], some believe in God [the English word, namely, the god of the Christians], some believe in Sai Baba."

It is also an interesting sociological description. The major religious communities of Mumbai are conventionally defined as Hindus, Muslims, and Christians—Amar, Akbar, and Anthony, to cite the metonyms made popular by a well-known Hindi movie.[1] Identifying a fourth category and naming it after Sai Baba, however, might seem like a departure from the script to anyone not familiar with the city.

Who is, or was, this Sai Baba? In the usage of somebody like Azad—a representative of subaltern Mumbai, a labor migrant, like so many others, from a backcountry village—what does he stand for? Is the name functioning here as the signpost of a fourth confessional division, in supersession perhaps of Jains, Parsis, or Buddhists (to name three other Mumbai constituencies)? Or is "Sai Baba" rather being deployed as a sort of taxonomic punch line, a final term to encompass or transcend the others? Azad's verb, *maanna*, can also be rendered "to submit to" or "to honor / to revere." How would one of these alternative constructions recast the relation he draws between religious communities and the objects of their devotion?

In a broader Indian context, the name Sai Baba (or title—the two words in combination are semantically rather slippery) can refer to more than one spiritual master. But there can be no doubt that the contender named in Azad's lineup of heavyweights is Sai Baba of Shirdi. To say this figure commands a high profile in Mumbai would be an understatement. The portrait of the lean, bearded saint, circulated in a handful of stereotyped forms, is virtually ubiquitous in urban space. A visitor to the city will encounter the Baba printed on stickers, labels, and the surfaces of wall-mounted tiles; enthroned as a tiny effigy on dashboards; and, above all, enshrined in a myriad of structures, from makeshift altars to booths to open-sided rooms, on the public streets. And the first point of information (again, given that quality of slipperiness I will be remarking on, it could also well be the last) that the visitor will learn about the icon is that this eminently ordinary-looking old man—thin, unpolished, unpretentious—is recognized as an embodiment of divine presence by Mumbai residents regardless of their religious affiliation.

Indeed, it would not be going too far to state that an ecumenical compass has become the defining characteristic of the saint's public. In the Mumbai area the cult—or more precisely, as I will argue, the image—retains a crossover appeal that makes Sai Baba emblematic of a reified notion of Hindu-Muslim accord. This aspect of his persona is summed up in the Hindi maxim that circulates in citation of the sum of his teachings: "Sab ka malik ek" (the Lord of All is One). A widely reproduced portrait bearing these words superimposes a temple, a mosque, and a church on the Baba's breast; the image of the One Lord who encompasses the sectarian trio is the graphic equivalent of Azad's exposition, presenting Sai Baba as trumping Amar, Akbar, and Anthony alike.

A saint who preached a gospel of tolerance and inclusion—how remarkable, yet how fitting, to find evidence of dedication to his creed in every corner of this city! How eloquent of the possibilities of urban cosmopolitanism, as critiqued in the Mumbai context by Arjun Appadurai (2000), Sunil Khilnani (1997, 135–44), and others![2] Tempting, however, though it may seem to read Sai Baba's visual proliferation as an embrace of his teachings, it would be a delicate task indeed to map any such move onto the complex social geography of the city, where *Hindu* and *Muslim* not only continue to inscribe bounds of identity but do so in more than strictly doctrinal terms, their circumscriptions overlapping with other categories, including those of class, caste, and ethnolinguistic loyalty. More delicate yet, once contextualized historically, any such proposition would contend with a disjuncture between what can be tracked chronologically of the icon's spread and Mumbai's unfortunate record of sectarian strife.

Just who, then, among the population makes such a point of displaying allegiance to the Baba? And what does it mean to believe in him? Pivoting off a critical engagement with discourse and belief—as conventionally foregrounded in religious studies approaches to saints—my argument here will take in a brief survey of the scholarship on Shirdi's holy man. I will then move on to offer an argument that runs along the following points.

First, understanding the Sai Baba phenomenon begins with reframing it as a problem in visual culture, which is to say, per this book's wider argument, that it is a problem of the organization of space. Second, the spread of the Sai Baba icon, a distinctly modern kind of image, is related to Mumbai's standing as a distinctly postcolonial kind of space, with a history of contestation over the configuration of the public, as discussed in chapters 1 and 2. Third, understanding how the icon works in public among diverse constituencies of viewers requires a theoretical engagement with *darshan*, or the practice of visual worship. I will propose a model of the *darshan* encounter on the paradigm not of faith or belief but rather of recognition.

In so arguing, I will advance through three historical scenarios. In the first, a turn-of-the-twentieth-century moment, I will look to the circuit of pilgrimage to the Baba's seat at Shirdi as described in the cult's central scripture, the *Shri Sai Satcharita*. In the second, I will invoke Indian public culture in 1977, the last year of Indira Gandhi's Emergency, when two hit movies introduced subaltern publics to authoritative figurations of the saint. Finally, I will revisit some of my fieldwork research from 2003, recalling the November morning when, acting in the name of the public interest, the government launched a demolition campaign against "illegal religious structures" that was visited primarily on Sai Baba sites.

Serious academic treatments about the Baba published in English include articles by Charles S. J. White (1972), Smriti Srinivas (1999), and Karline McLain (2011); and book-length biographies by Antonio Rigopoulos (1993) and Marianne Warren (1999). McLain (2016) has recently completed a book about Sai Baba worship in a contemporary and global frame, and Kiran Shinde and Andrea Pinkney (2013) have published an article-length study of the cult's center at Shirdi. To say that none of this scholarship affords much explanatory purchase on the question of Sai Baba's ubiquity in Mumbai is not to situate myself in opposition to these projects (I am particularly indebted to the work of McLain and Warren). Rather, what my criticism indicates is the inadequacy of traditionally favored approaches to the study of saints and their cults—in South Asia and elsewhere—to the task of analyzing the dissemination across urban space of this particular saint's image. The metropolitan embrace of the country preacher from Shirdi is, in my view, best studied at the nexus of visual studies and urban ethnography. Accordingly, I have looked to anthropological and semiotic perspectives for guidance in thinking through two vectors of the way the sacred image operates: (1) its relation to its spectator, or addressee; and (2) its relation to the space that surrounds it.

The threefold Site/Sight/Cite device will be recalled from the previous chapter. What I have chosen to leave out of the formula here is the third term, *cite*. And in de-emphasizing what the image represents, or describes—the historical individual Sai Baba, the corpus of his teachings—I am taking a position, not strictly speaking against meaning as such, but perhaps against mimetic representation (see Foucault 2010). This is not so much a statement of philosophical principle as a response to that sense of semiotic shallowness that kept bemusing me in my encounters with the Sai Baba icon. In what remains of this introductory section, I will consider some of what might be brought to the surface by biographical, theological, and iconographic lines of inquiry and then move to my own, historically and ethnographically grounded excavation, directed not at beliefs or teachings but effects.

Biographically speaking, then, Sai Baba was a charismatic who was based in the village of Shirdi, in Ahmednagar District in what is now central Maharashtra State, well into the twentieth century. Marianne Warren (1999, 35–49), the most academically rigorous of his biographers in English, dates his fleshly career from the late 1830s to 1918. It may be noted that the period coincides with the advent of modern technologies of mass reproduction in India and elsewhere, as well as with the heyday of colonial rule (with its implications for the development of the region's infrastructure and the imposition of a bureaucratized taxonomy of religious identity on the populace). Over the last century, even as the site of Sai Baba's tomb has been built up in the style of a conventional Hindu temple complex, the record of his words and works has become overgrown with the no-less-conventional tropes of Hindu hagiography. But on the basis of a contextualization of the record within the religious milieu of the day Warren argues that the historical Baba of Shirdi, who made his home in a ruined mosque, preached and comported himself in accordance with norms observed by contemporary Sufi masters.

Warren's case for situating him alongside other Muslim mystics active in the period thus lays down a marker against the saint's present-day adoption as an object of devotion within mainstream Hinduism (see also Shepherd 1985, 2011). One tried-and-true tactic used to assimilate heterodox or antinomian charismatic figures within the orthodox caste hierarchy is to endow them with Brahmin birth parents—once separated from whom they commence their dharmic missions among low-caste or otherwise marginal groups—and in the case of Sai Baba the story seems to have attained the status of something like conventional wisdom (Sikand 2003, 119). Ritual and rhetorical interventions along these lines notwithstanding, however, not even the staunchest Hindu chauvinists have yet succeeded in erasing his Muslim antecedents altogether.[3]

Indeed, Sai Baba finds good company among other mavericks rehabilitated as Brahmin foundlings, of whom the most illustrious names are perhaps the fifteenth-century North Indian poet-saints Kabir and Ravidas. Contra the blurb copy on my edition of one popular hagiography, *Sai Baba of Shirdi: A Unique Saint*—"In all of India's history, there has never been another like him. He is not a conventional saint. . . . He made no pretensions to scholarship yet he had a profound insight into both Hindu and Islamic scriptures. . . . He performed 'miracles' but in no manner of means to impress anyone. . . . Sai Baba in every way remains unique" (Kamath and Kher 1991, back cover)—the profile actually fits many other historical and modern individuals, especially those whose popularity in subaltern contexts involves the attribution to them of healing powers (see, for example, Assayag 2004; Bellamy 2011; Ferrari 2011; Kakar 1982; Sikand 2003). In asking why it is Sai Baba, of all these personages, whose visage should end up installed in public as the universal access point to divine power, I invite attention also to the flip side of the question: what is it about him that has made his gesture of universal address so open to co-optation by Hindu elites, and possibly others?

Reading his actual teachings is unlikely to yield the answer to either question, because such lessons as the sage has left us are cryptic or confrontationally gnomic in style (Rigopoulos [1993, 297–305] develops the comparison with Kabir). They have been transmitted as utterances or exemplary gestures, narrativized by his followers in anecdotes that correspond to well-established patterns found in South Asian hagiographical texts. The corpus offers thin gruel to any prospective devotee looking for instructions to follow, much less a substantial doctrine to believe in.

As collected in the *Shri Sai Satcharita*, the closest thing the cult has to a canonical text, a "recurring lesson encountered in these stories is Shirdi Sai Baba's all-pervasiveness and accessibility" (McLain 2011, 27). Indeed, what is at stake in the anecdotes frequently hinges on the Baba's appearance—the manifestation and recognition of his authentic, divine image—to a devotee in a moment of pious anticipation or, conversely, of alienation. This is the visual relation glossed in the *Satcharita* with the (principally) Hindu term *darshan*. It can be said that the blessing of the guru's vision in itself satisfies a host of questions, and I will examine the apparitions described in the *Satcharita* in some detail below. Again, however, my point is that coherence at the level of doctrine is not an emphasis of the text. Nor is there any overarching institutional structure that could direct coherence in interpretation, let alone mobilize a proselytizing campaign. The body that administers the pilgrimage complex at Shirdi, the Shri Saibaba Sansthan Trust, runs all of one official temple in Mumbai. None of the myriad outposts that enshrine the Baba on the city's streets and walls are subject to a central authority.

It is this very mimetic shallowness, I would argue, that has made possible the assimilation of the Baba's distinctive legacy within the ritual norms of modern Hinduism. In fact, as I illustrate toward this chapter's end, the Shirdi site has itself become thoroughly made over in this way by none other than the legacy's executors, the trustees of the Shri Saibaba Sansthan. (To gesture at a touchstone of Hindu studies, it could be said that the Sansthan's priorities lie with orthopraxy rather than orthodoxy.) Here it remains to add that a close reading turns up the familiar combination of Hindu-Muslim crosscurrents and semantic poverty in the saint's very name: *sai*, meaning "master," "god," or "Muslim ascetic," plus *baba*, an informal term of address for "father," "grandfather," or "holy man"; thus, *sai baba*, "Master Father" or possibly "Reverend Dad" . . . with the curious detail that the *Oxford Hindi-English Dictionary* traces the part with the specifically Islamic association to an Indic derivation, *svaamin* (as in "swami"), and the thoroughly colloquial *baba* back to Persian.

Belief, again, in an exemplary life or a body of ideas—in anything describable or interpretable—is somehow beside the point. To make free with some Weberian language, what is going on might rather be conceptualized as the transference of the prophet's charisma from his physical person, not to a codified body of scripture, but to his visual trace as manifested in graphic or plastic form. I look again to the opening statement presented by my interlocutor Azad, and to his use of the multivalent verb *maanna* as a cue. I question whether he was actually stating that people "believe in" the Sai Baba image.

An iconographic survey of Sai Baba pictures produced over the decades would turn up some interesting mimetic referents, many having to do with the conversion of the fakir persona into a form more consistent with the typological standards of Hindu god poster art. This now-hegemonic visual idiom has been studied by Christopher Pinney (1997a, 2002, 2004), Kajri Jain (2007), and Sumathi Ramaswamy (2010), among others; the style could be described as a sort of fabulous hyperrealism, with bright colors, flattened perspective, and smooth, rounded surfaces among its features. Anthropomorphic figures are typically given a static presentation that, citing the formal contours and positioning or staging of cultic objects (*murtis*) in temples, invites the adoring gaze of the viewer. In line with these norms, devotional prints of Sai Baba limit themselves in the main to a few standard postures: Full-Frontal Standing, Full-Frontal Seated Cross-Legged, Full-Frontal Facial Portrait.

In her article on the Baba, McClain (2011, 32–38) has presented a nuanced reading of a representative set of images, with one line of interpretation stressing the Hindu or Muslim coding of particular motifs and graphic details.[4] It is important to note that successive editions of images can incorporate all sorts of formal interventions, notably in color. It thus becomes possible to track Hinduization across reissues of devotional pictures. For example, the white kerchief donned by the saint in a style typical of a Muslim mendicant has in many contemporary renditions been given a Hindu-coded saffron color. For my purposes, however, it is even more important to note that all iterations of mass-market Sai Baba art are derived from a small pool of source images: a set of historical photographs.[5]

Let me state briefly what I see at stake here. A charismatic figure in whom devotees recognize an embodiment of divine power (in terms of Hindu doctrine an incarnation or *avatar*; in Sufi terms a saintly dispenser of *barkat*) has been photographed at a particular moment in colonial modernity. Photography, at the turn of the twentieth century, was one technology whose artifacts were becoming established in circulation among an Indian public; the chromolithographic process behind poster-style art was another. Sai Baba's capture on film at this juncture presented his followers with a challenge that, I propose, went beyond matters of mere interpretation. They did not start by asking: What does this image describe or resemble? What does it *mean* in its formal details?[6] Rather, I will argue, the question ran along the lines of: If the trace of a person who is himself a material trace of the divine has been imprinted within this new medium, does that secondary trace contain power? And to that I would add my own question: What happens when it transmits that power?

Koi Sai Baba ko maanta hai: "Some ~~believe in~~ Sai Baba." Let me wrap up this introductory section with an alternative translation of *maanna*. I suggest that in Azad's formulation, the relation that connects a religious subject to an icon is one of *recognition*. What the worshiper does is "submit to" it, perhaps even "heed [its] call." In the pages to follow, my analysis will take up Sai Baba not as a historical figure or theological voice but as an image—as a reproducible artifact that, mediated by locally prevailing forms and organs of visual culture, presents an ideological address to members of its viewing public and helps to construct the city as a shared space.

To restate a commonplace, all visual signifiers occupy space, just as all aural signifiers take up time. All such spaces are materially constituted—even the pages of books and television screens—and are modified by the signs that mark them, although the relation of that mark to the space it occupies has not traditionally been the main concern of visual studies, let alone religious studies. Presenting some elements of textual and ethnographic research, then, I will engage ideas advanced by anthropologists regarding certain kinds of images typologically identifiable as sacred in modern Indian visual culture (see Gell 1998; Pinney 1997a, 2004), exploring the operations of the Sai Baba icon within culturally contingent ways of seeing and of marking space, and foregrounding the mediation of these operations by the legal-bureaucratic system and technologies of visual reproduction.

Bombay to Shirdi: The Circuit in the *Shri Sai Satcharita*

The *Shri Sai Satcharita*, which consists in large part of a chronicle of events from the Baba's historical lifetime, was compiled a hundred years ago. Bombay city occupied roughly a third of the geographical area claimed by present-day Greater Mumbai and had less than a twelfth of its population. Yet the city's broad ambit is suggested in many episodes recounted in the *Satcharita*. If the general purport of the text's many pilgrimage tales is that all roads lead ultimately to Shirdi, it could be said nevertheless that on their way through the hinterland many connect with Bombay-bound junctions. The city's prestige as the defining locus of modernity was if anything more salient in this period. As capital of the Bombay Presidency it was the administrative hub for approximately one-third of British India, as well as the region's principal port and center of industry and commerce. And if the *Shri Sai Satcharita* chronicles the collection around the master's feet of an eclectic group of rustic disciples—women as well as men; low castes as well as high; Muslims, of course, as well as Hindus—there is a contrast to be noted with another set of devotees, whose travel to Shirdi in quest of the divine presence is relayed in one tale after another. Many of these seekers set out physically from Bombay and its environs, while others on the path do not. They can be grouped together, however, under the mark of a different kind of origin: a shared place within colonial modernity as members of a nascent middle class.

These pioneer witnesses to the Baba's authenticity are pillars of the community. Indeed, they are nothing less than professional men: lawyers and doctors; managers in the textile industry and in a Greek-run trading firm; functionaries in the colonial bureaucracy's postal, railway, and revenue services. The very author of the *Shri Sai Satcharita*, Govind Raghunath Dabholkar—styled "Hemadpant" by the guru himself, after a medieval hero of Marathi letters—worked as a "servant of the Bombay Government and his last appointment was as a magistrate in the Bandra suburb of Bombay" (Dabholkar 1999, foreword). Most of the exemplary devotees Hemadpant identifies are Hindu men like him, with Maharashtrian family names and honorifics. Their common business is the management of knowledge as mediated through paperwork. Paper circulates within their offices as the material bearer of meaning to be documented, duplicated, and authenticated; paper circulates beyond their offices to generate effects of value and power. It was precisely such colonial moderns as these, I contend, who constituted the public in this period for the products of technological processes like photography and chromolithography.[7]

As I have already proposed, the characteristic movement of the *Satcharita*'s edifying tales is to stage a question, "Is the Master truly divine?" and, working through narrative, to deliver an affirmative resolution: "Behold the proof—he is indeed divine!" These tests and demonstrations are glossed, in a term from Hindu philosophy, as Sai Baba's *leela*, or "play"—his gracious intervention into the ultimately illusory fabric, *maya*, of phenomenal reality. Overwhelmingly, the evidence thus adduced is made manifest visually; the revelation generally involves the display of the guru's person, which enacts the authenticating gesture in itself. In some stories Sai Baba's form is a vision, confined as an image to the interior of the devotee's mind and revealed to the rest of us through verbal testimony. This is, to be sure, a standard motif in devotional literature in India and elsewhere. But in other stories Sai Baba is materially instantiated within narrative action as a picture or photograph.

Hemadpant was tasked by the Baba with writing the *Shri Sai Satcharita* in the 1910s, as the author himself chronicles. He published it in 1929, the year of his own death. The Marathi original is in verse. The most common English version, the slim volume published and distributed by the Shri Saibaba Sansthan, is a prose translation and abridgement by Nagesh Vasudev Gunaji (1996). In 1999 Indira Kher completed the full, line-by-line translation I rely on in this chapter. The Sai Baba biographer Marianne Warren, who gave support to Kher's project, has noted of the older, Sansthan-certified redaction that Gunaji seems to have edited away much of the Sufi language present in the original, thus re-inscribing the Baba's historical words and works with a Hindu, and specifically Vedantic, emphasis (see also Shepherd 2011; Sikand 2003, 133).

The first thing to remark in examining the place of photography in the *Shri Sai Satcharita* is its documentation of a specific image that has become central to the Shirdi-based cult. The Baba gazes pensively into the lens, seated with his right leg crossed over his knee at the ankle, left fingers draped across his right foot. The photograph (a life-size print that was likely overpainted with gouache, per the typical Indian practice)[8] was mounted in one part of the pilgrimage complex at Shirdi while the saint was still in residence.[9] After his physical passing in 1918, it was reinstalled at the center of the tomb-cum-temple space (*samadhi mandir*). In 1957 it was replaced in its turn by a three-dimensional copy executed in marble, which occupies pride of place to this day at Shirdi as the central object of cultic attention (*murti*) (Wakchaure 2004, 37).

This definitive Baba pose has subsequently been disseminated across Mumbai and, to a lesser extent, the rest of India in a range of graphic and plastic media. Hemadpant (Dabholkar 1999) singles it out as a form that lends itself to meditation in chapter 22, verses 9–25, comparing the Baba's right toe as seen through his left fingers to the new moon framed in a tree—a luminous point on which the practitioner can train his or her focus. Elsewhere in the text, the master himself affirms that the portrait enshrined at Shirdi is to be equated with his presence (and, more broadly, with the presence of the divine). In chapter 28, verses 187–214, Megha, one of the Baba's intimates, worships the photograph, which is mounted inside the building of which he is the caretaker. One morning Megha "had a vision as he lay awake on his bed. . . . [A]lthough his eyes were closed, his mind was fully awake, when he clearly saw Baba's figure" (28:190–91). The guru speaks, commanding him to draw a trident, a symbol of Shiva. Opening his eyes, the disciple sees the doors are all locked; he gets up and visits the adjacent mosque, the master's living quarters. "Megha narrated his vision in detail. Baba then said, 'What vision? Did you not hear my words. . . . Calling it a "Vision," are you trying to evaluate my words?'" (28:196–98). Chastened, Megha returns to his room and draws the trident on the wall. The next day a pilgrim arrives with a stone Shiva *linga*. The master passes it on to Megha, instructing him to install Shiva's worship object next to Shiva's graphic symbol and, of course, next to his own photographic emanation on the wall.

The *Shri Sai Satcharita* contains other tales in which the Baba's power is made evident or accessible through the device of a physical picture. In 9:70–115, a factory manager in suburban Bandra, member of a reformist sect that abjures Hindu *puja* as idolatry, becomes persuaded by his son to practice the ritual before a "drawing" of Sai Baba (9:74). In 28:24–35, an employee of a Bombay trading house sees an old, bearded man in a dream and subsequently recognizes the saint in a photograph during a performance of devotional music. In 33:45–50, the victim of a scorpion sting prays before the guru's photo and is cured by ash from the incense burned before it. In the same chapter, verses 141–232 tell of a well-known singer of *kirtan* hymns from Bombay—a story I will cite further on—and also of a government official in Thana District, north of the city, who practices Sai devotion through worship of a photograph and is rewarded with a visit from an enigmatic bearded man. In 46:22–90, a member of the circle of intimates at Shirdi sets off on a pilgrimage to the distant sites of Banaras and Gaya. He seeks Sai Baba's blessing, is told the master will precede him, and is appropriately schooled when he encounters the Baba in pictorial form at the house of a Brahmin in Gaya. And in 51:17–96, the same devotee is dispatched to a nearby town with the sacred photograph from Megha's wall to have the glass in the frame repaired. There he meets an impressive figure, a London-returned political candidate, and gives him a revelatory preview of the *darshan* to be attained at Shirdi by lifting the dust cover off the photo.

There is another story, one that deserves closer attention. Verses 113–75 of chapter 40 narrate a story about Hemadpant himself that is continued in the following chapter through verse 73. On the morning of the Hindu festival of Holi in 1917 the author—who, it will be recalled, lived in Bandra, adjoining Bombay proper—is visited in a dream. The guru announces to his devotee that he will be joining Hemadpant's family for lunch. Hemadpant instructs his wife to lay an extra place, and the Holi guests—family members and close friends—assemble in anticipation. "[S]uddenly, footsteps were heard on the staircase.... As I slowly unbolted the door, I saw two persons on the stairs. One of them was Alli Mohamed and the other, a disciple of [Peer] Maulana, Ismu Mujawar by name" (40:139–41). The Muslims apologize for interrupting the holiday meal and ask the author to accept an item that belongs rightfully to him. "So saying, Alli took out a parcel from under his arm and . . . began to untie the knot. As he removed the newspaper wrapping, in that instant was seen a bas-relief of Sai"

(40:145–46). Alli and Ismu then excuse themselves, leaving the Hindus to celebrate with their guest of honor.

Nine years pass before Hemadpant meets Alli again, in a chance encounter on the street. Finally Alli explains himself. He had purchased the Sai Baba image from a trader in Bombay and used to take *darshan* of it alongside the portraits of four Muslim charismatics.[10] But Alli fell ill and left his house to convalesce with his brother-in-law, Noormohamed. Some time before, he had given Noormohamed a portrait of his own spiritual master, Baba Abdul Raheman, which Noormohamed took in his turn to a Bombay photographer's shop. "He got a fine picture made from it, of the great Baba Abdul himself, in order to take it to him as a present. . . . He got copies made and gave them to all the relatives and close friends" (41:37–38). But Noormohamed finds, to his great distress, that when he presents the picture, he is accused of idol worship and driven from Baba Abdul's assembly. He takes the lesson: "Even though much money has been spent to collect these pictures, there is no other way now, but to immerse them in water" (41:47), and not content with drowning his own photos, he reclaims the copies he had given away.

"I too, was ill at the time and staying with him. So he advised me similarly, saying that, 'these pictures bring calamities. Hence when you collect all of them and immerse them in the sea, only then will you get rid of your illness'" (41:55–56). Alli sends for his servant to remove the images from his own house and dispose of them. When at length he returns home, recovered, it is to find that the bas-relief of Sai Baba mysteriously remains on the wall. "It was no use keeping it in my house, for the moment my brother-in-law would see it, he would immerse it. But I could not give it away, with any certainty, to someone who was not a devotee" (41:63). He consults with Ismu Mujawar, the disciple of a different Sufi master, and together they arrive at the happy resolution to entrust Hemadpant with the miraculous image.

By this point the didactic purport of the story will appear familiar. Sai Baba's image manifests itself in one medium (a dream) to test his disciple's faith—or perhaps *trust*, in the authority of the image, is a better formulation—and that trust is then confirmed and rewarded through a second, gracious manifestation in a different but equally authentic visual medium (a picture). But recall Azad's *maanna*: not "belief" but "submission." The question implied in this story, and the others, is not of the correctness of doctrine or the persuasiveness of argument but of the legitimacy of a claim to power. Let me invoke, as a metaphor, the sort of office papers these early patrons of the Sai Baba cult had been processing in their work lives. At stake is not the accuracy of the information communicated through language on a given sheet of paper; what is at stake is rather the imprimatur, the validating stamp at the bottom.

If the stamp is legitimate, then what it certifies is true. It may then be asked whether the system or dispensation that backs the stamp up (the credit guaranteed by a banker, the writ of the British Raj) is to be recognized as having a claim over the subject. And yet further, the kind of work the stamp does in citing that regime of value or power might also be brought into question. In other words, to move back from rubber stamps to sacred pictures, one concern these stories share is with the efficacy of photography as a medium. In fact, photography is coming into its own, I argue, within a novel sort of praxis that mediates the devotee's relation of submission to the master. I will have more to say about the master-slave relation further on. Here, the clearest way to refine the point about visual praxis is to return to some basics of Peircean semiotics, as introduced in previous chapters.

Peirce's *iconic* mode connects a sign to its object on the basis of a formal resemblance. Thus, a picture of Sai Baba "is" or "means" Sai Baba because it looks like him. The *indexical* mode connects the sign to its object via a relation of causality or contiguity. Thus, the ash produced by the sacred flame he tends "is" Sai Baba, as is his trace on the plate that comes out of a camera he has posed in front of. Tales like the "Visitation at Holi" are told to justify the iconic operations of devotional pictures through the indexical logic of the narrative of events. The point is to make a photograph as legitimate a way for Sai Baba to make his person apparent as the traditional mode of appearance in a dream. In the inaugural event of this tale the Baba arrives in a dream. And then x happens, and then y follows . . . until at the chain's conclusion the equivalence is established with his return in a photographic image.

Of course, this reading relies on the premise that indexical logic was adduced by preference, in this period, in discourses about religious signs and phenomena and their connection to the powers behind them—and, correspondingly, that turning to iconic logic would have been a relatively less intuitive move. But this latter premise is supported by the historical milieu as depicted in the *Satcharita* itself. It is one in which devotional pictures, relying for their effects on iconic resemblance, were modern novelties. As such they were both scarce and precious.

One point of conflict in this story about how sacred images work has to do with the proscription of idolatry in dogmatic Islam and with the diversity of positions represented by the Muslim characters, well-to-do citizens of Bombay and Bandra. It will be noted that not even the convinced iconoclast,

Noormohamed, considers the pictures of the saints to be false, in the sense that they are empty or worthless. They contain power, but of a sort that will project harmful effects onto those exposed to it. Accordingly, they must be eliminated, and not simply discarded on the nearest rubbish heap but neutralized in the manner approved by pious Muslims and Hindus alike when parting with ritual objects at the ritual's conclusion: through immersion. And just as Noormohamed and Alli had expended substantial sums in obtaining their newfangled photos in the first place, so too are they prepared to pay to dispose of them. They hire boatmen and, "sailing as far into the water as [they] could" (Dabholkar 1999, 41:28), have them jettisoned in the Arabian Sea.

Once instructed that religious pictures are dangerous, the brothers-in-law know the solution. But the depiction of Muslim Bombay here is a multivocal one, where resident Sufi saints differ on the religious implications of the new technologies. The distinctly Hindu language of the text, in which the Muslims represent their interactions with the pictures in terms of *darshan* of their *gurus*, can perhaps be attributed to Hemadpant's paraphrase of their words. But it should not be missed that Noormohamed enters the story assuming he is doing honor to Baba Abdul by commissioning the photo as a prestation. Alli, the original enthusiast, never doubts through the course of events that the pictures are charged with power. Sai Baba's wondrous endurance on his wall does not so much provoke a change of heart as bring it home to him that Sai, of all the saints, is very powerful indeed.

We who learn the story from the *Satcharita* know that it is Sai Baba's person that presents the devout with an authentic point at which divine presence can be recognized in this phenomenal world. But let me go against the grain, for a moment, of my own argument about the text's emphasis on the charisma of the Baba's imprimatur. It can't be denied that this story does cast Sai Baba as the exponent of a distinctive doctrine. And what marks him apart as a teacher from his Sufi peers (who must look very similar as images, with their beards and unkempt attire) is his unequivocal position in favor of the use of pictures. In fact, elsewhere in the *Satcharita*'s pages he demonstrates over and over a teaching that is easy to miss in the absence of narrative contestation—and it is easy to miss precisely because it has been embraced as a central truth of Hinduism as practiced in the present day. It is this: worship pictures. The cultivation of *darshan* through the iconic products of modern technology is both sound in principle and efficacious in practice.

I conclude my reading of the Holi story, and the *Shri Sai Satcharita* as a whole, by remarking on two aspects of the production and consumption of sacred images as observed among Muslims and Hindus of Bombay in the 1910s. The first is that there is no indication that the pictures circulating in this story—or elsewhere in the *Satcharita*—have been consecrated at any stage by a ritual specialist. The photos' consumers evidently bring them home from the shop ready-charged, untouched by the hands of priestly middlemen, their power a direct effect of their iconic relation to the divine. The second point is that they bring them *home*. It is clear that the *darshan* images described in the *Satcharita* share their effects on a very limited circuit. Outside of Shirdi, where the cross-legged portrait is enshrined at the cult's very center, photographs of Sai Baba appear almost exclusively on the interior walls of middle-class homes in Bombay. The Sai Baba icon cannot yet be said to circulate in public.

It should prove useful to hold on to these two points as I return from Bombay to Mumbai. If the first point (that the icon can be recognized as sacred without any ritual consecration) continues to hold true, then the second (that images of Sai Baba—and other claimants to divinity—do not circulate in public) is emphatically no longer the case. The proliferation of technologies of visual reproduction, such as improved processes of photographic and lithographic printing, not to mention injection molding and resin casting—multiplicity in three dimensions!—has led to the mass dissemination of devotional art products. The technical aspects of this transformation are not as germane, however, to this book's argument as the way that the expansion of the city's built environment and its twelvefold growth in population have combined to complicate the location of the public. In a colonial city whose masters considered the native quarter to be a secondary category of urban settlement, the boundary between public and private had a certain conceptual clarity, for those who cared about such things. But how is public space demarcated in the twenty-first-century city? And just who, out of Mumbai's vast demographic diversity, constitutes the public as a social formation?

The Mass Invades the Media: Bombay in the 1970s

In the recollection of many downtown residents, the Baba's popularity as a cultic figure—along with the corresponding plethora of public shrines—was not even a discernible Bombay phenomenon until the mid-1970s. This period was dominated, politically and culturally, by Prime Minister Indira Gandhi's imposition of a state of Emergency Rule for nearly two years from 1975 to 1977, when civil liberties were suspended and the Congress Party's enemies squashed. The day's public discourse was marked by something of a moral panic about the growth of slums, which figured as the symptom of a breakdown in the national project on several levels. The great promise of the Nehru years, that a centralized development policy would create prosperity for all, was deemed to have failed. The contours of a national modernity given shape (albeit imperfectly, from the first) by Bombay as India's showcase city appeared increasingly flimsy. And the jerry-built "encroachments" that seemed to keep expanding, out of control, into the zone of the public came to be connected with several of the Emergency's key themes. These included Congress's vaunted restoration of law and order as well as the simultaneous efforts it made, in a populist vein, to mobilize the newly prominent masses. Most notorious was the Congress government's campaign of coerced sterilization—the regime's bid to control that undisciplined and immoral tendency of the masses to keep making more of themselves. In two well-known novels that deal with the era, some of the bitterest passages are reserved for the slum clearances that brought the Emergency home to many residents of Indian cities: Delhi in Salman Rushdie's *Midnight's Children*, Bombay in Rohinton Mistry's *A Fine Balance*. The demolitions advanced under the slogan "Garibi Hatao" (Eliminate Poverty)—words that perhaps seem less ironic in an alternative translation: "Banish Poverty" (from the middle-class gaze, at any rate).

An underexamined aspect of the political scene in 1970s Maharashtra is the association that seems to have developed between the Congress Party and the Sai Baba icon. Then as now, the party marketed itself as the champion of Indian "secularism," an ideology comparable with multiculturalism in the US context, whose instrumentalist applications involve appeals to voting blocs defined by religious or caste identity. (The paradigmatic example is the "Muslim vote.") Thomas Blom Hansen and others have commented to me on the suggestive role played in this period by the Maharashtra party chief Y. B. Chavan, one of whose many accomplishments was victory in the March 1977 election that concluded the Emergency (the contest resulted in a rout for Congress almost everywhere else in India, to the shock of most of the party's leaders, if not perhaps the rank and file). Sai Baba's blessing of the party's secularist vision—and, reciprocally, the party's blessing of whoever exhibited the Sai Baba emblem— has been identified by some of my interlocutors in the graphic motif of the Baba's right hand. In devotional images of the present day, the hand is conventionally shown blessing the viewer in a raised position. Thus, the reasoning goes, it also marks homage to the Congress Party, which adopted the open hand as its symbol before the election of 1980, Mrs. Gandhi's great comeback.[11] Iconographic research that could pinpoint this detail's emergence in the post-Emergency period is lacking, but it is beyond doubt that the gesture is the result of an artistic intervention. None of the historical photographs show the saint performing it—not even the cross-legged image, however natural the view has come to seem of the seated Baba with his palm held up.

Studies of Hindi film have made much of its transformation in this period by the incursion of themes and character types identified with the urban poor, such as the Angry Young Man persona of the star Amitabh Bachchan. But in cinema the moment was also notable for a different sort of encroachment. Film industry leaders and critics in the English-language press were taken by surprise when representatives of a neglected and moribund-seeming genre captured the imagination, and the box-office receipts, of mass audiences. The very first films made in India had been "mythologicals," which brought the Hindu deities to the screen from epic and Purana literature, and "devotionals," inspired by the lives of historical saints. But from dominance in the silent era the genre had become relegated, in the main, to bottom-tier productions. Indeed, the breakaway hit of 1975, *Jai Santoshi Maa* (Vijay Sharma), was itself a modest effort, its overall look distinctly down-market (see Lutgendorf 2003). The crude special effects and stagey mise-en-scène begin to make sense, however, when the film is examined alongside its evident source of visual inspiration: mass-produced devotional art. At the formal level, *Jai Santoshi Maa* realized a cinematic encoding of the god poster aesthetic (and the phenomenally successful *Ramayana* epic that debuted on television twelve years later marked the apex, perhaps, of the modern *darshan*–motion-picture form).[12] Transposed to the screen from a cult circumscribed until then by bounds of geography and caste, the persona and mythology of an obscure goddess were re-presented iconically and circulated on a translocal scale.

Two years later, not long after the Emergency's end, the Hindi film *Shirdi Ke Sai Baba* (Ashok Bhushan, 1977) was released. To the extent that it followed *Jai Santoshi Maa*'s pattern in converting the object of a local cult into the icon of a metropolitan deity, it seems to have made its mark on a more modest scale. A key distinction on this score is that, as I have argued above, from the time of the Sai Baba cult's routinization with the compilation of the *Shri Sai Satcharita*, the saint had already been accessed customarily through his icon. What *Shirdi Ke Sai Baba* appears to have done is to have disseminated that icon across Bombay and beyond, making it legible in terms of an associated personality and narrative. And possibly in synchrony with the tactics of the Maharashtra Congress Party, the film seems to have encouraged the image's adoption among a wide swath of the populace, including the residents of slum colonies and otherwise at-risk neighborhoods.

Shirdi Ke Sai Baba stars Sudhir Dalvi in a role he was to repeat in at least one subsequent feature, although the name first identified with the movie is generally that of a more mainstream actor, Manoj Kumar, who plays a devotee in the frame narrative.[13] (Kumar has subsequently been quoted as saying that film and television "have put Baba on the world map.")[14] The film's titular hero is portrayed as the mouthpiece of the conventional discourse of secularism as espoused by the Congress of the day.[15] In one memorable song sequence, a policeman who has converted to Sai Baba's service sings his praise in verses that take on visual form as religious symbols: the Aum, the Islamic crescent, the Christian cross, the wheel of the Buddhist Law, and even a sacred flame for the Zoroastrians are successively animated across the frame. My friend Azad would have recognized that tune.[16]

Sai Baba's best-known and most cherished Bollywood moment, however, is a guest appearance in a different hit of the same year, *Amar Akbar Anthony* (Manmohan Desai, 1977). This playful and exuberant film, which like the Sai hagiography was released only once the Emergency was lifted, narrates a message of communal brotherhood under the guiding hand of the state that can in fact be read as squarely in accord with the party line. Three brothers of Bombay, Hindu by birth, have been raised by foster fathers in different religions. Akbar, the Muslim brother, is a comic imagining of the sort of Sufi mystic whose declamations are set to music in the *qawwali* style. In the sequence in question, he officiates at a prayer service convened at an artfully visualized space of syncretism. In its main outline and architectural idiom it seems to be a Sufi tomb, or *dargah*, but saffron-colored flags fly overhead and installed within is a *murti* swathed in saffron cloth. This is a life-size marble replica of Sai Baba in the cross-legged pose derived from the photograph.

Akbar is singing Sai's praises before a mixed congregation when a mysterious blind woman crashes the party. She seeks refuge from a pair of racketeers who chase her all the way to the gate, where they are warded off by a cobra. Stumbling at the threshold, she continues toward the Baba on her knees; in her blindness she performs another involuntary gesture of obeisance, knocking her head on the floor. This is the gesture that initiates a miracle. The woman raises her face, now streaked on the forehead with blood. The splash at once connotes *balidan*, a sacrificial blood-offering to the deity; a *teeka*, the mark that certifies ritual purity at the conclusion of *puja*; and a *bindi*, the adornment signaling a Hindu woman's married status (the next scene will reveal to the character that she not only is still married but can also claim three strapping sons). Two flames kindle in the idol's eyes; they fly across the compound and enter the eyes of the supplicant. "Baba! I can see now," she cries rapturously. "I can do your *darshan*."

Some of the trademark motifs of Sai Baba worship will be noted from prior exposition. Take, for example, the grounds of equality on which Hindus and Muslims meet, united in submission to their common master. There is also the photorealistic form in which the Lord of All is made present—and the film's endorsement of it as unexceptional, with the *murti*'s adoration by Muslims exciting no remark. Another element brings up a question I will address in the next section: the saint's gaze is penetrating, and it does not recognize everyone as good. Sai Baba, it seems, welcomes all to his court—except those who approach with evil intent. The threshold of the refuge is patrolled by a cobra, which might be thought of as an autochthonous minor deity. Is it significant that the chief racketeer is a Christian, depicted as a deracinated sort of Anglophone sahib figure? Or that, simply put, he is a rich man—a parody of the postcolonial elite that calls the shots in the city?

The part I focus on here, preparatory to the theoretical inquiry in the next section, is the petitioner's recovery of her vision. To interpret this as a lesson about the Baba's extension of grace through his image, per the script made familiar by the *Shri Sai Satcharita*, poses no great challenge. But there are features from the film's wider narrative that distinguish it as a 1970s-vintage telling. The exemplary subject is no longer a colonial modern blessed with access to a novel visual form in which to catch a glimpse of the Truth. Bharati, the mother figure in *Amar Akbar Anthony*, is a woman of the masses (of the servant classes, to recall Suketu Mehta's [2004] self-indicting phrasing from chapter 1) who is cast onto the streets when her husband's boss, the Anglophone villain, separates her from her slum colony home. The curse of blindness attends her descent into urban anomie, and the film's depiction of Bombay as the stage on which a fantastical plot then unfolds in a series of stunts, gags, musical numbers, and masquerades suggests that—entertaining though much of the urban pageant may seem—blindness is the actual condition of one who encounters this flimflam as reality.

In this allegory Bharati, with her rustic-looking sari and somewhat hapless affect, is of course a subaltern subject, a representative of the throngs of villagers who have migrated to the city in this period. Blindness is her reaction to the dazzling play of surfaces (although it could also be read as symbolic of her invisibility in the eyes of others). The madcap vision of Bombay brings to mind the philosophically resonant nickname Mayapuri, City of Illusion, as well as the poetic image of the *rangmahal*s, the urban mansions with their colorful and reflective façades. And where all is fleeting, even meretricious illusion, it develops that the *leela* of Sai Baba opens up a redemptive window. The abject Bharati does not so much find her own way to the holy man's visage as she is driven to it in extremity. But once placed in a position to behold the master, she has but to demonstrate submission for the Baba to recognize her as a subject and endow her with the agency to recognize him. What results is less a miraculous transformation than a restoration to order and stability as configured by a conventional idea of a Hindu woman's dharma: home, community, respectability, sons.

Once again, Sai Baba emerges as the prophet of a modern dispensation in which pictures are not blank—nor faces anonymous. In the antic chaos of the postcolonial city the message has become, if anything, more urgent. The public reach of modern media has expanded, as has the range of media forms in dazzling variety and color, with paperwork and newspapers joined by corporate branding, advertising, and, above all, popular cinema.[17] In a parallel movement, the mass traffic of bodies in rationalized public spaces has rendered village- and caste-based performative modes and marks of identity atavistic and, to most, illegible. (The shift to this norm of anonymity invokes the scenario from chapter 1 where the light boys enter the studio space.) Urban modernity has reached a stage, it seems, where the Baba's affirmation to the likes of Hemadpant that self-presentations such as pictures are to be seen as persons—with histories, relationships, agency—comes to make sense to real-life Bharatis too.

This is the ascendancy of the Peircean iconic. At the start of his praise song to the saint, the Akbar character declaims:

Zamane mein kahan tuti hui tasveer banti hai
Tere darbar mein bhigadi hui taqdeer banti hai

[In this age, where can a shattered picture be made whole?
Your court is where ruined destinies are repaired.]

A conventional interpretation contrasts the mundane frustration of the first line with the sublime promise of the second. The contrast hinges on the rhetorical or ironic use of *kahan*, "where," in the first line: *where* in the dismissive sense of "where the hell," with an implication of "probably nowhere." In this modern age, that is to say, we have fallen to such lows that even if something as cheap and flimsy as a picture (emblematic of the age in its very cheapness) were to require repair, we wouldn't find anyone with the integrity to fix it. All the more miraculous, then, that such a one as Sai Baba should deign to show us wretches grace!

But there is also merit to an against-the-grain interpretation, one that actually hews more closely to the literal sense of the words. In this complementary reading, the *where* is asking a straightforward question. The second line gives the answer—go to Sai Baba's court!—and the tawdry-seeming "picture" (*tasveer*) and the grandiose "destiny" (*taqdeer*) are set forth as parallel terms. For ours is indeed an Age of the Picture, a dreamscape of glimpses among which we drift directionless, like sleepwalkers. But what the master reveals is a true picture, an ontologically fixed point around which to assemble our coordinates. Once we have submitted to the Lord of All, the big picture falls into place— each of us in our proper place within it.

Perspectives on *Darshan*

When I say that an artifact of visual culture (for example, a sacred picture) exerts an effect on the subject who views it, what shape does that process take? For guidance at the nexus of visuality, desire, and identity, I follow the lead of several anthropologists of South Asia in looking to the psychoanalytic models of Jacques Lacan. Brian Keith Axel (2001) has examined mass-mediated images, most notably a web-based genre of photos of bodies exhibiting marks of torture, in his delineation of a Sikh "diasporic imaginary." Closer to home, the thematic core of Thomas Blom Hansen's (2001) ethnography of the Shiv Sena in Mumbai is the party's project of renaming the city, an ideological move Hansen relates to the Lacanian subject's quest for recognition.

Most illuminating for me has been Katherine Pratt Ewing's (1997) study of Sufism in late twentieth-century Lahore. Among her positions is a considered rejection of the Symbolic Order, the matrix of signification and repression within which, in Lacan's scheme, most social relations are enacted. As a unitary edifice, to be sure, the Symbolic Order has been assailed by the champions of a diversity of selves it seems to shut out—most prominently theorists of gender and sexuality but also ethnographers and other critics of Lacan's cultural parochialism. I find Ewing's sensibilities in this regard to be very much in tune with my own. Following a line of critique initiated by Gilles Deleuze and Félix Guattari, she maps out a postcolonial milieu in which multiple discursive and affective fields lay claim to an "elusive, multivocal shifting subject": "Nevertheless, the phenomenon of a fixed structure of signs remains—as an ideological formation, one of several that may coexist, which when enunciated fixes subjects as 'identities,' or subject positions in relations of power" (Ewing 1997, 32). Again: "I take from Lacan the idea of a subject that may be split by its entry into language, but language of a particular sort—the signifiers of an ideology that are fixed through the process of domination. This subject may be activated by a desire for recognition that passes through a Symbolic Order, constituted out of a linguistic structure of difference. . . . But this Symbolic Order is not, in my view, the overarching deterministic structure that Lacan assumes it to be" (36).

Now, retaining the point about the Symbolic Order's multiplicity (not to say multivocality), let's get to grips with the dynamics of recognition. I propose to do so by looking not so much to Lacan himself as to Alexandre Kojève, from whom Lacan derived the understanding of Hegel's *Phenomenology of Spirit* that would go on to underpin his theoretical framework. Indeed, the "Kojève-Hegel matrix in Lacan" seems deserving of more attention than it gets these days in the field of religious studies, for the model it provides of subjection and subjectification is one whose implications have not been exhausted.[18] For Kojève as for Lacan, the interpellation of the subject is theorized to turn on the desire for recognition. Exemplary of this movement, in my study, is the case of a sacred display mounted in public space that exerts its appeal on an unsuspecting pedestrian. To the degree that this moment of enunciation is experienced as effective, the subject—our pedestrian—attains a recognition contingent on subjection to a regime of power relations (which may be configured both discursively and nondiscursively, *pace* Lacan, through somatic and affective modes). To be specific, these relations take the contours of the master-slave dialectic, and in Lacan's schema this is inscribed as submission to the Law of the Father. More closely aligned with my own project, however, is Kojève's (1969) reading of the dialectic as an existential conflict between master and servant (see also Biles 2007, chap. 1).

Kojève reads Hegel's master-slave dialectic as a sort of unrequited romance. Through his refusal to recognize the slave, the master forfeits the fulfillment of his own desire for self-affirming recognition; by withholding "human reality and dignity" from the slave, he ensures his ultimate dissatisfaction (Kojève 1969, 20). Kojève casts the master-slave relation as analogous to the historical opposition of man and woman, and while straightforwardly binary and heteronormative, it seems this gendered approach to Hegel could lend itself well to the analysis of schools of Bhakti and other devotional and mystical attitudes predicated on the construction of the deity as an absent beloved (compare Ranajit Guha [1989] 1994, 259). Yet for the purposes of the present argument, what I want to stress is Kojève's insistence on the slave's dependence on subordination to the master for his or her identity. This arrangement finds its parallel in the hierarchical relationship between human subject and deified Other, construed theologically as normative in religious contexts in South Asia (among other places).

In relation to religious images, viewers occupy the subject position of the slave in Kojève's sense of the term. Submission to God is cast as subjection to a lord whose powers are celestial and terrestrial, otherworldly and mundane. Yet the desire for recognition is determinative, albeit imperfectly, of the autonomy of slaves and of the norms and bounds of social personhood. In fact, rather than rendering the slave passive and docile, the experience is said to endow him or her with a predisposition to "change, transcendence, transformation, education"—historical progress itself (Kojève 1969, 22). This corresponds with the citation of obedience to God(s) or patron spirits as a condition of possibility for human flourishing in a host of religious traditions.

One aspect of the Lacanian framework that has been enthusiastically taken up in the study of visual culture is its elevation of the visual as a privileged channel of enunciation. If the god given form by the *murti* be identified as the object of its devotee's gaze, it is surely suggestive that, according to Lacan and his more doctrinaire followers, the scopic relation is initiated not by the viewer as an agent but rather by the Other that affirms the viewer as a subject in the first place through the gesture of recognition: "[T]he subject of vision is itself an object of representation, because what determines the subject is a look that is outside—for Lacan, in the field of the visible: 'I am looked at, that is to say, I am a picture'" (Lapsley and Westlake 1988, 96).[19] Compare the *Shri Sai Satcharita*: "[T]he *darshan* of Sai Baba's photograph is the same as his *darshan* in person. But there has to be full, complete trust and you will receive the mark at the right time" (Dabholkar 1999, 33:150). Reminiscent of the *Amar Akbar Anthony* scenario examined in the previous section, this statement can be broken down in analytic terms that complement its theological assumptions. Sai Baba—the pictured object of desire whose reciprocating gaze is sought—is also the agent of enunciation, who extends the gesture ("the mark") that integrates, or interpellates, the desiring subject within an ideological dispensation. The condition of recognition is surrender to the guru's mastery. Number 8 of Sai Baba's "Eleven Assurances," which is printed in English on some of his images, offers a more succinct formulation. "If you look to me," Sai promises, "I look to you." If you recognize this picture as me, I recognize you as a picture.

There are other things to be said here about *darshan* that are not as theoretically abstruse as this Lacan-inspired model of recognition. The concept is central to Hindu thought and ritual discourse, although it is important to remember that not all the images that project a visual address on Mumbai's streets hail from Hindu traditions. A pithy summary of the process is supplied by Lawrence A. Babb (1981, 387): "Hindu devotees . . . wish to see the gods; and the gods evidently see their devotees in turn." The sequentiality implied by Babb's "in turn" is absent from the words of a Tamil peasant quoted by Valentine Daniel (1984, 84): "the deity must look at you in such a way that it has an effect on you." (Had he perhaps been reading Lacan?) Diana L. Eck (1981) makes a (non-Peircean) distinction between "iconic" and "aniconic" images, which provides the needful reminder that not all worshiped images are endowed with the eyes to look back. On the other hand, many aniconic objects are readily converted into icons through the simple expedient of painting eyes on them. Babb (1981, 387) notes that "even the crudest lithic representations of deities are likely to have eyes," and indeed, the common devotional practice of touching the surface of even aniconic *murti*s with the fingers and then touching one's own eyes can be cited in further support of a formulation of *darshan* as an exchange between worshiper and worshiped.

In line with my general emphasis in this chapter against discursive meaning, I resist theorizing this exchange as communication. Closer to the approach of my Mumbai interlocutors would be a rival model in which the spirit-presence that is one party in the transaction is conceptualized as a subtle emanation that fills the effigy or image. The eyes of both parties are homologized with other orifices that permit the transfer of substances such as food or sexual fluids from one body to another. What passes between them is thus not meaning but energy, or a material "flow." In the anthropology of South Asia there is an established line of inquiry theorizing the construction of personhood through ritual and other transactional relations (see, for example, Marriott 1976; O'Flaherty 1980; Gell 1998, 137–54; and, in a Buddhist context, Gombrich 1966, 23–25). And this line of thought is corroborated in Hindu literature, most notably in Tantric texts that project the operations of the gaze—and, more broadly, of the faculties of sensory perception—as emissions of light energy from the eyes of the perceiving subject (see D. White 2009, especially 151–61). When it comes to my own fieldwork, the connection has been matter-of-factly explained to me in terms of the flow of electricity between terminals. For my consultant in this matter, who lived in a slum environment and was something of an equal-opportunity visitor to the shrines of different creeds, the question of installation or maintenance by a qualified professional—a ritual specialist, Brahmin or otherwise—to ensure that the *murti* was switched "on" did not enter the equation.[20] Nor, indeed, did the question of faith, although there is a pleasing symmetry to the proposition that, in receiving a recognition normally withheld an anonymous subaltern in urban space, a desiring subject effectively refills the vessel through his or her own *darshan* gaze.

"And now, listen carefully," in the words of the *Satcharita* (Dabholkar 1999, 33:151), "to the narration of how the *darshan* of his mere photograph is the same as his actual *darshan*":

152. Balabua Sutar, the [well-known singer of hymns] from Bombay[,] . . . once went to Shirdi for Baba's *darshan*.

153. This was his very first visit. But . . . as soon as they looked at each other, Sai very clearly said to him.

154. "See, I have known him for the last four years!" Balabua[,] naturally, wondered why he was saying so.

155. "Baba has not left Shirdi and even I have seen Shirdi for the first time, today. . . ."

156. As he pondered on it, Bua suddenly remembered that four years ago, he had once made obeisance to Baba's photograph. . . .

158. "I had made obeisance only to the photograph and set eyes on his form, for the first time, today. But Baba recognized me, though I had forgotten all about it, long ago!" he thought.[21]

Given the sheer number of shrines occupied in the present day by effigies of the bearded old man, to attribute to the Baba the ability to gaze out of each local station is to concede panoptical powers that rival those of that other be-whiskered saint who sees you when you're sleeping and knows when you're awake.[22] And, of course, on streets that are traversed by a diversity of inhabitants, subject to diverse dispensations, it is far from everyone that can be expected to heed—*maanna*—Sai Baba as the master. Indeed, the logic of image-as-agent may well offer a corollary: perhaps Sai Baba's gaze is not welcoming of all it surveys.

To be sure, this is an inference that cuts against the basic principle of the saint's theology—namely, that the Lord of All is One (and I am that Lord). Or, to be more precise: the Lord of All is One (and in My form the Lord is effectively recognizable to All—however many rival figurations are out there addressing subsets of All). But to follow through on the connection I drew in chapter 2 between slum housing for humans and shrine housing for gods, I suggest that for many shrine builders and clients whose outposts mark an alternative, slum-based geography, the flip side of the *darshan* image's ideological address is an equally desirable surveillance effect. Boundary zones in the villages that many of the settlers of Mumbai shantytowns come from are made visible by the local stations of divine guardians. In other words, what marks the edge of "our" settlement is a shrine. The sentinel deities posted to them are discrete personalities, marked apart spatially and hierarchically from the *gaondevi* worshiped as the village deity. And rural Muslims are no strangers to this sort of cultic activity, as human or as deified participants; in some Hindu communities of the Deccan, for example, the spirit-horseman who patrols the marches is worshiped as a Muslim hero. (What is important, again, is that he's *our* Muslim hero.)

It might be thought: the old mendicant is himself a footloose migrant from rural Maharashtra; this makes Sai Baba a logical emblem for slum residents to identify with, perhaps new arrivals from Maharashtra in particular. But I doubt even this basic biographical detail comes into play. In the present day, at all events, the Baba's mimetic reach is shallower. On this field of contested urban turf, it seems likely that he is often deployed as a sort of placeholder. The saint is a signpost on the border, occupying a mediatory position: legible enough to gain attention from the public—and the neighbors—but not so aggressive as to throw down the gauntlet. It follows that at certain sites the Sai Baba icon must be functioning as a mask. For a given shrine's client community, the agent of surveillance emplaced in the neighborhood shrine may well be a less encompassing quantity than the Lord of All who adorns the surface; the actual resident would be a site-specific deity, its sovereignty coterminous with the local community that maintains it in its place. At the same time, this *indexical* groundedness in no way invalidates the image's effect as an *icon* on any members of the public who recognize it as the Baba. Visual operations in this scenario can thus be conceptualized along three vectors: forward, into the public; backward, into the client community; and sideways, in relation to other spatial markers.

Epilogue: Return to Shirdi?

My discussion concludes with this Peircean distinction between indexical and iconic modes of signification. I posit the indexical mode as fundamental to a subaltern spatial imaginary that maps urban neighborhoods on the plan of a village. Within this dispensation city blocks are constituted as habitable, not through certification by the paperwork of the state, but by a higher, if unofficial, imprimatur: the concretized presence of protective spirits. Subtly constituted settlers no less than fleshly ones require housing, and stations are built where such squatter gods have asserted their presence.

Yet the same generic quality that enables Sai Baba to cross over among religious traditions also liberates him from such an indexical commitment to specific locations. As I have argued, the real secret of his ubiquity, unbounded by spatial constraints, has to do with the way his form becomes manifest. Here is the return of Vidya Kamat's question from the previous chapter, about the Sai Baba shrine by the stock exchange. Did the Dalal Street shrine draw its power from the saint it enshrined or from the ground it occupied? How has the Sai Baba image's mass-mediated dissemination across the city—a movement contingent on elements of a complex social geography, as sketched in these pages—produced slippages in the symbol's relation to the space it marks, on the one hand, and to the personality it represents, on the other?

To begin by addressing the first question, I propose that the icon's proliferation helps accomplish a transition between two modes of imagining and experiencing the urban street: from a territorialized space that is monitored by resident gods to an iconographic field traversed by a viewing public. Not a public sphere for the exchange of Habermasian rational discourse, what I have in mind is rather a contested canvas on which the claims of diverse constituencies are marked through the display of religious and other kinds of valorized images. In this scenario, what a religious display signifies is a bid for public recognition on behalf of the community that owes it allegiance. Yet in the case of the Sai Baba image the sectarian affiliation is elided, with the claim being made on the simultaneously broader and shallower basis of a demarcation of generically or ecumenically (or even, to deploy the term in its Indian sense, *secularly*) sacred space.

These are both points I have argued in these pages. It will be recalled from the previous chapter, however, that of the initial total of 857 illegal structures counted by the Municipal Corporation, all but 99 had been identified as Hindu—a category within which Sai Baba was subsumed. The tabulation points to a problem that has as much to do with the icon's citation of the formal typology of Hindu images as with the ambiguous antecedents of the person it represents. For iconic *darshan* imagery has been instrumental to the ascendancy of devotional Hinduism across India in this age of mechanical reproduction. It should be asked: Has the dissemination of the Sai Baba image diluted the saturation of public space by the metonyms of a hegemonic Hinduism? Or, conversely, is proliferation in this field of citational effects actually converting the Baba into a stealth vehicle for the reinscription of Hindu norms? Does the fakir's beard mask a Brahmin after all?[23]

I think the answer can cut both ways. A visit to the pilgrimage center at Shirdi confirms the impression that mediation by technologies of mass reproduction has divorced his likeness not only from his history as a Muslim mystic but also from his place of origin and, effectively, from roots in any other place in particular. So detached has the icon become from its locally and historically grounded object that here, under the direction of the Shri Saibaba Sansthan Trust, the cultic center has become thoroughly Brahminized. Priests from Brahmin families, draped in saffron-colored dhotis, preside at four prayer services (*aarati*s) daily. What might once have been recognizable as a *dargah*, a Muslim holy man's tomb, has been built over in the idiom of Hindu temple architecture and now stands reconstituted as a *samadhi mandir*. Outside the complex the town consists in the main of hotels for pilgrims, some quite fancy, and a bazaar whose stock-in-trade takes the form of visual-cultural artifacts—posters, key chains, tote bags, stickers—marked with the figure of Sai Baba. As if to emphasize the indexical disjuncture between these duplicate forms and their place of fictive origin, much of the merchandise is stamped *Made in China*.[24]

On the other hand, why travel as far as Shirdi? The namesake village of Shirgaon offers a salient advantage over the original: its convenient location by an exit off the Mumbai–Pune expressway. At first glance this equally dusty little community would seem to have little to recommend itself as a pilgrimage site beyond the iconic resemblance of its name to *Shirdi*. But it was there that, sure enough, in the course of delivering an Independence Day speech on 15 August 2002, the local politician Prakash Devale was visited by the Baba and commanded to build an exact replica of the *samadhi mandir*. Devale followed up on the vision with a pilgrimage to Shirdi accompanied by an architect, an engineer, a video camera, and measuring equipment. The results are impressive. In iconic terms the copy is exact.

Pakka from the get-go: the only detail that disqualifies this feat of religious entrepreneurship from inclusion in the last chapter's list of illegal religious structures, perhaps as its crowning exhibit, is that there seems to have been nothing illegal about it. (In this regard, sponsorship by a highly placed lawmaker—a Shiv Sena party boss, no less—surely didn't hurt.)[25] Strategically placed on the thoroughfare, it courts a public of passersby; it recasts its rural host community as custodians of a sacred site.

Yet it cannot go unasked: is Shirgaon a real temple or a fake temple?

For the people who flock there to take *darshan* of the Baba as made present in his cross-legged, marble effigy, generating an atmosphere of intense enthusiasm to rival Shirdi itself, there can be little doubt that the site is efficacious. And although I have visited Shirgaon only twice, once in 2003 and again in 2008, it seems to me that the Baba's establishment has brought the locality material blessings, with the busy stalls trading in Sai Baba merchandise signaling the advent of a full-blown, *pakka* bazaar. The hotels so conspicuous at Shirdi are not to be seen at Shirgaon, however, and this absence indicates a strategic side to Devale's revelation. A visit to Shirdi from just about anywhere else reflects a commitment: it's a pilgrimage. A visit to Shirgaon, however, is no more than a detour if you live in either of Maharashtra's two most populous cities and own a car or the means to hire one. Shirgaon invites busy city people to spend only as much time as they can readily spare, and in the process maybe spend some money too.

There is another strategic side to the politician's dream, and it has to do with the way the saint's enshrinement off the highway bypass facilitates the exchange of cash and *prasad*, food-blessings, between well-off visitors and less well-off villagers. How many of the urban Hindus who recognize the Baba in his transplanted icon will even notice that, behind the colorful dhotis and sacred threads that replicate the priestly garb at Shirdi, the *pujaris* at this rival center have been hired from the local population? Should it matter? Given that the Lord of All is One, it seems only right that the ritual care of his image in the splendid new temple should be in the hands of Shirgaon's Muslims and Dalit Buddhists.

4

URBAN TRIBAL

AT HOME IN FILMISTAN

Lord, it's not easy
Getting by in this town—
Heads up! Watch your back!—
That's my Bombay, sweetheart.

MAJROOH SULTANPURI, "Yeh Hai Bombay Meri Jaan"

Take a guess, what's my name?
In the village at the river's edge
There's a tree in my yard dancing in the breeze—
You'll find cool, cool shade.

MAJROOH SULTANPURI, "Boojh Mera Kya Naam Re"

To walk through one of the more *kaccha* slums of Mumbai is to gain an appreciation of bricolage in its material sense. The condition of a settlement where people live in constant fear of displacement is reflected in the composition of its housing: scrap lumber, plastic sheeting, assorted mixed media. In Hindi, this cobbled-together quality is often described as *jugaad*. The term is generally applied to improvised quick fixes to mechanical problems; thus, a *jugaad* technician gets motors, plumbing, wiring, and even computers to work through the application of tape, twine, or pirateware, along with a little elbow grease.[1] But it's not a perfect fit for the French. For, of course, *bricolage*, in the Lévi-Straussian sense, has applications beyond the material. The concept can help explain some of the ways in which subaltern residents of Mumbai use words and other symbols, but there is an important distinction to note. In Lévi-Strauss's scenario, a tightly circumscribed pool of concrete phenomena supplies a "primitive society" with the symbolic building blocks of meaning. By contrast, postcolonial Mumbai engages the subjects who inhabit it with a heteroglossia of stimuli, images, and discourses, circulated across a diversity of spaces, idioms, and media.

Bricolage as practiced by Mumbai subalterns is thus a more diffuse project than one of assimilating such disparate elements within a putatively unitary structure—whether conceived as effective or merely aspirational. At this level, the city's lingua franca, Bombay Hindi (Bambaiya), is a work of bricolage. It establishes a system intelligible to people from diverse regional backgrounds by loading words and forms taken from discrete source languages, chiefly Marathi and English, onto the armature of a stripped-down Hindi. (Hindi's basic grammatical norms have been, if not formally taught to all the city's residents, at least circulated and reiterated through the cinema and other organs of public culture.) Bambaiya—along with other creole vernaculars, perhaps—reflects the twofold needs of a cosmopolitan speech community, providing at once a tight enough matrix to establish diverse interlocutors on common ground and a horizon elastic enough to accommodate expanding registers of reference, citation, and affect.

This chapter is a companion piece to chapter 1, a return to Filmistan Studios. I revisit the space through the eyes of a local guide, who appears here under the pseudonym Vikas. He is a member of the Warli community, which is classified by the Maharashtra State government as one of forty-seven Scheduled Tribes. He lives on a parcel of land that he understands to constitute an ancestral village. At the same time, the space is entirely enclosed within a Bollywood studio. When I first met him in 2002–3, he was in his midthirties; he is a person of strong opinions and our friendship was and is a difficult one.

By this point in the book, it may seem like an obvious thing to propose that Vikas lives in multiple worlds. More precisely, he inhabits distinct geographies, whose effects on sociality and the arrangement of urban space make themselves felt contingent on distinct modes and moments of visual address. And the way he expresses himself in these pages will demonstrate the eclectic range of a freelance bricoleur. Many of his formulations are idiosyncratic. Rather than coining neologisms for general circulation, what he is doing, it could be said, is striking his own, limited editions from unstable amalgams.[2] For all the abstruse content of our conversations, I never found him at a loss for words, even if the mot juste often turned out to be one of his own devising.

A defining moment in my efforts to orient myself to his perspective came in March 2003. Just the other side of the Arabian Sea, the armies of the United States and Britain were completing a massive buildup in preparation for the invasion of Iraq. Indian news media—print and television, English and Hindi—

gave the crisis extensive coverage. Most people I spoke with, from across different walks of life, were against the war, but not all of them. There was some diversity of opinion in the press as well. So it was only to be expected that the invasion would come up as Vikas and I were getting acquainted, and I wasn't really surprised when he told me of his support for the actions of "my people"—the Anglo-American coalition. What surprised me was the way he justified it.

Here's this man Saddam Hussein, he explained. He's the dominant leader in the area. He's been stockpiling oil for some time now. Your Britain and America—historical champions of the rule of law—have been putting pressure on him to export some of the supply to his neighbors, to places that could use it, like India. But in defiance of international law, Saddam sits on his hoard. And now things have come to a head: he's posing a hazard not only to his own people but to the rest of the neighborhood as well. Everyone knows oil is a volatile substance, and with a stash of the size this man has collected, all it would take would be one spark and everything would go up in flames. Now, finally, the English and Americans are stepping in to set things right with their Global War on Terror.

I joined Vikas in argument, only to find that our premises were so far apart as to be irreconcilable. (I since discovered this to be true with respect to most American supporters of the war as well.) But as I thought over his assertions and tried to trace where they came from—and as I got to know more about the conditions of his life—I came to see that he spoke with some authority, not about what was going on over in Iraq, but what was there before my eyes in Mumbai.

The Iraq War story combines a digest of newspaper articles with a projection of the world, or the Middle East at any rate, in the image of a Mumbai shantytown. Vikas has cast Saddam in the role of a key figure in the social organization of modern India. This is the *dada*, or "big brother," the strongman at the head of a local network of patronage and control. To an American observer, or really to anyone familiar with the picture of big-city life given in American movies, the readiest analogue to the "*dada* system," or *dadagiri*, is the Mafia. And indeed in Mumbai the gangster underworld is everyone's go-to example of a social order contested by factions pledged to one or another big brother (recall the identification of the underworld as "the Brotherhood" in chapter 1). But *dadagiri* can also be seen to drive Indian institutions that operate in other, ostensibly more transparent spheres. The political parties that compete for votes in the world's largest democracy; the business houses that jockey for profit; even the NGOs that bid for whatever tax-free funds are left over: from the point of view of someone like Vikas, all these demonstrate the *dadagiri* dynamic in action. In fact, the notion that *dadagiri* is a model that could productively be applied to the analysis of Indian society at large is one that I at once attribute to Vikas and join him in advocating; I believe the move could hold real promise for future scholarship.[3]

Be that as it may, the characterization of the Iraqi dictator as a Mumbai godfather does lead to distortions, of which the richest is the identification of his crime as the hoarding of oil. What Vikas has in mind is kerosene, which is a government-rationed commodity used as fuel for cookstoves and hence a staple of subaltern living. Between its ubiquity and its volatility, it's the origin of many shantytown fires; kerosene is also the weapon of choice when it comes to murderous attacks on riot victims or on inadequately dowered brides. In fact, among the urban poor, kerosene embodies the threat of mass destruction close at hand, and here some reflection is called for on that multivalent concept: terror.

Long before anyone in Washington came up with the notion of a War on Terror, the English word *terrorist* and its Hindi counterpart, *atankwadi,* had become integrated into the speech of ordinary Indian people. This is not only to be attributed to the daily reports of conflict between their government and armed movements in Kashmir and elsewhere. In the contemporary Indian context, where the tactics and also perhaps the agendas of separatist militants have become hard to distinguish from those of the private armies of propertied interests or local party- or caste-based groups, *terrorist* has become extended in public discourse to cover a multitude of actors who challenge the state's monopoly on violence. And in Mumbai, where the 2003 and 2006 bombings that killed hundreds on the streets and commuter trains are attributed to radical Islamist factions working through Muslim mob bosses, it is not surprising that for many like Vikas the categories of *terrorist* and *gangster* should have come to seem interchangeable. In his subaltern milieu, there is no exotic quality to terror; the management of everyday life involves constant negotiation with one *dada* or another, albeit none boasting the notoriety of a Saddam Hussein or Dawood Ibrahim.[4]

Clearly, one thing Vikas has done with the newspaper headlines is to translate them into local or domestic terms. But there is more at work in his creative reuse, for his Iraq War story owes a substantial debt to Bollywood as well. Where a slightly more prosperous person would have drawn on the authoritative images and narratives delivered by the broadcast news, Vikas does largely without television in his daily life, the canvas-and-sheet-metal quarters of his extended family having (at the time of our conversation) no electrical connection. However, as I have mentioned, those quarters do stand inside a film studio, and my interlocutor was, and is, thoroughly familiar with the output of the Mumbai film industry over the past several decades. And while very few others can claim what is in Vikas's case a concomitant knowledge—his insider's perspective on the production process—the commercial cinema is indeed a cultural touchstone for urban subalterns in India. The point that underemployed young men make up a particularly avid audience is borne out by ethnographic studies (see Derné 2000; Dickey 1993), as well as by the strategies of filmmakers.[5] Stock elements of the kind of tough-guy cinema that parallels the Iraq War scenario include muscled heroes and mustached villains, stern ultimatums, and big explosions.

In fact, this cinematically mediated picture of the invasion of Iraq may seem like a perfect illustration of Ashis Nandy's (1998) well-known thesis of "Indian popular cinema as a slum's eye view of politics." But on top of the bricolage of news text, celluloid, and the material circumstances of slum life described thus far, there is a final, somewhat incongruous element to consider. This is Vikas's identification of the Anglo-American forces with the principles of law and justice. More than the official statements of the US and British governments during the buildup to the war—rarely if ever reported uncritically, Indian editorialists on the whole being inclined to define Bush and Blair as the outlaws in the matter—a likely source of support for this idea is again to be found in cinema, although not the domestic one.

On its home turf, Bollywood's keenest competition is probably encountered in the action-movie genre. Indians form a big audience for the kind of internationally marketed productions in which a white hero at least nominally associated with a security or law enforcement agency squares off against an antagonist who plots the disruption of order on a global scale.[6] The paradigm was certainly cited in popular American imaginings of the Iraq War—and never more theatrically than in George W. Bush's uniformed photo op on an aircraft carrier in May 2003. As I have proposed, in Vikas's script Saddam has been cast as a relatively down-to-earth figure: the neighborhood *dada*. And yet if terror, and its agents, feel all too close to home, the seat of justice would appear to be far distant. Somewhat after the manner of the black fans of Tarzan movies in Frantz Fanon's (1965, 144n15) childhood Martinique, Vikas, it seems to me, has enlisted a postcolonial deliverer in the image of James Bond.

The exploits of 007 and his American understudies are not the whole story. Later conversations would establish that Vikas's support of the coalition troops as the guardians of the law reflected a deeply held conviction that the British were to be credited with introducing India to the principles of law and order. In the analysis that follows I will relate this idea (which might seem to owe less to Ian Fleming than to Rudyard Kipling) to a couple of conceptual moves that have important implications for the sort of city Vikas inhabits and the sort of tribe in which he claims membership.

The first move is his demarcation of a sphere of discursive production that encompasses modern Indian legal codes, the textual artifacts of their negotiation and adjudication, the paperwork that mediates the agency of state bureaucracies, and perhaps also the more authoritative registers of journalism—all this under the sign of the English language. This fund of illegible (to him) text and symbol, which produces effects that sustain and advance what I am calling the official spatial order, constitutes a source of power from which Vikas is alienated. The second move is the construction of an idiosyncratic narrative that glosses the current condition of his village-turned-slum and, by extension, of the city of Mumbai and of the Indian nation, in terms of postcolonial decline. In Vikas's version of the Kali Yuga, India has fallen from the golden age of justice and recognition—a regime that saw each constituent population assigned its own legitimate space—that was the British Raj.

A Day in the Life

One day some documentarian friends of mine, shooting footage in Filmistan for a project of their own, brought their video camera behind the scenes and turned the lens on Vikas. This was the real impetus to his collaboration with me, and to our friendship. My star did not fail to make the most of the interview, settling into the role with an air that suggested he had been biding his time on the back lot all those years in anticipation of the screen time that was his due. Working primarily from this record (Shepard 2003), I offer here an account of Vikas's daily routine and self-presentation.

The opening shots show a two-story building with a verandah at one side of a courtyard area. On the other side stands a fairly solid single-story shed; between these two *pakka* structures runs a low row of cabins with the makeshift roofs characteristic of Mumbai shantytowns: sheets of metal and plastic held down with rocks. Just behind these dwellings, beyond the compound's back wall, there can be seen a tall middle-class apartment house, looking almost shiny in its air of prosperity. The yard is traversed by chickens and a few incurious people; the camera passes a sleeping dog on its way to frame a slender man in his thirties standing stiffly in the foreground.

This is Vikas, and the environs shown are the corner of the studio everyone refers to as the Village. The camera's sweep reproduces the perspective from which most people—residents, workers, and visitors—customarily encounter the scene. Occupying its southwest corner, Filmistan's Village is cordoned off by studio buildings that leave open two points of entry. Of these, the left-hand one, approached through the permanent Central Jail set, is the more routinely trafficked path. My friend Sadia's camera did not record the Central Jail on the far left or the little shrine tucked just inside the gate, to which I will devote some attention further on.

The only part of the Village that actually serves filmmakers as a set is the two-story building on the right flank. Both this structure and the yard are interstitial zones. Film crews shoot at the building and set up in the yard as they please, but when the professionals and their gear are not present, both spaces come within the sphere of daily domestic life for the Warli residents. To the extent that these twenty-odd members of an extended family have private dwellings of their own, they are contained in the ramshackle row of cabins. When Vikas voices his right to occupy this corner of Filmistan, he is able to assert his residency within a structure designated by a specific address, and given the generosity of the city's tenancy laws, this is a factor that may have contributed decisively to his continued presence in the studio. But over and above that, his stake extends to membership in a village, with coordinates that are not represented textually but—for those who can recognize them—manifested visually and spatially.

Most of the video follows a standard interview format, with another friend, Ajit, addressing our questions from offscreen. Vikas begins by laying out the history of the settlement at Filmistan. "We," that is to say, the ancestors of the present residents, had been present on the grounds for at least 130 years. At that time, in the late nineteenth century, their village already occupied the spot. Subsequently, the British had entered the scene and caused Filmistan Studios to be built. Filmistan had expanded to encompass the whole village. The British had left at the time of Independence, and the Indian government, into whose custody the studio had fallen, created a "Film Society" to administer it, in charge of which they appointed a man named Jalan. Asked where the village's Warli founders had come from 130 years before, Vikas answers "Thana," going on to explain that "this full area" (*is* full area *jo hai*) from Bombay up to Selvasa and Nagar Haveli had been part of a unified Thana District (compare the region's administrative history as sketched in the next chapter). The "Central Government" had gone on to partition this territory into the units we now know as Selvasa, Thana, Bombay, and so forth. Technically speaking, political boundaries were already in place under the colonial regime, but Vikas's point is clear: what had been in historical times a unified territory called "Thana" populated by Warlis had since become, as the result of political intervention, fragmented, renamed, and reassigned.[7]

One hundred and thirty years ago, the area had suffered a drought, and many of its inhabitants had migrated south in search of work and sustenance.[8] A city of considerable size by that time, Bombay already offered economic opportunities; subsequently, it had acquired the "company factories" that offered yet more inducement for people to move and thus had gradually become transformed into an "international city." But when Ajit presses Vikas on the question of how many Warlis participated in the migration, Vikas resists the proposition:[9]

> Ajit: *How many Warli people came from out there?*
>
> Vikas: *I'm not going to say anything in terms of "how many came"; they were liv-ing here from before. Before, actually all this belonged to the Warli people—Bombay, Thana District. So I'm not going to say that the Warlis actually came from anyplace. They have been living in their own district; they have been coming to their own villages. They didn't come from some other place.*
>
> Ajit: *So this was strictly a Warli village from before?*
>
> Vikas: *This was strictly a Warli village from before.*
>
> Ajit: *In which you people—*
>
> Vikas: *In which we people are Warlis! The deal is, other people came in afterward. For example, Britain came, France came. After that, other people came; the Muslims; after that, all the different kinds of people who are present in Bombay today.*

In Vikas's representations of Filmistan as his patrimony, two aspects of his father's memory loomed large: as the Warlis' tightest link with the film industry (he had worked as the boom operator under a sound engineer) and as their senior, if departed, member. Of the four households (*ghar*) the Filmistan village contains, Vikas's father's widow and their son Vikas constitute one; the others are descended from his father's sisters and include their sons and their wives and children. Vikas does not hesitate to assert that in the eyes of the law (*kanoon ke zariye se*), responsibility for the whole village devolves to him as his father's son, since not only property but also the office of village headman, or *pramukh*, are handed down through the male line.

The interview moves on to a discussion of the parts played by the Village and its villagers in film productions. Vikas explains that since bit players, or "junior artistes," are unionized, they are reluctant to let others appear on camera, and consequently, when his home is used for shooting, he and his fellows are generally to be found on the sidelines. But on occasion they have joined in crowd scenes that needed to be padded.[10] His own longtime ambition was to follow in his father's footsteps in the audio department—ideally, to rise to become a sound engineer. The educational requirements have become more stringent than in his father's time, however, and Vikas finds himself unqualified for consideration.

For future employment prospects he looks to the management of Filmistan Studios, and it is at this point that he introduces a theme that would dominate many future conversations. This is "the case": a legal tussle that occurred years ago, during his childhood, when the studio management moved to have Vikas and his extended family evicted from "their home and their place" (*ghar aur jagah*) inside Filmistan. As he makes plain, the Warlis have had their day in court, and since by his reasoning the lawsuit—and the uncertainty it generated—prevented him from getting an education, he has a moral claim on Filmistan for support. The only thing holding him back, it seems, is getting them to recognize that claim.

In the meantime, he states rather self-importantly, he keeps busy consulting with lawyers on the case or discussing with the other villagers (*gaon ke log*) how to "accomplish the advancement of our [Warli] community." (The picture I subsequently put together of his routine would have made more room for the movies and for religious observances, and not much for lawyers.) And after dinner he studies the papers. He reads the *Navbharat Times*, a Hindi-language daily whose content is largely translated from the English of the Times Group's flagship, the *Times of India*.

But he's consuming stale news, remarks Ajit.

Vikas: *Many people tell me: I don't get why you wait till night to read the newspaper. And what I've said is: Look, bhai, I'm no James Bond. I'm one Indian citizen. [Main ek Hindustani nagarik hoon.] I'm not going to be able to fly in like James Bond to wherever . . . and save anyone. The only thing I can do is try and say: Bhai, what's going on over there shouldn't be*

happening. . . . That's what I can say as a citizen. But to go flying already
the way James Bond does, to just take off and get somewhere the way James
Bond does, to take off and get there the way Superman does, and stop it—I
can't do that. I'm a human being, not some kind of angel [farishta]. . . . I've
got no wings.

What he is keenest on is information that might have something to do with his
legal case. Also important is news that indicates which members of society are
following the wrong path and which course will move society forward. Interestingly, the word he uses here for "society," *samaj,* can denote Indian society as a
whole but might equally plausibly in this context be confined to the Warli tribal
community. It will develop that the distinction tends to get elided in Vikas's
discussion of matters pertaining to collective identity, the law, and the national
space. Also, given his expansive idea of the lawsuit's ramifications, questions
about polity have a way of becoming collapsed into questions about the case.

The video concludes with a statement about the particularity of the Warli
community and his own particularity within it as a modern Warli.

Vikas: *Look, what's special about the Warlis is that . . . just as every community*
has its method of farming, we Warlis have got our own way of farming. Just
as in the Indian tradition we honor the arts of song and dance . . . , in the
same way among us Warlis we have our own song and dance; for example,
we dance to the tarpa.[11] *And on top of that, just as different people pray to*
their own gods and have their own forms of worship, we—

Ajit: *So how would you talk about this: There are you Warli people who have*
been here at this spot at Filmistan for the past 130 years. And then there are
all the other Warlis in other places who have been leading very different
lives from you. How would you describe the difference?

Vikas: *Look, as far as we're concerned, our position is: at this time, we're in*
Filmistan Studios. So for one thing, we understand that we're in the mod-
ern style, so, bhai, that means there are certain kinds of rules that apply to
us. On account of the film industry, on account of the government, we've
become aware of this. But as far as those people who live on the outside are
concerned, they're not perfectly aware of the rules. . . . On the other hand,
take me—I live in the studio, and there's this case that's come down, and
as far as that's concerned I know perfectly under what laws I can claim my
rights, under what laws I have no rights and can't make any claim—I'm

> *perfectly aware of all this, but as far as this kind of thing is concerned, all those Warli people on the outside, they haven't got a clue.*

Submission to the law as the defining characteristic of a modern subjectivity, both among tribals and within the larger collectivity of Indians, was one of the themes I encouraged Vikas to expand on over the course of further fieldwork. He and I struck up a somewhat cranky rapport. We met regularly at Filmistan and other spots in Goregaon. We talked about the law and the British regime and Indian politics. We talked about temples and movies. We talked about what he saw in his dreams. I'm sorry to say I often found what he told me so strange as to be downright aggravating, and there were conversations we had, some in public parks, that descended into shouting matches. We must have put on quite a show for the retirees and young couples of the neighborhood as we nattered at each other in substandard Hindi from either end of a park bench.

For his part Vikas, I learned, shared his information because I had stepped into his frame of reference, with my digital voice recorder and Fulbright funding "from the US government," in the role of an international man of mystery. And this was one of the things we argued about. The more I protested, or offered rationalizations of the ethnographic method, the more I confirmed his suspicions about the nature of our work together. As I kept telling him, in spite of my apparent ability to fly here and there, my bankrolling by a superpower that had declared a War on Terror, and my occasional need to report downtown to the US Educational Service in India—a grim-looking office entered through a gauntlet of sandbags and heavily armed cops—I was no James Bond either.

Sixty years earlier, K. J. Save, the pioneering ethnographer of the Warli community, had lamented the chariness of his Warli informants, who had stonewalled his inquiries with such replies as "Why do you want to know the name of the 'jungli' man?" Vikas's contemporary attitude stands in sharp contrast with this old-time mistrust of the colonial state—the *sarkar*—its clients among the landlords and the estate agents, and perhaps the practice of record-taking itself: "You will take down all that we tell you and show it to the Sarkar. . . . We shall be caught in the writing" (Save 1945, 243–44). In his capacity as Special Officer for the Protection of the Aboriginal and Hill Tribes, Save embodied the authority of the English (and American) legal edifice that Vikas ascribed, via mediation by the *Navbharat Times* and action cinema, to me. The rural Warlis of Save's day, lacking access to such modern channels, had shunned the state's emissary. My friend, however, deliberately entered the role of informant, in much the same spirit in which he had addressed the camera lens, and with a desire that went beyond the level of instrumentalist purpose.

He had, and has, the sense that my translation of his self-representations into the prestigious registers of English prose could endow his person with agency—or at least with legibility or visibility—within the matrix of the law and its associated archives.[12] And in principle I can see now that there was nothing intrinsically grandiose or fantastic about this conflation of ethnography with surveillance. As stated on film, his point was that the aspiration for citizenship—understood as his recognized occupancy of a space under the jurisdiction of "modern rules" (to quote his own words)—is precisely what differentiates him from the rural Warlis, who are indeed by contrast with him *jangli*, or "wild," people. The Hindi word neatly maps the condition of barbarism onto habitation of the natural space of the forest: his uncouth fellows, beyond the pale, are not merely unlettered but illegible.

Ghosts of Filmistan: Studio Histories

"Wherever a village is founded," the old Kolaba District Gazetteer notes, "it is customary to establish a village deity as the guardian of the village" (*Gazetteer of Bombay Presidency* 1964, vol. 11 [1883], 164). To learn about a village temple is to learn about the village, and it will be recalled from chapter 1 that there are two sites on the Filmistan grounds that appear to be sacred spaces. One is prominently located in a garden adjacent to the main office building. It is well appointed and permanent looking—*pakka*—although its status as an *asli mandir*, a "real" or efficacious temple, is open to some question. The second is small and *kaccha* by comparison, an installation about the size of a public mailbox at the main entryway to the Village. The small shrine houses the tiger god Waghoba, the sentinel deity that patrols the boundary. Who, then, is to be named as Waghoba's boss—the sovereign deity that commands the center?

The identification can be made on the basis of sacred geography. In the settlements of Warlis and other tribal and lower-caste groups across the Deccan, it is a goddess site that typically provides the community with a common locus of cultic attention (as distinct from the worship of personal and household deities, who are seated within discrete households). Such morphological features as may be inferred from several people's description of the original display at the larger temple as "just some rocks" also bear out the inference that the site used to be occupied by a *gaondevi*, a village goddess.[13]

"The shrine of any mother-goddess without an *identificatio brahmanica* is outside the village," notes D. D. Kosambi (1962, 91–92). "Occasionally, and with her special permission, a representative stone may be brought into some temple inside the village to facilitate service during the rains. . . . Otherwise, finding the shrine in the middle of a town means that the place has grown from economic causes while the cult-spot remained unchanged." What Vikas told me of his village's shape—and its vicissitudes—actually cuts against this norm (or perhaps Kosambi's "economic causes" clause could be brought in here for some explanatory heavy lifting). For according to his account, the Warli settlement had formerly been located in the area of the big studio temple, which had indeed marked the seat of the *gaondevi*. (The small, secondary temple, on the present-day Village's outskirts, would still have been positioned on the old settlement's threshold—albeit on the other side.) The relocation of the village from its old position athwart the approach to Filmistan Studios, with the office building to one side and sound stages to the other, likely occurred at the time the facilities were first expanded, between 1958 and 1962, or possibly as early as the studio's groundbreaking in the early 1940s.[14]

Recall how Vikas had attributed Filmistan's founding to "the British," who took charge of the land in his grandfather's day and repurposed it for film production. He believes that after India gained its independence in 1947, control over the studio and its grounds passed into the hands of the Indian government, which in turn entrusted it to a businessman, Jalan. It is not hard to reconcile this subaltern history with a more official transcript of events. What is peculiar is the role Vikas assigns to the state—whether colonial or independent—as a principal in these transactions, and I think this emphasis can be attributed to two factors. The first is the salience of 1947 as a watershed moment in popular narratives of the times. (The trope is disseminated in public-cultural, as well as official, discourses.) The second is my interlocutor's regard for the rule of law as it pertains, specifically, to the apportionment of the nation's territory among its constituent communities. In subsequent conversations with Vikas, it emerged that for him the primary project of the law was precisely that: to recognize discrete communities in their own spaces. This was a project for which the British administration had laid down defining precedents. The problem was, and is, that its corrupt Indian successors have been lax in enforcing them.[15]

Be that as it may, the particulars of the studio's establishment in Goregaon, as documented by historians and journalists and wryly witnessed by the Urdu writer Saadat Hasan Manto in his screenwriting days, run like this. Filmistan was founded in 1942 by a cadre of film industry professionals who broke away from what was at the time the Indian cinema's premier outfit, Bombay Talkies. Led by that studio's general manager, Rai Bahadur Chunilal, the seceding team had made up one of its two resident production units.[16] As an in-house writer, Manto (1998, 109, 137) used to commute every morning to Goregaon "from Bombay," a distance of twenty miles the train took an hour to cover. After Independence not only Hindustan but also Filmistan changed masters, with the studio's purchase from Rai Bahadur Chunilal by Tolaram Jalan coming to pass in 1959.[17] Jalan's family, headed by his widow, operates the facility to this day.

Interestingly, around the same time that he acquired Filmistan, Tolaram Jalan also took over Bombay Talkies, only to have the senior concern shut down. And if the case at Filmistan is that the studio has subsumed the village whose territory it took over—stealing its heart, as it were, by appropriating its temple—Bombay Talkies presents the inverse case: namely, the studio's occultation from the landscape. There, the facilities have been stripped and the premises rented out to manufacturers, with the cavernous stage buildings subdivided among a multitude of small workshops. Of the buildings' old purpose, the present-day occupants have left nary a trace.[18]

Yet maps of the Mumbai suburbs will still show a corner of Malad, just north of Goregaon, labeled "Bombay Talkies." It is managed to this day by the Jalan family. For their part, neighborhood people with whom I spoke mentioned the old studio's name with a sense of local pride. The *Telegraph* printed a detailed conversation with an elderly contractor, Syeed Pappu, who remembered Tolaram Jalan as "Jalaram Tolaram" and his studio as a lush spot full of trees and men on horseback (presumably actors from historical movies). At the end of the interview, he added: "Some people say Jalaram Tolaram's ghost haunts this place. He comes on a horseback [*sic*] during the night. He cannot get over Bombay Talkies still" (Bhattacharya 2003).

There is a suggestive affinity between the facility's old business of producing visual traces and the lingering presence there of the studio's master and destroyer.[19] But I relay the story of Jalaram Tolaram because of a more explicit link with the lived geography of Filmistan. For Filmistan is also a space populated by spirit-presences, and along with the gods there are ghosts. According to my contact Azad, Stage Number Four was haunted by a foreign technician—likely a member of the German cadre who had come to India to work at Bombay Talkies in the early days—who had fallen to his death from the rafters. The violence of his demise and his separation from his native place, suggestive of both the "inadequate or incomplete funeral rites" and the "untimely . . . death of a person who dies with intense unfulfilled desires" (Stanley 1988, 28), are the elements that make this tale a persuasive Maharashtrian ghost story.

Ghosts (*bhut*), like demons (*shaitan*), are considered to circulate through the air, on occasion seizing the chance to house themselves in a human body that has become opened up through some sort of vulnerable condition. One way to tame, or contain, a wandering spirit is to give it recognition in its proper place—grounding it, like a live current, at a dedicated terminal, a space marked ritually and visually as such. What this means is that the perception by certain people—or by certain groups of people—of specific spots as haunted can somewhat counterintuitively be indexed to the very absence at those spots of the features marking the presence of spirits that have been properly installed.[20] The ghosts of Bombay Talkies and Filmistan are thus to be classified among other site-specific cultural phenomena as part of a distinct way of organizing space. In this model, spatial coordinates are set not by measurements of distance or abstract value but by qualities, for example, auspiciousness or inauspiciousness, that are held to be immanent at concrete sites, that are perceived as the indices of resident spirits, and that engage affective relations among members of the communities that inhabit and negotiate spaces so organized.[21] This is the stratum I have been discussing in this book under the label of sacred space.

In their invisibility and their narratively mediated emergence from out of studio history, the ghosts serve as useful reminders that not all the signposts of this spirit-geography are made visible in material form (except through bodily possession, a mode I discuss later in this chapter). Nor are they necessarily integrated within spatial relations specific to villages. That being said, however, the other examples I can identify at Filmistan are indeed traces, elided by the studio to varying degrees, of the Warli settlement. Some mark the present-day landscape only as memories: the tamarind and mango trees that used to stand over the approaches in two directions. And some amount to something more: two of the three village wells, rendered inaccessible since the studio's early years but still exerting effects across the overbuilt space. When a *Times of India* journalist investigated the continued popularity that Filmistan's aging and comparatively small facilities enjoy among Bollywood producers, she discovered "a superstition that Stages 3 and 4 . . . are lucky. 'Directors like Karan Johar and Inder Kumar may use locations around the world, but they shoot at least one shift at Filmistan because they believe it is fortunate for them,' says . . . the manager" (Iyer 2006). An interview with the manager's boss, Mrs. Jalan, reveals the reason: "Stages 3 and 4 have actually been built over wells, and this is probably why this place is so lucky. According to the shastras [Hindu scriptures], flowing water is considered to be very lucky" (Iyer 2006).[22]

This encroachment was completed between 1958 and 1962, well before Vikas was born.[23] As I observed above, it was also during this phase of Filmistan's development that the Warlis' original homes were most likely displaced from around the goddess temple. Let it be stressed, however, that physical houses— namely, shelters in which families store their possessions and inside of which they can sleep—are not the most important components of a Warli village. By itself, either at the old location or the current one, the Filmistan Warlis' meager housing could be dismissed as a bit of largesse allocated by the studio to Vikas's father in his capacities as an employee and the patriarch of a populous clan. What makes it the residential quarters of a community is its association with the village's other component units. There are the wells, the trees at the boundaries, and zones of impurity or conventional invisibility such as those reserved for the disposal of refuse or excrement. Above all, there are the spaces consecrated to resident deities.

Forest Hamlet to Urban Village

What did the settlement look like before the construction of Filmistan Studios? In what sense was it a "real" Warli village? Until 1957 Goregaon was not even part of the municipality; as a heavily wooded tract in the middle of Salsette, it was conventionally associated with Thana rather than Bombay. In describing the landscape, Vikas and my other interlocutors in Hindi and English habitually used the word "jungle" (*jangal*). Before Filmistan's establishment, the land it now occupies was part of an estate or plantation (*wadi*) belonging to a landowner named Maya Shankar Thakkar. What would eventually grow, or rather atrophy, into the peculiar show village of my interest was a *pada*, a tribal hamlet, adjoining the cultivated part of the property. Vikas's grandfather, Sukur, worked as a laborer on Thakkar's farm, and it seems likely that his kinsmen in the *pada* would have done so also. Such an arrangement was typical of the region in this period, with the Warli *pada*s that were scattered throughout the woodlands often being brought into relations of dependency with the capitalists who were developing parcels of land up and down the road to Thana, generally with the purpose of marketing cash crops such as fruit.[24]

Farther north, in the Thana subdistrict of Talasari, the Communist activist Godavari Parulekar was at this time helping to organize and lead Warli farm laborers in resisting the worst abuses of the plantation system. In her memoirs of that struggle, *Adivasis Revolt*, she defines a *pada* as a collection of ten to fifteen huts, with a complete Warli village comprising five to fifteen such *pada*s, spaced from half a mile to three miles apart from each other (Parulekar 1975, 12). Yet through the course of my own fieldwork in wooded parts of suburban Mumbai,

I was hardly aware of this broader rubric of *village* as an operative unit of social organization. For my Warli interlocutors, the primary referent of social and spatial affiliation remained at the *pada* level. The one instance I witnessed of a village identity being articulated through practice took the form of a religious observance. In October, Warlis celebrate a festive Gaondevi Puja, during which the residents of distinct localities collect at central goddess sites. The sovereignty of the *gaondevi* I visited at a forest shrine encompassed many, if not all, of the *pada*s in the Goregaon-Borivali area. I will have more to say about this in chapter 6; the point to mark here is that this invocation of cross-*pada* solidarity is the ritual exception, not the quotidian rule.

To understand this shift in the meaning of *pada*—from the outpost of a geographically diffuse village to something like the "tribal quarter" of a community populated by caste Hindus and others—the obvious step is to contextualize it within the history of Mumbai's northward expansion. In the area now known as the outer suburbs, the phenomenon reflects the density, diversity, and intensity of nontribal settlement, which accelerated in the years following Independence and became a full-blown process of urbanization in the 1970s. Yet the outlines of the shift can be traced back to the mid-nineteenth century, to the economic penetration that followed the construction of the Bombay–Thana rail line through the forest—indeed, to the very conditions of exploitation Parulekar describes in her book. The dissolution of the Warli village unit began whenever *pada*s enfolded within the colonial economy found themselves subordinated to larger social formations by relations of capitalist exchange, feudal clientelism, or both.[25]

The constrained circumstances under which the *pada* of Vikas's grandfather Sukur struggled into the 1940s on a portion of Thakkar's holdings can be situated within this sort of settlement pattern.[26] Of course, it was only after control had passed to Filmistan that the enclave acquired its eccentric character as a space redefined by other people's ideas of what a village should look like. Importantly, the deal from which this singular fate ensued was not an outright sale. In 1942 or 1943 Thakkar signed the plot to be developed as Filmistan over to Rai Bahadur Chunilal and his team for the duration of a ninety-nine-year lease. Most of Goregaon was still covered with jungle; real estate values across the area were, in the words of Bal Samant, a local lawyer familiar with some details of Vikas's case, still "worthless." When Vikas's father, Buddhaji, found a job positioning the boom for Filmistan's soundman J. B. Jagtap, the studio recognized the local lad as its "servant," according to Samant, and it was as such that he gained the informal right to keep a shelter as he liked on the property. Apparently, this commitment was not extended to his fellow Warlis, who had not secured such positions of service to the new masters.[27]

Vikas's narrative stayed consistent over multiple tellings, although some parts of his chronology remain fuzzy. He painted an appealing picture of the hamlet in the heyday of its symbiosis with the studio—that is, before he had himself been born. His father's cabin had been partitioned into a row of four chambers: the first for Buddhaji and his siblings; the second for their father, Sukur, and presumably their mother; the third reserved as a temple for the household gods; and the fourth set aside for the storage of firewood. Counterposed with the *pada*'s central temple was the Waghoba shrine, which had marked the southwestern quarter since the 1930s, when Sukur had installed the sacred stone he had brought there from his natal village. And Vikas also spoke of yet another temple, one that had stood at the foot of a banyan tree until 1978, when a storm knocked the tree onto it. This fourth sacred site had also housed a collection of rocks, some of which his father salvaged and brought into the new structure into which his family had been moved by that date.[28]

The list of special trees that helped define the village space did not end with tamarind, mango, and banyan. There had also been cashew trees to supply the residents with that much-remarked staple of tribal life, toddy. And if Filmistan's Warli villagers were apparently not alone in their enjoyment of this produce, neither was Vikas in his nostalgia for the sort of lush Indian backcountry idyll within which toddy consumption is an established trope. His statement that the liquor had flowed freely among the studio's in-house staff, crew, and talent was corroborated in the reminiscences of others. And it echoes in many of the village-based dance numbers featured in the Bombay cinema of the period, in which the formulaic evocation of a state of gay abandon—*masti*—had acquired a tribal signature, much in the same way that affective modes such as "soul" or "natural rhythm" were racialized as qualities essential to African Americans in Hollywood musicals.

Alongside Buddhaji's household, several other families had been based in the *pada* into the Filmistan years, but in time they left for elsewhere in Goregaon. Those who stayed amounted to an extended family centered on Buddhaji and his siblings: three sisters and one brother. Buddhaji and the sisters married and had children, all four sets of whom settled at Filmistan. In 2003 the community included children born to Vikas's cousins and counted about twenty members, with some individuals moving between their family homes and alternative dwellings beyond the compound. Within this group, Buddhaji's status as the favored client of the film studio would have been complemented by his position as Sukur's only male child to have married, stayed put, and raised progeny.

In 1969 Filmistan ceased to be a studio that produced films under its own banner. With the exception of a permanent skeleton crew, the in-house technicians and staff were released to seek employment on a shoot-by-shoot basis, as they do today. It is to be supposed that Buddhaji was able to continue in the industry, but whether or not the restructuring threatened his standing at the studio, it boded ill for Filmistan's viability as a business. A reluctant Tolaram Jalan was persuaded by his wife, then working as the studio's manager, to invest the funds to keep it competitive as a production facility. According to one report, she induced him to "sanction her Rs. 2 lakh [200,000] to infuse life back into the crumbling walls. Permanent structures like a police station, a jail, a village and a garden were created" (Iyer 2006). It was thus, in the 1970s, that the displaced housing of Sukur's *pada* ended up as one wing of what was reconstituted as a village set. The site was duly entered on the studio's roster of lots, slotted in after the stages and several other permanent sets with the official designation Number Eleven.

Almost to the end of the 1970s, ownership of the land itself was retained by the heirs of Maya Shankar Thakkar. On 6 August 1979, they sold the plot to Dipak Mahendra More and Dilip Mahendra More of Deodar Properties Ltd.[29] Vikas referred to the new owners as "More" and considered "him" to be the maternal nephew of Thakkar. He also held the strong conviction that More was a venal, *dada*-like figure, whose motive was (and continues to be) to cut a deal with a builder and have the studio razed for a housing development. I have no further information on either of these points, although I have no doubt that such a deal could be lucrative. Setting aside these particulars, however, the underlying reason why this transaction from 1979 has inspired such ongoing foreboding is clear: it was in this period that the development of Goregaon real estate got under way in earnest. To be sure, the party in the most direct position to threaten the Warli settlement was not the land's actual owner but the holder of the ninety-nine-year lease on it, Filmistan Studios itself. Yet given this context of rapid escalation in property values, it seems likely that negotiations over the sale did provoke, in one way or another, the studio management to take the step that would stand in Vikas's mind as a defining crisis.[30]

Sometime in 1978, Filmistan served the studio Warlis with a notice of eviction. It is uncertain whether the action was at this stage a legal matter, formally speaking, as opposed to a peremptory gesture lent authority by official-looking paperwork. Whichever the case, Vikas's father was not daunted. He sought legal assistance, probably through the good offices of his film industry patrons. Buddhaji and his little clan contested the studio's right to evict, took the sahibs to court, and carried the day.

This is the version told by the son, who was seven years old at the time. Bal Samant, the lawyer who inherited the practice consulted by the Warlis, told me the case had actually been dismissed because the studio's representatives had failed to appear. Be that as it may, for Vikas the decision was a famous victory— and something more. It was an official recognition of his *pada*'s right to the specific space it occupied, referring back to precedents set before the filmmakers' arrival on the grounds "at the time of Independence." And by extension it was also a vindication of the Warli community as a whole—a recognition of the Warlis' historical title to all the lands they inhabited under the panoptical gaze of the British Raj. For recall that in Vikas's mind, it was the colonial administration that had imposed the law over Indian space in the first place. In fact, one of his more eccentric opinions involved a large group of other *adivasis*, people who were facing the threat of displacement from their homes in the forest on Goregaon's borders. (This is the constituency with which chapter 6 is concerned.) Vikas contrasted their entanglements with state authority with his own, as he thought of it, legally validated position. To him, the apparent lack of documentation certifying those other Warlis' presence in the forest meant that they must have migrated there after the crucial date of 1947—independence from Britain. The area was thus, by his definition, not legitimate tribal territory.

Pakka-fication

"No, I don't allow anyone to stay here," was the comment of the general manager of Filmistan Studios when I had finally steered the interview around to what I was really interested in—namely, the story of Vikas and his fellow villagers. I found several other ways to ask the question before satisfying myself that his position was that the studio's resident community of tribals simply did not exist. It seemed a step beyond the casual marginalization of the settlement I had encountered at the Filmistan office during my first visit to the studio, as described in chapter 1: "They are nothing. They are little people. Why don't you talk to . . . the people who are making the films?" Yet then again, the statement did stop short of an outright erasure, one implication of the absence of authorized tenants being the possibility of unauthorized ones.

The tribal presence at the studio surfaced at one other point in the interview, albeit obliquely. When I commented on the existence of temples on the grounds, the manager confined his remarks to the larger one by the entrance. Yes, it was a working temple; yes, people did worship there, as their consciences stirred them; yes, it was also convenient to film there when a script called for a *puja* sequence. And the temple had indeed occupied the site from the time of the studio's establishment. But it had long been an eyesore, even as it commanded people's devotion: an unsightly pile had framed a crude display consisting of nothing more than a number of rocks. The manager had seen it fit to clean up this heap, erecting a polished-stone structure with pillars, a Maharashtrian-style tiled roof, and a floor raised on a stepped platform. The rocks were replaced with a naturalistic, polychromed statue, and the whole was dedicated, with the prescribed Brahminical ritual of installation (*pratishtha*), in 1998—an event commemorated by a plaque on one of the pillars.

When I reached the Jalan matriarch on the telephone, she echoed her employee in professing ignorance of the presence of tenants on the grounds. And she spoke with similar pride of the upgraded temple, assigning the key role in its reconstruction to herself. It is hardly surprising that each should claim credit for what can be seen as a highly conventional, even definitive, act of charity: the endowment or expansion of a place of worship. But it must be noted that the photogenic new structure has not, through raising its profile, actually reconstituted the site as an authorized Hindu temple. No administrative body for it has been registered as a trust with the state, nor is there any *pujari*, Brahmin or otherwise, to officiate at rituals.

Relocating the example, however, within the alternative category examined in chapter 2, that of "illegal religious structures," makes it easier to see that the refurbished shrine's fortunes have nevertheless followed an established pattern. Let's call the pattern "*pakka*-fication." This is the makeover of a *kaccha*, makeshift-looking structure—a contingent element of the environment from which it emerges—into something progressively more defined, solid, and independent. Recall that the *pakka* quality of a religious structure does not only record patronage and the investment of capital. It also indexes a degree of permanence to the claim the temple makes to its space as an occupant and, more provocatively, the legibility of that claim as a visual signal. One could say that from a mark *of* the landscape, such a structure moves to being a mark *on* the landscape. The cleaner lines, brighter colors, and sharper contours shift it into a different visual register and transform it into a different kind of display, with corresponding implications for the sociology of its effects as a signifier and the theology of its function as a place of contact with God.

Pakka-fication, then, is to be glossed as a process not of renovation or restoration but rather of development, in the sense of what a real estate developer does in gentrifying a neighborhood. The gentrification scenario seems particularly appropriate to the case of Filmistan, where the development of the site has been bankrolled and executed by interests external to the temple's original cult community—namely, by the studio management. This sort of appropriation is generally not evident on the streets, where capital improvements tend to be introduced by the shrine operators themselves. But it is a characteristic method used by Hindu nationalists in proselytizing among lower-caste or tribal communities under the banner of *ghar wapsi*, or "return home" (that is, to the Hindu fold).[31] The *pakka*-fication of a shrine reframes what it enshrines and, in so doing, transforms it. From a symptom of spirit-presence recognizable to a bounded constituency of local initiates, the *murti* moves to an image made meaningful, and potentially powerful, through visual codes legible to the public at large.

And along with this conversion at the level of semiotic form, does not a local, non-Sanskritic site subjected to modernization in this way also undergo a more literal conversion? Who, let's ask, is the god now in residence at this upscale temple development on the grounds of Filmistan Studios? The display includes an assortment of icons, including a print of Krishna, plaques of Durga and Ganesh, and a Shiva *linga*. But the central *murti* is a colored stone statue, executed in the standard style of idealized realism, depicting a slender, dhoti-clad youth with three heads and six arms. The heads form the *trimurti*, or triad of Brahma, Vishnu, and Shiva. This is the conventional depiction of the god Dattatreya, whose cult is popular in Maharashtra and parts of Karnataka and Gujarat and largely obscure elsewhere, not least in the English-language literature.[32] And yet to identify the site's new occupant as Dattatreya is just to get started answering the question.

For one thing, the protean tendency indicated by the god's physical attributes—the Apollonian figure with its Dionysian members—is complemented by a certain slippery or amorphous quality. In an essay written with Charles Pain, Eleanor Zelliot introduces Dattatreya as "clearly the ultimate syncretistic god, an *avatār* (incarnation) of Brahma, Vishnu, and Shiva" (Pain and Zelliot 1988, 95), while specifying elsewhere in the same volume that the contemporary worship community is "urban and Brahman-dominated" (Zelliot 1988, xvii). This apparent delimitation of the cult in terms of geography and social constituency can actually be read as a statement of its translocal scope, since metropolitan culture and Brahmins alike are distributed across Maharashtra. Without much of a stretch, one way to define the domain Zelliot indicates would be *middle class*; another might be *modern*. And while the cult has a long history, with a sixteenth-century revival spurred by the composition in Marathi of the *Gurucharitra*, which put an orthodox Brahminical stamp on the norms of Datta worship (Lubin 2001, 86; see also Raeside 1982, 498), the god's other two important praise texts are both relatively recent, datable to the nineteenth century (Pain and Zelliot 1988, 106).

The mythology of Dattatreya supports a view of the god's imprint on the landscape as pervasive but not deeply rooted. Peripatetic within set bounds, in the guise of an ascetic he traces a daily circuit inscriptive of a sacralized Maharashtra: he is said to take his morning bath at Panchaleshwar in the central region, meditate at Girnar off in Gujarat to the west, beg for alms at Kolhapur in the south, and retire for the night at Mahur in the northeast. A key feature of this itinerary, Zelliot points out, is that although they are celebrated pilgrimage centers, these sites are not principally sacred to Dattatreya. Rather, they are historical bases of goddess worship (Pain and Zelliot 1988, 96). Datta thus emerges as a supplemental presence, bestowing a *pakka* gloss on sites already consecrated to deities with a claim of autochthony.

One more observation of Zelliot's sheds light on this deity's signature transferability. "Not only is he three gods in one, he is the divine archetypal guru, reincarnating himself as guru time after time. He . . . combines three figures highly revered in Hinduism: the *sannyāsī*, the guru, and the *avatār*" (Pain and Zelliot 1988, 98). If this (doubly?) three-faced god has shown a remarkable catholicity in surfacing at sites across Maharashtra, the theological mechanism by which Datta's predominantly Brahmin sponsors have rededicated the ground in his image has been the appropriation of locally seated personas as his incarnations. And alongside autochthonous deities, these include historical ascetics. Thus, the main pilgrimage center of the contemporary Maharashtrian cult is located just across the Karnataka border at Gangapur, the resting place of the holy man Narasimha Saraswati, whom the *Gurucharitra* celebrates as an avatar (see Raeside 1982, 498, 498n73). And while that is an instance of a saint from the fifteenth century being claimed through a text from the sixteenth, it is telling that the dates of many other historical Datta avatars can be placed within the modern period. Yet more telling is the fact that Maharashtrian Hindus recognize several Muslim holy men as avatars of Datta (Deák 2005; Pain and Zelliot 1988, 98). The most notable of these is—surprise!—Sai Baba of Shirdi. As I argued in the previous chapter, he is Mumbai's principal example of a masklike icon, ubiquitous by virtue of his semiotic shallowness.

My argument about Filmistan advances with an identification of Dattatreya as the sort of deity that flourishes under conditions contributing to Hindu modernity. These include urbanization, Sanskritization—or, to be precise in this case, an accretion of regional cultural prestige through literary treatment in Marathi—and the translocal circulation of text and image accelerated by technologies of mass reproduction. The point is supported by G. S. Ghurye's (1962, 125–26, 218) tabulation of the god's temples in Pune. Of the eleven sites he counted in 1956, only one had existed at the beginning of the nineteenth century. For his part, Pain comments that "[m]ost of the Datta temples in Pune were built shortly after the turn of the [twentieth] century" (Pain and Zelliot 1988, 102).[33] At the visual level, I suggest that the codes that dictate the representation of the deity, combining as they do eclectic, mimetically dense elements within a naturalistic idiom, are exemplary of the kind of icon favored by replication through the characteristic modern processes—lithographic printing, resin casting—that have come to mediate devotional worship across India.[34]

In the context of the present day, the story of the Filmistan temple is not anomalous. *Pakka*-fication in a modern visual-cultural idiom is commonplace wherever there are patrons to invest the money. And it is easy to understand the sensitivity to appearances that is likely to have motivated the studio management, for the site's central location makes it impossible for visitors to overlook. On the one hand, the down-market look of the old Warli display must have signaled "primitive" and "backward"; on the other hand, simply to have torn it down would have looked impious, and not only to the local people but to industry professionals as well. Neither precedent nor logic, however, should be allowed to obscure the invasive character of this usurpation of space.

Dattatreya's installation has moved the site from a subaltern form of localized folk-Hindu practice to a translocal, Brahmin-dominated cult well integrated within metropolitan Hinduism. But that is to state matters conservatively. *Adivasi* activists and their political allies would advance a sharper formulation: that it cements a hostile takeover by Hindus of a tribal site that was never Hindu to begin with.[35] Moreover, the conversion of this temple is not merely symbolic of Filmistan's colonization of the Warli village. Or rather, it is not merely symbolic in an illustrative sense; it is powerfully symbolic at an ideological level, for it is the pivot of a project of spatial reconfiguration. It is there that the immanent deity around whose presence the Warlis organized their village has been paved over, displaced by a Hindu icon whose integration within prevailing codes of visual culture annexes the site to an alternative visual-spatial regime. This is the regime of spectacularized space within which the studio's sets and façades function simultaneously as components and images. I will have more to say about this cinematically mediated register further on. What needs to be asked all over again about the Filmistan temple is whether it still operates as a sacred site—that is, whether it is still felt to seat some sort of god—and if so, which god, and by which people among the diverse groups that traverse the studio?

Several non-Warli workers, including a trio of Dalit sweepers and a light boy, Nilesh from chapter 1, told me they took *darshan* at the secondary temple at Filmistan, the unequivocally tribal tiger shrine marking the boundary of the current Warli settlement. Although Nilesh stated he worshiped daily at the re-furbished Dattatreya temple, explaining that it was "equal" (*barabar*) to the Warli boundary shrine, others expressed the contrary opinion that the Datta temple was not a real temple because film crews used it for shooting. The skep-ticism shown its employment in the service of the camera seemed to consign it to the status of a simulacrum (Baudrillard 1993). Filmistan's temple is a copy without an original, or rather a copy with an original that is not a materially constituted, geographically emplaced temple but rather a set of mass-mediated visual forms.

And elaborating on this judgment, some people told me that for shooting purposes Datta was routinely dislodged by whatever other god a given script might call for. It was left to Vikas to spell out the details for me: a screen (*parda*) would be set up before the effigy to mask it off, and the image of the deity that had been cast would be placed in front of that. In fact, as applied to the filming of *puja* sequences, the routine has become so well established that the film-makers themselves have made fun of it. The fabrication of back-lot temples was mocked, for example, in the comedy *Chachi 420* (Kamal Haasan, 1997), which opens with a bride and her film industry groom praying to Ganesh to bless their marriage—only for the god to be whisked away in mid-*darshan* by stagehands, exposing the shrine for the Bollywood illusion that it is (compare Meyer 2015, 232–35).

Let me close this discussion of the Filmistan temple by noting that nobody ever named the deity that had been embodied in the sacred rocks before be-ing replaced by Dattatreya. The rocks' own rockness was evidently more ger-mane to the way they were dealt with, or discussed, than the personality they once emplaced. I should also make it clear at this point that, although I often noticed the marks of devotions paid the *murti* of Dattatreya—garlands, traces of red powder, and the like—as far as most of the Warlis were concerned no trace of sacrality remained at the site. Vikas's cousins made a clear distinction to me between their Waghoba shrine as a "real" (*asli*) place of worship and the Dattatreya temple as "fabricated" (*banaya hua*) and therefore "false" (*nakli*).

Oddly, aside from Nilesh, the broad-minded Gujarati Hindu, in my time at Filmistan there was only one other person I ever saw taking *darshan* at the site, and that was Vikas himself. It's time to ask how and in what capacity he was connecting with the power he still recognized there, and how he understood the questionably sacred image's work of visual mediation.

Vexed Virtuoso

When I first met Vikas, I was keen to see if he would introduce himself as a Warli, thus confirming the identity signaled by a settlement's placement of a tiger god on its threshold. He told me instead that he was an "*adivasi* Brahmin." The self-description left me bemused. At least part of what he meant, though, I realize now, is that he is distinguished within his *adivasi* village by hereditary station and also by individual capacity as somebody who enjoys a privileged intimacy with divine powers.

Vikas asserts his status as the *bhagat*, the tribal medium or priest, on the basis of patrilineal succession. He also advances a more contentious claim to visibility: as the patriarch's sole resident grandson he is also the *pramukh*, or village headman. This means that his person is vested with representative authority on behalf of the entire settlement—as he makes clear to me—by virtue of not only tribal kinship hierarchy but also, significantly, the property rights bestowed by the law (see also Sundar 2007, 28–29). But the big problem for Vikas is that within neither the internal regime of tribal custom nor the public jurisdiction of the law are these bids for recognition returned. He is a quixotic figure, a vexed virtuoso. I see him less as representative of other individuals in his community as of urgent political and theoretical concerns.

Within the village Vikas's kinfolk do not take him seriously, and just to go by his own account, it's not hard to see where the fault lines lie. Kinship relations in this *pada* do not follow the pattern to be expected among the conventionally patrilocal Warlis. The descendants not of his deceased father's brother but rather of the father's three sisters head up the three households that make up the rest of the settlement. There are many contending interests and claims to be parsed in these examples of what Warlis call a *gharor* marriage, in which a woman's husband, typically for want of brideprice, moves into his wife's natal place in a position of subordination to her primary relatives.[36] And without lingering on this issue, I should add that Vikas's cousins' children did not strike me as inclined to be impressed by anyone courting attention as a traditional authority like a *bhagat* or *pramukh* in any case. Rather, they had their sights set on assimilation within broader social formations as posttribal, generic Marathas.

If you are engaged in a project of self-refashioning of this sort, however, which negotiates questions of modernity and backwardness along with caste, tribal, or religious identity, the question of how to redraw the bounds of endogamy—who provides an appropriate marriage partner?—presents a major challenge. And in late 2003, cross-cousin's offspring or no, the *pada* was getting busy with arrangements for the marriage of Vikas's aunt's grandson Bhushan to a suitable Warli girl. The staging of the wedding at the groom's residence is in fact an anomalous feature, but that need not hold up the discussion here. Much of the information required at this point is conveyed in an image I introduced in connection with an earlier stage in the Village's history. Recall the scenario of a tribal celebration with its festive elements of drumming, drinking, and dancing—the model for those scenes of rustic *masti* that used to feature in the movies. And now consider its enactment under the Warli settlement's changed circumstances, as documented in the preceding pages.

There is one thing to add. This sort of scenario is the locus classicus of spirit-possession activity in western India. It may come as a surprise to learn that Vikas, the self-designated medium, viewed its onset with trepidation. A childhood tendency, connected with his spiritual sensitivity, to fall into fits had incited beatings at the hands of Bhushan and other cousins. The beatings, in turn, had made him more susceptible to fits. Previous experiences with spirit-possession mediated through ritual and alcohol consumption had likewise ended either in violence or in offense and scandal. I can infer some of what he must have voiced on those occasions. He used habitually to complain to me about his relatives and the way they dismissed his legal and customary right to represent them as a village—that is to say, as a human collectivity emplaced in a space made sensible and habitable by certain powers. For if the law of the Raj had been established to be on his side, Vikas nevertheless had the corruption of its present-day successors and the covetousness of local power brokers—*dada*s and "terrorists"—to contend with. Ever since they had lost the case, the people in charge of Filmistan had targeted him for black magic. Likewise, the landlord, More, had long wanted the Warlis to abandon their birthright. In furtherance of this aim he had been instigating Bhushan and others against Vikas, the lawful *pramukh*.

In this connection, Bhushan's upcoming wedding was fraught with intrigue as well as potential peril: "Is mein kuchh *suspense* ki baat hai" (There's cause for some suspense here). Where had Bhushan raised the money for brideprice? What had he offered the property's owners in return for their permission to mount a wedding in the *pada*? Again, a by-the-book wedding was hazard enough, given the ritual drumming that would summon the village deities and the subject's unhappy history, even under the correct circumstances, of spiraling into booze-fueled excess. But cause for further alarm lay in the possibility that Bhushan or one of Vikas's other persecutors, versed in witchcraft, might seize the occasion and call out not a local god (*ghar ka bhagwan*) but an evil spirit (*shaitan*) to visit his body.

There are a number of points to develop here. The first is that in its outlines, this scenario invites comparison with many cases from the anthropological literature in which the ritual of possession creates an opening for a normally voiceless person to speak unwelcome truths. In reconfiguring agency, desire, and social and material interests in relation to a decentered subject, possession invites the attention of scholars concerned with marginalized or subordinated identity categories—paradigmatically, with gender—and with avenues for resistance.[37] But my emphasis here is not on Vikas's truth statements, nor on his empowerment as a human subject through possession performance, although I don't deny that his professed receptivity to spirits indicates some ambition to greater physical and legal autonomy (even as it threatens to foreclose the possibility of self-possession). In bypassing questions of voice or discourse, I take my cue from his ideas, as I understand them, in favor of an interpretation that foregrounds the dimension of the visual.

What is at stake here is not Vikas's personal visibility as an individual within a larger Warli community. It is rather his bid to make visible, and thus recognizable, an ordinarily invisible domain or network of power. This is the domain of the village's resident gods, whom the *bhagat* represents in the sense that elected politicians represent their constituents. The exhibition of his possessed body, in this view, is an assertion of the divine order's sovereignty over a particular space and thus a reinscription of spatial coordinates. By way of comparison, consider the circuits of urban neighborhoods traced at ritually prescribed times by the mendicants known as *zogua* or Potraj, as introduced in chapter 2. The *zogua*s with whom I spoke in Mumbai all identified themselves as Mahadev Kolis, a Scheduled Tribe allied with the Warlis. Their performances were cursory. Through a few economical gestures—cracks of a whip, steps shuffled to a drummer's accompaniment—they cited for the audience the image of a possession that was not actually being experienced. But they served to re-mark the city blocks in the image of the deity: to make manifest a trace of the immanent, if normally invisible, sovereign force. The *zogua*'s dance on the street is a symptom, like a rash (in village goddess cults, pox is diagnosed as divine possession)—an index of an Other's power.

The second aspect of this episode that calls for some discussion is Vikas's fear that his enemies might make use of black-magic techniques to call a devil into his body instead of a god. Now as the readers of (especially South) Indian village ethnographies will know, devils and the smaller fry among non-Brahminical gods are closely related kinds of parahuman persons, as are ghosts and occulted saints. They are kindred spirits, so to speak. That Vikas should own to anxiety that his person, once transformed through ritual and stimulus into a receptive vessel, should prove vulnerable to infiltration by the wrong kind of powerful agent is no longer surprising to me. I do confess to ignorance of the degree to which his cousins might be implicated according to their own lights, however. Setting aside the problem of conscious intent (which academic theorists of witchcraft have found notoriously tricky), his cousins' own subjection to the jurisdiction of the local spirit-regime remains for me an open question.

What I can expand on here is Vikas's formulation of spiritual power on the model of electrical power. What goes on when witches divert its transmission to him is like scrambling his circuits, hijacking his frequency. In his terms, possession may be conceptualized as a technology for the transmission of power. Power flows from a locally grounded source to the appliance plugged into it—namely, the possessed human subject, which turns visibly "on" if it's working. Is possession a communications technology, a means for the delivery of authoritative discourse? My answer is yes, but secondarily so. The semantic content of the utterances sent through Vikas can be considered authoritative to the extent that their sacred origin is recognized as valid. And by the same token, the successful manifestation of the spirit-presence through its highly localized receiver-slash-speaker is (1) a validation of the system's continued functioning and (2) an affirmation of Vikas's place within that system. Again, any directives or ideas that are sent carry a "charge," so to speak, only to the extent the local wires are live and the receiver is correctly connected. The recognition that the *bhagat* is actually performing as a working appliance is a gesture of subjection to the local system.[38]

I am reminded of an exchange in which Vikas laid out for me the relations between temples, the spaces they occupy, and the kind of cult objects they house. A shrine set up at the wrong spot was a hazard to its environs, he stated, because it could invite a *shaitan*. So could a correctly stationed shrine if you made a mistake in how you addressed your prayers—the demon would intercept the god's transmission. The latter scenario worked "like a short circuit," an exposed line that a nimble-fingered *shaitan* could tie into like a slum colony electrician. He actually drew me a diagram of two terminals connected by a wire.

It seemed to me then that within subaltern communities in this part of India the invocation of electricity with reference to religious phenomena must have a particular purchase. To be sure, until a decade or so ago, Mumbai enjoyed an exceptional status as the one city in India (never mind the rural sector) whose residents were *not* subjected to regularly scheduled power cuts. But even in Mumbai, the flow of electricity has never been something to take for granted if you live in a slum. And the relative ease of access to it enjoyed by rich people is one of many privileges that set us apart.[39]

Mujictions: Technologies of Possession

Dressing up the Warli *pada* to re-present the façades through the medium of cinema as the landmark sites of a considerably grander spatial order—that is to say, the Indian nation—is the daily business of the Filmistan staff and the crews that shoot there. In so doing they confer on the mask a recognizable legibility and relegate the face behind it to a generic, even fungible, blank quantity. The camera's imperatives have at once destabilized the gods as terminals of the local power grid, ungrounding them and possibly even threatening them with home-lessness, and opened up the possibility of access to a different system of order-ing people in their proper place.

How does the colonization of his village by this alternative regime, at points spectacularizing, at points spectralizing, recast Vikas's predicament? Touching back on the discussion of possession, it is no stretch to connect the image of the person as a receptive vessel (or perhaps an empty dwelling, the door open to the first migrant in search of a squat) with the sense of anxiety about displace-ment that pervades Vikas's language about Filmistan. And recall that his project is a bid for a sort of double recognition. If there is a new source of power, or sys-tem of directing and distributing power, with effects that have become manifest in space, his challenge as the local virtuoso is to gain recognition as someone connected to that system. In other words, what he requires from human society is exactly the recognition that he is already recognized as a vessel or communi-cant by that system's distant agents. In this sense his subject position is indeed that of medium: he mediates the flow of external power into local space.

But I want to retain the place in my own analytic scheme for *medium* in the sense of an interface through which the human subject invites the external power. Time and again, I observed a pronounced attraction on Vikas's part to visual media of several kinds: to the sacred images of Hindu and other traditions; to photographs reproduced in his precious newspapers, some of which he identified as particularly auratic; above all, to films. I lack the space to do more than touch on the transports Vikas has described experiencing in the practice of film spectatorship.[40] I have never been in his company during such exalted states, let alone participated in them. But reflecting on our conversations and nowadays his letters, which often feature screenplay treatments, imagined interviews with Bollywood personalities, and the like, I have come to think that he understands the address of mass-mediated imagery, like cinema, along the lines of the visions he receives in the grip of spirit-possession.

I asked him once what the difference was between the figural *murti*s that predominate in Hindu temples and the aniconic forms that tribals had historically worshiped. He said, "It's only now there are different *murti*s for different gods. It used to be just rocks. You could approach them as whatever god you had in mind." But if the aniconic sites were more convenient, it also appeared that they were less effective. He described them as outposts of the premodern past—and small wonder, given how the rocks that had helped stake out the turf of his ancestral *pada* had been erased from the landscape. He concluded with a statement about where he, as a modern, looked for power: "Nowadays the power [*taakat*] has moved from religion to the law [*kanoon*]." But when I followed up by asking whether the gods had become weaker in the modern age, he demurred. It was not exactly that they had become weaker, but rather that they had become absorbed within "science."[41]

Science in his thinking was a colonial bequest, a mode of access to power that was mediated by techniques and artifacts marked by the sounds and signs of the English language. More specifically, Vikas's "science" was strongly identified with technologies of visual reproduction. His principal example—indeed, I would hazard, his paradigm—of a scientific mechanism that produced power effects was what he called "mujictions." The neologism combines *music, magic,* and (I think) *motion,* as in motion picture. He used this word to denote the operations of citation and address he had witnessed from various positions as an intimate of cinema. What we all see in the movie theater is mujictions in action: heroes and heroines and, of course, villains, projecting their glamour in stereotyped roles that have less to do with anything contained in the script than with the stars who go through the motions. You laugh and fight along with the hero, and in India you sing with him too. You fall in love, via him, with the heroine. A truly powerful, effective hero will even travel back with you from the theater, to shape your dreams and possibly inspire your actions. In fact, it might even be said—recalling my own responses to the examples of policemen and temples—that the test of whether a matinee idol is a *real* idol or not is his power to compel you this way.

Mujictions were surely what was on Vikas's mind when he drew an equivalence for me between *darshan*—seeking contact with distinct divine personalities through their respective, distinctly configured icons—and television. "Bhagwan bhi aajkal *channel* ho gaye hain," he told me (These days the gods have become channels).

Here at the chapter's close I refocus on the concept of possession. What leverage does it offer on Vikas's positionality as representative of other Mumbai-area Warlis—and perhaps urban subalterns more generally—within the various domains they traverse? One way to answer this begins with a simple schematic, a view of his possession activity as the convergence of three elements. The first is Vikas himself as a human subject, the self-proclaimed *bhagat* and lineage head. Second are the media and methods through which he gains access to power: in addition to *darshan*, and to the drumming, dancing, and drinking that attend Warli weddings and other observances, this category also includes film spectatorship. The third element is the source of that power: namely, the parahuman family of spirit-presences who have settled the land in compact with the human community, some of them sovereign and legitimate, others malevolent interlopers. Note that this three-part scheme replicates the recognition relation as theorized in the preceding chapters.

Expanding this model of Vikas's possession to an analysis of Mumbai's dispossessed begins with these three points as nodes of inquiry. First, there is the question of the emplacement of persons who become possessed relative to those who do the possessing and the implications of this relation for territorial organization and sovereignty. Second is the question of mediums and media: that is to say, not only of the human subject as the vessel of possession but also of images and other devices that, in "opening up" the human medium through sensory stimuli, themselves mediate access to various external powers. Finally, there is the question of this power, of its quality as imagined in the slum neighborhoods of Mumbai, very likely on the model of electrical power, with its attendant technology of connections, channels, and terminals. In Vikas's case, it would seem, possession has become an idiom in which to enunciate the distance between the rapidly receding past and the invasive present, not to speak of the fantastic and elusive futures glimpsed in the darkness of the movie theater.[42] Yet in airing the voices of his gods and other masters—past, present, and future—whom else might Vikas turn out to be speaking for?

Having reviewed my fieldnotes many times in my attempt to do justice to the

insights shared with me by the most imaginative and demanding of my interlocutors, I am struck by a recurring theme. This is the lack of agency he owns
to in his capacity as a normally configured human subject. Vikas, who stands
out in my mind as a remarkably forceful personality, readily concedes mastery
over his subject position to a host of powerful Others, including gods, witches,
and the masters of visual-cultural mujictions. I think it could be said that for my
informant, power, *taakat*, is a quantity whose source is by definition alien and
whose ports of access are occluded—increasingly so. Also increasingly, what
at once separates him from the agents of power and promises to reveal the ap-
ertures to him are the processes and artifacts of modern technologies of representation.

His experience of some of these agents of power is initiated through the contemplation of affectively charged iconic images. Alongside Hindu deities, these
extramundane persons include Hindi film stars, who in themselves embody
icons of the heroes they portray.[43] And then there are other, somewhat less
glamorous agents, whose intervention he solicits in affirmation of the modern
order he inhabits in his quotidian life as an Indian citizen: "Main ek Hindustani
nagarik hoon." (A caveat: by the terms of my own analytic, Vikas is of course
no citizen but rather a subaltern at the margin of civil society, and he inhabits
this rationalized order aspirationally, at best.)

This latter class of agents is accessed not through glossy icons but via an inky
tissue of paperwork. Its members wield the power to manipulate English text
and perhaps even secure him recognition within it: officials and lawyers are
the primary examples. Perhaps not surprisingly, lawyers are ambiguous figures.
How is Vikas to gain the attention of a proper advocate, as opposed to someone
whose interest in him extends to no more than self-interest, who sees in him no
more than a rube to be fleeced? How even to get past the white-collar sentinels
known as "secoritaries"—those impassive figures stationed with their files at
the threshold, whom Vikas encounters not so much as secretarial but as security personnel?[44]

Alienated from his own village-family, which withholds recognition of what
he considers to be his rights as defined by customary law, he has no regard for
local efforts to organize tribals as a politically effective subaltern population.
Participating in any such project would involve his own subordination within
alternative hierarchies he considers illegitimate—in other words, within *dadagiri*, the big-brother system. But over and above that, as this chapter has illustrated, he rejects political society as a matter of principle. For where the self is
configured in relation to the sovereign state, Vikas is subject to a cruel contra-

diction: he recognizes the legitimacy of a postcolonial civil society that refuses to recognize him.

And yet this book has already indicated a further step to be taken into the theorizing of recognition. Let's wrap up this story on a different note. To cast Vikas as the protagonist in a Kojèvian master-slave drama is also to revise, suggestively, the roles of medium and agent. The terms of Kojève's analytic were laid out in the previous chapter, mapped onto the ideological terrain of postcolonial Mumbai. Within this scheme Vikas is, of course, the subaltern subject who seeks recognition from the citizen class, the masters of the modern legal regime. But the new scenario has recast the lawyers he petitions. From masters in their own right, they have become relegated to the role of supporting players, accessories to his quest. And in like manner, so too do I find my own place in Vikas's drama—the ethnographer he summons back through his letters on intermittent visits to Mumbai. No longer a secret agent, I have myself become a medium, in the sense that I embody the technology that can give his person form through English words. This book is one attempt at making him visible.

FIGURE 1. "Central Jail" at Filmistan Studios, with shrine visible inside archway. (Photo courtesy of Sadia Shepard.)

FIGURE 2. Real and fake shrines at Filmistan. The shrine on the left seats Waghoba, the tiger god. The shrine on the right has been fabricated for a set. (Photo by author.)

FIGURE 3. Nepeansea Road, Sai Baba shrine. (Photo courtesy of Elizabeth Pérez.)

FIGURE 4. Renascent Sai Baba shrine on Nepeansea Road after demolition. (Photo by author.)

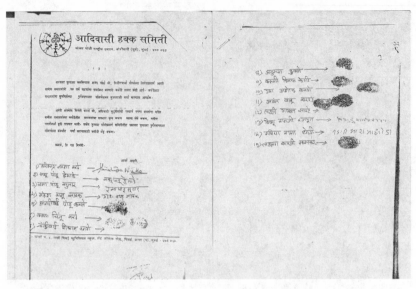

FIGURE 5. Adivasi Hakka Samiti letter, pages 2–3, dated 16 December 1998.

FIGURE 6. Warli *gaondevi* stone, Film City. (Photo by author.)

FIGURE 7. Child's painting in Warli style: police brutality at Whistling Woods Film Academy, Film City. (Photo by author.)

FIGURE 8. Warli-inspired YouTube office décor, Whistling Woods Film Academy, Film City. (Photo courtesy of Tony Elison.)

FIGURE 9. *Blue Sky Romancing the Sea*, from Alicja Dobrucka's series "Life Is on a New High" (2014).

FIGURE 10. Warli village set, Film City. (Photo by author.)

5

EXPANDING CONTRACT

TRIBAL SPACE AND OFFICIAL KNOWLEDGE

In the seventh Tretā Age, when all the worlds were controlled by Bali and the de-
mons had occupied the triple world, the dwarf appeared, Viṣṇu's third avatar. Con-
tracting himself in all his limbs, he went . . . to the place where the lord of demons
was performing a sacrifice. . . . "You are the king of the triple world. In you every-
thing is firmly placed. O king, you should give me the space covered in three strides."
"I grant this," answered the king, Bali the son of Virocana, and since he thought
him to be just a dwarf he himself was very pleased about it. But the dwarf, the lord,
stepped over the heaven, the sky, and earth, this whole universe, in three strides. . . .
The great-armed Viṣṇu who excites men shone forth, illuminating all the world,
and stole away the demons' prosperity as he stole away the three worlds. . . . Bali,
with his friends and relations, was bound with great cords, and the whole family
of Virocana was sent to hell.

Vayu Purana, translated by Wendy Doniger O'Flaherty

The Trivikrama, or "Story of the Three Steps," is a well-known Hindu myth,
circulated across India and beyond in myriad tellings: Sanskrit and vernacular; textual, oral, visual, and ritual. Cited above is Wendy Doniger O'Flaherty's
([1975] 1994, 178–79) translation of one of the myth's several appearances in
Puranic literature. As the fifth of the exploits in which Lord Vishnu takes an
avatar form to restore dharma to a world out of balance, the tale is integral to
the mythology and theology of Vishnu. But it is not limited to his cult. As with
many other myths upheld as canonical by the orthodox (Indologists no less
than Brahmins), the Trivikrama story also incarnates itself in a range of avatars
to engage a range of contexts and questions.

What is the story about? I first learned it as part of the sequence of Puranic
myths that narrate Vishnu's incarnations, and I'm sure my version was typical
of the tale as relayed through public-cultural or instructional media. In this sort

of telling the moral of the story is, well, moral: it deals with good and evil, gods and demons, with the appearance of power and actual power.

But it is also a story about sovereignty, about the right to rule and the sort of people who claim that right. And it is a live one. Even as I was writing these words in September 2016, Amit Shah, the president of the Bharatiya Janata Party (leading the ruling coalition at Delhi), found himself in hot water in Kerala, where the festival of Onam inaugurates the ritual calendar. Noted as a celebration of regional culture that brings the state's Hindus, Muslims, and Christians together, Onam unfolds over ten days. Its theme is Bali's return from the netherworld. Shah's offense was to send greetings over social media naming the occasion as Vamana Jayanti—Vamana being the name of Bali's nemesis—complete with a graphic depicting a Brahmin boy placing his foot on the king's head.[1] The implications of a gesture like this in the contemporary contexts of Hindu nationalism and caste politics will only become more apparent as this chapter gets under way.

What's more, it will develop that tellings which cast Bali as the sympathetic character and the dwarf Vamana as somewhat less than heroic—his dimension as an incarnation of Vishnu perhaps left out of the equation—are not merely inversions of a hegemonic norm. Let's return from Kerala to Maharashtra. In this chapter I will discuss a Warli story as a citation of the Trivikrama myth. As related in distinct rhetorical registers, what I am calling the "Oxhide Tale" (or Tales) will serve as a vantage point from which to explore a range of contexts, themes, and enunciative fields. The questions guiding this exploration have to do with the modern construction of tribal identity in western India and, more specifically, of Warli identity in the Mumbai-Thane area. Now, to be sure, neither the demon king Bali nor the crafty dwarf Vamana is named in this story, and my unpacking of it will yield little in the nature of any theological claim. But as with the case of the 2016 Onam controversy, the concern of my variant is not with God or metaphysics. The tellings I offer have been taken from sources that present them as narrative glosses of material conditions pertaining to the organization of space. And in fact, I would have hesitated to link the "Oxhide Tale" with the Trivikrama myth at all if not for the work of Michael Youngblood (2016), who conducted an ethnographic inquiry in rural central Maharashtra into the myth's local adoption as an allegory of caste relations and a heuristic for evaluating questions of sovereignty and space.

So let's lay out what is at stake here with a recapitulation of the Trivikrama myth. Vamana, imagined as a dwarfish Brahmin mendicant, is generally understood to have spanned the whole earth with his first giant stride and done the same for the heavens with the second. Having thus marked his claim over all extant space, he asks Bali what room there is left for his promised third step. The demon king, who has won world sovereignty as the fruit of his attendance on dharma, bows his head in obeisance before the revealed lord. Vamana plants his foot on it and crushes him through to the netherworld.[2]

These elements of the story are current among metropolitan and rural Hindus of all castes across Maharashtra. But like the celebrants of Onam in Kerala, Youngblood's lower-caste informants assign their sympathy unequivocally to Bali, whom the local tradition embraces as a purehearted son of the soil, as opposed to Vamana, here the archetype of the devious Brahmin. Particularly suggestive is the device of crushing Bali (back) into the soil of his territory and burying him underneath it, a figuration evocative of rhetorics typical of both nativist movements among peasants and indigenist movements among tribals—rhetorics that naturalize the bond between the land and its rightful occupants. This is one theme I will develop in this chapter.

"Maharashtrian agricultural and laboring subjects commonly express personal identification with the demon king—so much so that individual agriculturalists regularly greet each other as 'Bali,' and village folk songs often use the name 'Bali' as a reference to village cultivators or toilers" (Youngblood 2016, 205). Youngblood explores this inversion through oral retellings and ritual interventions that recast even such mainstream festivals as Navaratri and Divali as occasions to commemorate the subjugation by trickery of Bali—and, by extension, the lower castes—by Vamana, acting on behalf of Brahmins and other elites. Some of these observances even culminate in the burning of effigies of Vamana (238). Arguing that "Bali is a metaphor for a non-orthodox social and spiritual worldview—[that] of the least advantaged segments of rural society" (236), Youngblood moves on to examine the political mobilization of the Bali trope by an agrarian reform movement among Maharashtrian farmers, emphasizing the millenarian promise derived by many of his informants from the myth: "Bali will rise again." The future is to bring the restoration of the golden age of *Bali rajya* and with it the recognition of the cultivating classes as masters of their own plots. This aspirational identification of subalterns with Bali and the valorization of his reign as a model polity are said to be characteristic of village-based perspectives across a broad stretch of Maharashtra.[3]

This register of millenarian ideology and cosmological counternarrative— the grandest aspect of this Trivikrama variant told among Maratha-Kunbis and others—is not evident in the more modest version of a neighboring community, the "Oxhide Tale" of the Warlis. Indeed, the question of whether the story told by the Warlis is to be understood as a myth at all is one I will address in these pages. Certainly, it is no longer a Hindu myth, for as tribals the Warlis owe even less allegiance to the Puranic archive than the cultivating castes whose intervention here has taken the form of a symbolic inversion of the Brahminical elements. What has remained constant, along with the narrative structure, is the story's use as an image of contestation between rival groups over the same space. The Warli innovation is to develop the hint that the victorious side's advantage lies in its innovative, perhaps unnatural method of organizing and mediating that space.[4]

Tracing the Tale in Ethnographic Literature

Ajay Dandekar introduces a study of the myths and rituals of the Warli tribal community by citing a foundation myth of sorts: "Once upon a time, there was a king who ruled over the kingdom of Jawhar. He was the ruler of the Warlis. His Kingdom was attacked by a neighbour, Popera, the Koli king. Popera demanded that he be given only that much of land that could be covered by a cattle hide. The Warli king agreed to this demand. Popera then covered the entire Warli land with a cattle hide. Thus the Warlis lost their kingdom" (Remedios 1998, 11). This story valorizes the claim that the Warlis made to the land as autochthons, a claim that the rival Kolis usurped. It is not the foundation of a kingdom that is glossed by this myth but rather the reverse. What is narrated here is the foundational loss of a territorialized polity—the seminal event that results, in this case, in the spatial marginalization that is typical of the tribal condition.

Let me clarify this proposition, which is not, I think, particularly tendentious. Tribal identity in India is defined by spatial relations. To be an *adivasi*, an "original inhabitant," is literally to be beyond the pale, to belong to the kind of people who belong in remote areas on the periphery of caste Hindu society. In counterpoint, *caste society* is conventionally positioned as "civilization" in Brahminical texts, modern Indian public culture, and much ethnographic work from the colonial and Nehruvian periods.[5] Indeed, it could be said that caste Hindus and also, as I will discuss further on, many among the tribals themselves understand the tribals' relation to the wild lands they occupy— paradigmatically, the Forest or the Hills[6]—as something *natural* as opposed to *cultural*. Defined against city and village alike, neither civilized nor cultivated, people like the Warlis are in this construction an organic feature of the wilderness, their cabins sprouting from the soil like the woodland herbs they gather or the trees and anthills they worship. This naturalizing logic gives rise to the images and figurations that cast India's *adivasi*s in the mold of local fauna: as pests, as a natural resource, as an endangered species.[7]

The interesting thing about the oxhide story is that it contradicts this conventional framing, establishing the relation of the Warli community to its living space as the product of a cultural intervention. The Warlis' claim to the land they occupy is legitimized by invoking the mythohistorical kingdom that had originally demarcated the space—that is, made it culturally distinct and intelligible. They attribute their condition of marginalization within that space to the kingdom's loss of sovereignty. They are deprived of polity not because they dwell outside history in a state of nature but because a rival group has usurped the space over which that polity held jurisdiction.

The method of usurpation is also noteworthy. The Warlis have not been displaced (after the manner of Native Americans in a certain kind of US history textbook) through processes such as physical violence or demographic pressure that can be rationalized as part of a natural or inevitable dynamic of competition between rival populations. Rather, they have been swindled out of their rights through the distinctly cultural mechanism of a crooked contract. To drop the legal term, their land has been *alienated*; the Warlis have "signed" it away. In this connection, one recognizes in the motif of the all-encompassing oxhide the image of a piece of paper. Each of that paper's successive clauses, recorded in unintelligible script and referring to the arcane laws of others, advances an insatiable encroachment.

A community relieved of its territory and political autonomy by an unequal treaty: the scenario seems classically colonial. It is also all too typical of postcolonial conditions in contemporary India—conditions I have theorized in previous chapters and will illustrate further in the next—that relegate tribals and other subalterns to a status, not so much of second-class citizenship, but of a social invisibility that prevents them in effect from being recognized as citizens at all. I thus propose this myth as an allegory of relations of power, representation, and space that obtain currently among Warlis of my acquaintance. Before I move on to explore these problems as they have taken shape in their experiences, however, I will make some observations about the way the myth has been presented (or not) in the extant scholarship on the Warlis. This should highlight some of the tensions and ironies attendant on my interlocutors' odd situation as residents of Mumbai and, hence, as incongruously urban tribals.

So where does the story cited above about the kingdom of Jawhar come from? There are two answers: (1) Jawhar, which is a real place; and (2) Ajay Dandekar, who wrote my source text. In addition to the source mentioned above (Remedios 1998), Dandekar also reproduces the same tale in another essay about Warli settlements and forest management policy in contemporary Thane District. He concludes this telling with the remark, "The Warlis even today remember this legend fondly and the folk memory thus preserves whatever remains of the past in their mind-set" (A. Dandekar 1998, 108). And that, unfortunately, is the extent of his own attribution of a source for the myth. The apparently well-known tale does not appear in either of the two principal ethnographic studies published to date: *The Warlis* by K. J. Save (1945) and *The Painted World of the Warlis* by Yashodhara Dalmia (1988). The oxhide myth's absence from the two books is the more telling given the emphasis they share on recording myths, songs, rituals, and other artifacts of a traditional culture.[8]

Or, perhaps better: of a traditionalist ethnography. In presenting the Warlis as a tribal people distinct from caste Hindu society, both Save and Dalmia, separated though they are by a generation, privilege the Warlis' stories, arts, and religion as vehicles that express a collective voice and vision. A distorting effect of this approach is that the stress on the Warlis' cultural integrity tends to imply a corresponding social autonomy. The scenario that prevails is that of a placid community that dwells in isolation from other people and in harmony with the natural environment of its homeland, the primeval forests of Thane District, Mumbai's frontier. It seems the attribution of stasis, temporal as well as spatial, is basic to the figuration of indigeneity; tribals are authentic tribals insofar as they cleave to timeless folkways in lands occupied since time immemorial.

I should make it clear that I don't think of this essentialistic model of indigeneity as destructive or disempowering in and of itself. As I mentioned above and will move on to explore further on, there are Warlis who represent their tribal identity in the terms of the model and even seek to exploit it to strategic advantage. Nor would I argue that Save and Dalmia sequester the tribals of their pages from history altogether. Save, who at the time of his book's publication was Thana District's Special Officer for the Protection of Aboriginal and Hill Tribes,[9] provides a fund of information about the Warlis' economic exploitation by traders, moneylenders, and large farmers in the late colonial period. Dalmia's study, focusing on visual art, was published by the Lalit Kala Akademi, the Government of India's organ of support for traditional arts. Perhaps somewhat subversively in light of the academy's preservationist mission, it does relate the transformation of Warli graphic motifs and patterns to the changing context of their production over the course of post-Independence decades. The point about history I want to entertain is more specific. What is missing from these descriptions of tribal culture is a notion of the tribals as political subjects, and what is missing from their identification of Thane as the Warli homeland is the sense of a landscape configured by polity.

Thane's very name bespeaks a certain amorphousness. The derivation attributed to it from the Sanskrit *sthana*, "place," conveys the impression of a land without intrinsic qualities—an afterthought, or perhaps a blank to be filled in. Since colonial times, when most of India's modern administrative boundaries were drawn up, the name has denoted both a district and its capital city, with the official shift to *Thane* from the more Hindi-sounding *Thana* being an example of the same Marathi-ization of place-names that has replaced *Bombay* and *Poona* with *Mumbai* and *Pune*. As a geographical designation *Thana/Thane* does in fact antedate the colonial regime. But a well-known folk etymology has built on the homophonic match between both versions of the name and the Hindi and Marathi words for "station" to identify the area with those twin metonyms of the British presence on the Indian landscape: the train station and the police station, or jail.[10] To take a quick look back to the earlier chapters for the terms in which to theorize this, it could be said that the part of Thana that is *pakka*—and thus nameable—is a sort of outpost, a colonial fort on the frontier of the *kaccha*. (And it could also be said that it was precisely the organization of space by the colonial state that set forest land aside as pristine or virgin wilderness to begin with. But that is to anticipate the next chapter.)

All of this notwithstanding, for Maharashtrians who do not actually live in the district the primary quality to define the place is surely a relational one. Thane is the land bridge that joins Mumbai to the rest of India, but it is not of Mumbai. Until well after Independence, the district and municipal boundaries of Bombay were coterminous with the geographical contours of the historical "island city," the dense wards built up over what had once been seven islands and their adjoining landfill. The eighth, much larger island-become-peninsula of Salsette that extended from the mainland to join the city at Mahim Creek was administered, and thought of, as part of Thana District. It was in 1920 that the colonial administration redesignated the southern half of Salsette as a Bombay (Suburban) District, which, however, remained administratively subordinate to and dependent on Thana for many years. In 1950 the jurisdiction of the Bombay Municipal Corporation was extended over the southern half of the Suburban District, composed of villages that had grown into the only-slightly-outer boroughs familiar to present-day Mumbaikars as integral parts of their city: Bandra, Andheri, Ghatkopar, and Kurla. Lastly, in 1957, in a move known as the "incorporation of the extended suburbs," the municipality absorbed the northern half of the Suburban District, including Goregaon, the neighborhood in which Filmistan is located (C. Rajagopalan 1962, 36–37). And yet in contrast with Bandra and the other closer suburbs, the northern areas remained thickly wooded and retained a relatively rustic character into the mid-1970s, when urban development finally commenced in earnest. While jurisdiction at the municipal and district levels may have technically passed to an entity known as "Bombay," in other words, for many years the extended suburbs continued to feel, to the urbanites down the line and local residents alike, more like "Thana."

Now, the casting I have suggested of Thana/Thane as Nature opposite Bombay/Mumbai as Culture supplies the context for a conventional association of the district with the Warlis as a sort of native territory. The association is well illustrated by the last page in Dalmia's book, on which a small inset map of coastal Maharashtra and Gujarat, showing a shaded patch to indicate the "area with Warli population," is dominated by a much larger image captioned simply "Thane." Thane's subdistrict units, or talukas, are indicated with labels but no boundary lines; oddly, the names of the constituent talukas to the south fall outside the shape's outline. The area identified as Thane thus turns out to represent no more than the northern half of the district. The message seems clear: any consideration of the district as Warli territory need not take its southern portions into account. Geographical features such as roads, railroads, and cities—built infrastructure—have been left out altogether. The choice seems notable given that Thane District's eponymous capital not only is a major city, with a current population well in excess of a million, but also served as the northern terminus of India's first rail link, the Bombay–Thana service on the Great Indian Peninsular Railway, inaugurated in 1853.[11]

The railroad is, in fact, another example of a historical factor that refigured the geography of the district, for it bound Thana to Bombay as the hinterland of a burgeoning commercial and industrial center. Not least of its effects was to open a channel for traffic in local produce, particularly fruit, grown on plantations where the labor was often supplied by local Warlis pressed into service under conditions approximating slavery.[12] Dalmia herself offers a compact encapsulation of the history of the area with reference to the poverty pervasive in contemporary Warli life (a fact that, for all its consonance with the well-worn trope of the "downtrodden tribal," is not to be ignored):

Thane, for all its rugged and isolated appearance, has been touched by history many times. It has been under an early Hindu rule (upto 1300 A.D.) followed by the Muslim period (1300–1600 A.D.), the Portuguese rule (1500–1670 A.D.), the Maratha period (1660–1800) and finally the British (1800–1947). Each successive rule brought little for the tribals except the imposition of taxes on their meagre land and with the last three rulers a class of landholders came into being over and above the actual tillers. With the British a uniform land settlement was imposed, with some concessions, to encourage the tribals to till their land. This only seems to have marginally benefitted them as the easy terms of the settlement attracted hordes of outsiders from other areas. Much of the land was thus appropriated by Gujarati, Marvari and Parsi landlords, while the Warlis were more often found working on their farms for little or no wages. (1988, 14)

The periodization here follows the conventional scheme established by colonial-era historiography and conforms in its dates (except for the irregularities in the text) to the example set by the *Thana District Gazetteer* (*Gazetteer of Bombay Presidency* 1985–, vol. 13 [(1882) 1986], chap. 7 passim). Again, I think credit is due Dalmia for including such material as contextual information. Yet the contrast implied even in this passage between Thane's "rugged and isolated appearance" and history's sporadic "touch" is indicative of the received conceptions about nature and culture that continue to pervade much thinking about Indian tribals.

Along with the occluded history of the tribal homeland, there is a complementary theme to be teased from the Save and Dalmia ethnographies, and I want to discuss its implications. This is the proposition that even indigenous populations may shift their places of settlement in historical time. Of course, it is hardly to be expected that the distribution of any minority population in space would conform evenly with political or administrative borders, and Save (1945, 1, 5) does identify Warli populations beyond the boundaries of colonial Thana District. To the east, he indicates Nashik and Jalgaon Districts in what is now Maharashtra. To the north he names Daman, Dadra, and Nagar Haveli—Portuguese possessions in his day, administered since 1954 by Delhi as union territories—and Dharampur, formerly a petty princely state and now part of Valsad District in Gujarat.[13] And he even makes a reference to the south, where the 1931 census is seen to have identified some 4,566 residents of the Bombay (Suburban) District as Warlis (2). To be sure, when Save specifies the northeastern part of Thana District as the Warli "stronghold," he is reflecting the demographic distribution as reported in the census. Nonetheless, while I can cite no source to claim that conditions on the ground in pre-Independence Thana actually contradicted his picture, my acquaintance with Government of India methods of data collection among present-day Warlis (to be taken up in the next chapter) does lead me to suspect that Save might have shared something of a blind spot with the census officials when it came to looking for tribals to the south.

The Warli enclaves located north and east of Thana fell beyond Save's official purview in the district administration, hence do not figure in his presentation of ethnographic work. The exception is a passage that names Dharampur and the surrounding Portuguese territories as the area "many Warlis claim" as their "original home" (1945, 5). In step with the conventions of the ethnography of his day, Save derives from this informant testimony and from philological evidence an originary narrative. He proposes that the tribe, "of non-Aryan origin," came from a northerly direction, "descend[ing] to the hilly forests of Dharampur" and thence southward (5). Dalmia (1988, 19) follows Save's lead and adds that her own informants, a generation later, "point to the north and state that their ancestors fled from there because of coercion."

I find this trope of the originary migration, and its continued life among tribals and ethnographers alike, to be of interest because it complicates the conventional paradigm of tribal identity at several levels. First, at the level of history: by privileging an ancestral place of origin over areas of present settlement, the narrative destabilizes the principle of indigeneity as it is cited in defense of contemporary tribals' claims to their lands. And what if an ongoing process of settlement over a diffuse area was to have endured to the present day, as the testimony of one of Dalmia's (1988, 19) old informants suggests? Contextualizing the Warlis' settlement of discrete spots within historical time would entail a reconceptualization of the production of tribal space as a dynamic practice enacted by tribals themselves, in interaction with other groups (see also Sundar 2007).

Second, at the level of polity or, more precisely, the relation between the production of space and the colonial (and postcolonial) production of knowledge: Save (1945) produces a scrupulous ethnography of the Warlis as tribal inhabitants of Thana District. But both the category *Warli* and the broader category of which it is a subset, *tribal*, are official designations employed and inscribed by the state apparatus of which Save was a part. Might it not be significant that the main areas of Warli settlement beyond his jurisdiction— Dharampur and the other petty Gujarati principalities of the Surat Agency; Portuguese Daman, Dadra, and Nagar Haveli—were sequestered from the archive of the Raj? What's more, what amounts to an official lacuna seems to have cordoned off Bombay and its environs as well. Might not what it meant to be recognizably "tribal" have been a different epistemological proposition outside the colonial regime of knowledge organization and production that held sway over rural British India?[14]

Third, in terms of language: as part of his project to mark the tribe apart as an independent cultural group, Save devotes much attention to distinguishing the lexicon used by his Warli informants from standard Marathi, and his case for a northern origin is made in part by remarking the Gujarati influence on the dialect recorded in villages to the north. Contrariwise, what seems more suggestive for the purposes of my own project is the dependency evinced by tribal "poaching" on the vernacular of the linguistic-cultural majority in a given area. Hence, Warlis in Gujarat speak a rustic Gujarati, while Warlis in Maharashtra consider the Warli language to be more or less the same as Marathi. (As for Warlis in Mumbai, where this book is concerned Vikas's bricolage as recorded in the previous chapter will have to serve as an illustration of their argot.) In opening this question, I point to the malleability and slippage among such rubrics of collective identity as *language, religion, region*, and *caste*, all of which carry political resonances and enunciative force in postcolonial India. Let's add to the mix, as a no less constructed term, one more category: *tribe* (see also Alles et al. 2015).

Fourth, and to my mind most compelling, is a question about narrative genre. Academics are accustomed to think of myth as a discursive form appropriate to a tribal way of life, in which narrative functions as a vehicle for disseminating messages whose verities—whether psychological, ideological, or metaphysical—are cloaked in metaphor and allegory. But Dalmia's gloss on the tale of the Warlis who fled their ancestral lands "because of coercion" does seem suggestively to accord with a historical account of dispossession. Does it belabor the point to invoke, again, the "Oxhide Tale"?

Tribal Kingdom

As with Dharampur and its environs and the Portuguese territories, Jawhar, the kingdom mentioned in the myth, was technically not subject to direct administration by the British regime.[15] In colonial days a minor princely state, it occupies the northeastern corner of Thane District and has been incorporated as a taluka since 1948. Much of the territory of Jawhar spreads over a plateau, and thanks to its high elevation, its capital is nowadays touted as a hill station, an ideal destination for middle-class urbanites in need of a weekend retreat. "One of the few tribal kingdoms in Maharashtra," reads the copy provided by the state tourism department, "Jawahar is famous for its vibrant Warli paintings. It invites you to forget your daily grind and all the turmoils that go with it" (Dhruva 2002). Nothwithstanding the salience of Warli art in this sort of tourist-oriented branding, however, the crown of this tribal kingdom has in fact remained in the hands of a Koli lineage since the end of the thirteenth century. Indeed, Jawhar's historical record would appear to begin with the "Ox-hide Tale."

Jawhar is called a tribal kingdom in two senses. The first has to do with the composition of its population. Recognition as a princely state did not keep Jawhar independent from the ledgers—and the categories—of the colonial census. "According to the 1881 census," reports the old colonial gazetteer, the population was 48,556, and of these, 41,095, or 84.63 percent, "were early tribes." Of these, 21,816, or 53.08 percent, "were Várlis." In addition to "the early tribes," there were 5,943 Kolis (*Gazetteer of Bombay Presidency* 1985–, vol. 13 [(1882) 1986], 700). The corresponding figures from the 1991 census are 122,833 inhabitants belonging to Scheduled Tribes—a category embracing both Warlis and Kolis—out of a total taluka population of 140,671, a tribal majority of 89.30 percent (*Census of India 1991* 1995, pt. 12, vol. 23, 6, 34). The key point to note is the near-absolute majority the Warlis appear to have maintained in this area over more than a century, but I will mark some other details that will reemerge to inform discussion further on.

The suggestive colonial designation *early tribe*, which situates Warlis along with other groups at the beginners' end of a telos of advancing development, is no longer part of official taxonomy.[16] The analogue in contemporary usage is *primitive tribe* or *primitive tribal group*, formulated in the 1970s in connection with India's fifth Five-Year Plan, but the Warlis do not fall within this category (N. Jain et al. 1995, 8). Warlis are, however, members in good standing of a more expansive official list: that of *Scheduled Tribes*. An individual certified as belonging to a Scheduled Tribe is eligible to claim certain rights and benefits from the state on the basis of official recognition of that tribe's historically underprivileged status. The state apparatus that administers this system will receive some attention later in this chapter; the point to be made here is that whereas in 1881 the Kolis of Jawhar were distinguished from their less advanced compatriots among the early tribes, according to the present-day taxonomy there are Koli subgroups that have been listed as Scheduled Tribes, and among those scheduled Koli groups is the community that claims the ruling house of the old kingdom: the Mahadev Kolis.

What this observation throws into relief is the malleability, previously remarked, of categories such as *tribe, caste,* and *region*. Where do the Kolis fit in?[17]

The best represented among the communities who call themselves Kolis are undoubtedly the Son Kolis, who have historically been settled along the coast of Maharashtra. The identification of a cluster of fishing villages as the original nucleus of Mumbai, and hence of the Kolis as the first inhabitants of the city, is a well-established trope (many of these fishing settlements, or *koliwada*s, endure to this day as enclaves on the edges of intensive urban development). Despite this attribution of original occupancy, however, nobody calls the Son Kolis *adivasi*s, and over the course of several decades' worth of nativist politics, the community has shifted from identification as a distinct, if Marathi-speaking, Hindu caste to assimilation within the greater body of Marathas.[18]

Unlike the Son Kolis, the less metropolitan Mahadev Kolis, who are dispersed across much of inland Maharashtra, are counted among the Scheduled Tribes. In Jawhar the Mahadev Koli families most closely associated with the ruling house asserted a distinct identity as "Raj Kolis" (*Gazetteer of Bombay Presidency* 13:701). The Koli identity of the lineage that ruled Jawhar throughout its history as a princely state furnishes the second sense in which it can be described as a "tribal kingdom," and the appellation trades on a certain incongruity. The idea that tribals can be kings runs counter to their conventional representation as children of nature, as well as their identification within the colonial taxonomy as potentially fierce—even warlike enough, in some cases, to qualify for military recruitment as "martial" peoples[19]—but hardly aristocratic. To recognize a tribal in the king's role would also seem to go against the grain of *varnashramadharma*, the naturalized social order espoused by orthodox Hindu thinkers, in which kingship is assigned to castes that claim Kshatriya status. And then again, to be sure, claiming Kshatriya status has been throughout history the preferred strategy of Sanskritizing groups seeking entry or promotion within the caste hierarchy (see M. Srinivas 1989).[20]

Far from any Brahminically sanctioned redrafting of its caste lineage, however, what Jawhar's ruling house cited as its principal source of legitimacy was the recognition extended to it, in historical times, as a sovereign vassal by the Muslim emperor of Delhi. Indeed, 5 June 1343, when Muhammad bin Tughluq bestowed the title of shah on the ruler Nemshah, was observed in Jawhar as the foundational date of a local calendar kept in use through colonial times. Nevertheless, the *Gazetteer of Bombay Presidency* makes it plain that the true architect of the dynasty's rise to power—de jure as well as de facto—was the father of Nemshah. The feat is chronicled in the authoritative voice of late-colonial historiography:

Up to the first Muhammadan invasion of the Deccan (1294) the greater part of the northern Konkan was held by Koli and Várli chiefs. Jawhár was held by a Várli chief and from him it passed to a Koli named Paupera. According to the Kolis' story, Paupera . . . had a small mud fort at Mukne near the Tal pass. Once when visiting a shrine at Pimpri, he was blessed by five Koli mendicants and saluted as the ruler of Jawhár. Paupera thereupon collected a body of Kolis, marched northwards, and was acknowledged by the people of Peint and Dharampur. . . . On his return . . . he went to Jawhár and asked the Várli chief to give him as much land as the hide of a bullock could cover. The Várli chief agreed, but when the hide was cut into fine shreds or strips, it enclosed the whole of the Várli chief's possessions. Gambhirgad about twelve miles north-west of Jawhár and the country round were given to the Várli chief, and Paupera became the sole master of Jawhár. (*Gazetteer of Bombay Presidency* 13:703)[21]

In thinking over the "Oxhide Tale," I stress three critical components: the kingdom, the tribes, and the hide. Both tellings of the story, as relayed here and at the start of the previous section, speak of (1) the construction of a particular kind of space; (2) the assignment of sovereignty over that space to a particular kind of group; and (3) the authoritative representation that mediates the relation between the first two terms. In the Warli myth, the hide that expands suggests a paper that contracts—a document, that is, whose clauses are binding. In the Koli folk history, by contrast, the motif of the strips demarcates the contested space by enclosing it in an outline. The figuration is evocative of technologies of mapmaking and surveying.[22]

In pursuit of the tale, I have described an excursus through a miscellany of maps, census data, and officially sponsored expository texts. But however eclectic the sources, the findings that promise to reward further inquiry fall along the same three axes. First there is the question of configurations of space. The assumption is pervasive that such people as Warlis and allied tribals belong to places defined as hinterlands—namely, Thane and, at a further remove, Daman, Dharampur, princely Jawhar—rather than places defined as centers, which is to say, paradigmatically, Mumbai. Second, there is the question of who is and who is not a tribal and the role that polity, whether in the form of the rajah of Jawhar or the modern state with its schedules, plays in the definition. Third is the question of the genre or medium in which the tribal presence is embedded and the degree of authority with which such visual and representational artifacts assert their effects. This question applies to maps, quantified data, myth, historiography, and other official modes of representing space and its inhabitants. But looking to the theoretical framework I set up in the earlier chapters of this book, I should also broaden the question to consider two other classes of media: spectacularized images, and images and marks imbued with the charge of the sacred.

In this connection, the ethnographer's potential role as the amplifying mouthpiece of a tribal voice becomes a loaded alternative. Of all the texts examined in this section, only one—the version of the "Oxhide Tale" cited at the beginning of the previous section—claims to offer a Warli voice, ventriloquized though it was by the ethnographer Dandekar. Something of the fraught quality of the ethnographic project as undertaken in an *adivasi* context comes across in an anecdote reported by Save, who was combining research with his administrative duties as a tribal affairs officer. What begins as a discussion of his Warli charges' attitudes toward the *sarkar*, or Government of India—conceived of not as "a machinery or . . . organization [but] . . . some powerful individual"[23]— becomes a personal lament on the part of the *sarkar's* frustrated emissary. And then it becomes something more: an almost endearingly artless confession of a methodological dilemma for the ethnographer and the suggestion of something like an existential crisis for his informants.

> An average Warli always evinces a vague fear of the *Sarkar*. He is also afraid of the officers of the *Sarkar*. A stranger in their locality is suspected to be a Government servant, especially if he is in Western dress. . . . A Warli does not disclose even his name to a stranger. When one meets a Warli on the way and asks his name, the Warli replies, "why do you want to know the name of the 'jungli' man"? It is because of this fear and general ignorance that they are most reluctant to supply anyone with information regarding their customs and beliefs. With great persuasion and through the influence of the local land-lords or their estate-managers, they were prepared to tell me something about their life. But the moment I took out the pen and paper, they got terrified and exclaimed, "you are deceiving us. You will take down all that we tell you and show it to the Sarkar. Sarkar will then arrest us. What can we tell to Sarkar then? We shall be caught in the writing." (Save 1945, 243–44)

The poignancy of the last line, with the figuration of entrapment glossing the usurpation of the subject's identity by his or her own textual representation, will not be lost on most people who have experienced either end of the ethnographic encounter.[24]

Some readers will also, however, recall it from chapter 4, where I contrasted it with the attitude of my Mumbai-based Warli friend Vikas. For Filmistan's outspoken *adivasi*, the goal was to get himself well and securely "caught in the writing"—to gain recognition from the *sarkar* and its associated elites, to get counted and thereby count for something, to be put on the map. A big part of the challenge, of course, was and is that for him, as an urban tribal, the place he desires is on the wrong sort of map.

"The Warlis hardly know of anything outside their own world. . . . Some of the settlements come down to within fifty miles of Bombay. But there is hardly one in a thousand who has ever seen Bombay" (Save 1945, 242). When Save made this observation in 1945, to be sure, the city of Bombay circumscribed a much smaller area. And if the adjacent zone administered as the Bombay (Suburban) District was still a dependency of Thana, it was nevertheless a southern corner in which the author, to judge by his fifty-mile metric, appears not to have expected to encounter any tribals. Yet my own contact with Warli people has in fact been limited to settlements that fall within that zone, in other words, within contemporary Greater Mumbai. Among my urbanized interlocutors the telling of traditional stories was not esteemed as a means of sustaining a distinct tribal identity. Nobody ever volunteered me a telling of the oxhide story. I have never heard it. But its themes resonate in the outlook and concerns of Vikas and others. My interlocutors have been smothered, as it were, beneath an oxhide document, and now they seek a way to emerge, to make their own marks on its surface.

Constructing the Natural: Hindu Discourses

Here is a thought experiment, and it pivots on an irony. If your identity is defined by the space you inhabit, and you belong to a space set beyond the bounds of civilization, you are placed ipso facto at a remove from civil society. Suppose you are a subaltern striver like Vikas (or any number of other Warlis resident in the Mumbai suburbs). If your aim is to win recognition as an individual with a full complement of citizenship rights, why would you desire recognition *as a tribal*? There are two good reasons, both in need of some unpacking. The first is that official certification entitles a member of a Scheduled Tribe to claim certain benefits and accommodations from the state, in token of redress for structural disadvantage. The second reason goes back to the opening premise: tribal implies indigenous, and indigenous implies a place of origin. At stake in your name on a list is your place on a map, and that can be a claim to a home.

Tribal as a designation of a kind of Indian collective identity has meanings at once specific and diffuse: specific because the word's use in India has little in common with its applications in, say, the Middle Eastern or Native American contexts; diffuse because its field of reference nevertheless remains ill defined. In modern India the claim of tribal identity is an official matter, adjudicated by government bureaucracy. There is an important overlap here with academic anthropology, one that remains to be investigated in some detail, but the crux is that recognition of tribal status is the government's prerogative to extend: to collectivities, on the basis of their membership among the tribes listed in the "schedules" appended, state by constituent state, to the Constitution of India; and to individuals, on the basis of documentary evidence that names them within lineages so certified and circumscribed.[25] At both levels, the enactment of official recognition is mediated by paperwork.

The official schedules of tribes have become established over generations as lists of essentialized identities. It is a point central to this book's argument that the state has the power to create tribals by naming people as such. But—to make a Foucauldian distinction—to say this is to stress the category's enunciative power over its mimetic function, its effect over its denotation. It's time to ask: what does the term *tribal* describe, and what characteristics do the diverse tribes on the schedules have in common? The answers to these questions do not primarily have to do with the social organization or economic relations of a given community. Rather, as the discussion of the "Oxhide Tale" has already suggested, the identification rests chiefly on a figuration of marginality: a spatial figuration, to be established both in geographical terms and metaphorically through relegation of the tribal to the outer fringe of civilization.[26]

Let's step back and revisit the organizing scheme of this book. As with the illegal religious structures downtown, so too with the case of the invisible tribals of the suburbs: I am interested in a threefold distinction in ways of organizing space and in the kinds of media in which those orders are made visible. In the first part of this chapter I focused on the official construction of tribal space as narrativized in the spreading of an oxhide, symbolic of legal documents and maps. In these further investigations into the tribals-as-children-of-nature construct, the discussion will remain with official, rationalized space and its apparatus of paperwork. To the extent that religion enters this picture, it will be in the form of classical Hindu discourses that support the Othering of the forest and its people. The next chapter will examine a counterhegemonic trajectory, the potential of religious practices to sacralize space as an alternative to its rationalization. Finally, the cinema cannot be ignored as the source of images that have historically defined what the tribal looks like for the public. The spectacularization of tribal space in popular visual culture will be analyzed in the conclusion.

Now, given the conventional equation, previously noted, of caste society with Indian culture itself, it is no surprise to find that when it comes to official formulations of tribal policy, the colonial and postcolonial archives have built on antecedents in the ancient texts of Hinduism. As Günther-Dietz Sontheimer (1989, vii–viii) succinctly observes, "in Sanskrit literature a major role is played by the opposition between, on the one side, the established settlement / regularly ordered land / established social system, and, on the other side, the jungle/ forest, where there lives the ascetic who has left society" (see also Malamoud 1996). In the wilderness are also to be found others who live in rejection of society: outlaws and tribals. These two categories have been and are frequently conflated, the most enduring such formulation for the modern era being the official classification by the colonial regime of such groups as the Pardhis and Chharas as Criminal Tribes.[27] But here is an important point. This dichotomy between the pale of social order and the wilderness beyond, spanning classical and modern ways of imagining Indian space, does not necessarily mark the periphery as godless. On the contrary, as its association with the figure of the renunciant indicates, precisely because of its sequestration from the compromises and transactions of social life—spiritually corrupting, substantially polluting—the wilderness serves as a site of redemption, purification, and liberation.

In other words, it may be established that the *adivasis* are savages. But are they noble or benighted savages? And here is a related question, which has historically framed the relations of caste society to tribal communities: are India's *adivasis* practitioners of their own, autonomous religions, or are they adherents of untutored (or degraded) forms of Hinduism? With regard to the policy of the Government of India, this debate was famously joined in an anthropological idiom by Verrier Elwin and G. S. Ghurye in the years following Independence.[28] In orthodox terms, the logic of *varnashramadharma* can be seen to place tribal groups in a caste-like category, albeit one standing outside the caste hierarchy: *adivasis* are relegated, not to a distinct level within a vertical structure, but rather to a horizontal annex. It is crucial to note, however, that tribals are peculiarly intimate outsiders; as recognized neighbors, they are more readily assimilable within the system than, say, Turks or Europeans. The process of absorption within the hierarchy has been discussed, not to say advocated, by Ghurye (1963), among many other scholars. The most influential theoretical approaches are perhaps those supplied by M. N. Srinivas (1966) and D. D. Kosambi (Kosambi 1985 is exemplary). As a colonial-era example of assimilation close to home for her project—and mine—Dalmia (1988, 13) cites the case of the Malhar Kunbis, a Maratha subcaste who "are known to be nothing but reformed or Hinduized Warlis who have upgraded their status."[29]

Accelerating this process of religious assimilation in the present day is the outreach, or "uplift," activity, carried out by NGOs, that is glossed in the rhetoric of development. Such programs characteristically stress temperance, literacy, and norms of modesty centered on female dress. Many are carried out by Hindu organizations as part of the nationalist project of *ghar wapsi*, or "return home," and make no bones about their missionizing purpose. Indian Christians, particularly those from Scheduled Caste families whose conversion occurred within recent generations, are another target of *ghar wapsi*, and nationalist rhetoric has identified even Muslims as brethren who, while essentially or substantially still Hindu, have set themselves apart artificially with their adoption of perverse standards of hygiene, diet, sexual morality, and costume.

In fact, to go by the letter of Hindutva ideology, the tribals are, in a sense, the most authentic Hindus of all, for when V. D. Savarkar ([1923] 1969) laid out the theoretical principles of the movement in his *Hindutva—Who Is a Hindu?*, he answered his own question with a naturalized formulation of identity that collapses race onto space.[30] Hindus are the native population of the subcontinent, and they embody a reverent attitude toward the spiritual power immanent in the soil from which they have sprung. Ancestral race-feeling for the fatherland: this is the essence of Hindutva, "Hindu-ness." In its Romantic reliance on the bond of blood and soil, Savarkar's argument is in step with other radical nationalisms of its day; but the text also incorporates a great deal of Sanskrit, examples of classical literature cited as the purest expressions of the Hindu's homage to the holy land (*punyabhoomi*) of India. The basis for *ghar wapsi* is laid down plainly enough in these pages. Tribal estrangement from caste society is an impediment to the attainment of racial and national solidarity; thus, India's tribal populations must be mobilized and brought to national consciousness through integration within Sanskritic cultural norms. Again, the spiritual bond the tribal enjoys with the land is a matter of direct experience—authentic but *kaccha*. To be made manifest and thus recognizable to others, it must be mediated by the symbols of a *pakka* Hinduism.

My argument has not seen the end of formulations like that one. But so much for Savarkar and his political agenda. *Ghar wapsi* and related Hindu nationalist policies are indeed matters of pressing concern for contemporary *adivasi* studies,[31] but for this book's purposes let's retain the key points about the natural spirit-force and its need for cultural mediation to give it form, and move on. What remains to be discussed is a different source of ideas—one intimately implicated within the production of archival knowledge about *adivasi* popula-tions, including the Warlis. This chapter's last section will take up the Maha-rashtra government's reliance on state anthropology. In a Northeastern tribal context, Indian state anthropology has been given a sustained and incisive anal-ysis by Townsend Middleton (2016) in his recent book about Gorkha political society in Darjeeling. But let me supply my own gloss of the concept as it will be used in the following pages. What interests me here specifically is the con-tribution of anthropologists to the state's generation of paperwork and the gen-eration by that paperwork of power effects over the populations they study.

Scrutiny Committees and Vigilance Cells

Like other polities for which *tribal* or analogous terms such as *native* are used to mark apart a distinct category of subjects under their jurisdiction, the Govern-ment of India retains anthropologists to help various state agencies determine who is and is not a tribal for administrative purposes. I was able to observe this consultative relationship at work in two contexts. The first is the Tribal Re-search and Training Institute, a Pune-based agency of the Tribal Department of the State of Maharashtra. The second was a training seminar held in Pune over two days in November 2003, in which anthropologists lectured officers of the Maharashtra police on interactions with *adivasi*s. Central to both contexts was the administrative concern of how to evaluate the legitimacy of applicants for tribal certification. This is a problem laid out neatly in a booklet issued at the seminar: "Firstly, there is an absence of a statutory definition of 'Tribe' or 'Tribal.' Similarly, there is a dearth of clearly formulated criteria for verifying the tribal origin and status of a group" (YASHADA 2003, 11). And from it de-rives my own question, as an ethnographer among the ethnographers: what *are* the criteria that officialdom uses in determining who is a tribal?

Even in principle, the way the registry system for members of Scheduled Castes and Tribes is supposed to work is fairly arcane. On paper, it is the dis-trict collector or subdistrict officer to whom members of Scheduled Castes and Tribes alike apply for their caste certificates. What complicates matters, bringing other government bureaus into the picture, is the question of verifica-tion. It is feared, and with good reason, that members of groups not named on the schedule may claim the places reserved for others by obtaining certificates fraudulently, often through taking advantage of homophonic matches in caste names. (A case often cited is that of the Thakurs, a Maharashtrian Scheduled Tribe that unfortunately shares a name with one of the dominant Kshatriya groups of North India.) For this reason, an applicant who seeks one of the slots reserved for tribals in a college or in government employment, or a candidate for political office who wishes to (or is required to) demonstrate tribal bona fides, finds that a tribal certificate by itself is not enough.[32] It must be supplemented by a validity certificate, a separate document that is issued by an agency of the state government's Tribal Department known as a Scheduled Tribe Caste Scrutiny Committee.

These are six regional bodies, based in Pune, Nashik, Nagpur, Aurangabad, Amravati, and Thane. These report to a central authority: the director of the Tribal Research and Training Institute. Along with supplying validity certificates, the committees also serve as courts of appeal for tribals whose applications for certification may have been dismissed out of hand at step 1, the collector's office. This is where the police come in. To pursue its inquiries each committee retains an investigative unit called a Vigilance Cell, staffed by officers of the Maharashtra police. The official Tribal Department website describes the relation between the Scrutiny Committee and its police arm like this: "In case of doubtful claims, the Cell makes necessary enquiries and *after collecting copies of relevant documents* submits a report to the Committee. A copy of the report is made available to the applicant who is given an opportunity for personal hearing *and to adduce any evidence*. The decision given by the Committee is final and can be challenged only through a writ petition in the High Court." The emphases here are my own. Note that the data the police investigators are tasked with collecting takes the form of a paper trail. Note also that the protocol leaves open a step for the applicant to respond by presenting evidence of his or her own. Let's mark down the slippage here between the "relevant documents" that record tribal identity and the "evidence" that could signify or embody it, as a site of potentially productive tension. (Foreshadowed here are both the end of this chapter and the story to be told in chapter 6, which follows a lawsuit filed by a community of Warlis against a government agency bent on evicting them from their forest homes.)[33]

Over the period of my fieldwork I visited the Tribal Research and Training Institute (TRTI) several times, to be received hospitably by various members of the staff. The TRTI is quartered in a two-story building. The upper level consists of a research library and offices, most prominently the Caste Verification Office of the Caste Scrutiny Committee. The lower level houses a Tribal Cultural Museum, which has exhibits open to the public. The spatial bifurcation is reflected in the hybrid composition of the staff, which includes anthropologists alongside the bureaucrats and clerical personnel. The enduring impression with which I left the institute was of an organization with a split personality.

Upstairs the offices are strangely uncrowded. Large, dusty rooms house rows of desks assigned to Tribal Department officers. Attending some of these officers are their tribal supplicants, who are for the most part stiff, rustic-looking men wearing Gandhi-style caps and tight, patient expressions. It is all very quiet. Any indication of bustle on the premises is to be found in the lumpy jute sacks piled along one wall of the main room, giving it the look of a loading dock. Threatening to spill over and engulf the functionaries at their desks, the mass has moved laterally to annex a stairwell, which it is on its way to filling up. The fabric is coarsely woven and worn away in places; what the sacks contain is bundles of files.

Downstairs, the museum is modest but kept to a professional standard. Among a range of attractions the collection features "(4) Gods and Goddesses," "(5) House patterns," and "(11) Warli paintings." A courtyard contains not-quite-full-scale models of *adivasi* building styles, including a dwelling with a thatched roof and mud-and-reed walls painted inside and out with Warli graphic motifs. A turbaned mannequin erected next to it has been accessorized with a *tarpa*, the flutelike instrument whose image circulates widely (second only to the paintings) as an emblem of Warli culture. A note of continuity with the office is supplied by the *adivasi* visitors who come filing by the exhibits on breaks from their vigils upstairs. Do they recognize themselves in the items that government curators have displayed as metonyms of their culture?[34]

In following the operations of the Caste Scrutiny Committee upstairs, I heard much criticism of its conduct of business from the anthropologists. Many of the research officers were said to be underqualified, with only a reported fifth of their number having completed the master of social work degree considered a professional desideratum. Each committee is assigned a law officer alongside its research officers, and at the time of my research it was also grumbled that Pune's law officer had obtained his post through bribery, and that in fact the man knew no English (if so, that would have certainly put him at a disadvantage in dealing with Indian legal documents). In the milieu of suspicion that pervaded an organization whose mission hinged on the widespread abuse of credentials, such allegations did not surprise me. But the on-the-books policies of the Scrutiny Committee were giving me food for thought in themselves.

I am indebted to one of the committee's research officers for most of the information I have about the verification process. According to Mr. Kulkarni, as I will call him, the job began and all but ended with paperwork. Per the protocol, admissible evidence was limited to seven kinds of papers: (1) the applicant's birth certificate; (2) his or her primary school certificate; (3) the father's birth certificate or primary school certificate; (4) in the event of the father having been in "service" (that is, government employ), the first page of the "service book," or paybook, in which caste or tribal origin is recorded; (5) land records; (6) documents pertaining to older generations in the family; (7) a validity certificate issued to a relative of the applicant.[35] All applications, once submitted to the Scrutiny Committee, were referred to the Vigilance Cell to be investigated; once the police returned the files, the committee made its evaluation. The whole process typically took six months (a pair of applicants I had spoken with, who had been counting on a one-month turnaround, appeared to be in for a rude awakening). "Any person who wants to apply for verification has to have two or three documents," Kulkarni told me.

There was one established departure from this procedure, the germ of a concession, it seemed to me, to the paperless condition endemic to *adivasi* life. In the case of "primitive tribes"—in official terms, a subset of particularly marginalized groups listed on the schedule—the TRTI organized teams of research officers to conduct fieldwork in remote *pada*s. (Such a visit would not ordinarily be undertaken to a settlement of Warlis, who do not rate among the "primitive" subset.) Mr. Kulkarni had himself served on such expeditions. The research teams made observations of such telltale symptoms as the settlement's "customs and architecture" and compiled reports on the basis of which the Tribal Department might send a recommendation to the local collector regarding the bestowal of tribal certificates. (The distinction between the tribal certificates to be dispensed in this kind of scenario and the validity certificates that are the TRTI's normal sphere of concern is an important one, but not germane to my argument here.)

These ethnographic fact-finding missions, then, pose an exception to the principle that evidence of tribal identity begins and ends with official documentation. They open up a sort of bypass off the closed loop of paperwork. Another potential exit is signaled in the description, cited several pages before, of the job assigned the Vigilance Cells. Once a request for a validity certificate moves from the research officer's desk to a field investigator, that is to say, a police officer, room is indicated within the protocol to accommodate evidence in forms unmediated by paperwork. In other words, within this narrow window, visual or material artifacts of an ethnographic character may come into focus as *pakka*. To encourage the police to recognize data in such alternative, nontextual forms, a seminar was convened on 8–9 November 2003 at which the personnel of Maharashtra's Vigilance Cells were brought together with state anthropologists.

This event was attended by thirty-five officers of the Maharashtra police, all of them inspector grade, and took place at the Yashwantrao Chavan Academy of Development Administration, a state of Maharashtra organization whose purpose is to train administration cadres. Introducing them to ethnographic methods were anthropologists working for TRTI and the University of Pune. For the mustachioed inspectors, whatever else it represented, the weekend at YASHADA's clean and airy campus must have come as a welcome junket, although it bears mention that the watchmen were themselves being watched, and note was to be made of each man's attendance record in a report filed with his superiors.

In a previous era, the fund of evidence consulted by police investigators at work among tribals and other subaltern communities would have included official files of visual material. In his book *Camera Indica*, Christopher Pinney locates photography alongside anthropometrics and fingerprinting as one of several visual recording techniques the British Raj put to work in classifying its imperial subjects. Stressing the intimate shared history of anthropology and forensics with specific reference to "fragile" tribal cultures, Pinney (1997a, 45) observes:

> Throughout the nineteenth century, two rather different photographic idioms emerged in India: a "salvage" paradigm, which was applied to what were perceived to be fragile native communities, and a "detective" paradigm, which was more commonly manifested when faced with a more vital caste society. In the "salvage" paradigm a scientific and curatorial imperative was dominant— "fragile" and "disappearing" cultures and communities had to be recorded ("captured") before their extinction....
>
> The "detective" paradigm, by contrast, presumed the continuing vitality of sections of Indian society and stressed the value of anthropological depictions and physiognomic observations as future identificatory guides.

At YASHADA in 2003, anthropologists and police officers revisited these categories. India's diverse tribal communities, which in a previous era had boasted such a panoply of distinguishing visual marks as to have warranted the compilation of a photographic archive, had lost their looks, even as the salvagers had expected. Nevertheless, they retained their designation under the state as a collectivity apart, and recognizing them in their particularity remained a job assigned to the police. In the present day, the physiognomies of tribal subjects could hardly be checked against the colonial archives of photographs and measurements. But were there nevertheless traces of some kind to be salvaged, visual clues independent of paperwork that could be made legible to a discerning eye?

Several specialists, with distinct methodological orientations, made the case that there were. The aspect of the seminar most relevant to my argument was the delineation of these sets of facts. Before moving on to an engagement with this privileged information, however, I want to pause and consider a more reflective register, which supplied the weekend's secondary theme. This was the emphasis on empiricism—or, more precisely, on the retrieval of facts from the field—as an epistemological mode as proper to police work as it was to social science research. There was an element of consciousness-raising that attended this project of reforming (or reviving) Indian police forensics along ethnographic lines. The presenters repeatedly identified ethnographic training as the solution to the reported abuses in the verification system.

The most eloquent statement to this effect came from one scholar who related how familiar his own fieldwork had made him with the trope of the policeman as a figure of fear (shades of the bogey-like *sarkar* imagined by the Warlis consulted by K. J. Save). After urging the cultivation of an attitude of cultural relativism, the professor discussed methods of working with tribal informants to elicit data that could supplement the evidentiary paper trail: observational technique, interviewing, genealogical mapping. This last-mentioned procedure turned out to be a hit with the inspectors, but as I watched them sketching away in their notebooks, I was left wondering what means their pursuit of verifiable information ordinarily entailed.

For concision's sake, in drawing my lessons I will cite the work of just two of the presenters. It is fair to say, however, that there were two things that characterized the program as a whole. These were (1) an emphasis on the classification of tribals as a cultural group to be recognized as distinct from the rest of Indian society; and (2) a supporting emphasis on religious imagery and practices as a particularly visible subset of recognizably tribal attributes. The lectures did in fact dispense a great deal of information about intertribal diversity—how to tell, for example, a Warli from a Mahadev Koli. But those details were not allowed to disturb the central assumption that *adivasi* communities belonged together as a class, and that the definition of that class against the majority was a matter of substantive Otherness.

"Tribal religion," one speaker pronounced (in implicit defiance of Hindutva orthodoxy), "is entirely different from Hinduism." He displayed a slide divided into halves: "Caste Group" as opposed to "Tribal Community." The attributes listed on the right side of the ledger included "primitive traits," "distinct culture," "animism," and "shyness by nature."[36] Another slide bore the title "Relation of Other Social Organisations with Religion" and itemized religious practices that served as the visible faces of distinct aspects of social life: tribal attitudes about health, for example, were manifested through therapies that addressed supernatural causes; the settlement of space was made visibly tribal through house-raising rituals. Next, having delivered a thoroughgoing exposition of the diversity of beings venerated by Mahadev Kolis and the traits marking each one's cult (the tribal deities being sorted according to a threefold scheme of village goddesses, nature spirits, and ancestors), the presenter closed with a slide headed "Changing Tribal Cultures."

Changing self-identity among *adivasis* in the present day posed a challenge for the project of their identification by others, he conceded. But in connection with this problem there was a distinction that could usefully be drawn between the "hard core" and the "soft core" of culture. The soft core was the material stratum, increasingly tricky to differentiate from the features of caste society. Beyond that, however, lay the "hard core" of the "ideational" stratum, which was the authentic repository of self-knowledge, albeit elusive of access by others. In other words, a tribal man might be wearing a shirt and trousers, a woman might be wearing a sari—just like everybody else—but the essence of their alterity would still be there, under the surface. Yet if difference was a matter of personal interiority, how then to take its measure, make it *pakka*? In practical terms the answer, it seemed, lay in the careful observation of sites and moments of religious expression.

The other speaker I describe here was in accord on this point but pressed the question of evidence in more concrete terms. Contemporary tribal life continued to reveal materially instantiated signs of cultural particularity—and those signs became particularly visible, he affirmed, during the performance of rituals. He termed such signs "ethnographic indicators." When properly decoded they served as synecdoches of distinct tribal identities. The bulk of his session was given over to an enumeration of these indicators. For example, in divinatory ritual, the use of an earthen pot would mark the participants as Thakurs; of rice grains, as Warlis. The characteristic medium of decorative expression among Bhils was basketry; among the Warlis it was (predictably) wall painting.

He flagged two other areas for inquiry that seemed promising, both relating to spatial practices: settlement patterns and housing styles. The list of factors to be taken into account included the site's location; the dwellings' architecture, including the rituals surrounding their construction and the materials used; visible manifestations of cosmological principles and directional symbolism; and, finally, the delineation of village boundaries and the stationing of local deities. I could have asked for no more by way of a statement about the visible instantiations of a *pada*-based sacred geography.

Other "indicators" were proposed as well over the workshop's two days. Taken all together, the criteria introduced by the event's speakers correspond well with a list compiled by one of their number, Robin Tribhuwan, along with some anthropologist colleagues and published in a collection of essays by the TRTI in 1995. I will conclude this chapter by reproducing and commenting on this list, which aims "to summarize in a nut shell the views of experts about the attributes [of] tribals."

1. Tribals live in an isolated area as culturally distinct groups.

2. Tribals trace their origin from the oldest ethnological section of the population.

3. They follow primitive methods of occupations such as hunting, gathering of minor forest produce and therefore they are backward economically as well as educationally.

4. Members of tribal society profess a primitive religion and are not always within the Hindu-fold in the traditional sense.

5. Tribals have their own common dialect. Their dialect has no written script.

6. Tribals love, music, dance and liquor.

7. Members of tribal society dress scantily. (N. Jain et al. 1995, 3)

Let's run through these items in order. The first is just the sort of figuration of spatial marginality—distance from the center being a matter of both geographical and cultural isolation—that has been examined in this chapter as the dominant trope in the construction of tribal status. Similarly, number 2, the attribution of tribal origin to the "oldest ethnographic section of the population," can be identified with the move to sequester *adivasis* in a time outside history as discussed in the exposition of the oxhide myth. Number 3 concerns the economic life of tribal communities. Given the site-specific nature of the activities named, I classify this point alongside the first two, as an extension of the spatial figuration of tribals as inhabitants of the wilderness "out there."

The list's second half involves some departures from that standard, and these call for some elaboration. Number 4 describes "primitive" religious practitioners who are delicately located "not always within the Hindu-fold in the traditional sense." The spatial figuration is present here as well. Yet, as the discussion in these pages has demonstrated, religion poses a special case as a site of tribal alterity. On the one hand, it invites study as a repository of marks, attitudes, and performances of difference normally kept under wraps. On the other hand, the promise of "tribal religion" for the researcher is complicated by the ambiguity characterizing its relation with Hinduism and the politics with which that relation is fraught. Next, number 5 states that *adivasi*s speak their own dialects. But given the range of local variation in language use among non-metropolitan Indian communities in general, this is too diffuse a proposition to be helpful as an index of tribal status.

The last two points are "Tribals love, music, dance and liquor"[37] and tribals "dress scantily." Now, to go by contemporary moral norms as disseminated through Indian public culture, both sets of attributes are somewhat offensive. And to go by liberal attitudes regarding the politics of representation—in India and elsewhere—it is the assignment of such attributes to a minority group, of course, that is offensive. But I think that both of these items are important, and without editorializing further on questions of morality, probity, or frivolity, I flag them for critical engagement here and in the conclusion to this book.

What sets them apart from the rest of the list is that they make substantive propositions about tribal persons, and these propositions are advanced as criteria against which tribal subjects are evaluated when presenting themselves before the eyes of others. That is to say, they are questions of visual culture. "Does so-and-so look like a tribal?" is thus to ask, "Does so-and-so exhibit natural rhythm / appear drunk / expose overmuch skin?" It is in the context of state anthropology that these stereotyped images have surfaced in these pages, so let me reinforce this connection by calling out textbook illustrations and museum exhibits as visual resources whose authority bears a government stamp.[38] (Alongside such official channels, a proper reckoning would also take into account the tribal image as disseminated by popular entertainment media, especially Hindi cinema.)

Now let's wrap up the list with an observation about all seven of its points: they add up to a portrait with limited descriptive power when it comes to the everyday life conditions of Mumbai-area Warlis. Twenty-first-century Warlis and their neighbors from other tribal groups who live in and around Mumbai and Thane identify themselves by generically Maratha-sounding names. They speak colloquial Marathi and Bombay Hindi. All but the oldest women wear full-length saris of mill cloth and the men wear shirts, pants, and *lungi*s like everyone else. In the absence of the piece of paper that authoritatively labels such a person, how is tribal alterity to be signified in public? The scholar and arts administrator Jyotindra Jain (1998, 9) shares this sardonic take on the question of "indicators": "By the advocates of this brand of authenticity, tribals are conceived as a single timeless community whose women supposedly go bare-breasted, whose men smoke pipes and roam around in ceremonial attire, who are extremely fond of tattoos and ornaments, who possess a tremendous urge for age-old artistic expression, whose arts, crafts, manners, and customs invariably have a magico-religious content. . . . They do not just come from somewhere, but always 'stem' or 'hail' from it." Jain spent several years as the director of a government museum and knows intimately whereof he speaks.[39] But what remains to be added is that the more urbanized among my interlocutors are also pretty well acquainted with this reified portrait. And in this connection I'd like to address the predicament Maharashtra's *adivasis* face with respect to governmentality with a proposition of my own, rendered in the categories of the Peircean schematic.

Recall the two-tier layout of the TRTI, with its Caste Verification Office built on top of the Tribal Cultural Museum. Now, if you are an *adivasi* presenting yourself before the research officers upstairs at the TRTI, the prize you seek is *symbolic* representation, that is, the winning of credentials through entry into the official archive. At the same time, the anthropologists on staff downstairs at the TRTI have authenticated a select set of material artifacts and visual motifs in their museum as *indices* of tribal particularity. So here is the question: might not the *iconic* citation of such visual elements be a means for you to raise your profile in the eyes of others—to help define you as a *pakka* tribal?

In my several visits to the TRTI, I did notice one person who appeared to have had the same notion (I suppose she would not have expressed herself in terms of Peirce's trichotomy). The majority of the hopefuls I saw, with their stiffly pressed caps and no less stiff carriage, looked the picture of ill-at-ease rubes in the city. By contrast, this woman had decked herself out in chunky jewelry and colorful, folkish-looking fabric. A plainly dressed man waiting by himself in the stairwell (not the one full of sacks of files) turned out to be her husband. He told me that he was himself from a nontribal background; in the English phrase he dropped, he was there because of his "intercaste marriage." He was evidently keeping his own profile low while his wife attempted to demonstrate her bona fides as a Mahadev Koli to the officers' satisfaction. Her recognition as such, once won, would undoubtedly be of material benefit to the whole family.

It has occurred to me since that what I saw as the woman's savvier approach might have had something to do with the circumstance of her marriage into the majority community. Perhaps this sharpened both partners' awareness of the tactical dimension involved in the negotiation of cultural difference. The next chapter will investigate some of the specific tactics whereby Mumbai Warlis have engaged this peculiar imperative, at once postmodern and postcolonial: to pretend to be who you actually are.

6

IMMANENT DOMAINS

EXHIBITS AND EVIDENCE IN THE FOREST

I am like a man who disbelieves
The evidence of his eyes:
For all its obvious size,
He doubts the elephant exists—
Until there's no elephant, only prints,
And then he's suddenly convinced.

KĀLIDĀSA, *The Recognition of Śakuntalā*, translated by W. J. Johnson

To the north, the Mumbai city limits follow the district boundary that runs between the suburbs and Thane. Along nearly half its length the line bisects a forest. Most of this area, 103 square kilometers, has been set aside as a nature preserve, the Sanjay Gandhi National Park (SGNP). Adjoining the park to the south, flanking Goregaon, two contiguous tracts are also run by the government. The Aarey Milk Colony is a sprawling dairy farm complex that suggests what the trysting grounds of Krishna and Radha might look like if repackaged as a state of Maharashtra undertaking: the cows graze a green landscape oddly punctuated by barrack-like housing units, research facilities, and, looming over the fringes, corporate industrial parks. Uncannier still is Film City, five hundred photogenic acres administered by the Maharashtra Film, Stage and Cultural Development Corporation. Among the permanent sets housed on the grounds, a promotional pamphlet lists "helipad, artificial lake, temple, discotheque, aeroplane, village, town, church and court." Most of the woodland has been sectioned into lots for producers to lease and to erect on them whatever their shooting might require.

Located within walking distance of the older studio, Film City, in short, is Filmistan on steroids. There are two tribal hamlets inside Film City, with another settlement immediately adjacent. Together, these add up to 110 households, of which all but twenty-nine identify themselves as belonging to the Warli community or other *adivasi* groups. My source here is survey data collected in 2003 by the tribal-rights advocacy group Sramik Mukti Sanghatan, whose totals for an area encompassing Film City, the Aarey Milk Colony proper, and peripheral tracts controlled by private interests add up to twenty-six *pada*s comprising 1,027 households, 749 of them tribal families. For corresponding figures on the population living within the much larger area of the SGNP, I turn to the work of another community organization, Sramik Mukti Andolan, which in 2000 compiled a list of thirty-six hamlets on the Mumbai side and an additional twenty across the district boundary, containing an estimated total of 2,500 *adivasi* families.

Neither of these sets of numbers constitutes official data. *Census of India 1991* recorded no human habitation within the forest zone at all, with the exception of the dairy employees housed in the workers' quarters at the Aarey Milk Colony.[1] In fact, the case of these forest *pada*s presents an anomaly as far as the official organization of space is concerned. But it is a multifaceted anomaly, affording more than one angle to the forest's inhabitants—or, more properly, those who represent them in public—as they seek recognition within the official order.

The problem is not simply that human settlement is conceptually inadmissible in an area that, across most of its compass, has been designated a nature preserve. As I argued in chapter 5, given the enduring power of the nature-culture opposition as a structuring trope in Indian history, tribal communities and territory have become defined as such through a segregation both political and epistemic. To be tribal is at once to be beyond the rule of law and ken of civilization. And to the degree that forest management policies adopted in the colonial period have come to transform this scenario, what the Government of India's assumption of the role of steward over natural resources and, by extension, guardian of the children of nature has done is to reframe the wilderness as a kind of annex of the modern state.[2]

My approach to fieldwork in this area has owed much to the precedent of Arjun Appadurai's engaged ethnography in Mumbai slum neighborhoods. His essay "Deep Democracy" is a discussion of the mastery of techniques of governmentality by a grassroots coalition called the Alliance. For example:

> Not only has [population survey methodology] placed self-surveying at the heart of its own archive, the Alliance is also keenly aware of the power that this kind of knowledge—and ability—gives it in its dealings with local and cen-

tral state organizations. . . . All state-sponsored slum policies have an abstract slum population as their target and no knowledge of its concrete, human components. Since these populations are socially, legally, and spatially marginal— invisible citizens, as it were—they are by definition uncounted and uncountable, except in the most general terms. . . . Given that some of the most crucial pieces of recent legislation affecting slum dwellers in Mumbai tie security of tenure to the date from which occupancy of a piece of land or a structure can be demonstrated, such information collection is vital to any official effort to relocate and rehabilitate slum populations. (Appadurai 2002, 35–36)

Framing the Alliance's move as an appropriation, he develops his argument about the mobilization of shantytown neighborhoods in engagement with a Foucauldian critique of technologies of knowledge:

To those familiar with Foucault's ideas, this may seem to be a worrisome form of autogovernmentality, a combination of self-surveillance and self-enumeration, truly insidious in its capillary reach. But my own view is that this sort of governmentality from below, in the world of the urban poor, is a kind of countergovernmentality, . . . in short, this is governmentality turned against itself.

I read Appadurai to be stressing the agency involved in this enterprise—an agency exercised in the Alliance not only among its leadership cadre but also at the level of its grassroots membership—as the factor that grounds it as a practice of deep democracy. In that case, not only is the Alliance's bid for archival visibility a sort of translation project, one that converts slum-dwelling bodies as objects of representation into the officially legible register of numbers embedded in text. It also initiates a transformation at a subjective level—a conversion of subaltern toilers into aspiring or nascent citizens. And let me press this point further. The ritualistic or formulaic character of some of the methods whereby members' participation is regularized is suggestive: survey techniques are "codifi[ed] . . . in the form of a series of practical tips" (2002, 35); the practice of setting aside daily savings, which is given a "profound ideological, even salvational status," is "fram[ed] . . . as a moral discipline" (33–34). Per this book's argument, my intervention here would be to theorize these activities as practices of conditioning that produce interpellation via reiterated visual encounters with paperwork.

By comparison with Appadurai's Alliance, the *adivasi* groups with which I worked cannot be described as mass movements. To be sure, "consciousness-raising" featured prominently as a theme in the activists' rhetoric. Sramik Mukti

Andolan also goes by the name Jaag, meaning "awaken," and I was actually involved as a participant in an event convened by Sramik Mukti Sanghatan that was described as a consciousness-raising program. But, as will shortly become apparent, in 2003 organization work in the *pada*s was a hierarchized undertaking. And the surveys and maps of settlements in the forest zone whose results I present in this chapter were provisional efforts. Members of the most educated and urbanized cohort within the community came up with them in response to specific challenges mounted by powerful nontribal interests and in consultation with other actors from outside. I would thus hesitate to analyze the groups with which I worked in terms of democracy or civil society. To bring in the work of a different theorist, they are more like incubators of *political society*, in Partha Chatterjee's formulation.

This chapter is organized around two crises in the forest zone. The challenge in the case of the SGNP took shape in a sequence of lawsuits. An effort to expel human "encroachers" from the area of the forest preserve reached the Bombay High Court as a writ petition, 305 of 1995, filed by an organization called the Bombay Environmental Action Group (BEAG). Debate in *BEAG v. Maharashtra* centered on the question of how human settlement in natural spaces was to be regarded in the eyes of the law. The survey data compiled by Sramik Mukti Andolan / Jaag was submitted as evidence in the case that succeeded *BEAG*, Writ Petition 925 of 2000, *Sapte v. Maharashtra*, which reopened the question with particular reference to the park's tribal population.

Having considered the arguments of learned counsel in these cases, I will move on to discuss some aspects of Sramik Mukti Sanghatan's activism in the areas adjoining the national park, the Aarey Milk Colony and Film City. This part of the forest is characterized by conflict between *adivasi* communities and a number of development interests that, when not effectively blind to their presence, actively seek to erase them from the landscape. The scenario is most vividly illustrated by the fate of a Film City hamlet called Devipada, the uneasy neighbor of an expanding construction site. The development in question, the Whistling Woods Film Academy, is the brainchild of the Bollywood impresario Subhash Ghai, director of *Taal* (1999), *Black and White* (2008), and other films. To hem the villagers in, Ghai's crews have erected a stone wall across territory the Warlis claim as part of their *pada* and on one occasion in 2003 enlisted the support of the authorities in relocating the inhabitants; the police arrived with bludgeons and a bulldozer.[3]

The conflicts animating my case studies were fought on distinct semiotic fields. In the first case, the right to live on forest land—a rationalized space given visible form in maps and measurements—was contested by professional advocate-surrogates, each move mediated through files of printed paper. In the second, a material usurpation of space enacted one party's erasure of the indexical presence of the other. In the mind of my Filmistan interlocutor Vikas, the contrast between these two scenarios would no doubt have been sharpened as an opposition between the rule of law and the exercise of terror. But I favor a different analytic. At stake in both cases, I will argue, was the problem of *recognition*. Invisibility, which had so long defined the tribal condition, was no longer a refuge. Once the forest had been absorbed within the realm of polity, it became incumbent on the Warlis to claim recognition as fellow subjects in whatever terms were practicable, or be consigned to abjection.

The opening move made by both tribal organizations was to compile official-looking survey data to enumerate the populations whose homes had been brought under threat. The next step was to connect those abstract symbols with representations of tribals already circulating in legal discourse and other privileged channels. The need was for images and narratives that could frame the forest's inhabitants as a certain kind of community whose relation to a certain kind of space gave them rights of occupancy. While it was imperative to come up with numbers on a map, in other words, there also had to be a persuasive validation of those numbers' presence on that map.

In what follows I will explore some of the distortions generated by the system of archival registration. In parallel with my tour of Mumbai's street shrines, my analysis will advance toward an engagement with Peirce's typology of sign-object relations. The bulk of my exposition will center on administrative and legal actions and accordingly will emphasize the symbolic mode. At the chapter's end, however, it is the iconic that will emerge as the salient signifying logic in the efforts of Mumbai's Warlis to make their mark as a community with a distinct cultural profile.

And along the way, it will be vital to consider a bid for self-representation that relies on an indexical link between the population and its land—namely, that marked by the resident gods. In the past decades, a body of precedent in the adjudication of indigenous-rights cases has accumulated in other countries that share the presence of a Native minority alongside a heritage in British common law—Australia, Canada, the United States—to produce, at a transnational level, a reified construction of tribal culture. One of the defining marks of such a minority community is adherence to a particular kind of religious observance, one that (again, regardless of geographical or historical provenance) claims space on the basis of recognition of immanent spirits at specific sites.

These legal precedents could give the inhabitants of the SGNP a leg up on their subaltern counterparts downtown who, in building shrines and worshiping stones and trees on the streets, may have felt themselves to be communing with divinity in much the same way.

Or such was the calculation of the Warlis' lawyer in the *Sapte v. Maharashtra* case, Maharukh Adenwalla. Yug Mohit Chaudhry, her partner, laid out the essential challenge of the case for me: "What is *title*? If we say, 'Our gods live in these hills,' *that's* title. That's a claim."

Sapte's Context: *BEAG* and the Failure of Governmentality

Sapte v. Maharashtra was a writ brought in the Bombay High Court against the state of Maharashtra in its capacity as the administrator of the SGNP. Named as copetitioners were Manik Rama Sapte, a "Warli Adivasi, residing at Navapada, Opp. Mafco Factory, Borivli National Park, Borivli (East), Mumbai-400 060," and the NGO Sramik Mukti Andolan. It was filed in 2000 by Colin Gonsalves, an advocate working for a different NGO, the Socio-legal Information Centre. The case was argued three years later by a legal colleague, Maharukh Adenwalla. In the summer and fall of 2003 I followed the case from Maharukh's office, the High Court, and the forest.[4]

In this period, if Mumbai's English-language newspapers were reminding the public of the human presence in the forest preserve, they were doing so via an offbeat story line. Right at the city's doorstep, it seemed, there had arrived an influx of fierce jungle beasts. In September it was reported that the body of an Aarey Milk Colony resident half-devoured by a leopard had been recovered from an adjoining section of the SGNP (Express News Service 2003). In October the *Indian Express* revealed that leopards captured in areas where they were likely to molest humans were simply being released back into other parts of the park (V. Singh 2003b).[5] The theme had actually debuted back in June with the discovery of the pugmarks of a tiger. The *Express* reporter who spent a day in the forest in quest of the beast came across more than one *adivasi* hamlet, but no sign of his quarry (V. Singh 2003a).

There is actually such semantic slipperiness among the words used to designate large animals in Marathi, Hindi, and colloquial Indian English that it can be hard to tell which species is meant. On one of my visits to the *pada*s in Film City, I was told of attacks by a creature that my hosts described by the English term *tiger* but that I am fairly sure was what I would call a leopard. On the track of the rarer, more formidable beast, the *Express* correspondent pressed the tribals for information about the *pattewala wagh,* the *wagh* with stripes. As I have mentioned before, under the name Wagh, Waghya, Waghdev, or Waghoba, the tiger is worshiped and propitiated by forest-dwelling groups like the Warlis as the guardian of the village boundaries. Revealingly, however, in the context of rural religion, *wagh* can also mean a fierce domesticated animal—watchdogs, sheepdogs, or hunting dogs of the kind that attend the horseman Khandoba (Dhere 1995, 249–50; Sontheimer 1997, 52–53). Of course, Khandoba himself functions as a boundary god, patrolling the approaches to the homes of agriculturalist and pastoralist castes, and herein lies the twist that makes this spate of news stories a commentary on the situation of Mumbai's tribals. For the figure of a horseman may also be found incised or daubed on the posts and stones of Warli guardians, including those named as Waghoba.

In what form are the Warlis to imagine their protector? As the mounted man from the steppes who drives the four-legged marauders from his flock, and in so doing opens the wilderness to cultivation? Or as the wild forest creature that preserves the habitat by keeping just such interlopers at bay?[6]

The local people the *Express*'s Vijay Singh encounters in lieu of the tiger—in effect, they take over the story—are made to seem on familiar terms with the beast. "Over ten hours in the jungle, we met dozens of tribals, all of whom claimed to have seen the *wagh*." It is established that the wild animal's proper place is in the state-administered natural space—indeed, its romantic presence might be said to validate the space as such. But what of the wild people to be found there instead? Are the Warlis to be numbered alongside their tutelary deity as organic parts of the environment?

If the tiger hunt piece cites a naturalized tribal presence, the report about leopards filed some months later by the same, felicitously named writer cuts sharply against that figuration. In defining "the classic human-animal conflict," Singh (2003b) is in fact content to relay the position of the leading advocates of the expulsion from the SGNP of all its human residents. In the views of Debi Goenka of the BEAG and the park's deputy director, A. R. Bharati, the root of the leopard problem lay with "[w]ho the animals share their space with: Over 12,000 illegal hutments inside the 103 sq km of the SGNP." Bharati is quoted offering "the solution" to this incompatibility: "The state government should amicably rehabilitate all the forest encroachers to a different place. . . . We have to accept that jungle sanctuaries are only meant for wild animals." As it happens, this is an effective condensation of the arguments Bharati had submitted to the Bombay High Court just a few months before as a respondent in the case of *Sapte v. Maharashtra*. In fact, Bharati's position was also an affirmation of the ruling that had mandated action on his part in a previous lawsuit, one in which he had found himself on the opposite side from Goenka: 1995's *BEAG v. Maharashtra*. For it was the decision in that case, handed down in 1997, that had identified all human settlement in the SNGP as illegal "encroachment" and targeted it for demolition.

Acting on that court order, municipal and Forest Department workers and Maharashtra police had carried out a series of demolitions between 1997 and 2000. The brutality of these operations drew the attention of an organization called the Indian People's Human Rights Commission (IPHRC), which set up a tribunal composed of three retired High Court judges to pursue an investigation.[7] The IPHRC published the tribunal's recommendations along with its findings and a body of supporting evidence in the form of a booklet, *Crushed Homes, Lost Lives* (Sebastian 2000), in October 2000. The following month, this document was attached as Exhibit A to a petition filed with the SGNP Grievance Redressal Committee, a body that had been constituted as a result of the *BEAG* decision; this move complemented the lawsuit the park's tribals had by then introduced before serving members of the bench in the names of Sapte and Sramik Mukti Andolan.

Crushed Homes, Lost Lives sets the scene with map and survey data derived from official sources. These introductory dates and measures are not contested and supply some coordinates held in common by the two camps: on the one hand, the state and city agencies acting on the court order and, on the other, the IPHRC in its capacity as advocate for the displaced.[8] In 1995, the year the BEAG filed its suit, the Maharashtra Forest Department put the number of residential structures occupying land within the boundaries of this territory at between 78,000 and 86,000. From this estimate the IPHRC derives total population figures of from 390,000 to 430,000 individuals. By the time of the publication of the tribunal's report in 2000, Forest Department officials had reckoned the number of households displaced in compliance with the 1997 demolition order at just under 50,000, with the remaining approximately 30,000 families placed on notice (Sebastian 2000, 2–3). "This is one of the largest ever demolition[s] conducted in urban India," comments the IPHRC, "and [at least] four persons have died due to alleged brutal actions of the police and demolition squads. More than four lakh [400,000] people—equivalent to a middle-size township— have been rendered homeless in one fell swoop" (2).

The compilation of this survey data relies on a simple calculus. What the Forest Department has been counting—perhaps not using the most rigorous methodology—is houses. The IPHRC has extrapolated families from structures at a correspondence of 1 to 1 and derives an estimate of individuals at the ratio of five members to each family.[9] This sort of rule-of-thumb accounting is a far cry from the comprehensive self-surveillance practiced by the slum residents of Appadurai's description. Poignantly, however, in a development all too typical of this sort of eviction scenario, it turned out that many of these *kaccha* households were in fact registered with a variety of state agencies and in asserting a right to stay in place unmolested could produce a range of official documentation that linked name to address: "ration cards, voters identity cards[,] . . . names . . . included in the Electoral Roll" (Sebastian 2000, 6).[10]

Of the squatter colonies that had jostled the park's fringes in the 1990s, the IPHRC report observes: "The area supposedly within the National Park contains schools run by the [Brihanmumbai Municipal] Corporation, ration shops, dispensaries, structures having requisite facilities such as electricity, water, sanitation and telephone. Many of the homes are 'pucca' structures which have been provided with amenities by the concerned authorities. Many of the residents [*sic*] structures have been in existence prior to the area being declared a 'National Park'" (Sebastian 2000, 4). This description suggests the two propositions that supplied the subaltern settlers and their allies in the citizen class with grounds for argument against the eviction order. One point was that many residents could make the claim—backed by dated records—that their houses had stood in place well before 1983, when the government's notification of the area as a national park had yanked the ground from under their foundations, so to speak. The other move was to dispute whether the land they occupied fell within the SGNP's boundaries at all. This second line of argument was given credibility by the concentration of settlement on the protected area's margins. For as illustrated by the data and interviews the tribunal went on to compile, the majority of the park's residents fell into that class of Mumbai subalterns definable by Sandeep Pendse's (1995) term *toilers*—a fraternity united not by religious, linguistic, or caste affinity but rather in their daily experience of struggling to get by, generally in the informal sectors of the economy. Most of the people living on forest land, in short, were located where they were in spite of, not because of, the woods.[11]

Participants in the urban economy, the SGNP toilers considered themselves to be members of urban society. And they aspired to recognition as citizens. In their testimony, evictees often expressed shock that they had not been integrated within the grid of governmentality to the extent that the paper trails they generated had seemed to record. On top of the taxes levied on households in some neighborhoods, the bribes demanded by police officers, Forest Department officials, and other representatives of the state (the principal providers of electricity, water, and telephone service in Mumbai are public agencies) must have felt like quasi-official surcharges. "Ketkipada and Dharkhadi is situated on Survey No. 345A, and has been in existence since the last more than 60 years, [*sic*] About 1,30,000 persons reside there. The area contains 5 ration shops, 2 municipal schools 3 BEST sub-stations, telephone lines and 12" pipe supplying water. Residents are paying non-agricultural (NA) Tax and Assessment Tax indicating that the land is designated for 'agricultural' use and not 'forest' by the revenue department. Certain residents possess 7/12 Extracts [land title documents] in their names" (Sebastian 2000, 22–23). And if they looked to official paperwork to endow their habitations with definition against the green blank of the natural space, they also undertook the characteristic work of *pakka*-fication at a material level. In a movement parallel to the street shrine–to–temple development projects charted in previous chapters, the SGNP squatters invested their earnings and sweat in consolidating the component structures of their settlements—from flimsy to solid, from rough to smooth, from a contingent to a permanent or finished condition.

All, in the end, to no avail. The trust many had placed in typescript and numerals as a medium of proof—validating their presence in the space in question and at the right time—turned out to be misguided. As far as the history of occupancy went, the authorities decided that the only date that mattered was 1 January 1995. That was the cutoff that had been decreed throughout the metropolis by the terms of an urban-renewal policy inaugurated, with some fanfare, by the new Shiv Sena–led Maharashtra government. In the name of modernity and self-respect, Mumbai's eyesore squatter colonies were finally to be razed, with the key provision that claimants able to demonstrate residency in the city before 1995 would be grandfathered into legal and *pakka* housing.[12]

The way this policy was implemented in the national park in the aftermath of *BEAG v. Maharashtra* left a good deal to be desired. In its order dated 7 May 1997, the Bombay High Court directed:

(o) . . . persons whose names are not found in the electoral rolls prepared with reference to 1st January, 1995 or any date prior thereto shall be forthwith removed from the National Park Division and structures inhabited by them shall be demolished. . . .

(p) With respect to the slum dwellers residing with the National Park Division whose names appear on the electoral rolls . . . it is directed that the State Government shall within 18 months from date, relocate these persons outside

the boundaries of the National Park Division, in keeping with their present policies, and thereafter demolish the structures occupied by them. (Sebastian 2000,
8–9)[13]

In practice, however, in many cases recorded by the IPHRC, the squads of police and Forest Department and Municipal Corporation workers who initiated
the demolition campaign in October, once the monsoon had passed, could not
or would not discriminate between these two classes of squatters. The report
drily notes that "the heavy duty demolishing equipment like . . . earth movers
could hardly distinguish between the pre and post 1995 residents, and by an[d]
large those protected under the May 7 order also were felled in the aggressive
demolition drive" (16).

The SGNP resettlement scheme seems to have failed entirely, and in its report the tribunal is not above imputing bad faith to the Maharashtra government. The initial lack of any actual provision for accommodating evictees at
alternative sites resulted in a stay of demolition activity that was maintained all
through 1998 and into 1999. In August 1999 the court was finally informed that
appropriate land had been found in the Thane subdistricts of Kalyan and Ambarnath, on the other side of the forest from the city. "The state government
however bowled a googly by insisting that the slum dwellers also contribute to
their own rehabilitation by paying Rs 10,000 per family as a precondition to the
allotment of the rehabilitation plots" (Sebastian 2000, 52).[14] Then the demolitions recommenced. The anxiety in the beleaguered communities would only
grow over the following months as the pace of demolition escalated, and more
and more families struggled to raise funds in the belief that they might be able
to procure a reprieve—only to be rebuffed by an officialdom apparently dead
set on flattening their neighborhoods.

In the absence of comprehensive population survey data, the settlers and
their allies sought leverage in records certifying residency over set dates that
they expected to have legally binding implications. This was largely in vain. It
will be recalled that they also pursued a complementary tactic: to question
the extant land survey data. Over the course of the demolitions several different neighborhoods appealed to the court for relief on the grounds that the
acreage they had been building on was not the National Park Division's to re-
claim. In some cases, the bench found the lack of definition in the boundary
lines sufficient to justify stop orders. At other sites, however, "the High Court
accepting the Forest Department's interpretations without ground surveys . . .

elevated the forest officials to the status of both judge and executioners" (Sebastian 2000, 66).

But in fact, with the passage of time, the Maharashtra government itself came to concede that there were areas of slippage between the National Park Division's jurisdiction on the ground and the emplotment of lines on the map. The Forest Department and Revenue Department were duly ordered to collaborate on a survey of two such *kaccha* areas. I conclude this description of the SGNP squatter evictions with the report's comment on this point: "Survey No 42A in Kandivili covers Bhim Nagar and Damupada, while Survey No 239(1) covers Ambedkarnagar area, both of which have been reduced to rubble by demolition squads. It is ironical that the government should choose to begin boundary measurements *after* the demolitions have already been carried out" (Sebastian 2000, 66).

The Tribal Exception

By 2000 the slum rehabilitation initiative spearheaded by the new Shiv Sena administration had excited as much attention for its destruction of housing across the city as for its sponsorship of new, *pakka* units. In this climate the Indian People's Human Rights Commission was able to enlist a good deal of public support for the victims of the demolitions in the national park. Allies included such leading citizens as the film star and leftist icon Shabana Azmi, the reformist ex–prime minister of India V. P. Singh, and even the famously incorruptible and outspoken deputy municipal commissioner G. R. Khairnar. Khairnar had become known in the English-language press as the "Demolition Man" for his zeal in pressing forward with slum clearances in the name of the rule of law, but by the time of the ill-executed campaign in the park, he was falling afoul of his political masters and eventually found himself suspended from his duties.[15] I think that in theoretical terms what exercised a figure like Khairnar could be summed up as a breakdown of governmentality. But at the risk of seeming to romanticize the invisibility of the SGNP evictees—and I trust the material I have presented from the tribunal has conveyed an impression of the lawlessness and real terror with which they met at the hands of the government's agents— I'll say there does seem to be something conceptually fitting about their *kaccha* blurriness on the park's periphery, shadows in a liminal zone between polity and wilderness, before the surveilling gaze of the state.

In distinction from the urban migrants whose settlements seemed to infringe on the park's integrity, *Crushed Homes, Lost Lives* identifies two other resident communities within its borders. Both are groups whose place is in the forest, to go by the nature-culture dichotomy; both, moreover, are groups whose bond with the space is experienced and represented as a matter of religion. The first of these two classes of forest dwellers is of course tribals: thirty-six *padas* within Mumbai city limits, to revive one set of figures with which this chapter opened, and an additional twenty on the Thane side. It is the legal challenge put forward in the name of this constituency that I will examine in this section.

The second group, mentioned in a single paragraph, consists of religious figures who have retreated to the wild as hermits. Along with a general lack of regard for their claims, the notable thing about the way they are described by the IPHRC is the indiscriminate use of Hindu and Islamic terminology, implying that sectarian distinctions are beside the point when it comes to identifying such charismatics:

> It has come to notice from the depositions of the residents and several journalists that several hundred acres of forest land has been grabbed by land sharks and ashrams and babas posing to be godmen.[16] These dargas and ashrams are situated in both Goregaon and Borivali side of the Park. . . . On the Borivali side of the park, several babas and ashrams are prospering in the Kanheri caves area, and are said to be patronised by the local BJP MLA [member of the state legislature]. Reports by journalists indicate that many of these godmen have air-conditioned apartments and mobile phones at their disposal. No notices of eviction or any demolition operations have been conducted against these ashrams. Nor has this issue been pressed in court by the BEAG. (Sebastian 2000, 66–67)

However lax in the actual observance of their vows, ascetics of this sort are as essential a part of a self-respecting Indian jungle as tribals and tigers. I have no firsthand information about this subset of the forest's population. But I suspect that on top of the prestige the *babas* command within their cult communities, their patronage by such powerful interests as the right-wing lawmaker mentioned above has a good deal to do with the entente they evidently enjoy with forestry officials and perhaps even, as the report remarks, with members of the Bombay Environmental Action Group.

A comparison with the more established or *pakka*-fied sites among the city's unlicensed places of worship, as described in chapter 2, is instructive here. The builder of a religious structure on contested ground relies on some degree of culturally pervasive piety, that is to say, of recognition of the enshrined presence itself as a validating authority, as insurance against demolition. But attracting the interest of a locally powerful and connected human patron adds the promise of a level of hands-on security that could prove decisive. What's more, in its contrast between a set of principles or affective dispositions held in common, on the one hand, and the personal attentions of a power broker, on the other, this scenario replicates an opposition central to my friend Vikas's way of thinking: between the public code of law and the familial model of bullying and nepotism, *dadagiri*.

Finally, the case of the *baba*s brings up a practical consideration. This is the question of topography. As inhabitants of the park's rugged interior, the holy men occupied spaces that were neither as accessible to the bulldozers as the border areas nor as visible to—or potentially exploitable by—parties interested in the administrative and commercial development of suburban Mumbai. Of course, the same should have applied to the tribal habitations scattered through the forest. And more than any other factor it was perhaps the *pada*s' inaccessibility that kept the demolition crews at bay until 1999, when notices were posted in the woods informing the National Park Division's *adivasi* residents— those who could read, anyway—that they were being evicted subject to the same conditions dictated to the settlers of the periphery.

Provision was to be made, then, on a family-by-family basis, for resettlement at the Kalyan or Ambarnath sites contingent on payment of 7,000 rupees. The figure was well beyond the means of a community that lived, for the most part, at a subsistence level off forest produce. And payment, of course, was not the heart of the matter. If the policy of levying fees from families to be dispossessed of their jerry-built shantytown homes seems yet less well conceived when applied to the residents of jungle clearings, there can be little doubt that when word reached the tribals of just what sort of land they were getting relocated to, it was met with even less enthusiasm.

Both of these points are emphasized in the section that *Crushed Homes, Lost Lives* sets aside for tribal matters: four pages of testimony from *pada* residents and statements in their support by two experts, the activist Vithal Lad (himself a Warli) of Sramik Mukti Andolan and the sociologist Indra Munshi of the University of Mumbai. Two of the statements the tribunal collected refer to a precedent in the tribals' experience of deportation. Both Lad and Venu Soma Pagi, a seventy-year-old local Warli, noted that back in 1973 or 1974 the Forest Department had made a determination about permissible land use practices in four hamlets within the SGNP, identifying a number of families as tillers of cultivated plots as opposed to foragers. These offenders were removed to a distant site in Thane's Palghar Subdistrict. Just as in the later scenario, the land set aside for resettlement had been part of someone else's village. Finding it "barren [and] rocky," the reluctant homesteaders soon returned to their *pada*s.

The court order in *BEAG* dictated the removal from the SGNP of all persons duly and authoritatively determined to fall into the category of "encroacher." Documenting Maharashtra officialdom's near-blind application of this standard to the tribal as well as settler communities is the main point of the material reproduced in *Crushed Homes* from interviews with *adivasi*s. But even as the IPHRC frames its grievance in terms of the denial to both groups of rights due them in common, its report sets up the makings of a case for tribal exceptionalism. If the treatment suffered by the tribals comes across as peculiarly unjust, that is because its presentation relies on distinguishing details that support a conception of *adivasi*s as a peculiar sort of community.

To put the problem in analytic terms: both constituencies faced a crisis of misrecognition. But whereas the toilers, the great majority of the park's population, were stymied in a bid for recognition as fellow citizens, what was at stake in the tribals' claim to the space they inhabited was not commonality but difference. The two propositions on which Maharukh Adenwalla and her legal and activist colleagues constructed their argument in *Sapte v. Maharashtra* emerged clearly in the tribunal's report. First is the symbiotic, even organic, relation of the tribal way of life to the natural environment. Second is the culturally distinct character of tribal identity.

The two points overlap, of course. But for the sake of coherence, let's take up the question of spatio-economic practices first. "Tribals have been residing in SGNP since time immemorial," the report states, "i.e. prior to the rule of the Moghuls, Marathas, and British" (Sebastian 2000, 36). And in time-honored ways, the tribunal's informants imply, they have continued to make a peaceable living in the woods. Their statements stress the consumption and also trading, on a small scale, of the fruits of their hunting (crabs and fish, nothing requiring a gun) and of their gathering (roots, herbs, and dry wood, nothing requiring a saw). Their houses are built of mud and bamboo, "which is easily available and renewable." Indeed, they protect the environment against the real agents of deforestation: timber traffickers and forest fires. Such agriculture as tribals do practice is unobtrusive and sustainable, amounting to the tilling of patches of grain and vegetables for subsistence and the raising of some chickens and goats.

Complementing the theme that at a material level their way of life is integrated with the forest that surrounds them, at a cultural level they are to be distinguished from the larger society that crowds them—thus, the insistence among some informants, seemingly prompted by questions from the tribunal, that their settlements do not harbor any households from outside the community. For example: "Non-tribals do not like to reside in hamlets and nor do we permit them to live in hamlets" (Sebastian 2000, 37). As my inquiries at Filmistan have indicated, the history of settlement in the area does involve configurations in which woodland *pada*s have developed as satellites of villages and, eventually, urban neighborhoods dominated by other groups. In fact, some of the population clusters in the present-day Aarey Milk Colony are mixed enough to defy straightforward description as tribal *pada*s. Moreover, the image of autonomous hamlets suggested in the report elides whatever distinctions might structure relations on the ground among Warli and Kokana, Kathkari, and other *adivasi* groups. Similar objections could be raised to the report's rather romanticized image of sustainable cultivation in the forest.[17] But recall that *Crushed Homes* served the tribals' lawyers as Exhibit A in the petition they filed with the park's Grievance Redressal Committee in tandem with the lawsuit *Sapte v. Maharashtra.* What I want to drive home here is that behind the selective picture there is a design to use the established tropes of tribal life to advantage.

Now, given the weight placed on religion as an "indicator" of tribal alterity by state anthropologists and others, it comes as no surprise to find a corresponding stress in these pages. Kisan Chander Warthe, an *adivasi* employed as a watchman by the Forest Department, asserts the distinctiveness of tribal religion in its deviance from a Hindu norm: "Our main fe[s]tivals are Holi and Dassera, and we celebrate the same in a tribal manner." It is the Dussehra celebration that involves an arresting inversion: "Amongst us, Ravana is revered and his effigy is not burnt."[18] More adroit are the moves that situate religion as the tie that binds the population to its land. The same informant notes, "The dead amongst us are buried in SGNP. There is burial ground for four to five hamlets." This statement, too, marks a point of divergence, aligning *adivasi*s with Muslims and Christians as religious minorities that do not cremate.[19] And if generations of ancestors are embedded in the forest floor, so too, of course, are the community's gods. In Warthe's words, "Though we [have] no temples we have deities everywhere in the forest." Venu Soma Pagi's testimony makes the claim to space explicit: "They have close affiliation to the forest as their gods reside therein; they worship Himay, Hirva, Nanadev, Kansari, Waghaya" (Sebastian 2000, 37–38).

In chapters 2 and 3 I argued several points about the unauthorized erection of shrines in Mumbai neighborhoods. Mindful of the atmosphere of scarcity and anxiety that permeates the problem of housing in the city, particularly for poor people, I discussed this phenomenon as a project undertaken primarily by migrants from the rural hinterland. I argued that the structures should not be identified with the teachings of any particular religious community but rather viewed as manifestations of a pervasive sacred geography at odds with the liberal, postcolonial vision of the city. And adapting some elements of a Peircean semiotic vocabulary, I plotted the development of these claims to contested space on an axis running from *kaccha* to *pakka*, charting the progress of their operations within discrete fields of effects: their legibility as signs, their affective force as stations of presence. I think all three of these points are translatable to the situation in the forest zone as I have sketched it out in this chapter.

If the position of the SGNP tribals is evaluated in terms of space and recognition, it should emerge that the imperative confronting them and their lawyers in 2003 was, in a sense, the reverse of that faced by the downtown temple builders. In this case, the challenge did not lie in getting the legal system, and associated members of the citizen class, to recognize the logic that an immanent spirit marks a site apart as the territory of its cult community. This principle is fully in accord with received ideas and images of tribal spirituality that circulate nationally and transnationally through legal and public channels. Indeed, it also corresponds with the construction of the forest as a natural space. (As a home for spirits, the street has not, as chapter 2 should have made clear, been much of a contender in the bourgeois imagination.) But having once opted for distinction as authentic children of nature, as opposed to fellow citizens, where the park's *adivasi*s risked a failure of recognition was in having their discrete sites of worship noticed at all. The more *pakka* a street-front shrine is, the more effective its claim on public attention. How then, conversely, was a nontribal observer supposed to recognize whether a given spot in the forest preserve was sacred to the community or not?

Under the entry for "Várli" in the *Tribes and Castes of Bombay*, R. E. Enthoven (1920–22, 3:450) cites an authority from a previous generation of colonial scholarship: "In 1859, Mr. Boswell, the then Assistant Collector of Thána, described the religion of Várlis as follows:—Their religion consists chiefly in spirit worship. They think that every place is under the care of some spirit who lives in a tree or in a stone. Some they think unfriendly and spiteful, others friendly, and others indifferent, friendly or unfriendly according as they are propitiated or not." Most of this picture is corroborated by present-day contacts of mine within Sramik Mukti Sanghatan, modern Mumbai Warlis: "We used to believe trees and rocks were gods." (The smiles that would attend statements like this one had more to do with the leftist skepticism espoused by their organization than with the sort of patronizing take more committed Hindus might have expressed.) Again, as Warthe told the IPHRC tribunal, "We have no temples." Religious activity gets no more *kaccha* than nature worship. But here is the problem. If, at the rhetorical level, nature worship supplies the most effective device for connecting a tribal community to its land in the discursive space of the court, how were the Warlis to come up with visible gestures of that worship for others to recognize as evidence? To revert, once again, to the terms of Peircean semiotics: how was an indexical phenomenon to be made iconic?

Manik Rama Sapte v. State of Maharashtra

"In the High Court of Judicature at Bombay" runs across the tops of the official documents filed in the case of *Sapte v. Maharashtra*: writ petition, respondent's affidavit, written arguments, judgment. The physical space the words designate is a monumental neo-Gothic structure, a landmark of colonial architecture and also, to my outsider's eyes and ears, of colonial manners and locutions. Viewed from the street, the steep Gothic arcades, bustling with lawyers in black gowns and white stocks, look imposing, not to say forbidding. Only once up close do you see the stains and other signs of tropical weathering that embody the acclimation, over time, of this bastion of British jurisprudence. The High Court's police presence is revealed to be minimal; entry to its precincts, surprisingly easy. Possibly the grandness of the building has been deemed security in itself against intrusion by people who have no business being there.

My business on 17 July 2003 was the hearing at which Maharukh Adenwalla and her opponent R. M. Sawant, the government pleader, gave oral arguments before the bench. Chief Justice C. K. Thakker and Justice S. Radhakrishnan sat at a massive platform flanked by a bailiff in red livery and Maharashtrian turban; the dark-paneled room was adorned with portraits of the British jurists of previous centuries. The spectators in the gallery, diffident yet intent, had left standing room only. Most if not all must have been tribal members of Sramik Mukti Andolan. Although the language of the proceedings was English, I doubt I understood much more of what was being said than my neighbors. No decision would be forthcoming for another two months, and as the judges and the lawyers traded statements it was difficult to distinguish words of argument from protocol. The draped backs of the lawyers bobbed up and down, the big fans churned the air overhead; eventually I found myself a place to sit down, but most folk in the gallery stood through it all with uncomplaining patience.

Maharukh's predecessor, Colin Gonsalves, had filed Writ Petition 925 of 2000 on 23 March of that year. After identifying the petitioners and asserting their role as representatives of a community of 2,500 families, the document defines their grievance. The list of the fifty-six forest hamlets with which this chapter began—the places where those families make their homes—can be found annexed to the petition as Exhibit A.

Gonsalves's next step was to establish the tribal position as a question of customary law. In amplifying this point he summoned conventional tropes both of nature, as a condition that tribals unproblematically inhabit, and of culture, as a component of identity that marks the community apart: "The forest is a religious and cultural site for the forest dwelling communities and is the home or the natural environment of such people, just as the city is the home to the urban citizen. Ownership of this home is based on principles very different from the modern, legal notions of property. These principles are governed by customary law" (Sapte and Sramik Mukti Andolan 2000, para. 16). And in cementing the claim he made an appeal to precedents that have been set transnationally in the adjudication of Native land claims: "The emerging principle in the common law tradition from Australia, New Zealand, Canada, USA and South America is that communal rights in land are not dependent on legislation or administrative orders" (para. 22 [i]).[20]

At the end of the document the petitioners submit their "prayers" to the court. This section articulates three aims. The first is that the judges issue an order prohibiting the Maharashtra authorities from evicting any of the inhabitants of the settlements identified on the list in Exhibit A. The second aim is for an official judgment to be passed recognizing their status as legal inhabitants of their space. And third, in the interim pending the decision, the forest officers should be stayed from harassing any of the SGNP tribals. The second point is particularly important. The petition's request, in its own words, is "for an order directing the Respondents to regularise the occupation and possession of all the persons residing [in] the Adivasi padas listed at Exhibit A to this petition in the very same place and to grant full access to minor forest produce and to recognise the customary rights of the said persons" (para. 30 [b]). As the case proceeded, it would develop that the question of "regularisation" was the point on which the decision would pivot.[21]

The key move from the respondents' side was the submission of an affidavit to the High Court by the national park's deputy director, A. R. Bharati, on 14 July. Bharati's statement relies on two tabulations of population figures. The sources of those figures, while not purporting to represent comprehensive survey work, were nevertheless put forward as authoritative. The first is a signed and stamped Forest Department memorandum from 1977. The second is a letter from the members of a local tribal-rights NGO. This is the document attached to the affidavit as the respondents' own Exhibit A.

It will be recalled that two of the Warlis whose testimony was represented in *Crushed Homes, Lost Lives* had cited a previous attempt by forestry officials to have tribals removed from the park. In this initiatory event, which is remembered as having occurred in the mid-1970s, the authorities separated the alleged tillers of forest land from their foraging neighbors and deported them to a distant site. Bharati's first source text is an itemized list of the costs incurred by the Revenue and Forest Department in carrying out this operation.[22] It records the transport and resettlement of forty-two families in huts built on land in Palghar Subdistrict that had to be cleared of trees, stumps, and brush. (For some reason, Bharati's affidavit misreports this number as forty-six.) The second text is the work of a group called Adivasi Hakka Samiti, or Indigenous Rights Collective, an NGO that was apparently active within a subset of the forest zone's *pada*s at the time of the *BEAG* suit in the late 1990s. A letter dated 16 December 1998, it is the product of a meeting held on 4 August of that year between forestry officers and representatives of local tribal settlements concerning the court-mandated rehabilitation scheme. In the text, fifteen members of Adivasi Hakka Samiti bear witness that the number of *adivasi*s resident within the park's bounds amounts to some 260 families within eleven *pada*s (fig. 5).

The Forest Department's argument was simple. As the first of these documents could certify, the total tribal population of the SGNP in 1977 had been a mere 46 families. As of 1998, per the second record, it numbered 260 families.[23] The balance of the 2,500 families Sramik Mukti Andolan had estimated and whom the *Sapte* petitioners represented were thus—if present in the park at all—not tribals. Setting aside the eleven settlements legitimated by mention in the Adivasi Hakka Samiti letter, the fifty-six *pada*s the petitioners listed were not *pada*s but squatter colonies. And a further point to be inferred from Bharati's evidence—and chalked up in his favor—was the apparent fluctuation in the numbers recorded in 1977 and 1998 of a population claimed by the petitioners to have been inhabiting the forest since time immemorial.

The deputy director makes his position plain in paragraph 5 of the affidavit. In citing the passage, I add my own emphasis to what I take to be the key point: "I say that the petitioner's contention that the Tribal families have been the residents of the National Park for generations, cannot be accepted in view of the Revenue and Forest record, as stated hereinabove. I say that if the petitioner's contention is to be accepted, *the status of the said Tribals would have been amply recorded* to show that there are 2500 families who have been residing there for centuries and who have special customary rights over the said forest" (emphasis added). Bharati implies here that the Forest Department's failure of governmentality was somehow the *adivasi* community's fault. What's undeniable is that it had ended up being their problem. It should be noted that such tribal population figures as Bharati is able to muster in this affidavit were collected in the context of state-directed projects to reduce them to zero: a first time in the 1970s, a second in the late-1990s aftermath of the *BEAG* decision. It seems likely that at both junctures, survey work had been undertaken only once the authorities had already settled on eviction as their course of action.[24]

In comparing Bharati's letter with the petitioners' Exhibit A, the list of fifty-six *pada*s compiled by their own tribal-rights NGO, I reach for my Peircean toolbox. First, to put things in accord with my earlier propositions about governmentality and archival paperwork, I note that the signifying work both lawyers stressed with their deployment of these documents takes place at the symbolic level: the authoritative conversion of tribal subjects into numerals and typescript. (Roman type, the most prestigious register, was supplied in the case of the Marathi letter by an English translation.) However, the indexical and iconic operations of the *Sapte* exhibits are also part of the stories they tell as pieces of evidence.

The causal provenance of neither artifact is an official organ of archival data collection. Rather, at the indexical level, the claim of each to serve as a representation of local conditions rests on its validity as a statement by local people in the know—that is to say, by *adivasi*s. The petitioners' exhibit is an unadorned list (presumably transcribed from Sramik Mukti Andolan records by the lawyer's typist). The Adivasi Hakka Samiti letter, on the other hand, bears the traces of acts of witness: signatures and—perhaps more impressive as marks of both legality and tribality—thumbprints. And there is also an iconic dimension to the letter's superior force as a citation of both legal authority and tribal authenticity. Not only does it bear the impress of the rubber stamps of its recipients as well as of the inked digits of its subaltern coauthors, but it has been presented on the NGO's letterhead, which features a logo designed in the distinctive style of Warli graphic art. How are tribals qua tribals to be made recognizable in the eyes of the law? Between the indices of their physical presence and the icons of their cultural expression, the producers of this document had come up with not one but two answers. In the end I suspect that among the interested parties in the case, I was not alone in finding Bharati's evidence simply to look more like evidence.

In the oral arguments offered on 17 July, and in the written submissions with which she followed up on the thirty-first, Maharukh focused on two questions. The first was a question of legal recognition, of tribals as subjects of the state. What rights, if any, were indigenes who inhabited government-protected natural spaces entitled to? The second was a question of recognition in a more complicated, epistemological sense, of *tribal* as a category of identity. How many clients did she actually have, and how were the rest of us to know whether they were tribals at all?

On the first score her position was plain: the indigenes of the SGNP had a customary right to live in the forest. And in fact there was statutory language to back her up, contained in an amendment made to the Wild Life (Protection) Act of 1972 just one year before *Sapte* was heard, in 2002. Section 35 of the act is the legislation that established the category of *national park* in the Indian code. Its subsection 6, which is part of the later amendment, prohibits the exploitation of resources found in such spaces, including forest produce and other wildlife, "PROVIDED THAT where the forest produce is removed from a National Park, the same may be used for meeting the personal *bona fide* needs of the people living in and around the National Park and shall not be used for any commercial purpose" (Wild Life [Protection] Act 2003, 24). In her written submission to the High Court, Maharukh comments: "This proviso recognises that (a) people live in the National Park, (b) these people's bona fide needs are satisfied by forest produce, and (c) the forest produce may be used to satisfy these needs. 'People living in and around National Parks' who are depend[e]nt on forest produce relates to tribals."[25]

But as it developed, the main front in her battle would be the question not of rights but of legible identity. Referring to the testimony reproduced in the IPHRC report, Maharukh takes issue with Deputy Director Bharati's construction of the number of families deported in the 1970s as coterminous with the population of the SGNP's tribal residents. And, marking the Forest Department's failure to produce any evidence of survey work it had itself undertaken, in June 1996 or at any other time, she challenges the purview of the Adivasi Hakka Samiti as a representative organization:

> It is important to take note that in support of their claim that there are only 189 [*sic*] tribal families the Respondents have merely relied on a letter written by a non-governmental organisation who works with tribals residing in 11 tribal hamlets. This organisation was concerned with and had written a letter on behalf of those tribals in Sanjay Gandhi National Park with whom they are working. From the aforesaid it is clear that the First Respondent has no independent

knowledge of the number of tribal families or tribal hamlets contained in Sanjay Gandhi National Park.[26]

Justices Thakker and Radhakrishnan handed down their decision on 15 September 2003. *Adivasi*s were a group whose special interests had been duly recognized in the Indian courts as requiring special protection by the state. In principle, rulings in Maharashtra and elsewhere had set precedents for ordering regularization within national park territory as one such protective measure. Nevertheless, the justices stopped short of regularizing the homes of the *Sapte* petitioners. What they questioned was the estimated 2,500 families' standing as "bona fide tribals."

Bharati's affidavit and the letter attached to it had succeeded in their purpose, as I read it. This was to be taken just seriously enough that, if their erratic numbers did not actually secure official credence, they would nevertheless discredit the opposition's. Both sets of figures had been implicated in a project that was framed as intrinsically dubious: that of attempting an objective head count in the wilderness. The judges cited the Forest Department's data approvingly and concluded with the following words:

> 16. In view of the above facts and figures, in our opinion, a tall claim put forward by the petitioners cannot be upheld. There is no evidence, even of a *prima facie* nature, that the assertion made by the petitioners has substance.

Accordingly they dismissed the petition. They did, however, add the following proviso:

> 17. . . . It is however open to the State Government to consider the case of the petitioners and if it is found that they or any of them are tribals/adivasis, the respondent authorities will take appropriate proceedings in accordance with law for their settlement. . . .

In this way, the ruling created an opening for a fact-finding commission that could pronounce on the recognition of Maharukh's clients as tribals with official credibility. Seizing on the concession, she turned her energies to the search for an institutional body with the authority to host such a mission.

Her short list included a parliamentary standing committee in Delhi, a Mumbai-based research institute, and an agency of the Maharashtra government—none other, in fact, than the Tribal Research and Training Institute described in chapter 5. There was a model, after all, already in place at the TRTI for the sort of work the court had mandated: namely, the Caste Verification Office's protocol for fieldwork visits to "primitive" populations to evaluate their eligibility for tribal certificates. As the discussions advanced, Maharukh actually came to find partnership more feasible with Mumbai's Tata Institute of Social Sciences. But either way, it seemed, the future of the SGNP's *pada*s was going to hinge on their inspection by teams of official observers. Eviction procedures were scheduled to begin six months from the ruling.

Now, to address the question of what a bona fide tribal looks like is necessarily to ask, to whom? Efforts on the part of marginalized constituencies to gain visibility by appropriating symbols or images from more dominant strata may bring to mind the "poaching" discussed by Michel de Certeau (1984). But the moves I followed in my fieldwork tended to be more conscious exercises—more strategic than tactical, as de Certeau would have put it. Both the leaders of the area's *adivasi*s and their lawyers found they had to contend with a certain vexing lack of definition the *pada*s displayed by the standards of the hegemonically prevailing codes of representing space. Put simply, the tribal hamlets and the squatter colonies looked a bit too similar for comfort.

Back in 1995 the BEAG had presented photographs in support of the writ petition that had started all the trouble, stating at paragraph 16, "Large areas of the park look like slum colonies as is evidenced from the photographs at Ex. 'A' hereto." Of the same images, Maharukh asserted years later, "Photographs annexed at Exhibit 'A' of the [1995] petition *are* photographs of slum colonies." The passage (the italics are implicit in the original) appears in section B (b) of the written arguments she submitted in support of her own contention that her clients in *Sapte* were, not "encroachers" like those targeted by *BEAG*, but tribal villagers. She stopped short, however, of attaching the photographs she had of the petitioners' own dwellings. My own inability to tell the difference when her partner showed them to me might have had something to do with it. "It's a village," Yug had had to cue me, as if prepping a dull witness.

Gaondevi Puja

Ambassadors of foreign powers appointed to a monarchy are said to present their credentials at court. That, in a sense, is what was being demanded of the leaders of the forest zone's *adivasi*s in the aftermath of *Sapte v. Maharashtra*. I have laid out in some detail the impediments to their acquisition of visibility in the official archive. As an alternative to that, the arguments here and in chapter 5 have highlighted religion as a site of tribal difference. Tribals—it had been established in legal and public discourses—made their living space habitable by sacralizing it. (Per my argument in the first half of the book, in this they are actually no different from diverse other Mumbai-area subalterns, but never mind that.) Again, a tribal community's claim to a specific tract of land was understood to be experienced at a spiritual level; the distinctive ritual performances and visual symbols of tribal religion would be the means to express that spiritual bond and make it recognizable—*pakka*—in public. In the last part of this chapter I will investigate some of the complications that have arisen when tribal leaders looked to religion to mediate visibility for the community. I will also identify some alternative forms in which Mumbai's tribals have attained recognizable shape.

Above, I mentioned that the *adivasi* settlements in the national park exhibited no features legible enough to distinguish them in photographs from slum colonies. A *pada* may be experienced by its inhabitants as blessed or protected ground. The dwellings of its divine residents may conform to a sacred geography that generates effects according to a logic of indexical presence. And yet the villagers may stumble when faced with the imperative to translate their sense of home into terms recognizable to outsiders. For example, every settlement within the borders of the Aarey Milk Colony had been assigned a plot number by the administration. Sramik Mukti Andolan's Vithal Lad told me how hard he had had to struggle to persuade the residents to refer to their homes by the authentic-sounding *pada* names. When asked, "What is your village?" it was a matter of self-respect, Lad argued, to answer in Marathi, "Keltipada [Monkey Hamlet]," for example, instead of saying something like "Eighteen Number" in English.[27] Lad also surely thought of it as a matter of strategy. And this problem of the iconic signification, delivered phonically, of an authentically tribal claim to space applied not only to the *pada* as a unit but to the discrete dwelling spots of its gods. Time and again—and up to the present day—I have been told of how local Warlis had to be coached to respond to questions from outsiders. Whose place were they marking with their sacred stones? "You don't tell them, 'Ganesh,' 'Durga.' Make sure you say, 'Hirva,' 'Naran' [or Waghoba or Gaondevi]."

My interlocutor here was not Lad, of Sramik Mukti Andolan, but a leading member of its Film City and Aarey-based rival, Sramik Mukti Sanghatan. More modest in its scope and stressing a grassroots approach, Sramik Mukti Sanghatan had split from the other group in 1991 or 1992. It enjoyed some patronage from power brokers in the local party-NGO nexus (there appeared to be both Congress and Janata Party [Secularist] figures in the background), but its day-to-day operations were in the hands of a few local Warlis. Prashant, as I will call him, was one of these leaders, a dedicated social worker and a man whose leftist convictions had given him an ambivalent attitude toward religion as observed in the *pada*s. At the time of our first meeting he was in his late thirties.

The son of a schoolteacher, Prashant had a day job as a clerical worker at a hospital in the suburb of Jogeshwari. He did not live in the forest himself. The home he shared with his wife and two children was a two-room structure of cinder block and sheet metal—"Welcome to my hut," he had joked with me in English on my first visit—on a Jogeshwari hillside where every yard was covered in similar housing. In its own way this *pakka*-fied slum, home to people from a variety of Maharashtrian caste backgrounds, was as urban an environment as could be imagined. But in such time as he could reserve from his job and family, Prashant would walk down the motor road to Film City—no great distance—and make the rounds of his NGO's constituents in the woods.

Prashant's political sympathies were encapsulated in the greeting with which he announced himself in the *pada*s. He would raise his fist and call, "Zindabad!" This was short for *inqilab zindabad*, or "long live the revolution." In principle he adhered to a materialist disdain for religion. He wrote off the operators of the street shrines who had so excited my interest as hustlers who had hit on a clever way to turn a rupee by appealing to the credulity, as he saw it, of the masses. ("Opium of the people" sounds wonderfully narcotic when turned into Hindi: *awaam ka afeen*.) Yet one of the first episodes I followed of Prashant's enactment of his role as an urban advocate for the forest's residents involved a *gaondevi* shrine. A small structure marking a site in Film City, it had been damaged in a mudslide. Finding that the shrine (and perhaps its environs) was too *kaccha* to necessitate going through a formal registration process, he negotiated an informal agreement with the local police station to enable the site's reconstruction to go forward.[28] And on one sentimental occasion he remarked to me of his understanding that all religious beliefs and practices could be reduced to a simple principle of recognition. "I see you," he said in his basic English, gesturing at the sky, "you see me." Had he perhaps been inspired by the almost identically phrased maxim of Sai Baba?[29]

My friend embodies the image of a thoroughly modern, urban Warli. His wife had a white-collar job of her own, and their daughter and son had both gone on to higher education. Their little house on the hillside was known by a Sanskritized (and rather grand) name: Vidya Niwas, "the Home of Knowledge." Over the years I have known Prashant the structure has grown, with the acquisition of a second story, and indeed throughout the settlement the buildings have acquired a more glossy, *pakka* finish. His family has witnessed a steady improvement in their life conditions and prospects, and there can be little doubt that the sort of progress narrative in which they have been active participants, enabled by formal education and some judicious application of the levers of political society, was the pattern Prashant had in mind as he worked to ameliorate his kinfolk's marginalization.

In this context "religion," or *dharm*, meant two things to him, neither of them positive. It might refer to the doings of tribal *bhagats*—spirit-mediums like Vikas and his forebears—namely, possession activity, witchcraft, and blood sacrifice. Alternatively, it meant modern Hinduism in its hegemonic aspect—what Prashant liked to criticize in explicitly ideological terms as "Brahminism." The operative distinction for him, when it came to matters like the naming of village gods, would have been between superstructural "religion" (which the community would have been better off, in his view, dispensing with altogether) and "culture," *sanskriti*, as the authentic expression of tribal difference (see also Alles 2013). To follow up on the implications of this distinction for Prashant's activism, let's turn to a visibility-acquiring exercise he invited me to attend in the fall of 2003. In his leftist style, he referred to it as a "consciousness-raising program." He would be bemused to learn that I found the event, with its ritualized aspects and its central project of acquiring a portfolio of iconic images, to be something akin to religious proselytization.

Prashant, his colleagues in Sramik Mukti Sanghatan, and their counterparts in allied NGOs from Mumbai and Thane had planned the event as the statement of a rational, progressive *adivasi* sensibility. And they had scheduled it, calculatingly, on Gaondevi Puja, the central event of the Warli ritual calendar. This festival, which falls within a few days of Diwali, brings together the fellow residents of a tribal village from its component *pada*s, dispersed in the woods, to worship at the central station of the *gaondevi*, the goddess who personifies the space they share as a social unit.[30] Where the *pada*s within Sramik Mukti Sanghatan's sphere of operations are concerned, the cultic center is located at the foot of a hill in Film City.

This part of the grounds is well endowed with forest cover, and also with rocks, one of which houses the *gaondevi*. It is between three and four feet tall and stands in front of a larger boulder. Human hands have added some embellishments. To the front, the rock presents a surface that is mostly flat, but about halfway up, the contours have been shaped with some carving and painted to depict a female face (fig. 6). (It reminded me strongly of a Frida Kahlo self-portrait.) A very basic shelter, consisting of four posts and a sheet of corrugated metal, has been erected over it. On the day of Gaondevi Puja this frame was draped with bright cloth, the sacred stone inside was well garlanded, and the surrounding boulders were streaked with vermilion. The goddess's subjects assembled from their *pada*s to honor her with dancing, feasting, and blood.

It was as a supplement to, if not a substitute for, this religious observance that Prashant and his fellow activists had collected children on leave from school for the official Diwali holiday.[31] Their own show was aimed at invoking a sense of community solidarity that went well beyond the borders of discrete villages. Forty-two children had gathered at the venue rented for the occasion, a building normally used as a music school. Most were of grade-school age: well-scrubbed, name-tagged, and extremely cheerful. A banner hung across the room displayed the words "All-Bombay Adivasi Samaj." This was the coalition in whose name the event's various sponsors had come together; Prashant had been elected to its council as a delegate from his own NGO. *Samaj* can be translated as "society," which preserves the English word's dual sense of formal association and community, although the Hindi term is also frequently used in an intermediate sense as a synonym for caste, tribe, or other kinship-based group. Thus, the name All-Bombay Adivasi Samaj can be read in two ways. It could designate a select collective of Mumbai-area residents coming together in the name of *adivasi* interests. But more ambitiously, it could also denote the Mumbai subset of the entire collectivity of India's tribal populations. The language in primary use was Marathi. The day's agenda was to unfold in four parts: a lesson in Warli art; a consciousness development workshop; a training session in cultivating a scientific perspective; and a magic demonstration.

Let's dispense quickly with the latter two sessions. Although effective in context, they are not difficult to explain; they were two sides of the rationalist coin. The scientific-training session was directed at debunking superstitious practices and ideas, such as those associated with witchcraft, that were said historically to have kept tribals in a backward condition. The magic demonstration was an entertaining way of exposing the trickery behind the stunts used by the diviners and other charlatans who exploited superstition. Spirit-possession, animal sacrifice, alcohol: properly scientific-minded young citizens were to hold none of that in esteem. Indeed, had I arrived too late to catch the program's first half, I would have come away with the impression that the All-Bombay Adivasi Samaj had as its aim the erasure of much of what marked the tribal practice of religion apart from metropolitan Hinduism.

The program's first two sessions are more rewarding to consider because their purpose was to advance positive steps within the coalition's project of formulating a modern, translocal image of cultural particularity. One component of consciousness-raising was a series of interactive games in which everyone—

children, teachers and organizers, and interloper from *Foren* alike—was expected to participate, in a spirit of friendliness and mutual respect. I confess I was completely charmed by my young interlocutors; I tried to retain enough critical distance to recognize that something interesting was going on with the session's other component—an inauguratory ceremony that combined ritual with a didactic lecture.

The message went something like this. All India's *adivasi*s were one people. From here in Maharashtra to the tribal strongholds of the Northeast, the children of the soil were united in the shared experience of injustice suffered at the hands of "casteist," "Brahminist" society and were animated by a common cultural genius. This spirit expressed itself through talents even upper-caste people conceded to be natural tribal aptitudes: art and music. Tomorrow's tribals were not to consider themselves Warlis, Kokanas, or Mahadev Kolis; Gonds, Mundas, or Santals. They were alike members of the national community of *adivasi*s—of Original Inhabitants. And however marginalized they had been historically by their fellow Indians, they had won themselves a proud place in the national epic, the freedom struggle against the British Empire. (The usefulness of the Raj as an allegory for oppression closer to home, to be inferred as appropriate, has become well established in Indian political discourse.)

The exemplary *adivasi* who had sacrificed himself in the name of emancipation was named Birsa Munda. In the late nineteenth century he had led militant segments of the Munda community in an uprising against Christian missionaries and colonial authorities in the part of eastern India now known as Jharkhand. Captured in 1895, he died in prison in Ranchi five years later. Daniel J. Rycroft (2004, 63) has documented how, in commemoration of the centenary of his death, a Jharhkand political organization printed a poster based on a photo taken by his jailors; once introduced into public circulation, the portrait was adopted by a range of other groups with their own agendas. Indeed, a snowballing effect appears to have taken over the image, such that its reproduction and exhibition as a signifier of generically tribal resistance and pride may turn out to be the freedom fighter's lasting legacy.

A description of what the All-Bombay Adivasi Samaj did with Birsa's portrait will expand the point. First a framed chromolithograph of the image was garlanded and presented before the assembly for a collective moment of veneration. The gesture was familiar to everyone present. A standardized sort of modern rite, it cites the Hindu practice of *darshan* but is prescribed in a wide range of contexts in which Indians convene under the auspices of an organization—a political party, a school, a business—that can be represented by the image of an ancestor, guru, or hero figure. A comparison with the observance of Gaondevi Puja may yield useful insights. The one I want to develop has to do with the question of iterability, or reproducibility, as it pertains to the rather different objects of cultic attention in these two cases.

My points of comparison will call to mind the problematic I organized in earlier chapters around the axes Site/Sight/Cite. Let's begin with the tribal goddess stone, which functions primarily as an index of divinity. Even if modified by the hands of its worshipers and given eyes and other anthropomorphic features, as a cultic object it draws most of its power from its occupation of a particular spot and its concrete particularity, from the fact of its rockness. And the same thing could also be said of its power as a metonym of its cult community. Now, to *pakka*-fy the goddess stone at the iconic level would give it more definition to stand out from its jungle surroundings and also facilitate its picturization and thus its reproducibility. But as indicated in chapter 4, when it comes to giving visible form to divine personalities, the codes of Hindu iconography hold hegemonic sway in Indian visual culture, and legibility in the eyes of outsiders and reproducibility in public circuits would thus be gained at grave risk to the *gaondevi* as an image of tribal identity.[32]

(The question arises: instead of the goddess it embodies, why not picturize the rock itself—make an icon of that particular object? Ample precedents do circulate for use by Hindu publics: graphics of the *murti*s at the famous temples of Nathdwara and Tirupati, for example. But there are several objections to this, one being that the stakes are not as high for the Hindu adherents of those prestigious cults as for the advocates of a distinct minority religion. There is a knottier problem here too, one having to do with semiosis. The art historian Michael Meister [1995, 205–6] recounts how he once visited a temple to see a *murti* of the goddess Shitala that he had read about in the work of an earlier scholar. Failing to find any image with the correct iconography, he asked some local worshipers where Shitala's image was, and to his bafflement they showed him a little shrine containing two fragments of medieval sculpture. Meister "read" the carvings as mythological figures unrelated to Shitala or, indeed, to each other. "Yet," he concluded, "the worshipers are right: for centuries these images have conjured up the *vision* of Śītalā in the minds of the devout." I suspect that among the Warlis, in like fashion, what you "see" in the sacred stone at Film City is the goddess, not the rock. The problem thus goes back to the first consideration raised in this comparison of cultic objects: that of efficacy. A picture of the rock would likely just remain a picture of a rock, with no power to interpellate. You might be told that it represents a goddess, but would you *recognize* a goddess in it?)

And now let's return to the hero image. By contrast with the sacred stone (and much like the image of Sai Baba), the picture of Birsa Munda not only is copyable but is already a copy. For those who honor it, its power may not necessarily be a question of representation; the artifact marked with it may be considered the material embodiment or vessel of a presence, even as the stone is. But as a reproducible image that can circulate outside its cult constituency it also operates as a legible sign. And even if the object of its mimetic significa-tion is a nineteenth-century figure from the far side of the subcontinent, with a biographical narrative as yet obscure to most, the portrait's conventional asso-ciation with its partisans, the likes of the All-Bombay Adivasi Samaj, has the po-tential to become imprinted in public through repeated iterations. Again, along with the historical individual Birsa Munda, something else the image iconically cites is the formally similar images of everyone else's god or guru. Indeed, given enough reiteration, the day may well come when Birsa finds his place as the em-blem of a newly visible *adivasi* community alongside Hanuman and Mary, the Hand of Fatima and Dr. Ambedkar, as a tile on a rich Parsi's wall.

Birsa Munda was fêted in song, with lyrics set to melodies that had come the organizers' way, not from the context of *pada* life among the Warlis or any other tribal group, but rather out of the modern tradition of leftist protest music. And then it was time for the art lesson. A presenter, an art teacher from Palghar in Thane District, sketched on the board, demonstrating the proud status of the Warli graphic idiom as the direct heir of an aesthetic sensibility that could be traced back to the artifacts of the Indus Valley civilization. Art, in this narrative, was thus evidence. What documented continuity between India's prehistoric civilization and India's extrahistorical population was the Warli genius for line.

Here it is necessary to insert a sketch of the modern history of Warli paint-ing. The story involves the form's transformation in the 1970s and 1980s from the ephemeral traces of a women's wedding ritual into commoditized art products. The pivotal event was the recognition by bourgeois patrons of two men, Jivya Soma Mashe and his son Balu Mashe, as individual artist personali-ties.[33] Spearheaded by the art of the Mashes, compositions that worked with the motifs, formal principles, and even some of the media—rice flour and cow dung—that had till then been the preserve of *pada* women decorating nuptial cabins attained an international vogue in the 1980s. It is important to histori-cize what happened to Warli art in this period as one development within a broader phenomenon. The pertinent context is a Government of India policy that introduced the material-cultural products of rustic and tribal communities from across the country into public circulation through the patronage of state-based agencies called Handicrafts Boards.[34] The Madhubani painting of northern Bihar is an example of another well-known form that has followed a parallel trajectory. And indeed the comprehensive scale of this state initiative (in which support by local, national, and transnational NGOs has since come to feature prominently) bespeaks an investment from the government side in a complementary project: the visual and discursive construction of an India-wide *adivasi* identity. This is the field on which the All-Bombay Adivasi Samaj maneuvers as it champions Warli art as the authentic medium of a pan-Indian tribal spirit.

Let's call out some signal moments in the form's history. The Bombay art world became acquainted with the Warli idiom at an exhibition of the Mashes' work at the Chemould Gallery in 1976. Warli painting's high-water mark was probably the exposition of global styles called *Les magiciens de la terre* that was held at the Centre Pompidou in Paris in 1989.[35] Its fortunes in the market peaked shortly thereafter. By 2003 it was the opinion of most Mumbai patrons that the work had passed into kitsch. The point remains that circulation had established the form as a recognizable quantity within Indian public culture, and the artifacts it marked had come to be regarded as indices of a not merely Warli but generically tribal authenticity.[36] Furthermore, with a generation of practitioners having expanded its iconic capacity beyond the ritual domain of *pada* weddings to signify a wide range of themes and narratives, Warli art had potentially arrived as a reproducible idiom of tribal expression.

Characteristic of the Warli style is the depiction of minimally differentiated human figures in kinetic activities such as parading or dancing, a compositional feature that reminds my eye of the New York artist Keith Haring, whose star also rose in the 1980s. Haring was known for his involvement in public art projects and put his work at the service of various NGO-sponsored informational programs, including most notably an AIDS awareness campaign. *Adivasi* rights advocacy pressed along analogous lines may never attain the salience of Haring's landmark series, SILENCE = DEATH, although it seems to me that one could do worse for an opener than INVISIBILITY = DISPLACEMENT. But once the lecture portion of the art lesson was concluded, a display of the artistic efforts of Warli children showed that in 2003 in suburban Mumbai, at least, baby steps were indeed being taken in a leftward direction.[37]

One painting inverted the conventional depiction of the guardian of the forest by showing a tiger killing a village woman. It would have invited a smile as the product of an active imagination if it had not been an allusion to the actual attacks that had so excited the attention of the press that year. Another piece, whose political purport was impossible to ignore, depicted the hamlet of Devipada in Film City (fig. 7). Just the year before, the expansion of Subhash Ghai's Whistling Woods Film Academy project onto a plot inhabited by Warli families had led to their forcible removal by the police. The painting presented a sensational aspect of the incident: the beating of helpless tribal women by female officers wielding *lathi* rods. The young artist had successfully reduced the paddy wagon and the demolition crew's bulldozer to the spare graphic motifs of the Warli style. A Marathi caption ran across part of the picture: "Film City: Where pregnant women are beaten with *lathi*s."[38]

With the distribution of diplomas, inscribed to each child by Prashant and a woman colleague on hand-painted Warli stationery, the program came to a close. I went with my companions to visit the *gaondevi* on the Film City grounds, where they caught up with news of the festivities and teased me with the details of the exotic customs I had missed. The previous night had been dedicated to Waghoba, two of whose effigies flanked the goddess; the fierce god had arrived to "play," in the colloquial phrase, and possessed more than one heated supplicant. Earlier that day, the goddess's votaries had butchered goats and chickens for her. Some of the blessed meat was still there for the partaking, bubbling in huge cauldrons over campfires amid the trees. There was plenty of drunkenness in evidence, with the most conspicuous reveler being a non-Warli, a police officer, who offered me a shot of whisky. Prashant chided me for it later; I had let down the reformist side.

Overall, the scene was for him an illustration, I felt, of what he hoped his community would someday move beyond. But in one aspect, the festivities perfectly mirrored the program Prashant and his comrades had devised to supplant them. When I queued up for a plateful of the *gaondevi*'s bounty, I discovered that the meatiest-seeming ingredient in the gravy I was served was some kind of vegetable gluten product. Whoever had catered that part of the feast had hit on a way to deliver properly nonvegetarian tribal fare at an iconic level while remaining indexically pure by reformist (and upwardly mobile) standards. In other words, what tribal persons were actually putting in their bodies was new, modern, and hygienic. But the image they presented to outside eyes was traditional and non-Hindu. One might say: *bona fide*.

Some Concluding Ironies

This chapter will close on a couple of ironic notes.

Gaining visibility for the tribal populations of the Mumbai area—and exercising tribal agency within that project—was very much a live concern for activist leaders throughout the period of my fieldwork, as it is to the present day. But the plans discussed in the aftermath of the *Sapte* ruling to organize teams of ethnographic observers to visit the *padas* were inconclusive. And in the absence of inspectors to check out their bona fides, the need to remove residents whose authenticity had been found wanting also appears to have lost its urgency. Where the laws on the books are concerned, the eviction order from the *BEAG* ruling in 1997 is still in effect. But per a 2011 SGNP management plan cited by the geographers Émilie Edelblutte and Yanni Gunnell (2014, 2), the latest figures enumerate 1,795 *adivasi* families living in forty-three hamlets within the environs of the national park. For over a decade now, it would seem, an unspoken accommodation has been allowed to rest in place. The tribals have stepped back into *kaccha* obscurity, and the Forest Department—unimpelled by any further scrutiny of its own devices—has been content to go along to get along.[39] In this context, the courtroom drama of *Sapte* can be understood as a bid for recognition that foundered because the petitioners' position was so marginal that even when they stood up to be counted, the state could not be bothered to do so—never mind tag and label them as individual citizens![40]

Edelblutte and Gunnell wrap up their overview of the SGNP tribals' predicament with two tables that identify various "stakeholders" and the courses of action open to them. Outside the tribal community, they depict a conflict between "red" interest groups, which seek to secure citizenship rights for the *adivasis* through advocacy work, and "green" groups committed to the ecological restoration of the park—and hence the expulsion of human interlopers. The options available to the tribals themselves are four: (1) "bend the Park rules"; (2) "adopt an urban lifestyle"; (3) claim their rights through legal mechanisms; and (4) "gain support from NGOs and political elites" through "work[ing] on the 'good tribal' stereotype" (2014, 11). Between the two of them, points 3 and 4 map out much of the domain of my analysis in this chapter.

But here, against the grain of my own argument, I must mention a fifth model for action that has proven to be effective at least once. This is the mobilization and exhibition of tribal bodies in public space. Some years before the *Sapte* ruling, Vithal Lad became exasperated, as he tells it, by the way the application process for tribal certificates had trapped his constituents on a circular paper trail. Lad mustered two hundred members of Sramik Mukti Andolan and staged a *morcha*. A *morcha* is a protest march, the staple image of civil disobedience in India. It is also a recurrent feature of the Mumbai streetscape, a challenge so routine to the normal flow of traffic as to make the norm itself seem tenuous.

The producers of *morcha*s are thus faced with a delicate calculus, in which the arousal of desired reactions in some spectators—shame, outrage, sympathy—has to be factored against the inevitable irritation or boredom of others, along with a husbanding of resources, both on the ground and behind the scenes. Lad and Sramik Mukti Andolan appear to have struck the right balance. The *morcha*'s destination was the subdistrict headquarters. Marching in from the margins and onto the canvas of public space, the *kaccha* bodies took enumerable shape before the subdistrict officer. Here was the "brute fact" of indexical signification: empirical data in the flesh. And a second viewership constituency was the local public addressed at the iconic level, for the marchers' appearance cited a well-established idiom of protest—one shared by the Shiv Sena, labor groups, and other mass movements going back to the struggle for independence from Britain.

As a direct result of the demonstration, according to Lad, the subdistrict office issued two hundred Scheduled Tribe certificates. In its exertion of extralegal pressure to gain recognition from the state, the tribal *morcha* was a textbook example of political society in action. And so, given the apparent success of this move, it may well be asked: what accounts for the subsequent lack of militant activism during the period of the *Sapte* suit? I propose that the conditions of recognition had shifted. As established in this chapter, *Sapte* reframed the predicament facing the *adivasi*s of the forest zone. (In Edelblutte and Gunnell's terms, "red" interests had ceded ground to "green.") The tribal certificates won by the *morcha* activists were claimed on the basis of commonality as political subjects: "Look at us; we are an aggrieved subaltern population, much like other subaltern populations of the city." With the *Sapte* petition, it became imperative to demonstrate difference—to present evidence of tribal bona fides.

In several of the Mumbai-area *pada*s I visited, there would be one dwelling marked apart from the others by the care it showed for external appearances. The house's contours would be unusually *pakka*, and its surface well decorated—white paint on brown walls—with dynamic-looking Warli graphics. These invariably turned out to be structures refurbished for use by Sramik Mukti Andolan. Lad is recorded in *Crushed Homes, Lost Lives* as having "deposed before the tribunal that every tribal family has a house of its own made of mud and thatch with Mangalore tiles for the roof" (Sebastian 2000, 38). But again, the only *pada* structures I ever saw whose roofs were free of such items of bricolage as old tires and plastic sheets were the outposts of his own organization.

Here is the second site of irony. Both Lad, of Sramik Mukti Andolan, and Prashant, of Sramik Mukti Sanghatan, looked to Warli painting as a form that could mediate tribal authenticity before the eyes of the state and of the bourgeois public. In the preceding section and in chapter 3 I have discussed the importance of iterability in iconic representation. In the present day, the Warli style does indeed surface in public circuits as a legible idiom of tribal expression. But in fact its very versatility and reproducibility are factors that have led to its loss of cachet in the art market. And just because an image signals a tribal provenance does not mean, of course, that it has necessarily been drawn from some authentic wellspring of tribal spirit. It does not even mean that it has been drawn by a tribal hand.

The only structures in the *pada*s bearing Warli paintings are the offices of Lad's NGO. But within the area of the SGNP, Warli murals are to be seen on another building that is prominent indeed: the headquarters of the Forest Department. And in Film City, where the Whistling Woods Film Academy rents out space to corporate tenants, YouTube's Mumbai office has installed a wall covered in a rather witty Warli-inspired design, with the trademark everyman and -woman figures shown in a wide range of daily pursuits (fig. 8). YouTube: Bringing ordinary people the extraordinary promise of visibility, circulation, citation without limit!

In fact, in the present day, examples like these of the co-optation of Warli art by official and corporate interests are legion. They can cast a sharp light on the sorts of debates that are joined nowadays around questions of cultural appropriation, online and on campuses in the United States and elsewhere, debates whose critical terms are often somewhat blurry (not to say *kaccha*). Of the images that could have closed this chapter, I have chosen the one that seems richest to me in its layering of multiple ironies. It invites questions of indexicality, iconicity, and commodity. It comes from a set of desk accessories I found at a South Mumbai boutique, Contemporary Arts and Crafts.

What caught my eye was a pair of wooden trays. Their designs had been executed in line with the standard Warli technique, but the animal motifs seemed to mark a stylistic departure. More than that, the animals pictured didn't seem to be native animals. "That's a deer," said my friend Pritha, although I begged to differ; another tray showed some kind of lizard, but it wasn't an altogether *deshi* cast of lizard. When I spoke with the shop's buyers, they told me the work was sourced from artisans in Thane. Unfortunately, they noted, it had been a long time since Warli art sold as such; it simply wasn't in fashion anymore. But the tribal association had endured, so Contemporary Arts and Crafts was experimenting with what it called the "Afro Line."

All the same, I was sure the mystery icon no more showed an African antelope than it did the Indian deer of Pritha's fancy. In the end it took some consulting with April Strickland, a specialist in the visual cultures of Oceania, to confirm my hunch that the creature pictured was a kangaroo. What my Warli-painted trays were citing was an Aboriginal style, as introduced to the global market in tribal art by the Yolngu people of northern Australia.

CONCLUSION

Mumbai. The very name of the megametropolis evokes high-speed images of life in the fast lane. Commerce and culture, fashion and films, glamour and glitz: it is a city that revels in its this-worldliness. Little wonder then that it shines forth as a lodestar for millions, who throng to it, drawn by dreams of a better life.

EICHER CITY MAP 2002

The main phase of the fieldwork on which the previous chapters are based ran from 2002 to late 2003. Between then and the completion of this book I have returned to Mumbai several times. The inquiry is ongoing.

As a business, Filmistan seems to be thriving. And so—to go by raw numbers, anyway—is the Warli enclave inside the studio. When I last visited, in 2015, between marriages and progeny the population of this incongruous *pada* had doubled from where it was in the main period of my fieldwork to number around fifty people. The Village, the corner of the studio in which the Warlis live, has been kept busy in its capacity as Lot Number Eleven. I have seen it dressed up for the television show *Ammaji Ki Galli* (Momma's neighborhood) as a sentimentalized small-town block somewhere in North India. The set included a street shrine, built to the same dimensions as the Warlis' tiger-god *mandir* and planted mere footsteps from it; an effigy of Durga had been set up inside (fig. 2). When I returned to the space in 2015, I stepped onto a block with roughly the same coordinates but different storefronts with signs in Urdu script. The street was decked with festive strings of paper Pakistani flags. Compounding the sense of disorientation, there was a Hindu temple in this set too, but the location of the temple had shifted. A member of the production team explained to me that what was being shot was the pilot for a television series about a Hindu family in Karachi. Yet the look of the set was hardly metropolitan; the homey neighborhood that had been layered over the Village struck me rather as having been designed to demystify Pakistan by domesticating it. At bottom, Pakistanis, it seemed to be saying, were just folks like us.

On the streets of the real city, there has been no decline in the construction of illegal religious structures. Sai Baba is more popular than ever. One development that has altered the visual environment of the street is the proliferation of cash machines—another set of booth-like stations that command pedestrians' attention and dispense blessings of a sort. And the past dozen years have seen the rise of India's information technology sector to a position of global prominence, but the technological innovation that has made its mark on everyday life, especially where poorer people are concerned, is not so much the personal computer (Mallapragada 2010) as the mobile phone (Doron and Jeffrey 2013). As far as the implications for religious practice are concerned, I think it's fair to say that the digital mediation of *darshan* by cell phone screens and cameras exacerbates some trends identified early in this book: deterritorialization, reproducibility, the reconfiguration of mass publics.

The material conditions of Vikas's life these days remain meager, although he does own a phone (albeit a basic, cameraless model). His room has an electrical connection now. Some time back he attracted the patronage of a well-to-do businessman, a Goregaon mover and shaker, who gave him employment as an office "peon" at an office that was otherwise vacant. His benefactor also introduced him to the meditation-based cult of Guru Siyag, a contemporary "god-man" figure who espouses a practice centered, as Vikas understands it, on the visual contemplation of the portrait of the guru's own preceptor, a bearded ascetic named Baba Shri Gangai Nath. My friend told me with satisfaction of how he was being paid to perform daily *puja-path*, "prayer and reading," or in other words sitting in the little office absorbed in *darshan* of this photo for hours on end. In time, however, his patron's need to downsize some ventures brought this happy episode to a close.

Prashant and his family have sustained a modest degree of upward mobility. As described in chapter 6, this trajectory has been symbolized for me by the addition of a second story to their house and the general *pakka*-fication of their hillside shantytown. But corporate interests have also been busy developing this part of Jogeshwari, and in a sort of funhouse mirror image, the view from the hill has become dominated by high-rise apartment buildings. And in the shadow of the towers, Prashant's neighborhood, for all its newly raised profile, looks to me to be in some danger of relegation to *kaccha* all over again.

Sramik Mukti Sanghatan has continued to work with lawyers and politicians to secure the paperwork that would enable local *adivasi*s to gain access to resources from the state. A recent win Prashant told me about was the acquisition of Scheduled Tribe certificates and ration cards for just under fifty residents of the forest *pada*s. The passage in 2006 of a new law, the Scheduled Tribes and Other Traditional Forest Dwellers (Protection of Forest Rights) Act, does not seem to have affected the conditions of life on the ground—not so far, at any rate.

Nor has a potentially much farther reaching government initiative. Aadhaar is the name of a new form of official identification designed to streamline the process of recognition of Indian citizens by government officials. The Aadhaar card has a hi-tech format combining symbolic, iconic, and—with the incorporation of biometric data—indexical modes of signification. In concept, it is well positioned to cut through bureacratic demands for paperwork; its technocratic boosters in the government and civil society use watchwords like *fix* and *reboot* (Srivas 2016). But Aadhaar's implementation among populations whose archival representation has historically been spotty—in other words, precisely those people most in need of the initiative—does not appear to be working as envisioned.

The scheme is exciting a good deal of scholarly attention. One landmark is the multimedia Identity Project directed by Ashish Rajadhyaksha from 2010 to 2013, which has produced the volume *In the Wake of Aadhaar* (Rajadhyaksha 2013). The emphasis in this collection, which includes field reports from seven states, is on Aadhaar's implementation across a range of social contexts rather than on its policy goals or ideological implications. (Criticism in the press of the latter has been sounding an increasingly dystopian note, in that the Aadhaar agenda is seen to align with the authoritarian tendencies of the current government.) Theoretical interventions include those of Itty Abraham and Ashish Rajadhyaksha (2015); Ursula Rao and Graham Greenleaf (2013); and, most provocatively, Lawrence Cohen (2017a, 2017b). One thing that can be said is that, at present, the facts on the ground and the terms of debate are both in a state of flux. As far as the scope of my own study is concerned, however, it does seem to be the case that for many subalterns, Aadhaar is encountered as simply one more layer of those manifold papers that mediate their access to power (see also Rao 2013).[1]

In the end, what has changed over the course of the years, to be addressed in this conclusion? Let's recall, briefly, the ground this book has covered and note the work that Peircean categories have contributed to the analysis. In several of my chapters, the argument has traced an ascending movement in the interpellative power of the iconic. As the final move, what I would like to do here is to press forward with the comparison between 2002–3 and the present day and historicize this movement, which, I believe, has over the intervening years become the dominant tendency in Indian visual culture. The examples I cite will be eclectic but will center on the mediation of the experience of space in Mumbai by iconic and ideologized spectacles. I will bring together images from electoral politics, development policy, and cinema (while passing over other important sites like digital media, real estate development, and bourgeois environmentalism) to assemble an impressionistic picture. Taking up a conversation whose contours have been outlined by Ravinder Kaur and Thomas Blom Hansen (2016), Kajri Jain (2016, 2017), Shaila Bhatti and Christopher Pinney (2011), and others, I call this phenomenon the spectacularization of Mumbai.[2]

India Shining

During the main period of my fieldwork, a National Democratic Alliance government was in power in Delhi; that is to say, the ruling coalition was dominated by the Hindu rightist Bharatiya Janata Party (BJP). In the months leading up to the general elections of 2004, the government generated a great deal of attention with an advertising campaign in print, television, and web-based media organized around the theme "India Shining." It is a slogan that has lived on to be invoked, meme-style, to this day.

As it transpired, I had launched my inquiries among some of Mumbai's more marginalized residents at a moment that, according to many richer Indians, marked a turn in the country's fortunes. The economy had entered an unprecedented boom: in the last quarter of 2003, growth reached double digits for the first time in history. The India Shining campaign was designed to capitalize—in the literal sense—on the trends that had led to this good news. Its purpose was to imprint on the public the image of a prosperous, dynamic, and modern India, a *pakka* visualization of the development policy of the BJP-led government. Importantly, the public thus targeted was twofold. The first constituency was affluent urban citizens, holders of the surplus income that, once invested, would be the fuel for further economic growth. The second was the electorate at large.

In the spring of 2004, Indians went to the polls, and the pundits of prosperity suffered a comprehensive defeat at the hands of the Indian National Congress. The result caught much of the commentariat by surprise. Nowadays political and media professionals remember India Shining as a fiasco. "In fact, the BJP leadership itself cited the campaign as the prime reason for its electoral defeat" (Ravinder Kaur 2016, 622). But in a recent article called "'I Am India

Shining': The Investor-Citizen and the Indelible Icon of Good Times," Ravinder Kaur (2016) advances a contrarian thesis. She suggests that far from having been rejected, the fantasy of modernity to which the project gave shape continued to thrive through the BJP's loss. Kaur locates its vindication in the even more lopsided victory of Narendra Modi over the Congress Party ten years later. Noting that India Shining originated with a Ministry of Finance initiative in 2003 to explore ways of stimulating domestic investment, she focuses on the desiring subject interpellated by the "mega-publicity spectacle" (622). This, she argues, was a subject whose configuration in neoliberal ideology was consistent across the rival visions offered by the BJP and the Congress in 2004, and so on into the BJP's promise in 2014 of "Acche Din" (Good Times).

I cite India Shining in order to illustrate a point, not regarding continuity as such, but rather the present-day exacerbation of a trend that was already well under way by 2004. My framing is different from Kaur's. I look to India Shining as a particularly salient example—a synecdoche—of a pervasive, more general phenomenon of mass media: namely, the spectacularization of space. To return to the analytic framework laid out in this book's introduction, I assign India Shining to a class or family of visual forms that mediate the experience of space in a way that has ideological effects. The images of India Shining contributed to an already well-established interocular field that its affiliated discourses cited and reinforced. This was not the rationalized space of plans, projections, and maps (although the project's impetus, to be sure, was to be found in technocratic metrics). Nor was it the sacralized space of divine presence fixed at discrete points by material or representational forms (although Kaur does use terms like *icon* and *idol* to convey a sense of the power of the images' address). India Shining was a conspicuous spectacularization, in the years 2003–4, of Indian modernity under a neoliberal dispensation. And for me here, at the end of the book, the question is not so much "What does that modernity look like?" but rather "*Where* does modernity look like?"

Indian modernity looks like the city. To be precise, what it looks like cites a long string of cleaned-up, sharpened, and smoothed-out images of cities—and one city in particular. The conventional wisdom about India Shining's failure is that its urban idiom ignored or alienated already marginalized voters in the rural sector. This statement from the newsweekly *India Today* is representative: "Critics of the campaign, and there are aplenty, say the blitz crashed because of its 'lopsided' focus on urban growth story while neglecting the distress and backwardness of the rural landscape" (Bagga 2013). In other words, the spectacle may have been successful, to a degree, in interpellating members of one public. This would be the group I have described as citizens, who were being called on to affirm their position as stakeholders in the national enterprise: "Put your money where your mouths have been all this time." Where the spectacle failed, on the other hand, was in its address to subalterns. Their only skin in the game was in the form of votes, and they cast them for the other side. And let me be clear here. The dividing line between these two publics has less to do with the urban or rural environment physically inhabited by a person than with whether that person sees a place for him- or herself in the vision proffered—the shining city of the future.

Now, Ravinder Kaur is not the only scholar who would take issue with this reading. The critique would rest strangely with theorists in the public-culture tradition, for whom the city furnishes the topos of the modern precisely because of its accommodation of multitudes. The important collection *Pleasure and the Nation: The History, Politics and Consumption of Public Culture in India* begins with an introduction by Christopher Pinney (2001, 11), who observes: "A trope such as the journey from the village to the city (and vice-versa) is one of the ways in which diverse class and cultural experiences are overlapped in popular Indian culture. The city—the central fixation of Indian public culture—operates as a space of experimentation and critique." Again: "The metropolitan aspiration described here with its encoding of empowering realms of knowledge and divinity is *projective*. Its orientation is to an outside, to a realm beyond the familiar: although the familiar is all around, it is recoded in the glamorous language of the outside" (12). Pinney's framing here is particularly apposite when it comes to popular cinema (which could well be described as the central fixation of scholars of Indian public culture; no fewer than seven of the ten essays in *Pleasure and the Nation* have to do with film). In chapter 1 and at other points throughout this book, I have myself stressed cinema as the chief engine of spectacularization in India. But if the projection of the urban in visual media has become less inclusive than previously—less hospitable to contradiction, contestation, ambiguity—I think that can be read as an indication of historical changes, changes that were gelling in the period of my fieldwork. By 2003–4, I propose, something was already happening to the city of Mumbai, and this was both reflected and enunciated in what was happening in the movies.

I have touched on an ideological shift that India Shining indexed among members of the citizen class: from a classically liberal model organized around state sovereignty and participation in civil society to a neoliberal model that elevates participation in the form of financial investment. Where the corresponding alienation of the subaltern class is concerned, a sharp indictment of India

Shining is to be found in another piece by Pinney, cowritten with Shaila Bhatti some ten years after the essay cited above. This is a quotation: "We are polishing the exterior, but the interior is starving" (Bhatti and Pinney 2011, 233).[3] It is attributed to Sunil Dutt in his capacity as a Congress parliamentarian from Mumbai. Having succeeded to politics from a career in the 1960s as an A-list film star, however, Dutt must also be recognized as a person who knew a thing or two about glossy surfaces and about the course taken by Indian popular media in the decades following the cinema's Golden Age.

In their own analysis of India Shining, Bhatti and Pinney (2011, 233) emphasize a disjuncture made evident in the 2004 election: a contest "between surface and interiority, reflectivity and textures that absorb sheen and stickiness." It is a critique that will resurface (so to speak) further on in these pages, when I discuss some recent work by visual artists. But if this visual disjuncture is to be charted as part of a broader trajectory, it will be helpful to sketch out the context of the decade that preceded it.

In India, the 1990s were defined by the historical turn often described as "reform" or "liberalization." The signposts are familiar to scholars of modern Indian politics and culture: the decade began with the implementation of reforms that opened the nation's markets to global circuits of capital, commodities, and media forms; at the same time the government's long-held monopoly over the airwaves gave way to an explosion of televisual media; and of course, there was the advent worldwide of information technology, the principal area of economic development in which India's leaders have staked their claim as an emergent world power. In Bombay, as it was called then, Shiv Sena demagoguery and mob violence in 1992–93 shattered what faith was left in governmentality among the postcolonial bourgeoisie. In 1995 the Shiv Sena–led state government had the city's name officially changed to Mumbai. And at this point let me suggest that, given the context of India's integration within the global capitalist system, this renaming can be understood as a rebranding.[4]

Returning to the period of my fieldwork, let's consider another signal event for the city—another shining moment, one could say. In September 2003 the release of a report by McKinsey and Company, the international consultants, was met with much excitement and debate. Titled "Vision Mumbai: Transforming Mumbai into a World-Class City," it had been commissioned by a group of city leaders called Bombay First, and its recommendations were aimed, with a high degree of urgency, at shaping policy in ambitious ways. The "executive summary" that opens the document introduces the plan with eight bullet points and a throwdown. "Mumbai is currently at a critical juncture. It must implement these eight initiatives, and it must do so now. Otherwise it is in grave danger of collapsing completely" (McKinsey and Company 2003, 2).

Point 7 is the most germane of these initiatives: "Generate momentum through more than 20 quick wins to show visible on-the-ground impact in the next 1–2 years" (McKinsey and Company 2003, 1). The program outlined here is getting Mumbai to look enough like a world-class city so that investors—from India and parts beyond—will give it the funds to continue to bid for membership in the world class. How was Mumbai, in other words, to gain recognition in the eyes of the kind of subjects who count? Many of these proposed quick wins involved the beautification or upgrading of sites of potential attraction or their swift erection from the ground up: zoo, aquarium, "retail park," bus and train stations, parks and green spaces, and a "world-class indoor stadium and convention center." Major roads were to be "raise[d] to international standards"; widening them would facilitate traffic flow but also—implicitly—make the impression of the city as a whole more appealing from the viewpoint of people traversing it in cars.[5] Among whose number, it is safe to say, there would be few motorists indeed hailing from the "35,000 slum encroachments" (28) McKinsey targeted for clearing off the roadside.

As far as I know, the champions of the world-class city scored no "quick wins" as a direct result of the report. But the point is that this Potemkin's plan was part of a wider, pervasive development of reimagining Mumbai through *pakka*-fying it. And if visual mediation of the construct of the city as a whole (and, by extension, of the condition of Indian modernity) was not to be accomplished by manicuring the view from the highway, there were still the movies and advertising media. Much of the real work was being done at places like Filmistan and Film City and on the computer screens of Photoshop experts.

There was, however, one project that was eventually realized in a style and on a scale to win the approval of McKinsey and Company. The list of quick wins began with the imperative to "improve airport ambience and emigration/immigration clearance." For what a sense of discomfiture must have greeted the globe's financiers, arriving for the first time at Chhatrapati Shivaji International Airport, as they made their way through the old terminal—*Third* World Class, at best—with its uncurated surplus of detail, the seams showing beneath the surface, the stubbornly uninvisible sweepers mopping up (or not) the stains that blurred the façade of what a "real" airport should look like! Government authorities had already determined the need for an overhaul in 2003, independently of the McKinsey report. And when they announced their plans for an entirely new international terminal, it became clear that they were going to go big. The edifice, known as T2, finally opened in early 2014. The design by Skidmore, Owings, and Merrill emphasizes dramatic, swooping curves, and to travelers familiar with the older structure the concern for stage management is apparent. The terminal brings to mind an opera house (it has also been likened to a giant meringue). The easiest way to get there from suburban Mumbai is to take a motor rickshaw, but the drop-off point for rickshaws has been sequestered far away from the main entrance, several levels below. If you ride a subaltern conveyance, what you get is the service door. In a word, it is a spectacular facility.

In *Wages of Violence*, his landmark ethnography of the Shiv Sena, Thomas Blom Hansen (2001) has written poignantly of the aspirational modernity the city embodies for the party's cadres. My own spin on Hansen's thesis would be to emphasize the role of spectacle as the mediating term in the Sena's ideology. Consider two moments of crisis I have described in my ethnography. When in 2000 the Shiv Sena administration ordered the removal of the squatters on the outskirts of the national park, promising resettlement for a select number in tall new apartment buildings, it was not concern for law and order that spurred the decision, as the lawless follow-through well demonstrated. Rather, I would describe what animated the move as something along the lines of an aesthetic commitment, a pledge to the neoliberal vision of the shining city. And in 2003, when Sena politicians spoke out in support of demolishing the "illegal religious structures" on the streets only to self-correct days later, taking a stand on behalf of the aggrieved mass of Mumbai's Hindus, what came to light was an ideological tension: between adherence to the iconic image of the *pakka* city, on the one hand, and the indexical emanations of the sacred, on the other. This tension poses a challenge for the party leadership even as it fuels the activism of the rank and file. As with right-wing movements elsewhere, the Sena points the way ahead to the neoliberal horizon, but most of its members are traveling in rickshaws.

Celluloid Arcadia

Of the spectacle, Kaur and Hansen (2016, 270) have recently teamed up to write: "A distinct feature of 'new India' is its claim to represent a collective dream even when a major part of the population remains outside of it. The perception of newness . . . is precisely created by 'leaving behind' that which does not fit in with the imaginary of a prosperous, techno-friendly, mobile consumer nation." Again:

to participate in what is called the high stakes "global game" on a world-scale means that the level of expectation and anxiety may also be high. . . . In the post-colonial world order, India was categorised as a Third World country lagging behind the developed world. . . . But how can such rearranging ignore and occlude that the majority of the population was never part of this new India? We propose that the answer lies precisely in signifying this other India as the past, as "old India," and in the aesthetic force of the promise to overcome a humiliating past, tainted by colonialism, in order to realize a truer and more timeless "new" India. (266)

It's time to refocus, for a final time, on film. Fifteen or twenty years ago, Hindi popular cinema was only just starting to receive attention from academics as a field of serious study. But if "Bollywood, the mediator of mass entertainment, in the post-reform era constantly seeks to escape the popular," as Kaur and Hansen (2016, 271) put it, the occlusion of what they call the popular—the subaltern—was perhaps more evident to observers in the 1990s, when the trend was accelerating on the screen in front of them. As the fortunes of Filmistan's Village demonstrate, villages and small-town settings continue to figure in Hindi film and television in the present day (although surely with less concern for realist narratives and idioms than ever). Yet already in 2001, when Ashis Nandy published a set of psychoanalytically inflected readings of films called *An Ambiguous Journey to the City*, he was mourning the relegation of rural space to the recesses of the past: the second half of the title is *The Village and Other Odd Ruins of the Self in the Indian Imagination*.

And in thinking through the role of the movies in connection with the spectacularization of Mumbai, the framework I keep coming back to is one proposed by Ronald Inden back in 1999. In the essay "Transnational Class, Erotic Arcadia and Commercial Utopia in Hindi Films," he tracks the action of Bollywood narratives and song sequences across a recurring set of backdrops. Inden (1999, 44–45) draws a distinction between *utopia*, "a society that is fundamentally transformed by the use of machinery," and *arcadia*, "rural or even pastoral communities where life is simple and peaceful, based on an abundance provided by nature either directly or through the grace of a deity."[6] Spectators typically encounter these idealized spaces—what the author calls "paradises of modernity"—during the affectively charged musical numbers that are the hallmark of the Indian popular-film format. If the pairing seems obvious, it should be noted that the categories map onto the well-entrenched nature-culture dichotomy discussed and critiqued in the last two chapters of this book.

Now, the case for Bollywood's utopia as a facet of the spectacle of "new India" has, I think, largely been made in these pages.[7] And to the extent that the Mumbai-based film industry has dominated the production and dissemination of images across India, the urban locus of utopia has a mimetic referent in a concrete location: Mumbai. To say that all Hindi films take place in the city and that the city in question is always Mumbai, whether named as such in diegesis or not, would be an exaggeration, to be sure. And yet Bollywood has presented the inhabitants of Mayapuri, harried citizen and toiling subaltern alike, with an irony that viewing subjects elsewhere are spared: the projective site of glamorous and shiny modernity is an illusion fabricated at their doorstep. Surely, for many the disjuncture registers only in fleeting glimpses. But no one constituency in Mumbai can be more awake to the flimsiness of the spectacle than the people who actually make their homes backstage—the Warlis of Filmistan and Film City.

So what of Inden's other term: *arcadia*? I think that part of the story of the ascendancy of the neoliberal vision is in fact the accelerated reification and attenuation of the cinema's arcadias in the years that have passed since his article's publication. (In the 1980s and 1990s, it wasn't uncommon to hear Westerners dismiss Indian movies as a matter of the two romantic leads "chasing each other back and forth among tree trunks." But no longer—trees haven't been a defining image of Bollywood for some time.) Now, when it comes to village spaces, I have already written much that complicates the picture in connection with my fieldwork at Filmistan's Village. Let me, however, follow through here on the proposition made above: that the film industry's primary model for the image of urban modernity is the city of Mumbai. The premise implies a corollary. The model for arcadia would then be found in the natural areas the studios abut— the forested frontier of the suburbs.

Unlike the identification of cinematic representations of Mumbai with the mediatory spectacle of the Indian modern, the idea that the Warli *pada*s are part of the "original" arcadia cannot be backed up by any extant body of scholarship, never mind one that cites well-known and recent movies. A proper study of the trace that the Warli settlements have left in India's cinematic archive has yet to be written, and this is hardly the point at which to take on that project. But it should at least be mentioned that in the early decades of the Bombay film industry, before the stock of arcadian backdrops expanded beyond the repertory of woodlands, villages, gardens, and mountains[8] to include more exotic attractions like beaches and foreign locales, tribal-style musical numbers in wilderness settings were a recurring feature. As seen in a series of 1950s films starring the Golden Age heartthrob Dev Anand, the tribal number opens at a point when the hero woos the heroine in a forest glade that diegesis locates at a joy-ride's distance from the city. In other words, "Thana," as described in chapter 4. Mediating the lovers' desire for each other are the tribal maidens who happen on the idyll: sparsely costumed, rhythmic, and "naturally" erotic.

The more sensitive films have ways of cuing the audience to the possibility that tribal people may have lives that extend beyond singing and dancing in the background. Memories of the Communist-led revolt on the Thana fruit planta-tions were perhaps still fresh during the shooting of *Sazaa* (1951), a Dev Anand vehicle that takes place on just such an estate.[9] Somebody—maybe the direc-tor, Fali Mistry, who had leftist sympathies, or R. D. Burman, the Bengali music director—gave lyrics to the chorus in the tribal number that sound just like the gibberish the Hindi-speaking audience would expect. But the words ring loud and clear in Bengali: "(Let there be) lime and ink on your nose and face [*naake mukhe chun-kali*]." In other words, "Shame on you." *You* could refer to the tryst-ing lovers; but it could also mean *us*.

An early work by another leftist filmmaker takes the unusual step of ac-tually making the romantic leads tribal characters. In the heavily allegorical *Roti* (1943), the director Mehboob portrays their jungle home as an arcadia indeed, one innocent of property or social hierarchy, the better to draw the contrast with the industrial (and still colonial) city—a stark dystopia for In-dia's nascent proletariat. The best-known film I would include on this list is the Gothic-influenced *Madhumati* (Bimal Roy, 1958). Like *Roti*, it brings the tribal presence out of the scenery—and the musical novelty number—by making the heroine an *adivasi*, a mysterious "Santhal" woman (the hero is the standard, normatively modern, unmarked Hindu type). The diegetic location has shifted from Thana to some vaguely eastern milieu. But the delicate camerawork not only delivers on the narrative construction of the tribal character as a ghost but effectively suggests the occulted trace of her people on a landscape from which others have tried to erase them.

Comparably reflexive gestures in films made since then have been rare.[10] To the degree that the motifs of the old tribal numbers appear in contempo-rary mainstream Hindi films, they have been cited in a parodic mood, as in *Om Shanti Om* (Farah Khan, 2007) or *Chintuji* (Ranjit Kapoor, 2009). And yet, looking back from the present moment, what strikes me as important is not the record of the odd cinematic statement of critique but rather the normal-ization of the tribal presence, however stereotyped and accessorial, on the na-tional landscape in the first place. Nowadays, as I have indicated, there is no room within the frame of a properly shiny, world-class India to accommodate an urban slum. There may yet be a place for forest greenery somewhere in the picture, possibly as a decorative border, but to acknowledge its habitation by primitive indigenes would be to extinguish whatever ideological power arcadia still holds in the current configuration of the Indian modern.

By the same token, however, puncturing the shiny surface of the ideological bubble is a favorite project of visual artists working in India. It would be remiss of me to wrap up this conclusion without naming some artistic interventions that challenge the spectacle in ways that speak directly to my book's argument. I have chosen two projects grounded in photography: "Fields of Sight," by Gauri Gill and Rajesh Vangad, an ongoing series begun in 2014; and "Life Is on a New High," by Alicja Dobrucka, completed in 2014. Both series aim to destabilize the hegemonic image, opening it up to alternative subject positions as manifested in alternative visual codes. They do so not only by stretching the canvas, as it were, to bring in figural representations of marginalized presences; they also disrupt the photographic icon's smooth surface with textures that cite indexical traces. The struggle between surface and interiority noted earlier by Bhatti and Pinney is thus rejoined here, with acerbic insight and humor.

If the film *Madhumati* uses ghost-story tropes to hint at a tribal footprint in spaces claimed—and spectacularized—by others, Gill and Vangad's collaboration makes the hint explicit. Gill is a photographer. Vangad is a painter; he is also a Warli, and he paints in the highly stylized idiom that itself functions as an icon of tribal identity. "Fields of Sight" consists of black-and-white landscapes shot by Gill in and around the village where Vangad grew up in Dahanu, north of Thane; Vangad's person actually appears in many of Gill's compositions. Over her photos he has layered his graphics. Sprite-like human figures, animals, trees, and gods multiply across the land; and also trucks, airplanes, and tree stumps. Inderpal Grewal (2015) comments on this series: "Ecocriticism comes alive through the conjoining of photography and Warli painting, hoping to replace one modern history with another history, one that is contemporary. If the modern is marked by notions of progress, development, and nationalist discourses of decolonization, the contemporary moment, with its rampant inequalities and environmental destruction, calls for a politics outside of the modernizing narratives of the nation-state." If invited to edit Grewal, I would amend the last line to say: *the modernizing images of the neoliberal dispensation.*

Dobrucka, a Polish artist based in Mumbai, trains her own lens on the high-rise developments that are transforming the skylines of many neighborhoods (including my friend Prashant's) and on the media used to sell apartments in them. "Life Is on a New High," the title of the series, is taken from advertising copy Dobrucka found in the *Property Times*, a real-estate supplement that comes enclosed with the *Times of India*. Some of the works are conventionally shot compositions that show the new towers looming over the urban blocks that surround them (fig. 9). In two of these pictures the ground is occupied by slum housing, and the artist draws the eye to the colors and textures of the plastic sheeting material used by the construction workers and the street-level bricoleurs alike. But what gives Dobrucka's statement its edge is not this set of images but its witty complement: photographs of the photographs in the *Property Times*. With this additional iteration, the glossy representations of glamour and high living are imbued with an uncanny quality; the creases and nicks in the newsprint and the smudges of ink—the spectral impress of images from the facing page—suggest materiality, ephemerality, citational recess.

Behind the Beautiful Forevers

What sort of home do you find back there, behind the shiny surface of representation? Here is one more image. In 2003 it could be found in Film City, a stone's throw from Devipada, the Warli settlement bisected by the Whistling Woods Film Academy's wall.

Across the road there is an unscarred, much nicer looking *pada*. It includes six cabins, a main well, and an ancillary well (fig. 10). These features are arranged around an attractive and rustic-looking yet strangely *pakka* tiger temple. Despite its odd looks—and the off-putting placement of the border god's station at the village center—some of my tribal interlocutors expressed admiration for it. They said it was a faithful copy of a real Waghoba temple located some distance away in the forest's interior. The walls of all the structures are decorated with Warli painting. The director who had this set built, Nitin Desai, had made his name in the industry as a production designer, and the care taken with its realization reflects his expertise. Unlike the actual dwellings of Film City residents, it is made entirely out of materials that do not look like plastic. It covers more ground than the *padas* it borders.

The project for which it had been erected, *Desh Devi Maa Ashapura* (2002) was a mythological film, a votive gesture made in honor of the country goddess (*desh devi*) who had overseen the success of the famously devout Desai, a Gujarati country boy who made good in the big city. Once shooting had wrapped on the film, the tribal village went on to new fame on television as the ashram of a group of forest-dwelling ascetics. The series in question, *Gayatri Mahima*, aired in 2003 on Doordarshan, the government network, in the Sunday morning slot that has been set aside for programming of a devotional character ever since the *Ramayana* phenomenon of the 1987–88 season. Every week the pious viewers who tuned in were offered *darshan*, alongside the actors embodying Puranic gods and saints, of Desai's fabrication filling in as a forest hermitage—the locus of an arcadian sacrality.

For me as a sometime member of this audience, knowledge of what the set looked like before mediation by the camera threw the show's elaborately artificial style into sharp relief. Or, rather, it did the reverse; for what *Gayatri Mahima*'s producers were at pains to project was the distinctly flattened-out effect of Hindu devotional "god poster" art. In the process of being framed, lit up in the requisite warm glow, and transmitted to offer address from a screen, the icon became enchanted or sacralized, acquiring an aura wholly lacking in the material space behind it.

Not only did this Desh Devi *pada* look more like a "real" Warli hamlet than any real Warli hamlet I saw, its relatively *pakka* structures also seemed to offer better shelter. Yet none of the residents of the neighboring settlements, beleaguered though they may have felt in the shadow of Whistling Woods, had considered making use of it. Those I asked found my question absurd. There may well have been a threat of some kind of security measures in place, enough to ward off any such "encroachment." But I also suspect that this iconic site's lack of any indexical connection to local spirits precluded its adoption as a habitable space.

I will give the last word on the question of real and false idols to a teenage boy the Film City office assigned me one day to guide me around the lots. He was a nontribal local, a resident of a slum colony on the studio's periphery, but it is not hard to imagine his attitude replicated among his Warli neighbors.

One of the permanent outdoor sets is a large and well-appointed Hindu temple. It had been kept in continuous use for twenty-five years, my guide told me, but when we visited, there was no deity inside. At the time, my questions to him had specifically to do with whether an image installed there would be recognized as sacred without the mediation of a Brahmin priest. But our exchange speaks to concerns I have acquired since then. About appearances, about ideology, about how spectacles work; about branding, in the sense of what corporations do with products, and also of what ranchers do with cows; about a political regime in the present day that seems bent on branding a whole nation under the mark of a homogenized Hinduism; and about the characteristic and enduring tendency of so many ordinary Indian people to see through the surface:

"So," I asked, "I guess the production crews put their own *murti*s in it?"

"Sure, they bring whatever god they want."

"Do they ever bring along a pandit to consecrate it before they shoot?"

He laughed. "Even the pandit's an actor."

ACKNOWLEDGMENTS

This book has had a long gestation.

It originated in ideas I worked on at the University of Chicago under the mentorship of Wendy Doniger. Wendy has been a true guru to me, as to so many others, and an extraordinarily generous friend.

Yet she is not the only teacher to have had a guiding hand in this work. I thank Arjun Appadurai; William Mazzarella; and Christopher Pinney, who self-manifested in Chicago at just the moment I was most in need of direction. This is also the place to thank Tom Spear, who saw me safely onto the academic track in the first place.

An unhappy measure of how long this project has taken is the number of those I would like to thank who are no longer among us. I will name them alongside everyone else.

For their support through the Chicago years, I thank Cassie Adcock; Carey Arnholt; Brian Axel; Jeremy Biles; Carol Breckenridge; Peter Gottschalk; Sameera Iyengar; Bea Jauregui; Eliza Kent; Steve Lindquist; Amanda Lucia; Caitrin Lynch; Brian Malovany; McKim Marriott; C. M. Naim; Sarah Neilson; Sally Noble; Sandy Norbeck; Shreeyash Palshikar; Kym Pinder; Beth Povinelli; *Public Culture* and the Society for Transnational Cultural Studies; John and Jenny Quinn; Elias and Cristal Sabbagh; Mat Schmalz; Greg Spinner; Steve Theodore and Hai Han; Neda Ulaby; Rachel Weber and John Slocum; and Carrie Yury. Four friends, in particular, were fellow travelers: Allison Busch, Laura Desmond, Jen Higgins, and Blake Wentworth.

I am grateful to the Fulbright-Hays DDRA Program for funding my research in Mumbai in 2002–3 and to the United States Educational Foundation in India, particularly the staff in the Mumbai office. I thank the University of Pune (now Savitribai Phule Pune University), with which I was affiliated during the main period of my research. I also thank the Marty Center and the Committee on Southern Asian Studies at the University of Chicago.

Many of the Mumbai people I name here also appear elsewhere in these pages: Maharukh Adenwalla and Yug Mohit Chaudhry; A. K. Ali; Chandra Shekhar Azad; S. C. Bhambhri; Sidharth Bhatia; Neville and Ali Billimoria; Rani Burra and Subhash Dey; the Centre for Documentation and Research; Chandrasekhar; Rahul da Cunha; Celine D'Cruz; Falguni Desai; Alicja Dobrucka; Vidya Kamat; Mani Kamerkar; Kunal Kapoor; Shaukat Khan; Vithal Lad; Chandita Mukherjee and Comet Media Foundation; Suresh Naik; Bipin and Indira Patel; Sandeep and Aruna Pendse; Chandrashekhar Prabhu; Bhagvanji Raiani; Dhruv Redkar; Chandrashekhar Rokde; Murari Sakseria; Indra Munshi Saldanha; Babubhai Samant; Bal Samant; Ashish Sawhney; Dan Scholnick; Amit Shah; Meenakshi Shedde; Shiraz Sidhva; Pappi Sippy; Rahul Srivastava and Shekhar Krishnan at PUKAR; and Jay Vithlani. My fieldwork would have never gotten off the ground if not for four highly capable women-about-town: Rachel Dwyer, Pritha Murdeshwar, Rachel Reuben, and Sadia Shepard. And I owe special thanks to the members of Mumbai's Warli community whom I call out here (by pseudonym): Alok, Prashant, Priyanka, and, above all, Vikas.

Pune and Banaras have been my other bases in India. I thank Mike Bollom and Susan Renaud; Kumudini Dandekar; Rabindra Goswami; Ajit and Meena Harisinghani; K. S. Nair; P. K. Nair; the H. N. Pandey family of Lolark Kund, especially Amit Pandey; Sujata Patel; Andrea Pinkney; Rakesh Ranjan; K. S. Shashidharan; Virendra Singh; Robin Tribhuwan; and Michael Youngblood.

In the United States, I moved for some years from one academic base to another. These chapters took shape in various institutional venues—and so did I, as a scholar, along with them—thanks to the advice and critique of many friends and colleagues. I thank Shahzad Bashir; Bob Baum; Colleen Boggs and the Leslie Center for the Humanities at Dartmouth; Lawrence Cohen; miriam cooke and Bruce Lawrence; Sienna Craig; Dale Eickelman; Jamal Elias; Maura Finkelstein; Nancy Frankenberry; Thomas Blom Hansen and Stanford University's Center for South Asia; Linda Hess; Roger and Pam Jackson; Sunila Kale; Eliza Kent; Borayin Larios; Philip Lutgendorf; Rachel McDermott; Karline McLain; Sangeeta Mediratta; Lisa Mitchell; Satyajit Mukerji; Reiko Ohnuma; Anne Patrick; Sean Pue; Sumathi Ramaswamy; Daisy Rockwell; Parna Sengupta; Smriti Srinivas; April Strickland; Jill Tollefson; Raphaël Voix; and Eleanor Zelliot. Christian Novetzke and Karin Zitzewitz have been unstinting sources of moral and intellectual support.

Nowadays I am no longer a wandering spirit. I have a seat in an office at the University of California, Santa Barbara. I am deeply grateful to my colleagues in the Department of Religious Studies, who have made it such a place of welcome. I am especially indebted to José Cabezón, Juan Campo, Barbara Hold-rege, Kathie Moore, David Walker, Vesna Wallace, and David White.

With this book's publication by the University of Chicago Press, the project has returned to its place of origin. I have been truly fortunate to work with my editor, Priya Nelson: my appreciation for her dedication, care, and thoughtfulness has only grown over the course of a long process. It has also been a pleasure working with Dylan Montanari, Pam Bruton, and Henria Aton. Gauri Gill and Rajesh Vangad graciously provided the perfect cover image. I thank the anonymous readers who evaluated the manuscript for the South Asia across the Disciplines series, and I thank the readers who reviewed it for the Press (twice). The work is far stronger for their interventions.

Finally, I owe thanks to my family. I thank my brother, Tony, who fell under Mumbai's spell before I did, and my sister-in-law, Yasuko. I am deeply grateful to my mother, Toshiko Elison, and my father, Jurgis Elisonas. To put this book in their hands at last is the fulfillment of a promise long deferred. I won't itemize my debts to them, but there is one gift from my father—a gesture both scholarly and paternal—that should be recorded here. When I was a graduate student, I copyedited some parts of his publications, minor help for which he thanked me handsomely in print. When my own turn came, he read the entire manuscript before I made the final submission to the press. He caught many solecisms and errors, including a blooper of major proportions. The responsibility for any mistakes that remain is of course my own, but I feel grateful that, thanks to his rigorous once-over, I won't have to own that particular one. It's a secret between father and son.

Two children of my own, Raphael and Georgina, are now on the scene; they work daily to reenchant my living space. I thank them for showing me what is important to take seriously and what's not. I thank my mother-in-law, Ivonne Pérez, for her own daily efforts at policing the slapstick. And I thank my wife, Lisa Pérez, who helped bring this book to *pakka* form at every stage of the journey charted in these acknowledgments. No one has a sharper eye for details; no one has a quicker mind for connections. But she dreams the big picture.

Parts of this book have appeared elsewhere in article form. Material from chapter 2 is reproduced in "Site, Sight, Cite: Conceptualizing Wayside Shrines as Visual Culture," *SAMAJ: South Asia Multidisciplinary Academic Journal* 17 (2018). An early version of chapter 3 was published as "Sai Baba of Bombay: A Saint, His Icon, and the Urban Geography of *Darshan*," *History of Religions* 54 (2)

(2014). Parts of chapter 6 appeared in "'Bonafide Tribals': Religion and Recognition among Denizens of Mumbai's Forest Frontier," *Journal for the Study of Religion, Nature, and Culture* 4 (2) (2010). My ethnographic work with "Vikas," the basis of chapter 4, received a more literary treatment in the essay "At Home in Filmistan," featured in *The Believer* 119 (June/July 2018).

NOTES

Preface

1. In administrative terms, Greater Mumbai consists of the area governed by the Brihan-mumbai Municipal Corporation (BMC), which occupies two of the constituent districts of Maharashtra State. The official population counts given in *Census of India 2011* (2014) are as follows: 3,085,411 residents of Mumbai District and 9,356,962 residents of Mumbai (Suburban) District, for a total of 12,442,373.

Introduction

1. Kolatkar's bilingualism is the subject of a recent study by Anjali Nerlekar (2016).

2. At the start of 2017, to some fanfare, a new statue was finally erected in Edward's place. It depicts a riderless horse. The critic Mustansir Dalvi (2017) was among those unamused; see his short piece "The New Horse Statue in Kala Ghoda Embodies Mumbai's Efforts to Create a False Memory." On the role of horses and horsemen in South Asian mythologies of conquest and sovereignty, see Blackburn 1989; Doniger 1999. See also B. Singh 2015, especially chaps. 2 and 7.

3. As Dipesh Chakrabarty (2000, 88) observes: "Marx's thoughts, still the most effective secular critique of 'capital,' remain indispensable to our engagement with the question of social justice in capitalist societies. But my point is that what is indispensable remains inadequate, for we still have to translate into the time of history and the universal and secular narrative of 'labor' stories about being human that incorporate agency on the part of gods and spirits."

4. Church and state, God and Caesar: the opposition holds true, I think, as a way of il-lustrating the commitment to secularism that is taken very seriously in some sectors of Mumbai's population. But it should be stated right here at the start of the book that lo-cating worship within a sphere of private concern is a simpler proposition in the United States than in India. *Public*, as deployed in my argument, is a multifaceted concept, and in the next section of this introduction I will outline how I have chosen to complicate the term. In fact, the question of what sort of Hindu temple is public—and in what sense—poses a worthy challenge not only for social theory but also for jurisprudence. Succes-sive rulings handed down by Indian jurists have refined a distinction between legally recognized *temples* (public, in the technical sense that they are considered open to all Hindus) and *maths*, or monastic establishments (relatively more private). Fortunately, perhaps, the great majority of the religious sites with which this book is concerned are

not legally recognized, and thus, the niceties of the law in this regard are not germane to my argument.

5.   A Hindu worshiper customarily salutes a divine image with the *pranam* gesture, palms held together at chest level. It is not impossible to visualize a colonial subject enacting an interpellation by Cornwallis by presenting the effigy with a British-style military salute. (It does seem like something out of a Kipling story.) Compare the image of the black French soldier analyzed in Barthes 1972.

6.   See Lacan 1977a; Lapsley and Westlake 1988. Lacan's own model of recognition builds on Alexandre Kojève's (1969) interpretation of the Hegelian master-slave relation. I explore this connection in the context of *darshan* in chapter 3. I must also mark my debt to the work of Christopher Pinney (2002), who stresses that the subject has been conditioned to enter this exchange as an affective, embodied experience.

7.   At the levels of both embodiment and agency, interaction with the deity opens up the human subject. My ideas on this problem build on the investigations of the anthropologist Alfred Gell (1998) into what he theorized as "distributed personhood." A related concept is the "metaphysics of presence" developed by the religious scholar Robert Orsi in his research on cultic practices, especially those centered on saints, observed among Italian American Catholics. In his *Between Heaven and Earth* (2005) and other studies, Orsi traces networks of mutually dependent relationships that link the human members of the community with their (normally) invisible "kin." If I take the lesson from Gell that the individual subject may be distributed in space "beyond the bounds of the body," no less instructive for my work is Orsi's picture of distributed presence at the level of community.

8.   Mazzarella quotes Gangar's (1995, 210) "Films from the City of Dreams," which presents a tour of Bombay images from representative works of commercial and art cinema. For a meditation on the analogous US case, see the documentary *Los Angeles Plays Itself* (Andersen 2003).

9.   Mumbai's fickle enchantment is a theme shared by two books that introduce the city in very different but compelling ways: the historian Gyan Prakash's (2010) eclectic collage-portrait and Katherine Boo's (2012) journalistic account of slum life.

10.   Pinney (1997b, 855n43) credits the term "techno-juridical grid" to Ronald Inden.

11.   As for Horniman Circle—formerly Elphinstone Circle, after a governor of Bombay, but renamed for a British journalist who championed Independence—Rachel Dwyer informs me that cabbies habitually sacralize the name as "Hanuman Circle."

12.   Compare David E. Sopher's (1987, 366) "geometric" image of Hindu sacred space: "Place is replaced by sacred nodes and geography itself becomes a cosmic geometry. It is a geometry that is given life by the institution of pilgrimage."

13.   The quotation is adapted from a formulation at Appadurai 1996, 183, where the author himself credits Michel de Certeau (1984).

14.   Presenting his own scheme for theorizing the experience of multiple spatial orders in the Bombay of British days in terms of a "series of mental maps, co-existing or superimposed one upon the other," Jim Masselos (1991, 33–34) makes a distinction between external and internal templates: "one set related to urban form, an urban patterning of bounded shapes, no matter how indeterminate their form. Another set related to perceptions of space from within, not from a defined exterior but from an experienced interior."

15. Kinnard 2014, 3, citing J. Smith 1987, 107; with Smith himself citing Lévi-Strauss 1950, xlix. It is a distinct pleasure to be adding to this paper trail.

16. The proposition also implies "negatively sacred space": territory frequented by dangerous spirit-presences like demons and ghosts. Importantly, wicked or mischievous spirits are typically not emplaced stably and visibly, such that they can engage the recognition of the space's human residents. There is a strong connection between homelessness or lack of station, with its corresponding invisibility, and hostility—a connection that will be developed in the chapters to follow.

17. Smriti Srinivas's (2001, 17–18) typology of "ritual centers" in Bangalore opens by describing a dynamic characteristic of the sort of urban sites I have in mind, where a divine personality asserts the claim of one community to a particular space, on the one hand, and addresses a broader public, on the other:

> The first type of center is associated with cults of old village deities, Christian or Muslim saints, and holy personages. Such centers tend to be controlled by a single community but attract a multidenominational following. . . . Goddess shrines . . . often display an autochthonous relation to the land. . . . The goddess is believed to have appeared suddenly or manifested herself . . . at the time of the founding of the city. Although her shrine may be tended by members of a specific caste today, she attracts devotees across communities.

Viewed as structures, the Mumbai sites I will introduce in chapter 2 cannot claim to be of any considerable age. But the logics of autochthony and self-manifestation are, as I will argue, nevertheless central to the way they contribute to the organization of urban space. And regardless of whatever structure marks the spot, the immanence of a spirit-presence there may well be understood to antedate historical time itself, never mind the founding of the city.

18. For an erudite discussion of modern Indian visual culture that takes the connection with space in a different direction, see Sinha 2007.

19. For provocative reflections on the configuration of public space in the specific context of Mumbai, see Mazzarella 2015.

20. In the past quarter century, two special issues of the journal *South Asia* have been compiled around the problem of theorizing the public in specifically South Asian contexts. In addition to the introductory essays (Freitag 1991; J. B. Scott and Ingram 2015), articles from these two collections with which this project is in dialogue include Chakrabarty 1991; Gilmartin 2015; Masselos 1991; Orsini 2015; J. B. Scott 2015.

21. An exception must be made here for the nation-state as one such collectivity, to the extent that the Indian state retains a regulatory role over print, broadcast, film, and Internet media. The state's role in monitoring national publics is a central point of analysis for Habermas, for Appadurai and Breckenridge, and for Benedict Anderson (1991), among others. Since my project's purview is confined largely to a single city, the question of the national community as a really big public does not figure prominently within it.

22. See the work of Mikhail Bakhtin (1981) and Benedict Anderson (1991); Michael Warner (2002); and Christian Lee Novetzke (2011), respectively.

23. David Gilmartin (2015) constructs an argument about the public around South Asian conceptions of sovereignty across the historical transition from sacred kingship to colo-

nialism. See also Brighupati Singh's (2015, 42–44, 59–61) highly suggestive discussions of the sovereignty exercised by local deities.

24. A recent Mumbai ethnography that builds on a considered rejection of the subaltern model—and the school of thought that produced it—is Anjaria 2016.

25. When it comes to Peircean work in the anthropology of South Asia, the standard-bearer is surely Valentine Daniel's (1984) *Fluid Signs*. Other ethnographies following a rigorously Peircean approach include Keane 1997 and Parmentier 1994. In centering on the trichotomy of sign-object relations, my own ethnographic repurposement of Peirce follows the example of Rappaport 1967.

26. Khandoba's cultic domain actually extends beyond Maharashtra across the western Deccan; see Sontheimer 1989.

27. In a US city like San Francisco, it is common to see pedestrians navigating the streets with their eyes fixed on their mobile phones: they are making sense of the space they traverse via the symbolic interface of Google Maps. As for Mumbai, it is possible that things have changed since 2015, but the last time I experimented there with Google Maps, it really brought the resistance of the lived street to techniques of mapping and surveillance home to me.

28. In the final chapter of *Fluid Signs*, Daniel (1984, 233–87) offers a virtuosic breakdown of the pilgrimage he undertook to the sacred mountain of the South Indian god Ayyappan in terms of Firstness, Secondness, and Thirdness.

29. For a historical account of the Cornwallis statue and its cult, see Masselos 2012, 27–33.

Chapter 1

1. Some of Bapurao's images are in fact anticipated in a shorter work in Marathi from about a hundred years earlier, the fifteen-line "Ballad of Bombay" of Shahir Parsharam. Both Bapurao and Parsharam open with comparisons to Lanka, the marvelous citadel of the demon king Ravana in the *Ramayana* (Bhagwat 1995, 115–16; Chitre [1995] 2000, 29).

2. The great wartime hit *Kismet* (Gyan Mukherjee, 1943) is often cited in this connection. The film made the fortunes of Bombay Talkies, Filmistan's parent studio, and its story's influence extended well into the cinema of the 1970s.

3. The naturalized character of the police presence on the landscape is brought out well in a news item about Bill Clinton's state visit to India in 2000. On the eve of the president's stop at the Taj Mahal, the *Times of India* reported, the route he was to take through the Agra streets was subjected to a campaign of beautification à la Potemkin that even old-time residents declared to be unprecedented in scope. At the freshly scrubbed grounds of the Taj itself, no detail was neglected—except for a colorful row of flag-like cloths that proved, on inspection, to be the laundered undershorts of the Taj's police guard hanging out to dry. These were such a quotidian fixture that no one had noticed them (Dubey and Varadarajan 2000).

4. In Hindi, "Nakli pulis se sawdhaan." Real policemen have also gotten into trouble for impersonating bogus policemen. In 2014 it was reported that the police brass in Uttar Pradesh had found it necessary to censure members of the force who had eschewed the regulations in favor of wearing their uniforms after the style of Bollywood "heroes" playing police roles. Initially, "[t]wo constables . . . were suspended in Agra for wearing 'dark glasses and very tight pants'" (IANS 2014), but it was only the start of a statewide crack-

down. The number of Uttar Pradesh cops taken to task for this and a related offense—surfing their smartphones on duty—eventually reached 427.

5. In its early stages, the dissertation project was conceived as a study of Hindi cinema that would bring film analysis and an ethnography of film viewing together with research into daily life and work at the studio. I was never quite able, however, to map out the project coherently, and I had trouble finding published work to look to as a model. In 2015 Anand Pandian published *Reel World: An Anthropology of Creation*, a philosophically adventurous ethnography of the Tamil film industry, "Kollywood." It supplies answers to questions I didn't know I had.

6. His mustache was still black, however. Although Azad worked chiefly as a stagehand, he went by what was undoubtedly a *nom de théâtre*: in full, Chandra Shekhar Azad, a combination of a Hindu personal name with an Urdu handle, *azad*, or "free." He had named himself after a famous son of his hometown of Allahabad, a freedom fighter memorialized throughout India by the circulation on posters and other visual media of a single stereotyped image: flexing his muscles, the hero grooms his mustache in a bravura pose captured just before his showdown with the colonial police in 1931. For discussions of the iconization of the Chandra Shekhar Azad image, see Pinney 1997a, 177, 208–9; 2004, 175–78.

7. Illuminating in this regard is Dilip Gaonkar's (2002, 5) observation about modern—or public—forms of sociality: "[M]odernity in its multiple forms seems to rely on a special form of social imaginary that is based on relations among strangers. The stranger sociability is made possible through mass mediation, yet it also creates and organizes spaces of circulation for mass media." An implication here is that as the capital of modernity, Mumbai has public spaces, whereas other Indian cities are merely overgrown villages. The contrast between the public anonymity of Mumbai and the intimacy that characterizes provincial life is a classic Bollywood trope; Mani Ratnam's *Bombay* (1995) is a provocative example.

8. Few Bollywood productions explore the industry's own social dynamics with anything like an aspiration to realism. One exception is the flawed but endearing *Main Madhuri Dixit Banna Chahti Hoon* (Chandan Arora, 2003), in which the starstruck heroine, played by Antara Mali, narrowly escapes success as a junior artiste—a move that would have spelled doom for her hopes of the big time.

9. Or some variant thereof. The derivation is most likely spurious but nevertheless is cherished.

10. Before there was an official Mumbai, there was Bombay. And before there was a state of Maharashtra, there was a state of Bombay—heir to British India's Bombay Presidency—which included Gujarat. When Bombay State was split in 1960 along ethnolinguistic lines, the city was claimed for Maharashtra's capital. The populist agitation that compelled the partition is given a literary treatment in Salman Rushdie's (1981) *Midnight's Children*.

11. It may be said that caste names are intrinsically unstable terms, but the compass of *Maratha* as a descriptor is especially complex; see Hansen 2001, 31–33, for a discussion of the ways *Maratha*, *Kunbi*, and *Maratha-Kunbi* have overlapped historically and in the present day. The question will resurface in chapter 4 in connection with the Marathaness of the Kolis and Warlis.

12. Kaviraj (1997, 84n3) modestly defends this heuristic: "But in Calcutta this practical dis-

tinction is quite well understood: the *bhadralok* middle classes on one side and on the other all others who live in the city to serve them. This covered various types of people, from the really poor . . . to . . . bazaar people . . . who were often fairly well-off."

13. Hemalata Dandekar's (1986) study of the village of Sugao in Maharashtra's Satara District emphasizes the gendered character of the urban ties that developed as the result of post-Independence labor migration, as indicated by her title: *Men to Bombay, Women at Home.*

14. For a complementary discussion, see Swati Chattopadhyay's (2009) exploration of visual-cultural politics on the Kolkata streets, which centers on the graphics adorning bus transport.

15. For accounts of the Shiv Sena's populist vision and not-so-crypto fascist tactics, specifically its representation of an urban modernity in which are located the aspirations to middle-class citizenship of Maharashtrians and others—at the expense of yet others (since the 1980s, chiefly Muslims)—see Bedi 2016; Hansen 2001; Heuzé 1995. In recent years the Shiv Sena's claim to paramountcy has been compromised by a schism, with a breakaway party, the Maharashtra Navnirman Sena, bidding for the loyalty of its core constituency. As announced on its English-language web page, the Maharashtra Navnirman Sena is "committed to raising the State of Maharashtra, its people and the Marathi language to resplendent glory."

16. Writing of colonial and precolonial social formations, Ranajit Guha ([1989] 1994, 265–74) draws explicit connections between the devotional teachings of Bhakti and the formation of subjects in submission to the state.

17. In a trenchant analysis of the campaign that middle-class citizens' groups led in 2000 to have street vendors cleared from Mumbai's public spaces, Arvind Rajagopal (2001b, 91) deploys the term "'people like us' (or PLUS)."

18. See also Maura Finkelstein's (2016) discussion of the categories of *work* and *worker* in the contemporary context of Mumbai's deindustrialization.

19. In his study of the strike, Huub van Wersch (1995) emphasizes urban-rural ties between the workers and their villages in the Maharashtrian hinterland. In 1987 he surveyed a sample of 150 representative workers, of whom a majority, 86 percent, were categorized as Maharashtrians in terms of regional origin, and 75 percent as Marathas in terms of caste. (The Kunbi and Maratha identities are often conflated.) Only 10 percent of van Wersch's sample claimed the city of Mumbai as their place of origin. Interestingly, he cites a study from the 1950s that gave a picture of a much more diverse workforce, with large groups coming from Uttar Pradesh and Karnataka (1995, 67–68). The demographic shift would seem to be reflected in the declining optimism on the left, over the corresponding decades, in the Bombay mills' promise as the crucible of a modern Indian working class.

20. The star and auteur Raj Kapoor, whose figure loomed large from the 1950s through the 1970s as "the Great Showman," is said to have perfected the formula of "sex, songs, and socialism." It is a constant temptation for film scholars to read progressive politics into Bollywood productions, but on the whole I think it is fair to say that the attitude of the commercial cinema over the decades has remained comparable with the purported liberalism of Hollywood, hardly ever advancing beyond commonplaces of the "racism is bad" variety.

21. It must be said that the pastiche offered here of a typical story line fits the films of past

decades better than those of the present. The 1990s are understood as a pivotal moment in the development of contemporary Bollywood, and much has been written on this generic shift, relating it to economic and technological developments. See, for example, R. Dwyer 2000; Nandy 2001.

22. Azad's word for "illiterate" was *angutha*, literally "thumb," in reference to the thumbprint required by way of a signature from subalterns confronted with official paperwork on which they cannot sign their names. At the same time that he connected his relatively humble station to his lack of education, Azad implied that the film industry had given him better opportunities for advancement as an individual than he would have found elsewhere.

23. Given the theme of this chapter and the chronology of Azad's story, it seems appropriate to introduce the spectacular in these pages as a cinematic projection. Historically, cinema has dominated popular visual culture in India to a far greater extent than in the United States. But in the 1990s the opening of national markets and the advance of video and digital technologies combined to transform the media landscape—and the mediated landscape. Today the centrality of advertising to the dissemination of images of urban India is reflected in a glossy, globalized style of presentation, at once the fruit of corporate investment and bait for more such investment. I will have more to say about this topic in the conclusion to this book.

24. There are workers' welfare associations set up to deal with workplace concerns, collect funds for sick or elderly members, and so on; these are rival bodies whose local chapters are organized by studio and are not coterminous with the blanket organization of the Ciné Workers Union, which seems to function in a way analogous to the Screen Actors Guild in the United States. One such body is helmed by the film star Mithun Chakrabarty; another contender is the ciné workers' unit within the Bharatiya Kamgar Sena, the labor arm of the Shiv Sena.

25. The humbler toilers who perform maintenance work, such as the sweepers, who do indeed come from the sweeper caste, do not have union cards and are probably not on the payroll but, rather, are contracted informally.

26. This notice has been painted over and the whole gate cleaned up and given a makeover since 2003, when these details were current.

27. This is also to say, of course, that no one among their number is actually a boss.

28. Recent ethnographic studies of the Mumbai streets include Anjaria 2016 and Shah 2014.

29. Ethnographers of South Asia who have pursued research inside government offices offer much to complicate the picture. In the first chapter of *Pipe Politics, Contested Waters*, Lisa Björkman (2015) launches a close-grained analysis of the Mumbai water department's blueprints as aspirational statements. See also Matthew Hull's (2012) ethnography of the Islamabad city bureaucracy, *Government of Paper*.

30. Smriti Srinivas's (2001) *Landscapes of Urban Memory* and Raminder Kaur's (2005) *Performative Politics and the Cultures of Hinduism* are standout ethnographies of public rituals in urban space. I will address both arguments in the next chapter. For more recent perspectives on religious life in South Asian cities, see Bear 2013; Khan 2012; M. Rajagopalan 2016; N. Roberts 2016. Another recent entrant to the conversation is Daniel Gold's (2015) *Provincial Hinduism: Religion and Community in Gwalior City*, which stakes out an interstitial position as a small-city ethnography.

31. Through the Golden Age and well beyond, the mountains of Kashmir had pride of place

in Hindi cinema as a honeymoon destination. The snowy peaks were at once exotic and national; as Lalitha Gopalan (1993, 54) has observed, "the predominant presence of Kashmir in the Hindi love story film marks [it] as an integral part of India's geographical identity." Since the 1990s, however, its allure sullied by the newspaper headlines and the grainy images on the television news, Kashmir has yielded its place in the movies to location footage of other "arcadias." See the conclusion.

32. In fact, the private space that tenants allot to such employees often does not consist of much more than a cot: the *chowki* itself. The case of a subaltern resident expanding beyond such cramped quarters to become the impresario of a sacred display is—far from being unique to Azad's story—a characteristic Mumbai scenario. It will be taken up in some detail in the next chapter.

33. See Jaoul 2006 for an investigation of the erection of statues of the Buddhist leader B. R. Ambedkar as an assertion of Dalit (formerly "untouchable" castes) visibility and clout in Uttar Pradesh; see also M. Rajagopalan 2016 on controversy generated by subaltern Muslims' assertion of a right to worship at Delhi sites designated as historical monuments by the Archaeological Survey of India.

Chapter 2

1.   John James Blunt (1823, 43) writes of what would appear to be an exact precedent for the Mumbai solution to this problem as devised by the citizens of ancient Rome, who protected their property "against such as commit nuisances by consecrating the walls so exposed with the picture of a deity or some other hallowed emblem, and by denouncing the wrath of heaven against those who should be impious enough to pollute what it was their duty to reverence."

2.   Studies of subaltern practices of excretion as an aspect of the production (or corrosion) of urban public space in India have, as far as I know, emphasized defecation over urination. The ethnographic literature includes Appadurai 2002 and Doron and Raja 2015; see also Chakrabarty 1991. For policy-oriented discussions specific to Mumbai, see SPARC 2001; *Toilet Talk* 1997. Of late, the government of Prime Minister Narendra Modi has undertaken an extensive campaign to reform the defecating habits of India's poorer inhabitants. Critics in the press cite the invasive character of the plan's implementation and its emphasis on questions of appearance over public health or infrastructural development.

3.   I am indebted to Wendy Doniger for devising this threefold pun as an organizing rubric.

4.   Some of my observations in this chapter may be relevant to practices of framing and adoring Catholic imagery, whether installed by devotees or "self-manifested," in public space in US cities. Chicago's most celebrated example in recent years is undoubtedly the salt-stain Virgin Mary that appeared on the wall of the Kennedy Expressway's Fullerton overpass in April 2005, attracting attention from Catholics of diverse ethnic backgrounds and, in due course, city authorities concerned about traffic flow. Cases of images and objects venerated in a Hindu idiom offer more direct comparisons. In 1989 the adoption of an abandoned San Francisco parking barrier as a self-manifested Shiva *linga* became the nucleus of a shrine in Golden Gate Park. The site grew to attract an eclectic crowd of New Agers and others and to absorb in its structure, oddly enough, discarded materials from a different kind of sacred building—parts of a tenth-century Cistercian monastery, transported stone by stone from Spain in the 1930s and subsequently unloaded on the

city by William Randolph Hearst. The hybrid shrine's encroachment on public property led to legal action that was resolved in January 1994 by an interesting out-of-court settlement: the authorities agreed to truck the *linga* to the house of the man who had discovered it, local ashram leader and performance artist Baba Kali Das, alias Michael Bowen, where it could be reenshrined on private property (Hasson 2005, 3; Rix 1995). My thanks to Cassie Adcock for directing me to this episode.

5. It can be added that the neighborhood of Dadar, long a Shiv Sena stronghold, has some claim to being the citadel of the modern, ideologized Maratha identity and has thus itself become a rhetorical (if not visually signified) metonym. What Harlem is to New York and, at one remove, to African American culture in general, Dadar is to Mumbai and perhaps to Maharashtrian culture across India.

6. See R. Srivatsan's (2000, chap. 3) "Looking at Film Hoardings" for a theoretical discussion connecting cinema, spectatorship, and the streets as a space that engages public desire.

7. For an ethnography of advertising in Mumbai, see Mazzarella 2003. If there is one Indian advertising icon notable for its citation of forms conventionally identified with popular religion, it is the puckish "moppet" that has represented the Amul dairy cooperative's brand of packaged butter for over fifty years—the longest-lived brand ambassador in advertising history, in fact. With its wide-open eyes and avatar-like tendency to appear in myriad guises, Amul's doll-like mascot invokes Hinduism's most celebrated consumer of butter, the baby Krishna—*adorable* in more than one sense.

8. I owe much of my information about *zogua*s to personal communications with Nagaraj Paturi and especially to Sandeep Pendse. On the Potraj cult in Maharashtra, see Sontheimer 1989, 56–58; for related practices farther south, see Hiltebeitel 1988; S. Srinivas 2001.

9. On the historical role of processional spectacle as a mechanism for asserting institutional authority in urban spaces in South Asia, see Freitag 2001.

10. Smriti Srinivas (2001, 82–91) also notes the inclusion of Sufi and Christian sites within the circuit of the Karaga festival in Bangalore.

11. Smriti Srinivas (2001, xviii) estimates some two hundred thousand people in 1995.

12. Jim Masselos (1991, 52) attributes the general outlines of the Ganesh festival (that is, neighborhood crews build floats, exhibit them locally, carry them out to the thoroughfare on the tenth day to join in procession to Chowpatty Beach) to its "mimick[ing] . . . the format of another festival": Muharram, the most spectacular of Muslim celebrations in South Asia. As with its Hindu and Maratha counterpart, Muharram as observed in the nineteenth century also used to lay claim to the city in the name of an ethnoreligious constituency—but one whose bounds were also, to a point, fluid. See also Masselos 1982; Green 2011.

13. Neither do members of Maharashtra's Scheduled Caste and Scheduled Tribe communities, to the extent that they have embraced alternative politicized identities as Dalits and *adivasi*s. The Maratha-tribal relation will come in for some attention in the chapters to come.

14. Raminder Kaur (2005, 167) gives an estimate of 60–70 percent in preceding years. Her book contains an extensive exploration of Shiv Sena involvement in Ganapati Puja in Mumbai and Pune.

15. On 25 August 2003, bombs were detonated at two densely trafficked sites in the city,

killing fifty-two people. Whatever the accuracy of the official attribution of the crime to the usual suspects—Islamist militants—its perpetration the week before the holiday indicated that a desire to spread citywide terror by triggering sectarian violence was one motive. In the blasts' aftermath, national security was a theme that received attention from the Ganesh *pandals*' designers as well as from officialdom, politicians, and the press. One particularly lurid display, shown in a photograph by Dilip Kagda that ran in the *Indian Express* (9 September), depicted green talons emerging from a map of Pakistan to throttle saffron-colored India at its Kashmiri neck. On the festival's second day, the Shiv Sena and its ally, the Bharatiya Janata Party, acted on their cue by launching a series of *maha aaratis* (Mishra 2003; Olivera 2003; Times News Network 2003a, 2003b).

16. One of the most evocative contemporary picturizations of Ganapati Puja is the musical number "Deva Shree Ganesha" from the Bollywood film *Agneepath* (Karan Malhotra, 2012), a hard-boiled tale of the Mumbai underworld. To the accompaniment of a driving pop rhythm, the effigy is moved from its *pandal* in the courtyard of a *chawl*, a working-class apartment complex, and into the streets to the sea. Especially effective is the shift from the *chawl* thronged with female celebrants to the exclusively male environment of the streets, where shared fervor and clouds of colored powder erase what distinctions remain among the crowd's members—marchers, onlookers, and police alike. Amid the anonymity and ecstasy of the crowd, the film's hitman hero, played by Hrithik Roshan, recognizes his target and kills him.

17. Technically speaking, the widely aired observation about "the size of Ganeshes these days" was probably incorrect, inasmuch as the municipal authorities had imposed size limits on the images some years before. Of course, it could be said that the proscription merely proves the point being made. The critique fits neatly within the pervasive discourse of nostalgia for the more civilized, livable Bombay of yore, citation of which can itself seem like a ritualized gesture demonstrating membership within a distinct urban tribe, the Anglophone elite. See Deshmukh 2003.

18. Compare Lawrence Cohen's (1995) provocative analysis of the carnivalesque North Indian festival of Holi as celebrated in Banaras, in which an all-male and Hindu and predominantly young, poor, and lower-caste population of revelers converts the city's streets into a zone of license and inversion where norms not only of social hierarchy but also of sexuality and bounded personhood are renegotiated.

19. It may be objected that, far from demanding anything as abstruse or highfalutin as "recognition," the sort of exchange the *zogua*s, *hijda*s, and others have in mind is a cash transaction. But to take such a position is to dismiss the logic that glosses the petty sum that changes hands as an offering to the deity (typically a country goddess) whose temporal agent is the performer. The concept of *izzat*—honor or respect—is central to Gayatri Reddy's (2005) ethnography of the *hijda* community of Hyderabad, *With Respect to Sex*; see her third chapter for a discussion of *hijda* performance as a citation of classical discourses of asceticism.

20. At Kemp's Corner the women who provide this service are members of the Gondhali community, minstrels by hereditary occupation who hail from Satara District. They commute from their local base in Ghatkopar on the city's fringes, boarding the train in the morning with the bundles of grass they have cut and collecting the livestock at the other end of the line. The cows are rented from a North Indian businessman, a self-identified

Brahmin, who runs a rudimentary dairy in an apparently abandoned construction site in the otherwise densely packed neighborhood of Tardeo. For a description of the Gondhalis in their capacity as performers, see Dhere 1988.

21. Carla Bellamy (2011, chap. 3) analyzes the sacred fumes and establishes that the *lobaan* dispensed at her fieldwork site, a Shiite *dargah* in Madhya Pradesh, finds a market among Hindu as well as Muslim consumers. She also identifies the fuel that produces it as a synthetic compound whose manufacture can be traced to a factory in Ajmer, Rajasthan, the resting place of the Sufi saint Moinuddin Chishti. For ethnographic studies of cultic practices at other *dargah*s in South Asia, see Assayag 2004 (rural Karnataka); Ewing 1997 (Lahore); Kakar 1982, 15–52 (Delhi). See also Peter Gottschalk's (2000) discussion of *dargah*s as they feature in the production of sacred space in a Bihari village, especially the description at pp. 50–51 of a Muharram ritual in which a circuit is demarcated by the bearer of a sacred horseshoe (*na'l*) identified with the steed of the Shiite martyr Husain.

22. Not to mention overtly Anglophile names. The Piccadilly, Britannia, Churchill, and Prince of Wales restaurants number among these South Mumbai landmarks.

23. For a trenchant discussion of what is at stake in the reframing of a god image from the temple to the museum, see Davis 1997, chap. 1. See also Sullivan 2015.

24. Two ethnographically grounded studies of Hindu temple construction that are notable for their engagement with questions of form are Macrae 2004 and Waghorne 2004.

25. In proposing place of residence as a possible model for legal recognition of *mandir*s as social entities, I am not being entirely whimsical; there is a well-established tendency in Indian official discourse to define deities as legal persons. (Compare, in US legal usage, the recognition of corporations as persons.) A celebrated instance analyzed by Richard Davis (1997, 248–59) concerned a lawsuit the Indian government filed in London in 1986 in order to recover a smuggled art treasure, an image of Shiva. Davis writes:

> Later in the case the Indian side introduced still another plaintiff, Śiva. The god Śiva, acting as a "juristic person," would claim ownership of the Śiva Naṭarāja image that had originally resided in the Viśvanāthasvāmi temple. . . . Anthony Gardner, an antiquities dealer[,] . . . expressed this concern: "Anyone contemplating buying a Shiva Nataraja in future is going to think very carefully about its history, or else risk a writ from Shiva." . . . Indeed, Śiva's appearance in English court is also symbolically problematic, for—as the defense argued in their appeal—the United Kingdom is a Christian kingdom ruled ultimately by the queen under the Christian God, and this ought to preclude other foreign gods from bringing suit. (249)

26. Just in front of Sainath Granite, a stone and tile supplier in Dadar, stands a tree with an octagonal base the shopkeepers have transformed into an elaborate display. Tiled over with the business's own wares, each of the eight faces shows an image representative of a distinct religious community: Muslim, Hindu, Christian, Zoroastrian, Buddhist, Sikh, and Jain. The side facing the street has been reserved for the store's namesake, Sai Baba. The site is more a statement of Indian "secularism" or cosmopolitan comity than a *mandir*; it is also an ingenious advertisement.

27. As further remarks will demonstrate, popularization through film is one of several features the cult of Santoshi Maa has in common with that of Sai Baba of Shirdi.

28. Compare Christopher Pinney's (2004, 190) observation regarding the display in rural Madhya Pradesh of goddess imagery by the roadside purveyors of alcohol and non-vegetarian cooking—indulgences that are associated, along with sex, with qualities of heat and passion.

29. Andy Rotman's recent ethnographic work assesses the semiotics of branded merchandise in connection with the credit and piety of Hindu merchants in the bazaars of Banaras. See Rotman 2017 for some preliminary findings.

30. As a category within a psychoanalytical system, the abject owes its formulation to the post-Lacanian theorist Julia Kristeva (1982). Discussing the positionality of Sufi mendicants, *qalandars*, in modern urban Pakistan, Katherine Ewing (1997, 218) illustrates how Kristeva's concept can be put to work in an ethnographic context similar to that of my own study: "The selection of what in particular is to function as the abject is a process that is shaped by participation in a culturally and historically specific discourse. To the extent that an individual founds an identity on the respectability of being a proper Muslim and is constituted through that discourse, the qalandar functions as an abject. The qalandar is explicitly be-shar', without Law. As a sign, the qalandar is the antithesis of one who is 'subject' to the shari'at. The qalandar is 'not-Me.'"

31. See also the discussion of Hindu icons in the decades of Hindutva's ascendancy in Raminder Kaur 2005, chaps. 5–6.

32. *Janhit Manch v. State of Maharashtra* (2002), Bombay High Court, ordinary original civil jurisdiction, Writ Petition 2063.

33. Compare the points of contestation and convergence in the attitudes of street vendors, Brihanmumbai Municipal Corporation employees, and middle-class citizen activists as analyzed in Anjaria 2016.

34. Of the sets of relations that Peirce maps among signs, their objects, and their interpretants, the trio of relations that join signs to their objects—*symbolic*, *iconic*, and *indexical*—has traditionally commanded the attention of anthropologists and scholars of visual culture to the exclusion of his other trichotomies.

35. Compare Nikhil Anand's (2011) use of the term *settlers* in reference to the residents of Mumbai shantytowns.

36. In an essay about two different ways a community of Tamil potters provides its gods with vessels, Stephen Inglis (1985, 100) makes this observation: "The local deities are most active on the boundary of the village. They repel intruders, fight evil forces, and live in constant contact with darkness and pain." For a more recent ethnographic study of "fierce gods," see the eponymous book by Diane P. Mines (2005).

37. Günther-Dietz Sontheimer (1989, 187; see also 31, 93n84, 157, 189, 211) records numerous stories told by the Dhangars, pastoralists of Maharashtra and Karnataka, in which a cow finds the spot that hosts an immanent presence:

> One of the cows would always go to a certain place and stay there to lick a stone. The Gavlī asked himself, "Why does that cow go there every day? Why does it lick the stone?"
>
> One day as he was cutting grass, he came up close to the cow. He had his sickle, and he hit the stone with the point. And turmeric powder came out of the stone. The more he hit it, the more turmeric powder came out. So he thought, there must be a god here.
>
> He asked the other people . . . and they decided, "It's Khaṇḍobā." (187)

Chapter 3

1.   *Amar Akbar Anthony* (Manmohan Desai, 1977), a landmark of Hindi popular cinema, relates the adventures of three long-lost brothers who are brought up in different religions. (I am a coauthor of a book-length study of this film: Elison, Novetzke, and Rotman 2016.) One of the film's pivotal moments is a Sai Baba prayer service I will analyze in this chapter.

2.   In his review of two important collections edited by Sujata Patel and Alice Thorner, *Bombay: Metaphor for Modern India* and *Bombay: Mosaic of Modern Culture*, Frank Conlon (1997) questions the cosmopolitan ideal as projected onto urban life before the 1992–93 riots—riots that erupted even as the two volumes were in the process of completion. Conlon's very nuanced critique targets, not discrete arguments, but rather the assumptions behind their compilation.

3.   See also Rigopoulos 1993. Charles S. J. White (1972) and Smriti Srinivas (1999) have situated Sai Baba in relation both to his antecedents as a teacher and mythologized cult figure and to the subsequent holy men who have claimed his mantle: his disciple Upasani Maharaj, who established himself at Sakori, just south of Shirdi, in 1917; Meher Baba, who studied with Sai Baba and more extensively with Upasani Maharaj and went on to international fame; and the yet more famous (some would say notorious) god-man figure Sathya Sai Baba of Bangalore.

4.   The art historians Mary Nooter Roberts and Allen F. Roberts have curated a collection of Sai Baba images from India and around the world. A 2016 exhibition, *A Global Saint in a Virtual World: Devotional Diasporas of Shirdi Sai Baba*, will yield a forthcoming book. The Robertses also maintain an online archive of images at http://www.shirdisaibaba virtualsaint.org.

5.   The question of just how many photographs is a matter of some dispute. Somewhere between five and ten images can be identified as the issue of an encounter between the historical individual and a camera. Other black-and-white images circulate as Sai Baba photographs, but—although they must work perfectly well for devotees who regard them as such—their claims are open to two sorts of challenge: (1) Is the person pictured really Sai Baba? (2) Is the picture really a photograph? To expand on question 1, the details that figure as Sai Baba's distinguishing marks—the beard, the rags, the kerchief—are fairly commonplace attributes among spiritual teachers in the Baba mold. Question 2 stems from the popularity of techniques of retouching and overpainting in this period (and later), further compounded by a certain slippage among the categories of *photograph*, *print*, and *picture* in vernacular languages. See n. 8.

6.   Concomitant with the Sai Baba cult's valorization of the saint's picture was the proliferation in Bombay of what Francesca Orsini (2015) calls "religious print-objects," popular booklets mediating the words of other, more teacherly saint figures such as Kabir.

7.   It is easy to overlook the qualities of rarity and exclusiveness attributed by less prosperous Indians to devotional prints well into the twentieth century. A revealing indication is given in a text with a provenance comparable to Dabholkar's, *Indian Jottings, from Ten Years' Experience in and around Poona City*, by Edward Elwin (1907). The author, a Catholic missionary, writes of distributing mass-reproduced images from Europe—including old Christmas cards—among Hindus of Poona as a missionizing device.

8.   Or possibly an entirely hand-painted enlargement of the "original" photo. The term *foto*

in much colloquial Indian usage can be ambiguous, its referential range covering images produced by photography, by other printing processes, and even by painting and drawing. (The title of Christopher Pinney's 2004 book, *"Photos of the Gods,"* reflects this ambiguity, in that the images Pinney discusses are mostly lithographic reproductions of paintings.) What is not in doubt in the case of the central portrait at Shirdi is that all images of the cross-legged Baba, whether realized in two or three dimensions, are copies of the historical photograph. However stylized the reproduction, the idiosyncratic pose and the photorealistic contours (which might be smoothed out or rounded, to a greater or lesser extent, by the prevailing aesthetics of contemporary *murti* art) are traces of this indexical capture of the holy man by a camera.

9.   Mary Nooter Roberts, in a personal communication, gave the date of this photograph as 1911.

10. Baba Abdul Raheman, Maulana Saab (or Peer Maulana), Mohamed Hussain, and Baba Tajuddin, identified by Kher as contemporaries of Sai Baba based, respectively, in Bombay, Bandra, Bandra, and Nagpur (Dabholkar 1999, chap. 41, nn. 2–5).

11. Such graphic symbols appear on the ballot, enabling illiterate voters to identify the parties.

12. No Hindi film has so engaged the attention of Western scholars of Hinduism as *Jai Santoshi Maa.* In addition to Lutgendorf 2003, see Babb 1981; Erndl 1993; Lutgendorf 2012. For the *Ramayana* series that aired on Doordarshan, the government network, in 1987–88, see Lutgendorf 1995; Rajagopal 2001a.

13. Actors who portray gods and saints in Indian films tend to become confined to the religious genres. Typecasting, arguably more pervasive in Bollywood than in Hollywood to begin with, seems to be exacerbated when the personality represented or embodied by the actor is one shown on the screen for religious devotion. A cinematic god, or at least a successful one, is at once the object of an intensely affect-laden gaze and, through its extradiegetic cult, a social being whose authority places restrictions on the appearances of its impersonator on and off the screen.

In her seminal "Mythic Material in Indian Cinema," Geeta Kapur (1987) proposes that when framed according to the correct typological codes, an image that elicits the adoring gaze of *darshan* does so by rupturing diegesis. This alternative cinematic mode is what Kapur dubs *iconic.* In an interesting extension of this principle, it would seem that in moving out of diegesis, the iconic aura has a tendency to continue clear on out of the movie house in attachment to the person of the actor.

14. The quotation comes from the website of Mary Nooter Roberts and Allen F. Roberts, http://www.shirdisaibabavirtualsaint.org.

15. Complicating this picture is the persona of the star Manoj Kumar, who embodies a robustly masculine nationalist ideal. Kumar has been a prominent exponent of Hindu nationalist politics, and some of his more overtly nationalistic films also feature, in like vein, symbolic displays of religious diversity.

16. For more on this film, see McLain 2016, chap. 4.

17. Viewed as a historical process, the spectacularization of Mumbai entered overdrive in the 1990s, when economic globalization coincided with advances in visual technologies. See the discussions in chapter 1 and the conclusion.

18. The formulation "Kojève-Hegel matrix in Lacan" comes from Caroline Williams (2001, 94), quoting Macey 1988, 166.

19. Robert Lapsley and Michael Westlake, theoreticians of film, quote Lacan 1977b, 106.

20. Compare, however, the transfer, through Brahminical ritual, of the subtle essence of the god Vitthal (Vithoba) from his temple *murti* into a mundane pot, an operation enacted at the Maharashtrian pilgrimage center of Pandharpur in 1947 in response to Independence-era reforms. V. L. Manjul (2005, 186–87) recounts:

> When the Untouchables were allowed into the temple, my grandfather, Tryambakrao Manjul, and my father, Baburao Manjul, participated in the boycott of the temple. They, along with other orthodox priests, decided, in an astonishing ritual, to remove the divinity of Lord Vitthal from the idol, put it in a copper vessel, and take the pot to a Brahmin's home. The assumption was that the temple would be purified subsequently and the same divinity could be re-installed in the idol. But the ritual purification of the temple was impossible after the passing of the act, and hence the divinity of Lord Vitthal remained in the copper pot for over fifty years.

21. I am indebted to Elizabeth Pérez for highlighting this passage.

22. The comparison with Santa Claus may seem irreverent to some, but as recent ethnographic work by Joanne Punzo Waghorne (2014) demonstrates, it has enthusiastic proponents among Sai Baba devotees in Chennai (and possibly elsewhere).

23. I derive this image from the title of Smriti Srinivas's (1999) article "The Brahmin and the Fakir: Suburban Religiosity in the Cult of Shirdi Sai Baba."

24. Kiran Shinde and Andrea Pinkney's (2013) highly informative article "Shirdi in Transition" corroborates this picture of a place whose business is almost exclusively pilgrimage, and provides some figures. A town with a resident population of about 30,000 hosts 8 million pilgrims annually; the "floating population" of pilgrims ranges from 25,000 during the week to 75,000–80,000 over peak weekends (2013, 563). Shinde and Pinkney estimate that perhaps five hundred hotels cater to this trade, of which more than half "are concentrated around the main temple precincts. In this area, there are approximately two thousand commercial establishments that can be categorised into four types: (1) hotels; (2) shops offering Sai Baba novelties and religious trinkets, such as: laminated photos, lockets, picture frames, DVDs, VCDs, audio CDs, images, and devotional icons; (3) shops selling materials required for temple worship including garlands and flowers, sweets, coconuts, etc.; and (4) permanent and temporary restaurants (approximately 150 to 200 at any given time)" (564).

25. A similar dynamic on a more modest scale is demonstrated by a temple dedicated to Maruti (Hanuman) near the Mumbai red-light district. The structure started out as a shrine attached to the local Shiv Sena *shakha*, or neighborhood cell, and has expanded across legal boundaries to incorporate an interior compound of its own and now dominates the whole block.

Devale was himself a Shiv Sena politician. He had been elected to the Maharashtra legislative assembly in 1990 from the Pune area, with Shirgaon part of his constituency.

Chapter 4

1. Beatrice Jauregui (2014) works with the category of *jugaad* in the context of police administration in Uttar Pradesh.

2. To be sure, the tendency I find emblematic of his bricolage—that of devising local mean-

ings from lexical material drawn largely from technical registers of English—was likely exacerbated when he spoke with me, a native English speaker who often engaged him on speculative or esoteric matters.

3. A prominent voice in the developing scholarly conversation is Lucia Michelutti, who has led a team of researchers in a European Union–funded project, An Anthropological Study of Muscular Politics in South Asia; publications are forthcoming. See also Michelutti 2008.

4. Chief among the underworld figures whose names are invoked in connection with criminal outrages involving black marketeering, murder, and bomb blasts, Dawood Ibrahim famously coordinated his Mumbai operations from an overseas sanctuary in the Persian Gulf. (These days, although the boss is said to reside in Karachi, Dubai apparently remains a hub of operations for his syndicate.) Reports have implicated Dawood in the event known as 26-11, the attack by gunmen from the militant group Lashkar-e-Taiba that killed and wounded hundreds of people in South Mumbai from 26 to 29 November 2008. Targeting some of the city's best-known landmarks, including Victoria Station and the Taj Mahal Hotel, the militants carried out a spectacular rampage, much of it televised. Yet as an architect of terror, Dawood Ibrahim had likely already surpassed Saddam Hussein among Mumbai residents back in 2003. The conflation of the two is suggested by defining features of both: mustaches, swagger, personal handles combining two Muslim given names.

5. Critical work on Bombay cinema since the 1970s illuminates the connection. Fareeduddin Kazmi (1998) discusses the industry's appeal to this constituency in the form of the star Amitabh Bachchan and his persona of the Angry Young Man. See also Sardar 1998; Mazumdar 2000.

6. Compare the findings of Gregory Alles (2012, 643) concerning the sort of foreign films favored by the Rathva *adivasis* of Gujarat: the James Bond series, Arnold Schwarzenegger and Sylvester Stallone movies, and the 1981 Sam Raimi horror film *The Evil Dead*.

7. Events that can be fitted within this narrative include the absorption of the Portuguese colonies in 1954; the partition of Bombay State into Maharashtra and Gujarat in 1960; the reorganization of Dadra and Nagar Haveli as a union territory in 1961; and, probably most germanely, the extension of municipal authority over the whole of the Bombay (Suburban) District, at Thana's expense, in 1957. See chapter 5.

8. When asked which specific village within this old dominion of Thana had been his family's point of origin, Vikas gave the name Oha, describing the place as an entirely Warli village. He identified his mother's natal place as a village called Belad in Selvasa.

9. I have translated Vikas's words from the Hindi. In proper Mumbai style, his speech incorporates a good deal of English, and these English words are generally given in italics.

10. Some of Filmistan's other Warli residents, Vikas's cousins, stated to me that they readily accepted work as extras. But the settlement's female members were not to be brought similarly into the public domain.

11. The *tarpa* is a reed instrument that has become familiar to non-Warlis, largely through depiction in tribal art, as a metonym for Warli culture.

12. So definite was Vikas's purpose of getting himself "caught in the writing" that, in an ironic development, when I informed him about the institutional regulations that would guide my "human subjects research" work and assured him that his identity would be safeguarded through use of a pseudonym, he demanded to be represented under his real

name. In accordance with established norms of fieldwork ethics, however, I have disregarded his wish, although I am sympathetic to his stated position.

13. D. D. Kosambi (1962, 86) writes of the village goddesses of Maharashtra: "They have no images in iconic form, being represented by numerous shapeless little stones daubed with minium. . . . Similarly, the goddess Lakśmī-āï in many villages is a whole set of shapeless red-coated stones, apparently having nothing to do with Lakśmī, the beautiful consort of Viṣṇu." Again, of another Maharashtrian site: "The mother-goddess in her thicket is (as usual) several lumps of stone, coated with red" (87). Compare Whitehead 1921, 34–47, on the enshrinement of *gramadevata*s in South India, and the thoroughgoing typology by Cornelia Mallebrein (1998) of the iconic forms taken by the household deities of the Kokanas and Warlis, from whose number the normally aniconic goddess of the community is conspicuously absent. A recent study of village goddess worship with a broad historical and ethnographic compass is Padma 2014.

14. Filmistan was incorporated on 22 April 1943. The first production shot at the new studio was *Chal Chal Re Naujawan* (Gyan Mukherjee, 1944), released the following year (Rajadhyaksha and Willimen 1994, 91).

15. Vikas's principle of each community (*zaat, samaj*) belonging to its own proper place—its homeland—does of course resonate with both nationalist and counternationalist, separatist discourses of the sort that have defined geopolitical conflicts in South Asia since Partition. Importantly, however, it also seems to imply a subaltern logic that homologizes discrete territories with their native populations on the basis of a continuity of substance (see also, for example, Daniel 1984, 79–94). The point was brought home to me in a letter I received some time after I had returned to the United States, in which Vikas described an argument he had provoked by asserting that the Kashmir question could be resolved only with India's recognition of the area's essential character as the natal soil of Muslims. Elsewhere, he has inferred a link in some cases on the basis of an iconic affinity, as, for example, in his collapsing of *Parsis* with *France*. In his eccentric historiography, the Parsis/French feature as contenders with the British for colonial control over Bombay and hence as historical agents of disruption of the law. (The identification has force given the prominence of Parsis and Iranis among the entrepreneurs who carved fruit plantations out of the Thana forests in the late colonial period and exploited the tribal inhabitants for labor.)

16. For more about Filmistan's founding roster of talent, see "Films," n.d.; Manto 1998, 7, 107–8; Rajadhyaksha and Willimen 1994, 65, 91.

17. For the date of the purchase, I am indebted to Satyajit Mukerji (personal communication). Among Filmistan's founders, the buck seems to have stopped with Chunilal as far as business policy was concerned; Manto (1998, 172) describes him as "our owner." S. C. Bhambhri took over the sound department (including Buddhaji as boom operator) in the 1950s; in an interview with me he remembered differently, identifying the original owners as Shashadhar Mukherjee (producer), with a 60 percent stake, Chunilal with 20 percent, and Ashok Kumar (actor) and Savak Vacha (sound) with 10 percent each, which they sold to Mukherjee when they returned to Bombay Talkies in 1946.

18. In 2003 the Bombay Talkies industrial zone was said to host 850 registered factories, although one contractor claimed he shared the space with upward of 10,000 shops, not all of them authorized (Bhattacharya 2003).

19. More information about Syeed Pappu's story would be needed to address a pair of inter-

related points: the similarity of the studio's guardian-ancestor to the trope of the spirit-rider exemplified by the god Khandoba and the question of the informant's evidently Muslim identity as it pertains to such an identification.

20. A provocative take on this problem is Anand Taneja's (2013) article on the occulted Muslim landscape of Old Delhi, "Jinnealogy."

21. Of the mischievous spirits Jonathan P. Parry (1994, 226–48) describes in his account of possession activity in Banaras, perhaps the most suggestive in terms of the circuit of bodies, vessels, and geographical sites that he traverses is the *brahm*—the spirit of a Brahmin who has died a bad death—who was divined by the healer Panna to have followed a bride from her natal village:

> Panna's recommendation was that they should entrap the ghost in the effigy of a *brahm*, which they would then take to the wife-giving village from which it had originated. Here they would make it various offerings, instructing it to . . . "eat the sons, not follow the married daughters." They would then bury it in a hole adjacent to the shrine of the village's guardian deity (*dih*). The . . . effigy was to be put in a pot full of Ganges water with a lid on top. . . . They would then make offerings to the village protector who would ensure that the ghost remained firmly confined within its own territorial jurisdiction. (239)

22. It will be noted that the very building, Number Four, Azad named as the haunt of a deceased German is also one of the "lucky" stages that has sealed over a well. This raises the question: is there any perceived tension or contradiction between the danger produced by the ghost and the auspicious effects of the well?

23. My source for these dates is a personal communication with S. C. Bhambhri. Vikas's version dates the stages' construction more enigmatically to sometime after the production of the 1954 hit *Nagin* (Nandlal Jaswantlal). Judging by the timing, it seems likely that this expansion was planned by Tolaram Jalan when he acquired the studio. The customary description of Stages One through Four as Filmistan's "original buildings" (a figuration that distinguishes them from four additional, more modern facilities) elides the chronology of their construction in two stages. Oddly enough, a review of the film *Nagin* turns up the detail that "[i]t is believed that a nag-nagin actually live [*sic*] in Filmistan studios in Mumbai. The studio flourished as long as they were there, its fortunes nose-dived after they passed away!" (Salam 1999–2000). Were these resident water spirits supposed to have met their demise when the wells were blocked up?

24. Emphasizing the colonial government's administration of the forests as a determining factor, Indra Munshi Saldanha (1998, 717) focuses on an earlier phase in the integration of Thana's tribals into the plantation economy: "Even by the 1880s . . . a large number of tribals had lost their lands and become tenants and labourers to moneylenders and big landholders, the Marwari and Gujarati Vanis [*sic*], Parsis, Brahmins and others." See also Saldanha 1990; Ambasta 1998.

25. Although K. J. Save's (1945, 18) emphasis is on more independent hamlets—enclaves of a largely closed economy based on shifting cultivation and the gathering of forest produce—within specific geographical bounds he allows for the tribal satellite model of the *pada* as well:

> A hamlet is composed of a small number of huts, usually twelve to fifteen; four or five such hamlets make a Warli village. It may be noted that the Warli hamlets in the coastal

villages [that is, caste villages in coastal areas of Thana District, which would include Goregaon] are situated at their outskirts. Another noteworthy point about a hamlet is that it is not a segregated locality . . . and though Warlis prefer to live in a locality separate from that of the higher classes, they admit members of other tribes like Dublās, Dhodiās or Koknās in their midst.

Ashesh Ambasta (1998, 552) gives an arresting example of Kathkari men who avoided plantation overseers by the simple expedient of "render[ing] themselves invisible in the village. Their cluster of huts is . . . separate from the rest, and they keep themselves within its precincts."

26. Vikas frequently spoke as if his grandfather had arrived from a point of origin just north of what is now Maharashtra's border, in Nagar Haveli or in Gujarat's Valsad District, to settle in the Filmistan *pada* some 130 years before, that is, circa 1873. It remains an open question as to what is at stake in this date, which is hard for me to credit on its face; there seems to be room in his timeline for one or two extra generations. If 130 is not a formulaic figure of some kind, perhaps "grandfather" is a formulaic reference. The interpretation I favor is that Vikas is alluding to a collective narrative that sets the *pada*'s foundation at that particular site 130 years ago while enabling him to stay true to the picture of the whole of Goregaon as host to Warli *pada*s since time immemorial.

27. The original operators of Filmistan (in Vikas's conception, deputies of the British Raj) are said to have guaranteed Buddhaji's right to the site of his ancestral village, defined as the tract running from the shrine of the tiger god Waghoba at the southwestern boundary to a stand of mango trees at the north. The trees in question have not existed since the late 1950s, when Tolaram Jalan bought the studio and built Building Number Four on top of the well they had shaded.

28. Vikas did not specify whether the rocks were given a "god house" of their own in one of the new building's rooms, as before, or ended up sequestered in a basket in his father's own chamber, perhaps suspended from the ceiling, a typical method of securing household gods and other valued possessions.

29. These names are pseudonyms.

30. The real estate boom began at a time when Filmistan was going through multiple crises of its own. Following the demise of the old system of studio "banners," location shooting became the norm among Bombay filmmakers. In fact, the journalist who identifies Mrs. Jalan as the studio's rescuer credits her with "seeing that Filmistan was not sold to a real estate shark. 'There was a stage in the early '70s when it became fashionable to shoot movies in bungalows and at real locations,' [Mrs. Jalan] says. 'Studios went out of business, staff became a liability, and every big studio began selling out to builders'" (Iyer 2006).

31. Pralay Kanungo and Satyakam Joshi (2010) have produced a nuanced study of a *ghar wapsi* campaign centered on temple construction in the heavily tribal Dangs District of Gujarat. See also Tilche 2015.

32. Writing in 1982, I. M. P. Raeside stated: "Although an impressive bibliography in English and Marathi could be assembled around the name Dattātreya, most of it would consist of hagiographical works emanating from one of the modern cult-centres in Maharashtra and Gujarat" (439). Since then, work by Antonio Rigopoulos (1998) and Dušan Deák (2005) has moved scholarship forward.

33. Ghurye's numbers, however, are unlikely to have accounted for informal or illegally built shrines of the sort that can be thought of as private *puja* rooms that have spilled over into public space. Of conditions in 1969, Charles Pain writes: "The Datta temples of Pune are characteristically small, and many are inconspicuously hidden behind storefronts. Some are merely roadside shrines which can be viewed only from the outside" (Pain and Zelliot 1988, 101).

34. Making a case for the early-modern provenance of the god's *trimurti* form, Raeside (1982, 499) writes: "Dhere has shown very convincingly that one can find no certain reference to the modern Dattātreya—three-headed and representing an oecumenical fusion into one person of the trinity Brahmā-Viṣṇu-Śiva—before the *Gurucaritra* (c. 1550) and the hymns attributable to Ekanātha (1523–99)." His source is a study in Marathi by R. C. Dhere (1964, 28–33).

35. See Sontheimer 1989, 83–84, on related tactics of co-optation or appropriation of tribal sites. See also Kanungo and Joshi 2010.

36. Brideprice is basic to the transaction of marriage among Warlis, excepting minorities who have rejected it because of their embrace of Christianity or of a Brahminical or leftist program of uplift. Of *gharor* marriage Save (1945, 103–4) writes:

    > A young man goes and stays with one who has a marriageable daughter. He offers his services to him. This service period is regarded as probation or trial. If the girl and her relatives like him, the marriage takes place in due course. . . .
    >
    > Among the Warlis, a marriage in ordinary circumstances is a marriage by purchase inasmuch as a bride price has necessarily to be given to the bride's father. *Gharor* marriage is by service. . . .
    >
    > A *gharor* occupies a subordinate position in the family of his father-in-law. Sometimes he receives the same unkind treatment as a daughter-in-law receives in her husband's house. . . .
    >
    > A *gharor* inherits the property of his father-in-law, if the latter has no sons.

    The present-day configuration of households at Filmistan has thus grown from a constellation of no fewer than three *gharor*s around the patriarch Sukur, whose heir, Buddhaji, favored by patronage by the studio, has in turn been succeeded by Vikas.

    Vikas's aunts' appeal may well have been magnified in their suitors' eyes by the promise of alliance to Buddhaji, who could look to his film industry patrons for a foothold in the capitalist economy, not to mention a seemingly secure claim to a patch of the urbanizing Goregaon landscape. The acquisition of *gharor* relations undoubtedly redounded to the prestige of both Sukur and his son, although to the extent that bragging rights have come down to Vikas at the present day, they are dismissed by his cousins with indifference at best and at times with open hostility. In this context, Godavari Parulekar (1975, 94–95) saw in *gharor* marriage a solution to the debts incurred by brideprice, which sent many Warlis into indenture in the late colonial period.

37. See, for example, Comaroff 1985; Boddy 1989; Pérez 2011. For studies of possession in South Asian contexts, see G. Dwyer 2003; Nabokov 2000; F. Smith 2006.

38. Elizabeth Pérez has called my attention to the prevalence of electricity in the thought and symbolism of religious traditions sharing a heritage in the Yoruba cultures of West Africa. Electricity, particularly as a root metaphor for the movement of sacred energy through ritual activity and religious travel, is the organizing theme of Aisha Beliso-De Jesús's

(2015) recent ethnography *Electric Santería*. Her focus on spiritual currents in Cuban Santería/Lucumí complements the earlier insights of Andrew Apter regarding Yoruba rites of investiture as ceremonially recharging the battery of the king's body. As Apter (1992, 99) writes in an extended analogy: "ritual paraphernalia . . . transform, transmit, and store ritual power much as do electric condensers, cables, and batteries. . . . Ritual power, like electricity, is 'hot,' highly charged, and dangerous. Unbridled, it can kill. It must be contained, limited, and properly regulated to work productively for human society. Finally, ritual power, like electricity, possesses both positive and negative values." See also Harris 2006, 99; Probst 2011, 143–44.

39. Many of Vikas's concerns as identified in this section converge in a brief but highly suggestive essay by N. K. Wagle ([1995] 2000). Wagle's purpose is to reconstruct, from precolonial legal records, an archaic practice of Maharashtrian jurisprudence. In so doing, he discusses local gods, malevolent spirits, claims to territorial sovereignty, and the official recognition due the office of mediumship; the only piece missing is electricity. The historian finds that in several cases involving allegations of witchcraft—for example, where one party accused another of sending ghosts to haunt and blight his property—the adjudication of guilt, damages, and punishment was settled by tribunals of gods. They were convened from neighboring villages and given voice by teams of mediums. The Marathi name for this procedure, which seems likely to have had analogues in tribal and other contexts, was *padthal*.

40. By way of illustration, let me cite one early episode: an exchange between Vikas and Ajit from the video interview (Shepard 2003). Vikas sees a niche for himself in the film industry as a singer of Warli songs. Once in a while, at the cinema, he is visited by this sense of vocation when a musical sequence plays on the screen. Prompted for a Warli song, he complies, and surprises both Ajit and me. Isn't that a number from a Hindi movie?

Vikas's answer runs along these lines: There are Hindi words to the song, and then there are *adivasi* words whose meaning is very similar, and he has given the song an *adivasi* voice. Ajit queries: But what language has he put the song in? Is that the Warli language, or is it Marathi? The response is esoteric. There is a mapping of collective identity onto formations of space, as well as a gesture at summoning the authoritative valence of English words: "It's in Warli now, right? So actually Warli, this Marathi—there's a bit of a distinction. I mean, Marathi songs . . . that's the state [of Maharashtra] we're talking about. And then there's Warli songs. This is a district song [*yeh zilla gana hai*]." A perplexed Ajit wants to know in what sense a Hindi film tune, composed and written by Bollywood professionals, can be considered a "Warli song." Is it the melody, as opposed to the lyrics, that is the vehicle of some kind of Warli spirit? Was the composer perhaps inspired by some tribal folk song? But Vikas does not care to speculate about what others might have been feeling. It becomes clear that as far as he is concerned, it is precisely his own act of translating the lyrics into Warli/Marathi that accomplishes a cultural appropriation. In fact, what he is proposing is something like the reverse of Ajit's scenario. Moved by the music as circulated through the fantastic medium of the Bollywood cinema—and here *interpellation* is an apposite term—Vikas seeks a space for himself and his community within the spectacular fantasy by putting his mark on the lyrics.

41. Bhrigupati Singh (2015) theorizes the finite life courses, or "waxing and waning," of tribal deities. See, especially, his chapter 7, "Divine Migrations."

42. The transformative effects of media technologies on religious practice are not confined

to Hindu and related traditions, although they do appear to have particular resonance for practitioners of spirit-possession religions. Among the Sakalava of Madagascar, Michael Lambek (2003, 260) has described the far-from-salutary effect of television on an interlocutor's possessing spirit and muses on the man's relationship to television and reality: "There is some humor in the fact that he appears to mistake the one for the other. But this, in turn, produces reflection on the ontology of possession itself, its own relation, so to speak, to reality (costume or heirloom?), and ultimately on the relationship between television and spirit possession as alternate, and possibly competing, media for transmitting and juxtaposing images and for inhabiting and provoking reflection on the passage of history." See also Behrend, Dreschke, and Zillinger 2015.

43. And also, as already noted, the hero figures of occasionally viewed non-Hindi movies. I met Vikas one day not long after he had caught a screening of a film he called "Konarak" after the famous temple site in Odisha, which turned out to be *Conan the Barbarian* (John Milius, 1982). The impression was still fresh. "Do you know what that film is really about?" he demanded. "It's about God."

44. There is, in fact, a large and diverse group of people in Mumbai who make it their business to mediate between the spheres of the official and the subaltern. Social workers, party activists, neighborhood leaders: many of those who negotiate the entry of the poor into political society would fit the description. To the extent that he knows them, these are precisely the kind of people Vikas writes off as hopelessly corrupt.

Chapter 5

1. Coverage of this political flap can be found in the Indian news media, including the statement of Pinarayi Vijayan, the chief minister of Kerala: "By wishing Vamana Jayanti . . . BJP leader Amit Shah has ridiculed Kerala, Keralites and the culture of Kerala. Onam is the national festival of Malayalees. What is being reflected in this celebration is the unity of humanity, beyond the boundaries of caste and religion" (Sabith 2016).

2. As Wendy Doniger observes, the Trivikrama's antecedents can be found in the *Rig Veda* (1.154.1–6) creation myth in which Vishnu measures out—and thus creates—the earthly realms in three steps. The story acquires some characteristic features when it gets to the Brahmanas: "The gods and anti-gods were at war, and the anti-gods were winning, claiming the whole world as theirs. The gods asked for a share in the earth, and the demons, rather jealously, replied, 'We will give you as much as this Vishnu lies on.' Now, Vishnu was a dwarf, but he was also the sacrifice. The gods worshipped with him and obtained this whole earth" (*Shathapatha Brahmana* 1.2.5.1–9). A representative Puranic telling is cited above in this chapter's epigraph. Of the *Vayu Purana*, Doniger has commented:

> The cosmology implicit in the Brahmana myth is stated explicitly in this text: "Vishnu revealed that the whole universe was in his body." The anti-gods that appeared as a group in the Brahmanas are now replaced by the individual anti-god Bali, whose name, significantly, denotes the offering of a portion of the daily meal. That it is the Vedic virtue of generosity that destroys Bali may signal a challenge to that entire sacrificial world.
>
> In many versions of the Bali myth, Prahlada, Bali's grandfather, warns Bali that the dwarf is Vishnu (*Harivamsh* 71.48–72; *Vamana* 51; *Matsya* 244–46) and in one text, Prahlada complains bitterly that Vishnu as the dwarf deceived and robbed his grandson

Bali, who was "truthful, without desire or anger, calm, generous, and a sacrificer" (*Devibhag* 4.15.36–71). . . . The virtue of the demon king—his eternal *dharma*—leads him to lose everything, even his *sva-dharma* as king of the demons.

I have quoted this passage from a draft version of Doniger's *The Hindus: An Alternative History*. The words have been redistributed in the final edit (Doniger 2009, 318–20).

3. Youngblood (2016, 254n26) advances a further connection with the rural Maharashtrian practice of demarcating specific locations with reference to a host of other demons named in Puranic mythology. See also Feldhaus 1995, 181–84.

4. In his *Hybrid Histories*, Ajay Skaria (1999) pursues a subalternist historiography among the Warlis' tribal neighbors to the north, the Bhils of Gujarat's Dangs District. Skaria counterposes a genre of oral narrative known as *goth* to the official records of the colonial and postcolonial authorities, analyzing contested constructions of space and categories such as *wildness* and *tribal*.

5. This construction has received sustained critique in later scholarship that emphasizes a historical perspective (which is another indication, of course, of the trope's very salience). Where the literature on *adivasi* communities in western and central India is concerned, the landmark arguments have been produced by scholars working with the insights of Subaltern Studies to problematize the political agency of tribals in interaction with other groups: settlers, traders, religious movements, and—most germanely—precolonial and colonial state formations. In addition to Skaria 1999, cited above, these include works by Amita Baviskar (1995), David Hardiman (1987), Bhrigupati Singh (2015), and Nandini Sundar (2007). The nature-culture dichotomy has been no less important in defining the predicament of *adivasi* communities in India's Northeast, but the distinctive context of the Northeast has generated a specialized literature of its own.

6. Whether conceived collectively, as a distinct unit within the Indian population, or multiply, as the distinct tribes that make up that unit, the categorization of tribals is a project that owes much to the colonial census. This heritage in governmentality will receive attention in chapter 6. G. S. Ghurye (1963, 7) discusses the historical efforts of census commissioners to establish a workable taxonomy, with Athelstane Baines in 1891 considering separate *forest tribes* and *hill tribes* and J. T. Martin in 1921 opting for the unitary *forest and hill tribes*.

7. The Marathi travelogues mentioned by Anne Feldhaus (1995, 97) that warn of "the danger from tigers, tribals, robbers, and other denizens of the forest" are a specifically Maharashtrian example of a literary genre that casts tribals in this way. Feldhaus opens her discussion of a more prestigious genre, Sanskrit Mahatmya literature dealing with sacred river and forest sites, with a consideration of the demons portrayed in the *Ramayana* and *Mahabharata* epics: "The human counterparts of these demons are professional hunters and fishermen, highway robbers and tribals, natives of the forest and people who earn their livelihood from it" (103).

8. The ethnographic literature on the Warlis is not extensive. Along with the texts under discussion here, I have learned much from a dissertation by Ashesh Ambasta (1998) and articles by Cornelia Mallebrein (1998) and Indra Munshi Saldanha (1986, 1990, 1995, 1998). It is vital to consider the Warli material alongside work on other *adivasi* communities of Maharashtra and neighboring areas: in addition to the books cited in notes 4 and 5, and works by Günther-Dietz Sontheimer and D. D. Kosambi noted elsewhere in these pages,

valuable sources include Alles 2012, 2013; Damodaran 2006; Kanungo and Joshi 2010; Moodie 2015; Tilche 2015.

9. As such, Save (1945, iii) was an assistant to the Backward Class Officer within the colonial administration of the Bombay Presidency.

10. Satadal Dasgupta's (1986, 17–22) scheme of nested levels of spatial organization in use among Bengali villagers moves from *ghar* (household) to *pada* (a cluster or hamlet) to culminate at *thana*, the territorial bounds of the local police authority. As Doniger has pointed out to me in a personal communication, the Raj-era locution "out of station" has been adopted by speakers of contemporary Indian English as the standard way to say "out of town" or "not in the office."

11. Perhaps it is not to be expected for such a selectively cropped map to give any indication of the link's opposite terminus—Bombay, not thirty kilometers away. Yet in 1988, the year of Dalmia's book's publication, yet another administrative reform was passed to tie the suburbs more tightly to Bombay. After the manner, perhaps, of an expanding piece of leather, urban sprawl was continuing to make the boundary between Bombay and Thane less and less distinct. While Maharashtra's administrators redrafted their boundaries, Dalmia's own cartographer seems to have preempted this encroachment by simply discarding southern Thane as insufficiently Thane-like.

12. See the report of the official investigation, Symington 1950, as well as the powerful account by Godavari Parulekar (1975), the activist who helped lead a revolt of the plantation workers in the years immediately preceding Independence. For a study of women's roles in the Warli Revolt, see Saldanha 1986. The Parsi- and Irani-owned fruit plantations of colonial Thana also provide the setting for a highly original English-language play, Gieve Patel's (2008) *Mister Behram*—probably the most prestigious literary text to feature a Warli character to date.

13. It will be recalled that the states of Maharashtra and Gujarat date back as administrative entities only to 1960, with the partition of the old state of Bombay.

14. For the colonial "invention" of the village as an epistemic construct, see Bernard Cohn 1987. Cohn builds on the following provocation: "In some sense it might be argued that the British created the Indian village" (195).

15. The *Thana Gazetteer*, however, records more than one period in the nineteenth century when management of the state was taken over by the Government of India (*Gazetteer of Bombay Presidency* 1985–, vol. 13 [(1882) 1986], 705–6, 709).

16. More commonly encountered is an unofficial term that opts for a spatial index of Otherness: *remote tribe*.

17. "Among the various classes of inhabitants within the territory forming the Government of Bombay, the name of few is more familiar to us than that of the tribe of Kolies, more usually written *Cooly* by the English" (Mackintosh 1840, 189).

18. "In 1921 Enthoven wrote that a Kolī who takes up settled agriculture usually becomes a Kunbī, thus contributing to the recruitment of Marāṭhās. . . . The ocean fishermen of the coastal Konkan region, the Son Kolīs, are to be distinguished from the Kolīs of the Ghāṭs and the plateau, Mahādev Kolīs and Malhār Kolīs" (Sontheimer 1989, 69, citing Enthoven 1920–22 and Ghurye 1963). On Son Koli settlements in contemporary Mumbai, see Warhaft 2001.

19. Where colonial recruitment policies were concerned, hill tribes seem on the whole to have been favored with the attribution of martiality over forest tribes. Of the forest

dwellers of western and west-central India, the only example I know of a community targeted for military service is that of the Bhils of Khandesh, whose recruitment was initiated in the 1820s by James Outram, an officer in the service of the East India Company (Outram went on to direct the annexation of Awadh and was a leading commander in the conflict that followed it, the Revolt of 1857). Rudyard Kipling's ([1898] 1920) short story "The Tomb of His Ancestors" was inspired in part by this early phase in the career of the imperialist hero. Not one of the author's best, the story is nevertheless echt Kipling. Along with stock elements of the adventure-story genre it includes stock elements of the tribal milieu: the characterization of *adivasi*s as fey "little men," who appear uncannily out of the woods (138); the "aboriginal liquor" and "infernal music" that fuel a "Bhil orgie" (125); the tribal fear of the modernizing reach of the state, as manifested in law courts, the census, and inoculation drives (126, 133–34; the military presence, by contrast, is normalized); the quasi-magical power projected by English text on paper (143–45); even a tribal deity that incorporates in its features both horseman and tiger (136). The Bhils are described as "perhaps the strangest of the many strange races in India. They were, and at heart are, wild men, furtive, shy, full of untold superstitions. The races whom we call natives of the country found the Bhil in possession of the land when they first broke into that part of the world thousands of years ago. The books call them Pre-Aryan, Aboriginal, Dravidian, and so forth; and, in other words, that is what the Bhils call themselves" (111). For more on the Kipling story, see Radcliffe 2008.

Working primarily in South Indian contexts, Nicholas Dirks (2001) has drawn the connections between anthropological methodologies and policies of colonial administration. In his chapter 9, Raj-era constructions of "tribal barbarity," "criminal castes," and "martial races" come together in a comparison of the police force's interest in identifying malefactors with the army's interest in finding recruits. Dirks points out that the two arms of government often reached for the same people.

20. Bastar, the tribal-majority area whose history has been chronicled with both nuance and rigor by Nandini Sundar (2007), is a former princely state and as such could be described as a "tribal kingdom," although the ruling dynasty was not an *adivasi* family.

21. The gazetteer's source is Captain A. Mackintosh's (1840, 239–40) "Account of the Tribe of Mhadeo Kolies." Mackintosh's account, composed half a century earlier, is so different in style from the gazetteer's retelling as almost to qualify the latter as a translation:

> Having one day proceeded to pay his devotions at the shrine of the deity at Peemry, he met five Koly fukeers; one of these, placing his hand on Pauperah's head, bestowed his blessing on him, and said, "Go down to the Konkun, take possession of Jowair, and set yourself on the Gaddy there." . . . It is said that [he] paid a visit to Goozerat and that he prolonged his stay in Kattywar for seven years, at the termination of which period he proceeded to Jowair, and asked the Warley Raja to give him as much land as the hide of a bullock could embrace. The Warley Raja, seeing it would be impolitic on his part to offer resistance to a person of such power and influence, gave his consent to the proposal. The hide was cut into very fine shreds or strips, and when all were united and extended along the ground, the Warley Raja saw his small fort and dwelling embraced. (240)

The shift the translation achieves is a lesson in the relative prestige of distinct genres. Mackintosh's prose strikes a contemporary reader as nearly as archaic and quaint as the tone chosen by Dandekar for reproducing the story as a tribal myth. The anthropologist's myth, as cited at the start of this section, and Mackintosh's "Account" read like primary sources; the gazetteer stands out as a secondary source.

22. On a more diffuse level, stories similar to the "Oxhide Tale" could be said to include the *Aeneid* and Washington Irving's comic history of New Amsterdam. Of the purchase of Manhattan, Irving's ([1848] 1881, 130–31) Diedrich Knickerbocker recounts:

> The learned Dominie Heckwelder records a tradition that the Dutch discoverers bargained for only so much land as the hide of a bullock would cover; but that they cut the hide in strips no thicker than a child's finger, so as to take in a large portion of land, and to take in the Indians into the bargain. This, however, is an old fable which the worthy Dominie may have borrowed from antiquity. The true version is, that Oloffe Van Kortlandt bargained for just so much land as a man could cover with his nether garments. The terms being concluded, he produced his friend Mynheer Ten Broeck, as the man whose breeches were to be used in measurement. The simple savages, whose ideas of a man's nether garments had never expanded beyond the dimensions of a breech clout, stared with astonishment and dismay as they beheld this bulbous-bottomed burgher peeled like an onion, and breeches after breeches spread forth over the land until they covered the actual site of this venerable city.

Irving actually gives a citation for Dominie Heckwelder's version: manuscripts of the Reverend John Heckwelder held in the collection of the New-York Historical Society. The Heckwelders may indeed have "borrowed from antiquity": in the first book of the *Aeneid*, verses 365–68 tell of how Dido founded Carthage at the hill known in Greek as Byrsa, "hide," after *borsa*, a Phoenician word for "citadel." In John Dryden's translation of 1696:

> At last they landed, where from far your eyes
> May view the turrets of new Carthage rise,
> There bought a space of ground, which "Byrsa" called
> From the bull's hide, they first enclosed and walled. (Clarke 1989, 15)

I am grateful to Clara Hardy and Chico Zimmerman for directing me to Virgil and also to an essay by the classicist Raymond J. Clark. Clark (1970, 183) discusses a distinction I have attributed to rival Warli and Koli tellings of the story—that between blanketing and encompassing hides—as a motif operative within Virgil's own source texts, although one the poet himself delicately elides: "By writing not *tegere* ('cover') but *circumdare* ('enclose') Virgil passed lightly over the cunning in this event. But Servius *ad loc.* and other writers in antiquity explain how Dido's Phoenicians bought from the native Iarbas as much land as could be covered by a bull's hide and then cunningly shredded it into strips so that it might enclose a very much larger tract of land." Clark's source for Servius and his colleagues is Pease 1935. Citing James George Frazer's *Golden Bough* (1914, 6:249–50), Clark goes on to assert that "tales similar to Vergil's are found among the Hottentots, Saxons, and Danes, and in India, Siberia, Burma, Cambodia, Java, Bali, and Bechuanaland."

23. Along the lines of the puns and folk etymologies that characterize much subaltern repurposing of official terminology, the shift in meaning here is directed by a slippage in the word *sarkar*, which at once denotes government—*Bharat sarkar*, Government of India—and serves as a term of respectful address to social superiors. Compare the British "Guv'nor."

24.　A similar attitude greeted Ajay Skaria (1999, 34) in his attempts to gather oral narratives (*goth*) among Bhil elders in the Dangs region of Gujarat in the 1990s:

> As part of the sarkar's oppressive modernity, there was much reason to exclude me from spaces of intimacy, to not narrate too many goth to me. In one village, when other Dangi listeners urged a vadil to tell me more goth, he exploded: "What do you know about matters, telling me 'tell him the goth, tell him the goth.' . . . This was how the *saheb* [white man] came. . . ." Often, I was told primarily . . . the more playful vadilcha goth, and sometimes not even [those] where [they] involved hostility to the sarkar.

25.　Townsend Middleton's (2016) *The Demands of Recognition* is a reflexive double ethnography of a population that has mobilized to demand official recognition of tribal status—the Gorkhas of Darjeeling—and of the anthropologists retained to adjudicate such claims.

26.　Skaria (1997) mounts an elegantly historicized analysis of the category of *tribal*, ultimately to reject it. As I will move on to demonstrate, however, one of the most interesting contemporary developments in Indian identity politics is the reappropriation of the term by self-identified tribals.

27.　Criminal Tribes have been reclassified by the independent Indian state as De-notified and Nomadic Tribes (DNTs). Activist members of the Chhara community, a DNT group settled on the outskirts of Ahmedabad, are profiled in an ethnographic documentary by Shashwati Talukdar and P. Kerim Friedman (2011), *Please Don't Beat Me, Sir!* For a summary of the legal history behind the DNT designation, see T. Jain 2004.

28.　For a discussion of the rival anthropologists' positions on the relation of *adivasi* communities to caste society and the debate's implications for the tribal policy of the newly independent Indian state, see Ramachandra Guha's (1999) biography of Elwin, especially chapters 8 and 12. Summaries can be found in Skaria 1997, 740–42; and Sundar 2007, 180–83.

29.　Save (1945, 13) describes the foundation of the Malhar Koli community along lines that parallel the pursuit by caste groups of upward mobility as theorized by M. N. Srinivas (1966), Lloyd I. Rudolph and Susanne Hoeber Rudolph (1967), and others: "A few of the Wārlis . . . feeling that the designation Wārli was a term of degradation (which it is not), have lately styled themselves as Malhār Kunbis after the fashion of the Malhār Kolis (the latter word, *kunbi*, meaning the farmer or cultivator) in order to gain higher social status. They had convened a meeting of the people of a few villages and framed certain rules, particularly regarding the marriage laws and customs and resolved to abide by them. The rules were also printed in a small leaflet."

　　　Compare Rudolph and Rudolph 1967, especially 36–103.

30.　The following passage may be taken as representative:

> Out of a dozen Bhils or Kolis or even Santals, a youth or a girl may at times be picked up and dropped in a city school without any fear of being recognized as such either by a physical or by a moral test. The race that is born of the fusion, which on the whole is a healthy one, because gradual, of the Aryans, Kolarians, Dravidians and all those of our ancestors, whose blood we as a race inherit, is rightly called neither an Aryan, nor a Kolarian, nor a Dravidian—but the Hindu race; that is, that People who live as children of a common motherland, adoring a common holyland—the land that lies between the

Sindhus. Therefore the Santals, Kolis, Bhils Panchamas, Namashudras and all other such tribes and classes are Hindus. This Sindhusthan is as emphatically, if not more emphatically, the land of their forefathers as of the so-called Aryans; they inherit the Hindu blood and the Hindu culture; and even those of them who have not as yet come fully under the i[nflu]ence of any orthodox Hindu sect, do still worship deities and saints and follow a religion however primitive, are still purely attached to this land, which therefore to them is not only a Fatherland but a Holyland. (Savarkar [1923] 1969, 120–21)

31. A stark illustration of what is at stake in the Hindu nationalist mobilization of *adivasi*s can be found in accounts of the violence visited in 2002 on the Muslims of Gujarat by Hindu militants, many of whom were recruited from tribal communities. Parvis Ghassem-Fachandi's (2012) *Pogrom in Gujarat* is the definitive ethnography. Investigative journalists have tracked *ghar wapsi* campaigns in different parts of India; one illuminating long-form report is Sohini Chattopadhyay 2015.

32. Consider this cautionary tale from the political news: in 2003 the embattled chief minister of Chhattisgarh, Ajit Jogi of the Congress Party, found himself staring down both an unamused Sonia Gandhi and a local court, "the charge being that he used a fake Scheduled Tribe certificate to contest elections" (Chowdhury 2003).

33. The web page, which I accessed in 2007, did not appear to have been updated in the previous seven years, to judge by a number of details; even if one discounts this lapse, however, the last lines do not inspire confidence in the Tribal Department's own vigilance: "During the years 1997–98 and 1998–99, the three committees scrutinised 4472 and 3645 cases respectively. Around 55% of the certificates scrutinised by the committees are held invalid. Around 2200 writ petitions filed against the decisions of the committees are pending" (Tribal Department, n.d.).

34. Alice Tilche (2015) investigates a richly layered field site: an *adivasi* museum in Gujarat operated by Rathva *adivasi*s.

35. One of the lecturers at the Vigilance Cell training program also presented this list, with minor variations—for example, citing "land records" as a subcategory of "revenue records" and specifying birth and death registers as records pertaining to older generations.

36. On a critical note, a wholesale attribution of "backwardness" to the tribal side was paired up with "segmentary/divisive backwardness" on the part of caste society.

37. On stereotyping of Warlis and other Thane-area *adivasi*s as drunks, see Ambasta 1998, 542; Saldanha 1995, 2328–31.

38. During my first stay in India, when I was a college student, I visited the Indian Museum in Calcutta (as it was then spelled). The main thing I remember is the central hall, which was lined on either side with dioramas of tribal life. Life-size mannequins dressed in the styles of representative groups from across India had been posed in tableaux of hunting and dancing—quintessential representations of *adivasi* pursuits—for the edification of the public. I do not know if the exhibit is still there, or if it ever included a Warli tableau. I have already mentioned, however, the TRTI's exhibit of a model Warli dwelling and its inhabitant. There is also a full-scale replica of a Warli cabin at Shilpgram, the Rural Arts and Crafts Complex outside Udaipur. Shilpgram is one of a number of government-run museum–cum–theme parks that showcase live performances and material artifacts representative of the folk and tribal cultures of India's regions.

39. Jain was in charge of the Indian Crafts Museum for some years. This Delhi-based institution, officially known as the National Handicrafts and Handlooms Museum, is administered by the Ministry of Textiles; it can be seen as the model for the regional "crafts complexes" mentioned in the previous note. The Indian Crafts Museum was the site of a critical exploration by Paul Greenough (1998).

Chapter 6

1. The Census of India is undertaken every ten years and dated to each year ending in 1, although the bulk of the data is released subsequently. Accordingly, the published figures relevant to fieldwork data collected in 2003 are those from the 1991 census. Of the thirty-six settlements on Sramik Mukti Andolan's list, only one had been recognized in statutory terms by the Government of India, and in an affidavit filed in connection with the lawsuit *Sapte v. Maharashtra*, the administrator in charge of the SGNP stated that the place in question, the "revenue village" of Yeoor, actually fell outside the park's bounds. See Manik Rama Sapte and Sramik Mukti Andolan, petitioners, *Manik Rama Sapte v. State of Maharashtra* (2000), Bombay High Court, ordinary original civil jurisdiction, Writ Petition 925.
2. In a study of the construction of tribal space and identity in the colonial archive, Vinita Damodaran (2006, 162) lays out the historical background: "To be linked to the wilderness or the jungle, was by definition pejorative from ancient times down to the 18th century. It was not a recent phenomenon. It must be noted . . . that colonial epistemology aligned itself with Brahmanical knowledge resulting specifically in the depoliticisation and emasculation of many communities which came to be later termed as *adivasi*." See also Sundar 2007, especially 104–5, 128–30.
3. Ghai's project has been contested from more than one quarter. The controversy that is highlighted in the Indian press has nothing to do with the Warlis but rather concerns a dispute with a rival lessor (R. Mehta 2003; see also Wajihuddin 2003). Curiously enough, the one newspaper report I have seen that describes Film City's siege of Devipada appeared, of all places, in the Worcester, Massachusetts, *Telegram and Gazette*, the evident result of an AP reporter's conversation with Vithal Lad of Sramik Mukti Andolan (Misra 2003). I thank Andy Rotman, who came across the piece in his hometown paper.
4. The conflict surrounding human habitation in the SGNP has attracted recent study from a policy-oriented viewpoint. See Edelblutte and Gunnell 2014; Sen and Pattanaik 2016; Zérah and Landy 2013.
5. One implication of the reportage was that the leopards, though frightening, nevertheless belonged in the forest preserve—along with, arguably, other denizens of the wild. The unfortunate woman whose demise was reported in September was not an *adivasi* but an Aarey employee's wife whom the leopard had dragged across the park boundary. Of the twenty-three leopard attacks recorded in the greater Mumbai area in 2003, the twelve whose locations are actually listed in the newspaper article were all forays beyond the park's borders, with five particularly incongruous incidents occurring on the Powai campus of the Indian Institute of Technology. See also Zérah and Landy 2013, 28.
6. In a grotesque anecdote, Vikas told me that a young flower vendor in the market where his mother sold fish had been eaten by a "tiger" shortly after she had insulted his mother by lowballing the value of her catch. He described the girl's death as the punishment the

Warli god exacted for the affront to one of his own—even though the victim was a Kokana and thus a fellow *adivasi*.

7. The IPHRC is not an official body but rather a Mumbai-based NGO that commands some prestige within civil society. It is modeled on the National Human Rights Commission, which is part of the government.

8. The dispute's battleground, the Sanjay Gandhi National Park Division, had been set aside under some level of government protection since before Independence. It owes its present administrative status to a notification issued 4 February 1983. As a category of land management, *national park* was defined in Indian law by the Wild Life (Protection) Act of 1972. Technically speaking, 86.96 square kilometers of the SGNP's total of 103.09 square kilometers is administered as a national park, the balance being demarcated under the yet more restrictive designations of *protected forest* and *reserved forest*. These figures, however, give an impression of precision that is not borne out by the fuzziness of the park's boundaries as understood by the people involved (or even, apparently, at the highest administrative levels, as the course of this chapter will indicate). When the geographers Marie-Hélène Zérah and Frédéric Landy (2013, 26n1) began their research in the area, some years after I did, they "spent a certain amount of time finding out about official maps that would provide the official and uncontested boundaries of the park." They came up empty-handed. "The unclear delimitation of the park, that resists the desire of researchers to classify and delimit the area of study, explains as well the ambiguity of many residents' rights."

9. In the anthropology of South Asia, and perhaps more broadly in the field of postcolonial studies, it is the work of Bernard S. Cohn that put the census on the map, so to speak. Compare the SGNP scenario with Cohn's (1987, 233) discussion of the Census of India's genesis in East India Company efforts to extrapolate population figures from house counts:

> There is reason to believe that not only was the population of Banaras consistently overestimated in the first half of the nineteenth century, but that of other cities as well. Given the methods used it is easy to see why the population may have been overestimated. The reasons why the overestimations were believed is a more interesting question. I think the reasons lie in the perceptions of the cities by Europeans. In the early nineteenth century, as in the twentieth century, Indian towns and cities, particularly the *chauks* and bazaars, give a sense of huge crowds.

10. India's national rationing system distributes staples such as flour and sugar through a network of licensed shops. Ration cards, which are assigned to all Indian families within the purview of governmentality, thus function alongside voting rolls and birth certificates as signifiers of citizenship. A relic of Nehruvian socialism, the system has come to seem quaint to many members of the middle classes, who give their cards to their servants.

11. Per a list of occupations presented in the report:

> Majority of the people said they had come to Mumbai in search of work and to support their families. People were working as dhobis, rag-pickers, autorickshaw and BEST bus drivers, jewellery makers, cobblers, vegetable vendors, watchman, wardboy with ESIS Hospital, MMC and Aarey employees, and had small businesses, such as ironing clothes and hawking wares. Approximately 56% of the people were daily wager earners, they

did odd jobs or worked for contractors; 21% were masons, carpenters, plumbers, tailors, drivers; 12% were in the service sector; 7% were domestic workers—only 3% of the residents were unemployed. (Sebastian 2000, 20)

In terms of community identity, the primary group represented among the tribunal's interviewees was made up of Hindu peasants from the Maharashtrian hinterland. But among their neighbors were migrants from as far afield as Haryana and Nepal. And in at least one targeted settlement the majority were Muslim:

> In a bizarre case, the Forest Department completely demolished on November 22, 1997 a slum colony consisting of 500 families called Azad Nagar. . . . Ironically, the slum consisted mainly of 1992–93 Muslim riot victims who had been helped . . . to rebuild their houses after they had fled to the neighbouring Muslim locality of Pathanwadi. These residents had also been provided aid and material from the government as compensation for houses destroyed! (16)

12. Emma Tarlo (2003) has researched the paper trails generated by a similar policy, the demolitions directed in Indira Gandhi's name against the slum neighborhoods (*jhuggis*) of Delhi during the Emergency of the mid-1970s. See, especially, chapter 3, "Paper Truths," in her book *Unsettling Memories*.

13. Other stipulations of the ruling indicated the extent to which the colonies in question had made themselves extensions of the city:

> (a) BEST to stop bus services within the National Park Division. . . .
> (c) MTNL to disconnect all telephone lines with the National Park Division. . . .
> (q) BSES and BMC are directed to disconnect all electric and water supply connections in respect of hutments that will be demolished as per the above mentioned directions.
> (r) The Food & Civil Supplies Department is directed not to issue further sanctions to any more ration shops in the National Park Division area. All ration shops, schools and dispensaries presently functioning must be demolished within eighteen months from today. (Sebastian 2000, 9–10)

14. The court approved the program after reducing the fee to Rs 7,000, payable on a schedule of installments. However,

> most slumdwellers were outraged by what they considered a double imposition—forced relocation as well as a monetary penalty for being forced to relocate! Those who went to investigate the areas earmarked for rehabilitation were also appalled by the fact that it was nearly 60 kms from their existing locations and 15–20 kms from the nearest railhead. They also said the rural land was not even worth what they were paying as "rehab fees" and questioned why they should not buy better land at closer locations. Also, a large number could not afford the fees. (Sebastian 2000, 52)

15. More than one person with whom I discussed the city's 2003 demolition campaign against "illegal religious structures," described in chapter 2, invoked Khairnar's name. As a leading actor in previous efforts to clear the city's streets of scofflaw *mandirs*, he had become known for directing his municipal workers in person through the job of dismantling such offending structures and, if the final step to be taken met with pious reluctance

from his crew, for laying his own hands on the fallen idol to dispose of it. In his essay on *pheriwala*s, or unlicensed hawkers, Arvind Rajagopal (2001b, 101–3) gives a brief but powerful account of accompanying the Demolition Man on one of his errands.

16. One such journalist was the *Indian Express*'s Vijay Singh (2003a), who stumbled across a sage's retreat on his tiger hunt.

17. The report includes a paraphrase of some remarks by the University of Mumbai's Indra Munshi, who "states that the extraction by the tribals does not adversely affect the ecology" (Sebastian 2000, 39). Munshi is an authority on Warli agricultural practices and has authored a paper (Saldanha 1990) that gets into a good deal of nuance in discussing the mode of farming historically practiced in Thane's forests under less constrained circumstances. Known as *rab*, it is a form of slash-and-burn cultivation. Scholarly opinion on the method's relative kindness to wooded environs notwithstanding, it is easy to see that the compilers of *Crushed Homes* did not feel like getting into unnecessary detail about it. But I might add that what I myself saw of cultivation in the forest was modest indeed, the green thickets that turned out to yield vegetables being indistinguishable, to my eye anyway, from the growth surrounding them.

18. Warthe's contribution is the only indication I am familiar with of a Warli appropriation or rehabilitation of the *Ramayana* villain. But the inversion brings to mind the traditional tendency among non-Brahmin Hindus in Maharashtra to identify sympathetically with powerful figures who are anathematized in Brahminical narratives as demons. The Trivikrama myth discussed in chapter 5 is the definitive example. See also Alles 2012, 635, on the prominence of Ravana among the Rathvas of Gujarat, and also the discussion of the morphing identities of tribal and Sanskritic deities as a two-way street in Sundar 2007, 60–64.

19. It is my impression that burial prevails as the norm among Mumbai-area tribals. In the late colonial period, R. E. Enthoven (1920–22, 3:452) determined that the Warlis cremated their dead. He noted, however, an exception to the rule: corpses were buried when the funds to burn them were lacking. The scenario may well apply to the present-day inhabitants of the forest zone. Rather than emphasizing a doctrinal distinction, the best way to frame adherence to burial as an index of tribal religious practice may be to say that burying instead of burning is simply not a big deal for a Warli who isn't set on assimilation within modern normative Hinduism.

20. Among the rulings Gonsalves cites from North American jurisprudence are *Calder v. Attorney General of Canada* (1973), *Paulette v. Canada* (1973), *Narragansett Tribe of Indians v. Southern Rhode Island Land Development Corporation* (1976), and *Delgamuukw v. British Columbia* (1991). For ethnographic critiques of the adjudication of indigenous land claims in Australia and the United States, see Povinelli 2002; Clifford 1988, chap. 12. See also Daly 2005 for an ethnography of the Delgamuukw case.

21. Having been given access by Maharukh to her *Sapte* file, I can lay out the paper trail the suit generated from 2000 to 2003. As part of its order to expel the encroachers, the High Court's ruling in *BEAG v. State of Maharashtra* (1995), Bombay High Court, ordinary original civil jurisdiction, Writ Petition 305, had made provision for a procedural mechanism to deal with abuses: a SGNP Grievance Redressal Committee, which was instituted on 17 July 1999. On 14 November 2000, Gonsalves followed up on his submission of the *Sapte* writ earlier that year by filing a similarly worded petition with the committee, Application no. 16869 of 2000. It was to this petition that the IPHRC report *Crushed Homes,*

Lost Lives (Sebastian 2000) was appended as Exhibit A. As part of this parallel procedure the park's deputy director Bharati then presented the committee with an affidavit; although the date of his submission is unclear to me, the tribals' lawyers received their copy of the document from the committee on 7 February 2001. This ancillary skirmish reached a provisional conclusion on 13 March, when the Grievance Redressal Committee issued a statement to the effect that it would seek its cue from the High Court regarding the validity of the petitioners' claim on its attention.

22. Apparently, revenue and forestry occupied the same department within the Maharashtra state administration back in the 1970s. The document is a typewritten memo, filed under Administration Order no. FID 1173/77222-FI and dated 24 March 1977. Maharukh obtained her own copy and enclosed it in the *Sapte* file, although it is unclear to me whether the respondents' side actually forwarded it to her or not. The respondents do not appear to have entered the document formally as an exhibit.

23. The respondents' paperwork is inconsistent with regard to counts of tribal heads. The affidavit misquotes the forty-two families of 1977 as forty-six. And the English translation attached to Adivasi Hakka Samiti's Marathi-language letter as part of Exhibit A reports 216 instead of 260 families, and fourteen instead of fifteen signatories. I would say that this sloppiness in the presentation of what is purported to be authoritative data bespeaks a certain lack of regard for the petitioners in the case and for the project of enumeration, if not for the legal procedure itself.

24. The Adivasi Hakka Samiti letter actually takes the form of a correction of a survey the Forest Department had apparently carried out in June 1996 that put the *adivasi* population at 189 families in eleven hamlets. (A 1996 survey, of course, would have followed the 1995 filing of the writ petition in *BEAG*, albeit anticipating any court decision.) Having been summoned by forestry officers to the August 1998 meeting to be notified of their imminent removal from the park, Adivasi Hakka Samiti members then presented their letter in December confirming the number of *pada*s but marking up the number of inhabitants by an additional seventy-one households (and ergo, in the event of the relocation scheme going through, an additional seventy-one plots to be carved out of the distant village). For whatever reason, the Forest Department did not forward any record of its June 1996 survey. The only evidence annexed to the affidavit is the Samiti's letter.

25. Maharukh's submission also cites other texts, including the National Forest Policy presented by the Government of India in Parliament in 1988, and quotes liberally from Indra Munshi's views as reported in Sebastian 2000.

26. In a communication after the court issued its ruling, Maharukh informed me that the eleven *pada*s in which Adivasi Hakka Samiti was active—primarily in running preschool facilities—were all located in the park's recreational zone and that tribal settlement in the forest's interior had been entirely beyond the view and ken of the authorities. This focus on the periphery helps explain the Forest Department's insistence that the tribal residents were a minority in their own settlements. She also told me that the mysterious survey of June 1996, which had been confined to the eleven hamlets of the Samiti's interest, had been undertaken in the first place at the request of the Samiti, which subsequently went on to correct its figures.

27. It was in fact on a visit to Keltipada that I was surprised to see a Bharatiya Janata Party banner hung high on an isolated family dwelling. I had not thought that the party's brand of Hindu nationalism would command much of a following among Warlis; nor could I

understand why local party supporters would have chosen to advertise their allegiance in the middle of the jungle, where no one could see it. My guide, whose home it was, laughed. One of his brothers had a job with the Municipal Corporation, and a right-wing coworker of his had given him the banner. They kept it on the roof against the rain.

28. A brief description of this incident may prove useful in view of questions I raised with respect to extralegal religious sites in chapter 2. The shrine was the only structure in the hamlet that had even seemed *pakka* enough to require official permission to be rebuilt in the first place. Prashant knew that the spot it occupied was one the local officers passed on their jogging route, so its condition was not likely to have escaped their notice. (In fact, it was likely that, beyond the *adivasi* community, the only people even to know of its existence were the cops.) He had sent one of his workers, a resident of the *pada* in question, to the municipal ward office to initiate the registration procedure; the man had filed a form and deposited fifty rupees. The next step, which Prashant chose not to take, would have involved submitting photographs of the damaged structure.

    By way of explaining his assessment that no formal procedure would be necessary, several factors come to mind. As part of Aarey Milk Colony, the piece of land the shrine occupied was technically public property. Unlike the city streets, however, it was neither contested terrain nor was it visible to anything like a public constituency. More germanely, unlike the SGNP and the Municipal Corporation—answerable to the rulings of the High Court in *BEAG* and *Janhit Manch v. State of Maharashtra* (2002), Bombay High Court, ordinary original civil jurisdiction, Writ Petition 2063, respectively—Aarey was under no legal compulsion at the time to remove "encroachments."

29. More typical of his attitude was a quip he made after one old *pada* resident, comparing the penurious state of her community with the wealth and material comfort of the West (*Foren*), commented to me, "Our god hears our prayers half as much as your god listens to yours." Prashant added, "Ours is sitting in the A.C." (that is, in his air-conditioned office or limo, sealed off from his sweating constituents).

30. The most celebrated such site is Mahalaxmi Hill in Dahanu Subdistrict, Thane. In the past decades this goddess temple has come under the administration of a trust whose board consists of Gujarati Brahmins, but the officiating ritualists are Warlis. See Dalmia 1988, 52–53.

31. The children were from local *adivasi* families, but I was not able to learn what proportion of them lived in forest *padas*.

32. Chapter 2 of Townsend Middleton's (2016) *The Demands of Recognition* opens with the description of a sacred rock ensconced in Darjeeling's central plaza on the occasion of the Durga Puja festival. The rock was there in place of the customary Hindu icon. Middleton paraphrases the politico-religious message of this gesture by the leaders of the Gorkha community: "*To be tribal, one mustn't be Hindu.* The absolute dichotomy between tribes and Hindu castes was an ethnological fact in the public imagination" (57). As my own examples demonstrate, however, the dichotomy is much more slippery in the western Indian context, and the Warlis are far more marginalized than the Gorkhas.

33. For a sensitive presentation of the modern construction of the tribal artist persona by a curator who was centrally involved in the project, see Jyotindra Jain's (1998) introduction to the book released in conjunction with the exhibition *Other Masters*, which was mounted at the Craft Museum in Delhi under his directorship in celebration of the fiftieth anniversary of Indian Independence.

34. Fred R. Myers's (2001) essay about the roughly contemporaneous entry of Australian Aboriginal images into the art market sets out several issues it would be interesting to investigate in the Warli context: the role of state sponsorship, the development of consumer tastes, the emergence of high and low market niches, and the construction of tribal artist-subjects.

35. In offering this brief account of Warli art's market debut, I have benefited from consultation with Karin Zitzewitz, whose own research on Indian modern art has involved close work with Chemould's owners, the Gandhys. Zitzewitz sketches a scenario in which Khorshed Gandhy, taking her cue from the government's sponsorship of folk and tribal forms, cultivated a link opened with Jivya Mashe by the field coordinator of Maharashtra State's official Handicrafts Board. (Zitzewitz also points out that in the 1970s the Delhi branch of Chemould Gallery was actually housed in the capital's Handicrafts complex.)

    For a presentation of the Mashes' work in the context of *pada*-based ritual and myth, see Dalmia 1988. See also Mashe, Mashe, and Lal 1982, a volume that grew out of Chemould's Warli exhibition catalogs. I should add that while I myself find the Mashes' work attractive and evocative, when I showed my copy of this important collection of images to Vikas, the response was underwhelming. His principal comment was that a local fashionista from Bollywood's famous Kapoor family was marketing a line of jeans decorated with similar tribal designs.

36. Ajay Skaria (1997, 742) comments, "Consider one of the staples of radical chic in India: Varli painting. These paintings have come to be synonymous with *adivasi* art, and reproductions adorn many living rooms. Surely their ubiquity has something to do with the nature of Varli art, which . . . with [its] many stick drawings slip[s] neatly into our preconceptions of what primitive art is supposed to be like."

37. An anecdotal observation I can add is that at a sale of Warli paintings organized in South Mumbai in November 2003 by a Jesuit-affiliated *adivasi* group from Thane's Talasari Subdistrict, deforestation and other environmental themes featured prominently. The artists told me that what they painted reflected their own experiences, but I imagine that a consideration of the green politics likely to be shared by their target customers in India and Europe (the collective enjoyed exposure in Germany and Switzerland thanks to contacts made through Jesuit channels) would have been another factor.

38. My thanks to Christian Novetzke for translating the Marathi. The caption tempts comparison with the tagline printed on the cover of the promotional brochure I received when I visited the studio management: "FilmCity: Where we shape your dreams."

39. In the meantime a law has been passed that, in principle, extends new protections to bona fide tribals. The Scheduled Tribes and Other Traditional Forest Dwellers (Protection of Forest Rights) Act came into effect in December 2006 and it was supplemented with a body of Rules in 2008.

40. Compare, for example, the situation of the elderly *adivasis* of Thane reduced to penury as a result of their names' deletion from a list of government pensioners, as described in Ganesh 2003. Yet if exemplary, tribals are by no means unique in their vulnerability to the harsh fates that can follow on archival abjection, as the account of the SGNP slum clearances should have made clear. The effects of erasure attain a surreal quality in the cases of living individuals who have been registered as legally dead, generally by relatives who stand to gain property. The struggle of one such person to reinsert himself into the official gaze provided the theme for a play, *The Masrayana*, which was produced by Chi-

cago's Rasaka Theatre Company in the fall of 2005. Perhaps the most famous living dead Indian is Lal Bihari of Uttar Pradesh, founder of the Mritak Sangh (Association of Dead People) and 2003 Ig Nobel Peace Prize awardee (Debroy 2003).

Conclusion

1. I am indebted to Lawrence Cohen for filling me in on the scholarly state of play. The short essays of his I cite here are the preview of a larger project, but their ideas are germane to concerns of this study that go well beyond Aadhaar. For more on the view that Aadhaar is supplementing the old system rather than supplanting it, journalistic sources include Bhatnagar 2016; Dreze 2015; Yadav 2015a, 2015b.

2. Inquiries like these, bringing together urban landscape and ideological spectacle in the figuration of the *surface*, are indebted to Siegfried Kracauer's (1995) reflections on Weimar-era Berlin in "The Mass Ornament" and other essays.

3. The authors' attribution is to an article published in *India Today*, 19 May 2005, 28.

4. In the matter of the ideological shift, Naresh Fernandes (2013, 5–6) points the finger at Mumbai's own business elites: "not all Bombay fabrications have been salutary. Since the 1990s, the city's financial institutions and advertising agencies have seduced middle-class Indians into thinking that greed is good, that empathy for the less fortunate is unnecessary, that extreme individualism is a virtue."

5. What Kajri Jain (2016, 2017) has termed *automobility* is a guiding concern of her research on contemporary spectacularization, specifically the erection of monumental Hindu statuary chiefly viewable from the highway.

6. In *Discourses of the Vanishing*, her psychoanalytically inflected ethnography of Japan, Marilyn Ivy (1995, 1, 11n20) examines spaces like these in which "modernity's losses" can be recouped from its "rationalizing technologies, individualizing procedures, and totalizing apparatuses."

7. South Asia as the locus and inspiration for the utopian visions of urban planners is the theme of Smriti Srinivas's (2015) *A Place for Utopia*.

8. The topography of Mumbai's outer suburbs can offer no snowcapped peaks of the sort that have signaled "Kashmir" (and cued many a love duet) for generations of Indian filmgoers. But in fact the forest zone does contain a "little," or *chota*, Kashmir. This is a hilly tract next to Film City that has been landscaped in the style of a Persian garden; it even includes a small lake. Chota Kashmir is no longer much used by the production houses that used to shoot their lower-budget numbers there, but it remains popular all the same among Mumbai residents who can find the time for a picnic or a rendezvous. (Or for ethnography—I was introduced to Chota Kashmir by Vikas, who discussed the park's history in the movies as a backdrop for romance, observing, "In your country, love happens on the beach. In India, it happens in a garden.") Sramik Mukti Sanghatan's map of the area shows it flanked on four sides by tribal *padas*.

9. Another Dev Anand vehicle, *Munimji* (Subodh Mukherjee, 1955), whose story takes place on a similar estate, was shot at Filmistan.

10. One exception is *Satyam Shivam Sundaram* (1977), a Raj Kapoor film whose overtly sexualized treatment of the star Zeenat Aman struck many viewers as prurient. Lost amid the controversy (and the box-office returns) is the depiction of Aman's character—whose name is Rupa, meaning "shape" or "form"—as a tribal, or sometimes tribal, woman. Ka-

poor is very self-aware as he maps the nature-culture dichotomy onto the form of Rupa. In her persona as the respectable wife of a government engineer, she not only is wrapped in constricting saris but actually veils her face. This figuration is contrasted with the un-inhibited and largely unclothed "natural" Rupa, who retreats to her forest home, there to sing and dance with abandon.

WORKS CITED

Abraham, Itty, and Ashish Rajadhyaksha. 2015. "State Power and Postcolonial Citizenship in India: From the Postcolonial to the Digital Age." *East Asian Science, Technology and Society: An International Journal* 9:65–85.

Alles, Gregory D. 2012. "Tribal Chic: Crossing Borders in Eastern Gujarat." *Journal of the American Academy of Religion* 80:623–58.

———. 2013. "Are *Devs* Gods or Spirits: Some Quick Thoughts on Categories in the Study of Religions." *Din: Tidsskrift for Religion og Kultur* 1:111–18.

Alles, Gregory D., Lidia Guzy, Uwe Skoda, and Ülo Valk. 2015. Editorial. In "Contemporary Indigeneity and Religion in India," edited by Gregory D. Alles, Lidia Guzy, Uwe Skoda, and Ülo Valk. Special issue, *Internationales Asienforum: International Quarterly for Asian Studies* 46 (1–2): 5–16.

Althusser, Louis. 1971. "Ideology and Ideological State Apparatuses: Notes towards an Investigation." In *Lenin and Philosophy and Other Essays*, translated by Ben Brewster. New York: Monthly Review Press.

Ambasta, Ashesh. 1998. "Capitalist Restructuring and the Formation of *Adivasi* Proletarians: Agrarian Transition in Thane District (Western India), c. 1817–1990." PhD diss., Institute of Social Studies, The Hague.

Anand, Nikhil. 2011. "Pressure: The Polytechnics of Water Supply in Mumbai." *Cultural Anthropology* 26:542–63.

Andersen, Thom. 2003. *Los Angeles Plays Itself*. Thom Andersen Productions. Film.

Anderson, Benedict. 1991. *Imagined Communities: Reflections on the Origin and Spread of Nationalism*. Rev. and exp. ed. London: Verso.

Anjaria, Jonathan Shapiro. 2016. *The Slow Boil: Street Food, Rights, and Public Space in Mumbai*. Stanford, CA: Stanford University Press.

Appadurai, Arjun. 1995. "The Production of Locality." In *Counterworks: Managing the Diversity of Knowledge*, edited by Richard Fardon. London: Routledge.

———. 1996. *Modernity at Large: Cultural Dimensions of Globalization*. Minneapolis: University of Minnesota Press.

———. 2000. "Spectral Housing and Urban Cleansing: Notes on Millennial Mumbai." *Public Culture* 12:627–51.

———. 2002. "Deep Democracy: Urban Governmentality and the Horizon of Politics." *Public Culture* 14:21–47.

Appadurai, Arjun, and Carol Breckenridge. 1988. "Why Public Culture?" *Public Culture* 1:5–9.

Apter, Andrew. 1992. *Black Critics and Kings: The Hermeneutics of Power in Yoruba Society*. Chicago: University of Chicago Press.

Assayag, Jackie. 2004. *At the Confluence of Two Rivers: Muslims and Hindus in South India.* Translated by Latika Sahgal. Delhi: Manohar.

Axel, Brian Keith. 2001. *The Nation's Tortured Body: Violence, Representation, and the Formation of a Sikh "Diaspora."* Durham, NC: Duke University Press.

Babb, Lawrence A. 1981. "Glancing: Visual Interactions in Hinduism." *Journal of Anthropological Research* 37:387–401.

Bachelard, Gaston. (1964) 1994. *The Poetics of Space.* Translated by Maria Jolas. Boston: Beacon Press.

Bagga, Bhuvan. 2013. "What Makes NDA's 'India Shining' Campaign the 'Worst' Poll Strategy in Indian History." *IndiaToday.in*, 14 May. http://indiatoday.intoday.in/story/nda-india-shining-worst-poll-strategy/1/270916.html.

Bakhtin, M. M. 1981. *The Dialogic Imagination: Four Essays.* Edited by Michael Holquist. Translated by Caryl Emerson and Michael Holquist. Austin: University of Texas Press.

Barthes, Roland. 1972. "Myth Today." In *Mythologies*, translated by Annette Lavers. New York: Farrar, Straus and Giroux.

Baudrillard, Jean. 1993. *Symbolic Exchange and Death.* Translated by Iain Hamilton Grant. London: Sage.

Baviskar, Amita. 1995. *In the Belly of the River: Tribal Conflicts over Development in the Narmada Valley.* Delhi: Oxford University Press.

Bear, Laura. 2013. "'This Body Is Our Body': Vishwakarma Puja, the Social Debts of Kinship, and Theories of Materiality in a Neoliberal Shipyard." In *Vital Relations: Modernity and the Persistent Life of Kinship*, edited by Susan McKinnon and Fenella Cannell. School for Advanced Research Advanced Seminar Series. Santa Fe, NM: School for Advanced Research Press.

Bedi, Tarini. 2016. *The Dashing Ladies of Shiv Sena: Political Matronage in Urbanizing India.* Albany: State University of New York Press.

Behrend, Heike, Anja Dreschke, and Martin Zillinger, eds. 2015. *Trance Mediums and New Media: Spirit Possession in the Age of Technical Reproduction.* New York: Fordham University Press.

Beliso-De Jesús, Aisha M. 2015. *Electric Santería: Racial and Sexual Assemblages of Transnational Religion.* New York: Columbia University Press.

Bellamy, Carla. 2011. *The Powerful Ephemeral: Everyday Healing in an Ambiguously Islamic Place.* South Asia across the Disciplines. Berkeley: University of California Press.

Benjamin, Walter. 1968. *Illuminations: Essays and Reflections.* Edited by Hannah Arendt. Translated by Harry Zohn. New York: Schocken.

Bhagwat, Vidyut. 1995. "Bombay in Dalit Literature." In *Bombay: Mosaic of Modern Culture*, edited by Sujata Patel and Alice Thorner. Delhi: Oxford University Press.

Bhatnagar, Gaurav Vivek. 2016. "Aadhaar-Based PDS Means Denial of Rations for Many, Jharkhand Study Shows." *The Wire*, 9 August. http://thewire.in/64756/jharkhand-aadhaar-pds-nfsa/.

Bhattacharya, Chandrima S. 2003. "Bollywood's Birthplace to Factory Sheds." *Telegraph* (Kolkata), 9 December.

Bhatti, Shaila, and Christopher Pinney. 2011. "Optic-clash: Modes of Visuality in India." In *A Companion to the Anthropology of India*, edited by Isabelle Clark-Decès. London: Blackwell.

Biles, Jeremy. 2007. *Ecce Monstrum: Georges Bataille and the Sacrifice of Form*. New York: Fordham University Press.

Björkman, Lisa. 2015. *Pipe Politics, Contested Waters: Embedded Infrastructures of Millennial Mumbai*. Durham, NC: Duke University Press.

Blackburn, Stuart H., ed. 1989. *Oral Epics in India*. Berkeley: University of California Press.

Blitz Team of Investigators. 1982. "Pimping *Pujari* and the City's Gigolos." *Blitz*, 6 March.

Blunt, John James. 1823. *Vestiges of Ancient Manners and Customs, Discoverable in Modern Italy and Sicily*. London: John Murray.

Boddy, Janice. 1989. *Wombs and Alien Spirits: Women, Men, and the Zar Cult in Northern Sudan*. New Directions in Anthropological Writing. Madison: University of Wisconsin Press.

Boo, Katherine. 2012. *Behind the Beautiful Forevers: Life, Death, and Hope in a Mumbai Undercity*. New York: Random House.

Census of India 1991. 1995. *Maharashtra*. Series 14. Delhi: Controller of Publications.

Census of India 2011. 2014. *Maharashtra*. Series 28, pt. 12A, *District Census Handbook*. Maharashtra: Directorate of Census Operations.

Chabon, Michael. 2005. "Inventing Sherlock Holmes." *New York Review of Books* 52 (2).

Chakrabarty, Dipesh. 1991. "Open Space/Public Place: Garbage, Modernity and India." In "Aspects of 'the Public' in Colonial South Asia," edited by Sandria B. Freitag. Special issue, *South Asia: Journal of South Asian Studies* 14 (1): 15–31.

———. 2000. *Provincializing Europe: Postcolonial Thought and Historical Difference*. Princeton, NJ: Princeton University Press.

Chatterjee, Partha. 1993. *The Nation and Its Fragments: Colonial and Postcolonial Histories*. Princeton, NJ: Princeton University Press.

———. 2004a. "Are Indian Cities Becoming More Bourgeois?" In *The Politics of the Governed: Reflections on Popular Politics in Most of the World*. New York: Columbia University Press.

———. 2004b. "The Politics of the Governed." In *The Politics of the Governed: Reflections on Popular Politics in Most of the World*. New York: Columbia University Press.

Chattopadhyay, Sohini. 2015. "Inside a Hindutva Hostel: How RSS Is Rewiring the Tribal Mind." *Catchnews*, 19 December. http://www.catchnews.com/india-news/exclusive -inside-a-hindutva-hostel-how-rss-is-rewiring-the-tribal-mind-1450354461.html.

Chattopadhyay, Swati. 2009. "The Art of Auto-mobility: Vehicular Art and the Space of Resistance in Calcutta." *Journal of Material Culture* 14:107–39.

Chitre, Dilip. (1995) 2000. "Mumbaichi Lavni: The First Marathi Poem on Industrial Civilization." In *Folk Culture, Folk Religion and Oral Traditions as a Component in Maharashtrian Culture*, edited by Günther-Dietz Sontheimer. Heidelberg University South Asian Studies. Delhi: Manohar.

Chowdhury, Neerja. 2003. "Cong's Jogi Headache Worsens." *Indian Express* (Mumbai), 26 September.

Clark, Raymond J. 1970. "A Classical Foundation-Legend from Newfoundland." *Folklore* 8:182–84.

Clarke, Howard, ed. 1989. *Vergil's "Aeneid"; and, Fourth ("Messianic") Eclogue: In the Dryden Translation*. University Park: Pennsylvania State University Press.

Clifford, James. 1988. *The Predicament of Culture: Twentieth-Century Ethnography, Literature, and Art*. Cambridge, MA: Harvard University Press.

Cohen, Lawrence. 1995. "Holi in Banaras and the *Mahaland* of Modernity." *GLQ* 2:399–424.

———. 2017a. "Duplicate." In "Keywords," edited by Meera Ashar, Trent Brown, Assa Doron, and Craig Jeffrey, special section, *South Asia: Journal of South Asian Studies* 40 (2): 1–13.

———. 2017b. "Duplicate, Leak, Deity." *Limn* 6. https://limn.it/duplicate-leak-deity/.

Cohn, Bernard S. 1987. *An Anthropologist among the Historians and Other Essays.* Delhi: Oxford University Press.

Comaroff, Jean. 1985. *Body of Power, Spirit of Resistance: The Culture and History of a South African People.* Chicago: University of Chicago Press.

Conlon, Frank F. 1997. Review of *Bombay: Metaphor for Modern India*, edited by Sujata Patel and Alice Thorner; and *Bombay: Mosaic of Modern Culture*, edited by Sujata Patel and Alice Thorner. *Journal of Asian Studies* 56:831–33.

Cort, John E. 2012. "Situating *Darśan*: Seeing the Digambar Jina Icon in Eighteenth- and Nineteenth-Century North India." *International Journal of Hindu Studies* 16:1–56.

Dabholkar, Govind R. (Hemadpant). 1999. *Shri Sai Satcharita: The Life and Teachings of Shirdi Sai Baba.* Translated by Indira Kher. Delhi: Sterling.

Dalmia, Yashodhara. 1988. *The Painted World of the Warlis: Art and Ritual of the Warli Tribes of Maharashtra.* Delhi: Lalit Kala Akademi.

Dalvi, Mustansir. 2017. "The New Horse Statue in Kala Ghoda Embodies Mumbai's Efforts to Create a False Memory." *Scroll*, 28 January. https://scroll.in/article/827837/the-new-horse-statue-in-kala-ghoda-embodies-mumbais-efforts-to-create-a-false-memory.

Daly, Richard. 2005. *Our Box Was Full: An Ethnography for the Delgamuukw Plaintiffs.* Vancouver: University of British Columbia Press.

"Damning Verdict: Report of the Srikrishna Commission." n.d. Accessed 22 June 2013. http://www.sabrang.com/Srikrish/sri main.htm.

Damodaran, Vinita. 2006. "Colonial Constructions of Tribe in India: The Case of Chotanagpur." In *Europe and the World in European Historiography*, edited by Csaba Lévai. Thematic Work Groups, no. 6. Pisa: PLUS–Pisa University Press.

Dandekar, Ajay. 1998. "The Warlis and the Dhangars: The Context of the Commons." In *The Cultural Dimension of Ecology*, edited by Baidyanath Saraswati. Delhi: Indira Gandhi National Centre for the Arts.

Dandekar, Hemalata. 1986. *Men to Bombay, Women at Home: Urban Influence on Sugao Village, Deccan Maharashtra, India, 1942–1982.* Michigan Papers on South and Southeast Asia. Ann Arbor: University of Michigan Center for South and Southeast Asian Studies.

Daniel, E. Valentine. 1984. *Fluid Signs: Being a Person the Tamil Way.* Berkeley: University of California Press.

Dasgupta, Satadal. 1986. *Caste, Kinship and Community: Social System of a Bengal Caste.* Madras: Universities Press.

Davis, Richard J. 1997. *Lives of Indian Images.* Princeton, NJ: Princeton University Press.

Deák, Dušan. 2005. "Shah Datta—A Hindu God in Muslim Garb." *International Institute for Asian Studies Newletter* 37:20.

Debord, Guy. 1994. *The Society of the Spectacle.* Translated by Donald Nicholson-Smith. New York: Zone Books.

Debroy, Bibek. 2003. "Laugh, and Then Think." *Indian Express* (Mumbai), 5 November.

de Certeau, Michel. 1984. *The Practice of Everyday Life.* Translated by Steven F. Rendall. Berkeley: University of California Press.

Derné, Steve. 2000. *Movies, Masculinity, and Modernity: An Ethnography of Men's Filmgoing in India.* Westport, CT: Greenwood.

Deshmukh, Smita. 2003. "Ganesh Mandals Will Follow 10 pm Loudspeaker Deadline." *Times of India* (Mumbai), 19 August.

Deshpande, Haima. 2003. "Ganesh up for Grabs." *Indian Express* (Mumbai), 24 August.

Dhere, R. C. 1964. *Datta sampradayaca itihasa*. Pune: Nilakantha prakasana.

———. 1988. "The Gondhali: Singers for the Devi." In *The Experience of Hinduism: Essays on Religion in Maharashtra*, edited by Eleanor Zelliot and Maxine Berntsen. Albany: State University of New York Press.

———. 1995. "Folk Perception and Saints' Perception." In *Folk Culture, Folk Religion and Oral Traditions as a Component in Maharashtrian Culture*, edited by Günther-Dietz Sontheimer. Heidelberg University South Asian Studies. Delhi: Manohar.

Dhruva, Achal. 2002. "Jawahar: A Tribal Retreat." *Travel India: Express Travel and Tourism*, 1–15 August. http://www.expresstravelandtourism.com/20020815/travelindia5.shtml.

Dianteill, Erwan. 2002. "Deterritorialization and Reterritorialization of the Orisha Religion in Africa and the New World: Nigeria, Cuba, and the United States." *International Journal of Urban and Regional Research* 26:121–38.

Dickey, Sara. 1993. *Cinema and the Urban Poor in South India*. New York: Cambridge University Press.

Dirks, Nicholas B. 2001. *Castes of Mind: Colonialism and the Making of Modern India*. Princeton, NJ: Princeton University Press.

Doniger, Wendy. 1999. "Presidential Address: 'I have Scinde': Flogging a Dead (White Male Orientalist) Horse." *Journal of Asian Studies* 58:940–60.

———. 2009. *The Hindus: An Alternative History*. Chicago: University of Chicago Press.

Doron, Assa, and Robin Jeffrey. 2013. *The Great Indian Phone Book: How the Cheap Cell Phone Changes Business, Politics, and Daily Life*. Cambridge, MA: Harvard University Press.

Doron, Assa, and Ira Raja. 2015. "The Cultural Politics of Shit: Class, Gender, and Public Space in India." *Postcolonial Studies* 18:189–207.

Douglas, Mary. (1966) 2002. *Purity and Danger: An Analysis of Concepts of Pollution and Taboo*. Routledge Classics. London: Routledge.

Dreze, Jean. 2015. "Unique Identity Dilemma." *Indian Express*, 19 March. http://indianexpress.com/article/opinion/columns/unique-identity-dilemma/.

Dubey, Mohit, and Siddharth Varadarajan. 2000. "Hero No. 1 Came, Saw, and Was Conquered." *Times of India* (Mumbai), 23 March.

Durkheim, Émile. 1995. *The Elementary Forms of Religious Life*. Translated by Karen E. Fields. New York: Free Press.

Dwyer, Graham. 2003. *The Divine and the Demonic: Supernatural Affliction and Its Treatment in North India*. London: RoutledgeCurzon.

Dwyer, Rachel. 2000. *All You Want Is Money, All You Need Is Love: Sexuality and Romance in Modern India*. London: Cassell.

Eck, Diana L. 1981. *Darśan: Seeing the Divine Image in India*. Chambersburg, PA: Anima.

Eco, Umberto. 1986. *Travels in Hyper Reality: Essays*. Translated by William Weaver. San Diego: Harcourt Brace Jovanovich.

Edelblutte, Émilie, and Yanni Gunnell. 2014. "The Tribal Populations of Sanjay Gandhi National Park, Mumbai (India): A Brief Political Ecology." *L'espace geographique* 43:1–17.

Eicher City Map. 2002. *Mumbai*. Delhi: Eicher Goodearth.

Eliade, Mircea. (1954) 2005. *The Myth of the Eternal Return*. Translated by Willard Trask. Princeton, NJ: Princeton University Press.

Elison, William, Christian Lee Novetzke, and Andy Rotman. 2016. *"Amar Akbar Anthony":*
Bollywood, Brotherhood, and the Nation. Cambridge, MA: Harvard University Press.

Elwin, Edward Fenton. 1907. *Indian Jottings, from Ten Years' Experience in and around Poona*
City. London: J. Murray.

Enthoven, R. E. 1920–22. *The Tribes and Castes of Bombay*. 3 vols. Bombay: Government Central Press.

Erndl, Kathleen M. 1993. *Victory to the Mother: The Hindu Goddess of Northwest India in Myth,*
Ritual, and Symbol. New York: Oxford University Press.

Ewing, Katherine Pratt. 1997. *Arguing Sainthood: Modernity, Psychoanalysis, and Islam*. Durham, NC: Duke University Press.

Express News Service. 2003. "Panther Eats Woman in Goregaon." *Indian Express* (Mumbai),
26 September.

Fanon, Frantz. 1965. *Peau noire, masques blancs*. Paris: Éditions du Seuil.

Feldhaus, Anne. 1995. *Water and Womanhood: Religious Meanings of Rivers in Maharashtra*.
New York: Oxford University Press.

Fernandes, Naresh. 2013. *City Adrift: A Short Biography of Bombay*. Delhi: Aleph.

Ferrari, Fabrizio M., ed. 2011. *Health and Religious Rituals in South Asia: Disease, Possession and*
Healing. Routledge South Asian Religion. New York: Routledge.

"Films." n.d. Accessed 28 April 2006. http://www.indiasurabhi.com/exploreindia/filmsmain
.htm.

Finkelstein, Maura. 2016. "Landscapes of Invisibility: Anachronistic Subjects and Allochro-
nous Spaces in Mill Land Mumbai." *City and Society* 27:250–71.

Foucault, Michel. 1991. "Governmentality." In *The Foucault Effect: Studies in Governmentality;*
With Two Lectures by and an Interview with Michel Foucault, edited by Graham Burchell,
Colin Gordon, and Peter Miller. Chicago: University of Chicago Press.

———. 1995. *Discipline and Punish: The Birth of the Prison*. Translated by Alan Lane. 2nd Vintage Books ed. New York: Vintage.

———. 2010. *The Archaeology of Knowledge: And the Discourse on Language*. Translated by
Rupert Swyer. New York: Vintage.

Frazer, James George. 1914. *The Golden Bough: A Study in Magic and Religion*. 3rd ed. 12 vols.
London: Macmillan.

Freitag, Sandria B. 1991. Introduction to "Aspects of 'the Public' in Colonial South Asia,"
edited by Sandria B. Freitag. Special issue, *South Asia: Journal of South Asian Studies* 14
(1): 1–13.

———. 2001. "Visions of the Nation: Theorizing the Nexus between Creation, Consumption,
and Participation in the Public Sphere." In *Pleasure and the Nation: The History, Politics*
and Consumption of Public Culture in India, edited by Rachel Dwyer and Christopher Pinney. Delhi: Oxford University Press.

Ganesh, N. 2003. "Starving—a Way of Life in Mokhada." *Indian Express* (Mumbai), 30 November.

Gangar, Amrit. 1995. "Films from the City of Dreams." In *Bombay: Mosaic of Modern Culture*,
edited by Sujata Patel and Alice Thorner. Delhi: Oxford University Press.

Gaonkar, Dilip. 2002. "Toward New Imaginaries: An Introduction." *Public Culture* 14:1–19.

Gazetteer of Bombay Presidency. 1964. Rev. ed. (*Maharashtra State Gazetteers*). Bombay: Directorate of Printing and Stationery, Maharashtra State. Originally published Bombay:
Government Central Press, 1877–1904.

———. 1985–. Reprint, Pune: Printed at the Government Photozinco Press. Originally published Bombay: Government Central Press, 1877–1904.

Gell, Alfred. 1998. *Art and Agency: An Anthropological Theory*. Oxford: Oxford University Press.

Ghassem-Fachandi, Parvis. 2012. *Pogrom in Gujarat: Hindu Nationalism and Anti-Muslim Violence in India*. Princeton, NJ: Princeton University Press.

Ghurye, G. S. 1962. *Gods and Men*. Bombay: Popular Book Depot.

———. 1963. *The Scheduled Tribes*. Bombay: Popular Prakashan.

Gilmartin, David. 2015. "Rethinking the Public through the Lens of Sovereignty." In "Imagining the Public in Modern South Asia," edited by Brannon D. Ingram, J. Barton Scott, and SherAli Tareen. Special issue, *South Asia: Journal of South Asian Studies* 38 (3): 371–86.

Glushkova, Irina, and Rajendra Vora, eds. 1999. *Home, Family, and Kinship in Maharashtra*. Delhi: Oxford University Press.

Gold, Daniel. 2015. *Provincial Hinduism: Religion and Community in Gwalior City*. New York: Oxford University Press.

Gombrich, Richard. 1966. "The Consecration of a Buddhist Image." *Journal of Asian Studies* 26:23–36.

Gomes da Silva, José Carlos. 2010. *The Cult of Jagannātha: Myths and Rituals*. Delhi: Motilal Banarasidass.

Gopalan, Lalitha. 1993. "Cinema and the State: Coitus Interruptus and the Love Story." In *Institute for Culture and Consciousness: Occasional Papers 1*, edited by Susanne Hoeber Rudolph, Leela Fernandez, and Andrew Rotman. Chicago: University of Chicago Committee on Southern Asian Studies.

Gottschalk, Peter. 2000. *Beyond Hindu and Muslim: Multiple Identity in Narratives from Village India*. New York: Oxford University Press.

Green, Nile. 2011. *Bombay Islam: The Religious Economy of the Indian Ocean*. New York: Cambridge University Press.

Greenough, Paul. 1998. "Nation, Economy, and Tradition Displayed: The Indian Crafts Museum, Delhi." In *Consuming Modernity: Public Culture in a South Asian World*, edited by Carol A. Breckenridge. Minneapolis: University of Minnesota Press.

Grewal, Inderpal. 2015. "Gauri Gill and Rajesh Vangad: *Fields of Sight*." In "Vital Signs: Photography and Eco-activism in Asia." Special issue, *Trans-Asia Photography Review* 5 (2). https://quod.lib.umich.edu/t/tap/7977573.0005.205?view=text;rgn=main.

Guha, Ramachandra. 1999. *Savaging the Civilized: Verrier Elwin, His Tribals, and India*. Delhi: Oxford University Press.

Guha, Ranajit. 1983. *Elementary Aspects of Peasant Insurrection in Colonial India*. Delhi: Oxford University Press.

———. (1989) 1994. "Dominance without Hegemony and Its Historiography." In *Subaltern Studies*, vol. 6, *Writings on South Asian History and Society*, edited by Ranajit Guha. Delhi: Oxford University Press.

Gunaji, Nagesh Vasudev. 1996. *Shri Sai Satcharita; or, The Wonderful Life and Teachings of Shri Sai Baba, Adapted from the Original Marathi Book by Hemadpant*. 16th ed. Mumbai: Shri Saibaba Sansthan.

Haberman, David L. 2013. *People Trees: Worship of Trees in Northern India*. New York: Oxford University Press.

Habermas, Jürgen. (1962) 1989. *The Structural Transformation of the Public Sphere: An Inquiry into a Category of Bourgeois Society.* Translated by Thomas Burger and Frederick Lawrence. Cambridge, MA: MIT Press.

Hansen, Thomas Blom. 2001. *Wages of Violence: Naming and Identity in Postcolonial Bombay.* Princeton, NJ: Princeton University Press.

Hardiman, David. 1987. *The Coming of the Devi: Adivasi Assertion in Western India.* Delhi: Oxford University Press.

Harris, Hermione. 2006. *Yoruba in Diaspora: An African Church in London.* New York: Palgrave Macmillan.

Hasson, Kevin Seamus. 2005. *The Right to Be Wrong: Ending the Culture War over Religion in America.* New York: Encounter Books.

Headley, Stephen C. 2004. *Durga's Mosque: Cosmology, Conversion, and Community in Central Javanese Islam.* Singapore: ISEAS.

Heuzé, Gérard. 1995. "Cultural Populism: The Appeal of the Shiv Sena." In *Bombay: Metaphor for Modern India*, edited by Sujata Patel and Alice Thorner. Delhi: Oxford University Press.

Hiltebeitel, Alf. 1988. *The Cult of Draupadī.* Vol. 1, *Mythologies: From Gingee to Kurukṣetra.* Chicago: University of Chicago Press.

Hull, Matthew. 2012. *Government of Paper: The Materiality of Bureaucracy in Urban Pakistan.* Berkeley: University of California Press.

IANS. 2014. "Uttar Pradesh Cops Told to Refrain from Filmi Uniforms, Facebook." *India Today*, 4 November. http://indiatoday.intoday.in/story/uttar-pradesh-cops-no-facebook-filmi-bollywood-dabangg-singham-uniform/1/399100.html.

Inden, Ronald. 1999. "Transnational Class, Erotic Arcadia and Commercial Utopia in Hindi Films." In *Image Journeys: Audio-Visual Media and Cultural Change in India*, edited by Christiane Brosius and Melissa Butcher. Delhi: Sage.

Inglis, Stephen. 1985. "Possession and Pottery: Serving the Divine in a South Indian Community." In *Gods of Flesh, Gods of Stone: The Embodiment of Divinity in India*, edited by Joanne Punzo Waghorne and Norman Cutler. Chambersburg, PA: Anima.

Irving, Washington. (1848) 1881. *A History of New York: From the Beginning of the World to the End of the Dutch Dynasty . . . by Diedrich Knickerbocker.* Author's rev. ed. In *The Works of Washington Irving: In Twelve Volumes*, vol. 7. New York: G. P. Putnam's Sons.

Ivy, Marilyn. 1995. *Discourses of the Vanishing: Modernity, Phantasm, Japan.* Chicago: University of Chicago Press.

Iyer, Meena. 2006. "Studio-nama: Kal, aaj aur kal." *Mission Mumbai*, 19 July. http://mission mumbai.indiatimes.com/mission_articles1.asp?id=80&th=bollywood.

Jain, Jyotindra. 1998. Introduction to *Other Masters: Five Contemporary Folk and Tribal Artists of India*, edited by Jyotindra Jain. Delhi: Crafts Museum and the Handicrafts and Handlooms Exports Corporation of India.

Jain, Kajri. 2007. *Gods in the Bazaar: The Economies of Indian Calendar Art.* Durham, NC: Duke University Press.

———. 2016. "Post-reform India's Automotive-Iconic-Cement Assemblages: Uneven Globality, Territorial Spectacle and Iconic Exhibition Value." In "Aesthetics of Arrival: Spectacle, Capital, Novelty in Post-reform India," edited by Ravinder Kaur and Thomas Blom Hansen. Special issue, *Identities: Global Studies in Culture and Power* 23 (3): 327–44.

———. 2017. "Gods in the Time of Automobility." *Current Anthropology* 58 (supplement 15): S13–S26.

Jain, Navinchandra S., G. P. Ramteke, S. R. Shevkari, and Robin D. Tribhuwan. 1995. "Demographic Profile of Tribals in India, with Reference to Maharashtra." In *An Overview of Tribal Research Studies*, edited by Navinchandra S. Jain and Robin D. Tribhuwan. Pune: Government of Maharashtra Tribal Research and Training Institute.

Jain, Tarun. 2004. "Defying Labels, Defining Themselves." *India Together*, September. http://www.indiatogether.org/2004/sep/adv-dntlabel.htm.

Jaoul, Nicolas. 2006. "Learning the Use of Symbolic Means: Dalits, Ambedkar Statues and the State in Uttar Pradesh." *Contributions to Indian Sociology* 40:175–207.

Jauregui, Beatrice. 2014. "Provisional Agency in India: Jugaad and Legitimation of Corruption." *American Ethnologist* 41:76–91.

Kakar, Sudhir. 1982. *Shamans, Mystics and Doctors: A Psychological Inquiry into India and Its Healing Traditions*. Chicago: University of Chicago Press.

Kālidāsa. (2001) 2008. *The Recognition of Śakuntalā*. Translated by W. J. Johnson. Oxford World's Classics. Oxford: Oxford University Press.

Kamath, M. V., and V. B. Kher. 1991. *Sai Baba of Shirdi: A Unique Saint*. Mumbai: Jaico.

Kanungo, Pralay, and Satyakam Joshi. 2010. "Carving out a White Marble Deity from a Rugged Black Stone? Hindutva Rehabilitates *Ramayan*'s Shabari in a Temple." *International Journal of Hindu Studies* 13 (3): 279–99.

Kapur, Geeta. 1987. "Mythic Material in Indian Cinema." *Journal of Arts and Ideas* 14–15:79–108.

Kaur, Raminder. 2005. *Performative Politics and the Cultures of Hinduism: Public Uses of Religion in Western India*. London: Anthem.

Kaur, Ravinder. 2016. "'I Am India Shining': The Investor-Citizen and the Indelible Icon of Good Times." *Journal of Asian Studies* 75:621–48.

Kaur, Ravinder, and Thomas Blom Hansen. 2016. "Aesthetics of Arrival: Spectacle, Capital, Novelty in Post-reform India." Special issue, edited by Ravinder Kaur and Thomas Blom Hansen, *Identities: Global Studies in Culture and Power* 23 (3): 265–75.

Kaviraj, Sudipta. 1997. "Filth and the Public Sphere: Concepts and Practices about Space in Calcutta." *Public Culture* 24:83–113.

Kazmi, Fareeduddin. 1998. "How Angry Is the Angry Young Man? 'Rebellion' in Conventional Hindi Films." In *The Secret Politics of Our Desires: Innocence, Culpability, and Indian Popular Cinema*, edited by Ashis Nandy. Delhi: Oxford University Press.

Keane, Webb. 1997. *Signs of Recognition: Powers and Hazards of Representation in an Indonesian Society*. Berkeley: University of California Press.

Kent, Eliza F. 2013. *Sacred Groves and Local Gods: Religion and Environmentalism in South India*. New York: Oxford University Press.

Khan, Naveeda Ahmed. 2012. *Muslim Becoming: Aspiration and Skepticism in Pakistan*. Durham, NC: Duke University Press.

Khilnani, Sunil. 1997. *The Idea of India*. New York: Farrar, Straus and Giroux.

Kinnard, Jacob N. 2014. *Places in Motion: The Fluid Identities of Temples, Images, and Pilgrims*. New York: Oxford University Press.

Kipling, Rudyard. (1898) 1920. "The Tomb of His Ancestors." In *The Day's Work*. Garden City, NY: Doubleday, Page.

Kojève, Alexandre. 1969. *Introduction to the Study of Hegel: Lectures on "The Phenomenology of Spirit."* Assembled by Raymond Queneau. Edited by Allan Bloom. Translated by James H. Nichols Jr. New York: Basic Books.

Kolatkar, Arun. (1976) 2005. *Jejuri*. New York: NYRB Books.

————. 2010. "Breakfast Time at Kala Ghoda." In *Collected Poems: In English*, edited by Arvind Krishna Mehrotra. Tarset: Bloodaxe Books.

Kosambi, D. D. 1962. *Myth and Reality: Studies in the Formation of Indian Culture*. Bombay: Popular Prakashan.

————. 1985. "Combined Methods in Indology." In *D. D. Kosambi on History and Society: Problems of Interpretation*, edited by A. J. Syed. Bombay: University of Bombay Department of History.

Kracauer, Siegfried. 1995. "The Mass Ornament." In *The Mass Ornament: Weimar Essays*, edited and translated by Thomas Y. Levin. Cambridge, MA: Harvard University Press.

Krishnakumar. 2003. "Gods Who Have Encroached upon Govt Land." *Mid Day*, 7 October.

Kristeva, Julia. 1982. *Powers of Horror: An Essay on Abjection*. Translated by Leon S. Roudiez. New York: Columbia University Press.

Kulkarni, Sridhar Balkrishna (Patthe Bapurao). n.d. "The Ballad of Bombay." Translated by Christian Lee Novetzke and Shobha Kale. Unpublished.

Lacan, Jacques. 1977a. *Écrits: A Selection*. Translated by Alan Sheridan. London: Tavistock.

————. 1977b. *The Four Fundamental Concepts of Psycho-analysis*. Edited by Jacques-Alain Miller. Translated by Alan Sheridan. London: Hogarth Press.

Lambek, Michael. 2003. *The Weight of the Past: Living with History in Mahajanga, Madagascar*. New York: Palgrave Macmillan.

Lapsley, Robert, and Michael Westlake. 1988. *Film Theory: An Introduction*. Images of Culture. Manchester: Manchester University Press.

Lefebvre, Henri. 1991. *The Production of Space*. Translated by Donald Nicholson-Smith. Cambridge, MA: Blackwell.

Lévi-Strauss, Claude. 1950. *Sociologie et anthropologie: Précédé d'une introduction à l'œuvre de Marcel Mauss*. Paris: Presses universitaires de France.

Lubin, Timothy. 2001. "Science, Patriotism, and Mother Veda: Ritual Activism in Maharashtra." *International Journal of Hindu Studies* 5:81–105.

Lutgendorf, Philip. 1995. "All in the (Raghu) Family: A Video Epic in Cultural Context." In *Media and the Transformation of Religion in South Asia*, edited by Lawrence A. Babb and Susan S. Wadley. Philadelphia: University of Pennsylvania Press.

————. 2003. *"Jai Santoshi Maa* Revisited." In *Representing Religion in World Cinema: Filmmaking, Mythmaking, Culture Making*, edited by S. Brent Plate. New York: Palgrave Macmillan.

————. 2012. "Ritual Reverb: Two 'Blockbuster' Hindi Films." *South Asian Popular Culture* 10:63–76.

Macey, David. 1988. *Lacan in Contexts*. London: Verso.

Mackintosh, A. 1840. "Account of the Tribe of Mhadeo Kolies." *Transactions of the Bombay Geographical Society* 1:189–264.

Macrae, Graeme. 2004. "Who Knows How to Build a Temple? Religious and Secular, Tradition and Innovation, in Contemporary South Indian Sacred Architecture." *South Asia: Journal of South Asian Studies* 27 (2): 217–43.

Malamoud, Charles. 1996. "Village and Forest in the Ideology of Brahmanic India." In *Cooking the World: Ritual and Thought in Ancient India*, translated by David White. Delhi: Oxford University Press.

Mallapragada, Madhavi. 2010. "Desktop Deities: Hindu Temples, Online Cultures and the Politics of Remediation." *South Asian Popular Culture* 8:109–21.

Mallebrein, Cornelia. 1998. "Hidden Gods within the House: House Shrines of the Kokna Tribe of Maharashtra." In *House and Home in Maharashtra*, edited by Irina Glushkova and Anne Feldhaus. Delhi: Oxford University Press.

Manjul, V. L. 2005. "God in a Copper Pot." Translated by Sudhakar Kulkarni. In *Untouchable Saints: An Indian Phenomenon*, edited by Eleanor Zelliot and Rohini Mokashi-Punekar. Delhi: Manohar.

Manto, Saadat Hasan. 1998. *Stars from Another Sky: The Bombay Film World of the 1940s*. Translated by Khalid Hasan. Delhi: Penguin Books India.

Marriott, McKim. 1976. "Hindu Transactions: Diversity without Dualism." In *Transaction and Meaning: Directions in the Anthropology of Exchange and Symbolic Behavior*, edited by Bruce Kapferer. Philadelphia: Institute for the Study of Human Issues.

Mashe, Jivya Soma, and Balu Mashe, artists, and Lakshmi Lal, ed. 1982. *The Warlis: Tribal Paintings and Legends*. Bombay: Chemould.

Masselos, Jim. 1982. "Change and Custom in the Format of the Bombay Mohurrum during the Nineteenth and Twentieth Centuries." *South Asia: Journal of South Asian Studies* 5:47–67.

———. 1991. "Appropriating Urban Space: Social Constructs of Bombay in the Time of the Raj." In "Aspects of 'the Public' in Colonial South Asia," edited by Sandria B. Freitag. Special issue, *South Asia: Journal of South Asian Studies* 14 (1): 33–64.

———. 2012. "The City and Modernity 2: Portraying the Public Man." *Indica* 49:23–52.

Mazumdar, Ranjani. 2000. "From Subjectification to Schizophrenia: The 'Angry Man' and the 'Psychotic' Hero of Bombay Cinema." In *Making Meaning in Indian Cinema*, edited by Ravi S. Vasudevan. Delhi: Oxford University Press.

Mazzarella, William. 2003. *Shoveling Smoke: Advertising and Globalization in Contemporary India*. Durham, NC: Duke University Press.

———. 2015. "A Different Kind of Flesh: Public Obscenity, Globalisation, and the Mumbai Dance Bar Ban." *South Asia: Journal of South Asian Studies* 38:481–94.

McKinsey and Company. 2003. *Vision Mumbai: Transforming Mumbai into a World-Class City: A Summary of Recommendations*. A Bombay First–McKinsey Report.

McLain, Karline. 2011. "Be United, Be Virtuous: Composite Culture and the Growth of Shirdi Sai Baba Devotion." *Nova Religio: The Journal of Alternative and Emergent Religions* 15:20–39.

———. 2016. *The Afterlife of Sai Baba: Competing Visions of a Global Saint*. Seattle: University of Washington Press.

Mehta, Rajshri. 2003. "Ghai's Film Academy Plans Still to Take Off." *Indian Express* (Mumbai), 16 September.

Mehta, Suketu. 2004. *Maximum City: Bombay Lost and Found*. New York: Knopf.

Mehta, Uday. 1999. *Liberalism and Empire: A Study in Nineteenth-Century British Liberal Thought*. Chicago: University of Chicago Press.

Meister, Michael W. 1995. "Seeing and Knowing: Semiology, Semiotics and the Art of India." In *Los discursos sobre el arte*, edited by Juana Gutiérrez Haces. XV Coloquio internacional de historia del arte. Mexico City: Universidad nacional autónoma de México / Instituto de investigaciones estéticas.

Meyer, Birgit. 2015. *Sensational Movies: Video, Vision, and Christianity in Ghana*. Berkeley: University of California Press.

Michelutti, Lucia. 2008. *The Vernacularisation of Democracy: Politics, Caste and Religion in India*. London: Routledge.

Middleton, Townsend. 2016. *The Demands of Recognition: State Anthropology and Ethnopolitics in Darjeeling*. Stanford, CA: Stanford University Press.

Mines, Diane P. 2005. *Fierce Gods: Inequality, Ritual, and the Politics of Dignity in a South Indian Village*. Bloomington: Indiana University Press.

Mishra, Ambarish. 2003. "Ganesh Mandals Plan to Take Stock on Wednesday." *Times of India* (Mumbai), 26 August.

Misra, Neelesh. 2003. "The Seamier Side of Bollywood." *Worcester (MA) Telegram and Gazette*, 15 September.

Mistry, Rohinton. 1991. *Such a Long Journey*. New York: Knopf.

Moodie, Megan. 2015. *We Were Adivasis: Aspiration in an Indian Scheduled Tribe*. South Asia across the Disciplines. Chicago: University of Chicago Press.

Myers, Fred R. 2001. "The Wizards of Oz: Nation, State, and the Production of Aboriginal Fine Art." In *The Empire of Things: Regimes of Value and Material Culture*, edited by Fred R. Myers. Advanced Seminar. Santa Fe, NM: School of American Research Press.

Nabokov, Isabelle. 2000. *Religion against the Self: An Ethnography of Tamil Rituals*. New York: Oxford University Press.

Nandy, Ashis. 1998. "Introduction: Indian Popular Cinema as a Slum's Eye View of Politics." In *The Secret Politics of Our Desires: Innocence, Culpability, and Indian Popular Cinema*, edited by Ashis Nandy. Delhi: Oxford University Press.

———. 2001. *An Ambiguous Journey to the City: The Village and Other Odd Ruins of the Self in the Indian Imagination*. Delhi: Oxford University Press.

Nerlekar, Anjali. 2016. *Bombay Modern: Arun Kolatkar and Bilingual Literary Culture*. Evanston, IL: Northwestern University Press.

Novetzke, Christian Lee. 2011. *Religion and Public Memory: A Cultural History of Saint Namdev in India*. New York: Columbia University Press.

O'Flaherty, Wendy Doniger, trans. (1975) 1994. *Hindu Myths: A Sourcebook Translated from the Sanskrit*. Delhi: Penguin Books India.

———. 1980. *Women, Androgynes, and Other Mythical Beasts*. Chicago: University of Chicago Press.

Olivera, Roshni. 2003. "*Maha Aartis* Are Not an Election Ploy." *Times of India* (Mumbai), 2 September.

Ong, Aihwa. 2011. "Introduction: Worlding Cities, or the Art of Being Global." In *Worlding Cities: Asian Experiments and the Art of Being Global*, edited by Ananya Roy and Aihwa Ong. London: Blackwell.

Orsi, Robert A. 2005. *Between Heaven and Earth: The Religious Worlds People Make and the Scholars Who Study Them*. Princeton, NJ: Princeton University Press.

Orsini, Francesca. 2015. "Booklets and *Sants*: Religious Publics and Literary History." In "Imagining the Public in Modern South Asia," edited by Brannon D. Ingram, J. Barton Scott, and SherAli Tareen. Special issue, *South Asia: Journal of South Asian Studies* 38 (3): 435–49.

Oxford Hindi-English Dictionary. 1997. Edited by R. S. McGregor. Delhi: Oxford University Press.

Padma, Sree. 2014. *Vicissitudes of the Goddess: Reconstructions of the* Gramadevata *in India's Religious Traditions*. London: Oxford University Press.

Pain, Charles, with Eleanor Zelliot. 1988. "The God Dattatreya and the Datta Temples of

Pune." In *The Experience of Hinduism: Essays on Religion in Maharashtra*, edited by Eleanor Zelliot and Maxine Berntsen. Albany: State University of New York Press.

Pandian, Anand. 2015. *Reel World: An Anthropology of Creation*. Durham, NC: Duke University Press.

Parekh, Bhikhu. 1995. "Liberalism and Colonialism: A Critique of Locke and Mill." In *Decolonization of the Imagination: Culture, Knowledge and Power*, edited by Jan Neverdeen Peterse and Bhikhu Parekh. London: Zed Books.

Parish, Steven M. 1996. *Hierarchy and Its Discontents: Culture and the Politics of Consciousness in Caste Society*. Philadelphia: University of Pennsylvania Press.

Parmentier, Richard. 1994. *Signs in Society: Studies in Semiotic Anthropology*. Bloomington: Indiana University Press.

Parry, Jonathan P. 1994. *Death in Banaras*. Lewis Henry Morgan Lectures. Cambridge: Cambridge University Press.

Parulekar, Godavari. 1975. *Adivasis Revolt: The Story of Warli Peasants in Struggle*. Calcutta: National Book Depot, 1975.

Patel, Gieve. 2008. *Mister Behram and Other Plays*. Calcutta: Seagull.

Pease, Arthur Stanley. 1935. *Publi Vergili Maronis Aeneidos: Liber Quartus*. Cambridge, MA: Harvard University Press.

Pechelis, Karen. 2009. "Experiencing the Mango Festival as a Ritual Dramatization of Hagiography." *Method and Theory in the Study of Religion* 21:50–65.

Peirce, Charles Sanders. (1885) 1993. "One, Two, Three: Fundamental Categories of Thought and of Nature." In *Writings of Charles S. Peirce: A Chronological Edition*, vol. 5, edited by Christian J. W. Kloesel et al. Bloomington: Indiana University Press.

Pendse, Sandeep. 1995. "Toil, Sweat and the City." In *Bombay: Metaphor for Modern India*, edited by Sujata Patel and Alice Thorner. Delhi: Oxford University Press.

Pérez, Elizabeth. 2011. "Spirit Mediumship as Historical Mediation: African-American Pasts, Black Ancestral Presence, and Afro-Cuban Religions." *Journal of Religion in Africa* 41:330–65.

Pinney, Christopher. 1997a. *Camera Indica: The Social Life of Indian Photographs*. Chicago: University of Chicago Press.

———. 1997b. "The Nation (Un)Pictured? Chromolithography and 'Popular' Politics in India, 1878–1995." *Critical Inquiry* 23:834–67.

———. 2001. "Introduction: Public, Popular, and Other Cultures." In *Pleasure and the Nation: The History, Politics and Consumption of Public Culture in India*, edited by Rachel Dwyer and Christopher Pinney. Delhi: Oxford University Press.

———. 2002. "The Indian Work of Art in the Age of Mechanical Reproduction: Or, What Happens When Peasants 'Get Hold' of Images." In *Media Worlds: Anthropology on New Terrain*, edited by Faye D. Ginsburg, Lila Abu-Lughod, and Brian Larkin. Berkeley: University of California Press.

———. 2004. *"Photos of the Gods": The Printed Image and Political Struggle in India*. London: Reaktion.

Port, Mattijs P. J. van de. 2011. *Ecstatic Encounters: Bahian Candomblé and the Quest for the Really Real*. Amsterdam: Amsterdam University Press.

Povinelli, Elizabeth A. 2002. *The Cunning of Recognition: Indigenous Alterities and the Making of Australian Multiculturalism*. Durham, NC: Duke University Press.

Prakash, Gyan. 2010. *Mumbai Fables*. Princeton, NJ: Princeton University Press.

Press Trust of India. 2015. "Mumbai Police Ensure Incident-less Last Day of Ganesh Festival." India.com, 27 September. http://www.india.com/news/india/mumbai-police-ensure-incident-less-last-day-of-ganesh-festival-581974/.

Probst, Peter. 2011. *Osogbo and the Art of Heritage: Monuments, Deities, and Money*. Bloomington: Indiana University Press.

Radcliffe, John, ed. 2008. Kipling Society Readers' Guide notes to "The Tomb of His Ancestors." http://www.kiplingsociety.co.uk/rg_tomb1.htm.

Raeside, I. M. P. 1982. "Dattātreya." *Bulletin of the School of Oriental and African Studies* 45:489–500.

Rajadhyaksha, Ashish, ed. 2013. *In the Wake of Aadhaar: The Digital Ecosystem of Governance in India*. Bangalore: Centre for the Study of Culture and Society.

Rajadhyaksha, Ashish, and Paul Willimen. 1994. *Encyclopaedia of Indian Cinema*. Delhi: Oxford University Press.

Rajagopal, Arvind. 2001a. *Politics after Television: Religious Nationalism and the Reshaping of the Indian Public*. New York: Cambridge University Press.

———. 2001b. "The Violence of Commodity Aesthetics: Hawkers, Demolition Raids, and a New Regime of Consumption." *Social Text* 19 (3 [68]): 91–113.

Rajagopalan, C. 1962. *The Greater Bombay: A Study in Suburban Ecology*. Bombay: Popular Book Depot.

Rajagopalan, Mrinalini. 2016. *Building Histories: The Archival and Affective Lives of Five Monuments in Modern Delhi*. South Asia across the Disciplines. Chicago: University of Chicago Press.

Ramaswamy, Sumathi. 2010. *The Goddess and the Nation: Mapping Mother India*. Durham, NC: Duke University Press.

Rao, Ursula. 2013. "Biometric Marginality: UID and the Shaping of Homeless Identities in the City." *Economic and Political Weekly* 48:71–77.

Rao, Ursula, and Graham Greenleaf. 2013. "Subverting ID from Above and Below: The Uncertain Shaping of India's New Instrument of E-governance." In "Surveillance Texts and Textualism: Truthtelling and Trustmaking in an Uncertain World," edited by Gavin J. D. Smith, Mehera San Roque, Harriet Westcott, and Peter Marks. Special issue, *Surveillance and Society* 11 (3): 287–300.

Rappaport, Roy A. 1967. *Pigs for the Ancestors: Ritual in the Ecology of a New Guinea People*. New Haven, CT: Yale University Press.

Reddy, Gayatri. 2005. *With Respect to Sex: Negotiating Hijra Identity in South India*. Worlds of Desire. Chicago: University of Chicago Press.

Remedios, Avellino. 1998. *Mythos and Logos of the Warlis: A Tribal Worldview*. Edited by Ajay Dandekar. Castes and Tribes of India. Delhi: Concept.

Rigopoulos, Antonio. 1993. *The Life and Teachings of Sai Baba of Shirdi*. Delhi: Sri Satguru Publications.

———. 1998. *Dattātreya: The Immortal Guru, Yogin, and Avatāra*. Delhi: Sri Satguru Publications.

Rix, Kate. 1995. "Abbey Road." *SF Weekly*, 29 March. http://www.sfweekly.com/1995-03-29/news/abbey-road/.

Roberts, Mary Nooter, and Allen F. Roberts. n.d. *Shirdi Sai Baba: Visual Practices / Global Devotions*. http://www.shirdisaibabavirtualsaint.org.

Roberts, Nathaniel. 2016. *To Be Cared For: The Power of Conversion and Foreignness of Belonging in an Indian Slum*. Berkeley: University of California Press.

Rotman, Andy. 2009. *Thus Have I Seen: Visualizing Faith in Early Indian Buddhism*. New York: Oxford University Press.

———. 2017. "Who Moved My *Cheez*: Brandism, Bazaarism, and the Future of Indian Markets." Paper presented at Annual Conference on South Asia, University of Wisconsin–Madison.

Rudolph, Lloyd I., and Susanne Hoeber Rudolph. 1967. *The Modernity of Tradition: Political Development in India*. Chicago: University of Chicago Press.

Rushdie, Salman. 1981. *Midnight's Children*. London: Jonathan Cape.

Rycroft, Daniel J. 2004. "Capturing Birsa Munda: The Virtuality of a Colonial-Era Photograph." *Indian Folklore Research Journal* 1:53–68.

Sabith, Muhammed. 2016. "Anger in Kerala as Amit Shah Turns Onam into 'Brahminical Vamana Jayanti.'" *The Wire*, 14 September. http://thewire.in/65809/anger-kerala-amit-shah-turns-onam-brahminical-vamana-jayanti/.

Salam, Zia Us. 1999–2000. "Review of the Week: *Jaani Dushman, Ek Anokhi Kahani*." *Bollywood Best*. http://www.idlebrain.com/mumbai/reviews/mr-jd.html.

Saldanha, Indra Munshi. 1986. "The Political Economy of Traditional Farming Practices in Thana District, Maharashtra (India)." *Journal of Peasant Studies* 17:433–43.

———. 1990. "Tribal Women in the Warli Revolt: 1945–47: 'Class' and 'Gender' in the Left Perspective." *Economic and Political Weekly* 21:WS-41–WS-52.

———. 1995. "On Drinking and 'Drunkenness': History of Liquor in Colonial India." *Economic and Political Weekly* 30:2323–32.

———. 1998. "Colonial Forest Regulations and Collective Resistance: Nineteenth-Century Thana District." In *Nature and the Orient: The Environmental History of South and Southeast Asia*, edited by Richard H. Grove, Vinita Damodaran, and Satpal Sangwan. Delhi: Oxford University Press.

Sardar, Ziauddin. 1998. "Dilip Kumar Made Me Do It." In *The Secret Politics of Our Desires: Innocence, Culpability, and Indian Popular Cinema*, edited by Ashis Nandy. Delhi: Oxford University Press.

Savarkar, Vinayak Damodar. (1923) 1969. *Hindutva—Who Is a Hindu?* Bombay: Veer Savarkar Prakashan.

Save, K. J. 1945. *The Warlis*. Bombay: Padma.

Scott, J. Barton. 2015. "How to Defame a God: Public Selfhood in the Maharaj Libel Case." In "Imagining the Public in Modern South Asia," edited by Brannon D. Ingram, J. Barton Scott, and SherAli Tareen. Special issue, *South Asia: Journal of South Asian Studies* 38 (3): 387–402.

Scott, J. Barton, and Brannon D. Ingram. 2015. "What Is a Public? Notes from South Asia." In "Imagining the Public in Modern South Asia," edited by Brannon D. Ingram, J. Barton Scott, and SherAli Tareen. Special issue, *South Asia: Journal of South Asian Studies* 38 (3): 357–70.

Scott, James C. 1998. *Seeing Like a State: How Certain Schemes to Improve the Human Condition Have Failed*. New Haven, CT: Yale University Press.

Sebastian, P. A., ed. 2000. *Crushed Homes, Lost Lives: The Story of the Demolitions in the Sanjay Gandhi National Park*. Report of the Indian People's Human Rights Tribunal on the Sanjay Gandhi National Park Demolitions. Mumbai: Indian People's Human Rights Commission.

Sen, Amrita, and Sarmistha Pattanaik. 2016. "Politics of Biodiversity Conservation and Socio Ecological Conflicts in a City: The Case of Sanjay Gandhi National Park, Mumbai." *Journal of Agricultural and Environmental Ethics* 29:305–26.

Sen Gupta, Sankar, ed. 1965. *Tree Symbol Worship in India: A New Survey of a Pattern of Folk-Religion. Indian Folklore*, no. 5. Calcutta: Indian Publications.

Shah, Svati P. 2014. *Street Corner Secrets: Sex, Work, and Migration in the City of Mumbai*. Durham, NC: Duke University Press.

Sharma, Kalpana. 1995. "Chronicle of a Riot Foretold." In *Bombay: Metaphor for Modern India*, edited by Sujata Patel and Alice Thorner. Delhi: Oxford University Press.

Shepard, Sadia. 2003. Interview with "Vikas," Filmistan Studios, Goregaon, Mumbai. Digital video.

Shepherd, Kevin. 1985. "Hazrat Sai Baba of Shirdi." In *Gurus Rediscovered: Biographies of Sai Baba of Shirdi and Upasni Maharaj of Sakori*. Cambridge: Anthropographia.

———. 2011. "Shirdi Sai Baba and the Sai Baba Movement." http://www.kevinrdshepherd .info/shirdi_sai_baba_and_sai_baba_movement.html.

Shinde, Kiran A., and Andrea Pinkney. 2013. "Shirdi in Transition: Guru Devotion, Urbanisation and Regional Pluralism in India." *South Asia: Journal of South Asian Studies* 36:554–70.

Sikand, Yoginder. 2003. *Sacred Spaces: Exploring Traditions of Shared Faith in India*. Delhi: Penguin Books India.

Singh, Bhrigupati. 2015. *Poverty and the Quest for Life: Spiritual and Material Striving in Rural India*. Chicago: University of Chicago Press.

Singh, Vijay. 2003a. "Concrete Jungle." *Indian Express* (Mumbai), 8 June.

———. 2003b. "Where Do Trapped Leopards Go?" *Indian Express* (Mumbai), 9 October.

Sinha, Ajay. 2007. "Visual Culture and the Politics of Locality in Modern India: A Review Essay." *Modern Asian Studies* 41:187–220.

Skaria, Ajay. 1997. "Shades of Wildness: Tribe, Caste, and Gender in Western India." *Journal of Asian Studies* 56:726–45.

———. 1999. *Hybrid Histories: Forests, Frontiers and Wildness in Western India*. Delhi: Oxford University Press.

Smith, Frederick M. 2006. *The Self Possessed: Deity and Spirit Possession in South Asian Literature and Civilization*. New York: Columbia University Press.

Smith, J. Z. 1987. *To Take Place: Toward Theory in Ritual*. Chicago: University of Chicago Press.

Sontheimer, Günther-Dietz. 1989. *Pastoral Deities in Western India*. Translated by Anne Feldhaus. New York: Oxford University Press.

———. 1997. *King of Warriors, Hunters, and Shepherds: Essays on Khaṇḍobā*. Edited by Anne Feldhaus, Aditya Malik, and Heidrun Brückner. Delhi: Manohar.

Sopher, David E. 1987. "The Message of Place in Hindu Pilgrimage." *National Geographical Journal of India* 33:353–69.

SPARC. 2001. *Sanitation*. Mumbai: Society for the Promotion of Area Resource Centres. Digital video.

Srinivas, M. N. 1966. *Social Change in Modern India*. Berkeley: University of California Press.

———. 1989. "The Cohesive Role of Sanskritization." In *The Cohesive Role of Sanskritization and Other Essays*. Delhi: Oxford University Press.

Srinivas, Smriti. 1999. "The Brahmin and the Fakir: Suburban Religiosity in the Cult of Shirdi Sai Baba." *Journal of Contemporary Religion* 14:245–61.

————. 2001. *Landscapes of Urban Memory: The Sacred and the Civic in India's High-Tech City*. Minneapolis: University of Minnesota Press.

————. 2015. *A Place for Utopia: Urban Designs from South Asia*. Seattle: University of Washington Press.

Srivas, Anuj. 2016. "The Technocratic Visions of Nandan Nilekani: What an Aadhaar-Enabled Future May Look Like." *The Wire*, 17 March. http://thewire.in/24966/the-technocratic-visions-of-nandan-nilekani-what-an-aadhaar-enabled-future-may-look-like/.

Srivatsan, R. 2000. *Conditions of Visibility: Writings on Photography in Contemporary India*. Gender Culture Politics. Calcutta: STREE.

Stanley, John M. 1988. "Gods, Ghosts, and Possession." In *The Experience of Hinduism: Essays on Religion in Maharashtra*, edited by Eleanor Zelliot and Maxine Berntsen. Albany: State University of New York Press.

Stokes, Eric. 1959. *The English Utilitarians and India*. Oxford: Clarendon.

Sullivan, Bruce M. 2015. *Sacred Objects in Secular Spaces: Exhibiting Asian Religions in Museums*. New York: Bloomsbury Academic Press.

Sundar, Nandini. 2007. *Subalterns and Sovereigns: An Anthropological History of Bastar*. 2nd ed. Delhi: Oxford University Press.

Symington, D. 1950. *Report on the Aboriginal and Hill Tribes of the Partially Excluded Areas in the Bombay Presidency*. Bombay: Government Central Press.

Talukdar, Shashwati, and P. Kerim Friedman. 2011. *Please Don't Beat Me, Sir!* Four Nine and a Half Pictures. DVD.

Tanaka, Masakazu. 1997. *Patrons, Devotees and Goddesses: Ritual and Power among the Tamil Fishermen of Sri Lanka*. Delhi: Manohar.

Taneja, Anand Vivek. 2013. "Jinnealogy: Everyday Life and Islamic Theology in Post-Partition Delhi." *HAU: Journal of Ethnographic Theory* 3:139–65.

Tarlo, Emma. 2003. *Unsettling Memories: Narratives of the Emergency in Delhi*. Berkeley: University of California Press.

Tilche, Alice. 2015. "A Forgotten Adivasi Landscape: Museums and Memory in Western India." *Contributions to Indian Sociology* 49:188–215.

Times News Network. 2003a. "State Govt Faces Saffron Swipe from Puja Pandals." *Times of India* (Mumbai), 2 September.

————. 2003b. "Weak Govt Responsible for Blasts." *Times of India* (Mumbai), 2 September.

Toilet Talk. 1997. No. 1 (December). Mumbai: National Slum Dwellers Federation, Mahila Milan, and Society for the Promotion of Area Resource Centres.

Tribal Department. n.d. "Verification of Caste Certificates Issued to ST Candidates." Accessed 6 August 2007. http://www.maharashtra.gov.in/english/tribal/caste_certificate.html.

van Wersch, Huub. 1995. "Flying a Kite and Losing the String: Communication during the Bombay Textile Strike." In *Bombay: Metaphor for Modern India*, edited by Sujata Patel and Alice Thorner. Delhi: Oxford University Press.

Vasudevan, Ravi S. 2011. *The Melodramatic Public: Film Form and Spectatorship in Indian Cinema*. New York: Palgrave Macmillan.

Waghorne, Joanne Punzo. 2004. *Diaspora of the Gods: Modern Hindu Temples in an Urban Middle-Class World*. New York: Oxford University Press.

————. 2014. "Shirdi Sai Baba: A Saint for All Seasons, All Reasons in a Time of Indeterminacy." Paper presented at Association for Asian Studies Annual Conference.

Wagle, N. K. (1995) 2000. "On Relations amongst Bhūts, Gods, and Men: Aspects of Folk

Religion and Law in Pre-British Maharashtra." In *Folk Culture, Folk Religion and Oral Traditions as a Component in Maharashtrian Culture*, edited by Günther-Dietz Sontheimer. Heidelberg University South Asian Studies. Delhi: Manohar.

Wajihuddin, Mohammed. 2003. "This Mecca of Filmdom Puts Jha on Top of the World." *Indian Express* (Mumbai), 30 October.

Wakchaure, B. R., ed. 2004. "Shree Sai Moorti." *Shree Sai Leela*, September–October, 37.

Wallia, Kaajal. 2003. "BMC Seeks to Give Shrines Tree-Cover." *Times of India* (Mumbai), 10 November.

Warhaft, Sally. 2001. "No Parking at the Bunder: Fisher People and Survival in Capitalist Mumbai." *South Asia: Journal of South Asian Studies* 24:213–23.

Warner, Michael. 2002. "Publics and Counterpublics." *Public Culture* 14:49–90.

Warren, Marianne. 1999. *Unravelling the Enigma: Shirdi Sai Baba in the Light of Sufism*. Delhi: Sterling Paperbacks.

Weinstein, Liza. 2014. *The Durable Slum: Dharavi and the Right to Stay Put in Globalizing Mumbai*. Minneapolis: University of Minnesota Press.

White, Charles S. J. 1972. "The Sāī Bābā Movement: Approaches to the Study of Indian Saints." *Journal of Asian Studies* 31:863–78.

White, David Gordon. 2009. *Sinister Yogis*. Chicago: University of Chicago Press.

Whitehead, Henry. 1921. *The Village Gods of South India*. 2nd ed. Calcutta: Association Press.

Wild Life (Protection) Act of 1972. 2003. In *The Forest Laws*. LP's Bare Act 2003. Allahabad: Law Publishers (India).

Williams, Caroline. 2001. *Contemporary French Philosophy: Modernity and the Persistence of the Subject*. London: Athlone.

Yadav, Anumeha. 2015a. "JAM in Jharkhand: 'Apply Lemon Juice, Flour, Boroplus on Fingers and Pass Biometrics Test.'" *Scroll*, 23 November. http://scroll.in/article/769611/jam-in-jharkhand-apply-lemon-juice-flour-boroplus-on-fingers-and-pass-biometrics-test.

———. 2015b. "Jan Dhan Yojana: On Paper, a Radical Scheme, on the Ground, a Catalyst for Confusion and Coercion." *Scroll*, 24 November. http://scroll.in/article/769613/jan-dhan-yojana-on-paper-a-radical-scheme-on-the-ground-a-catalyst-for-confusion-and-coercion.

YASHADA. 2003. *Workshop on Issues in Tribal Identity: Anthropological and Ethnological Perspectives (Orientation Programme for Police Officers)*. Pune: Yashwantrao Chavan Academy of Development Administration.

Youngblood, Michael. 2016. *Cultivating Community: Interest, Identity, and Ambiguity in an Indian Social Mobilization*. Pasadena, CA: SASA Books.

Zelliot, Eleanor. 1988. Introduction to *The Experience of Hinduism: Essays on Religion in Maharashtra*, edited by Eleanor Zelliot and Maxine Berntsen. Albany: State University of New York Press.

Zérah, Marie-Hélène, and Frédéric Landy. 2013. "Nature and Urban Citizenship Redefined: The Case of the National Park in Mumbai." *Geoforum* 46:25–33.

INDEX